T0244127

Conquistadors and Aztecs

Conquistadors and Aztecs

A History of the Fall of Tenochtitlan

STEFAN RINKE

TRANSLATED BY CHRISTOPHER REID

OXFORD
UNIVERSITY PRESS

OXFORD
UNIVERSITY PRESS

Oxford University Press is a department of the University of Oxford. It furthers
the University's objective of excellence in research, scholarship, and education
by publishing worldwide. Oxford is a registered trade mark of Oxford University
Press in the UK and certain other countries.

Published in the United States of America by Oxford University Press
198 Madison Avenue, New York, NY 10016, United States of America.

This book is a translation of
Conquistadoren und Azteken: Cortés und die Eroberung Mexikos.
Munich: Verlag C.H. Beck oHG, 2019.

English translation © Oxford University Press 2023

CIP data is on file at the Library of Congress

ISBN 978–0–19–755246–9

DOI: 10.1093/oso/9780197552469.001.0001

Printed by Sheridan Books, Inc., United States of America

For my dear wife Silke,
for our many years together

CONTENTS

ACKNOWLEDGMENTS

I would like to express my gratitude to Susan Ferber, my editor at Oxford University Press; to Stefan von der Lahr, my editor at C.H. Beck in Munich; and to Christopher Reid, the translator of this book. I appreciate the support of the anonymous reviewers. Many thanks are also due to my student assistants and colleagues Daniela Celis, Nelson Chacón, Felipe Fernández, Lorena Jaureguí, and Karina Kriegesmann, who unwaveringly offered their assistance, and to the archives and libraries—especially the Ibero-American Institute in Berlin—which provided me with fundamental sources. Thanks are due to Stephanie Fleischmann for creating the Index. I received significant support through the Premio José Antonio Alzate, which the Mexican Academy of Sciences and the Consejo Nacional de Ciencia y Tecnología awarded me in 2017; this helped me to conduct my research in Mexico. I am deeply indebted to both institutions as well as to the more than one hundred former and current members from all over the world of our German-Mexican International Research Training Group "Between Spaces" and its successor "Temporalities of Future," which have provided a unique academic environment for more than a decade. Finally, thanks are due to my friends in the history department of the Latin American Institute at Freie Universität Berlin.

Conquistadors and Aztecs

Introduction

In March 2019, the newly elected President of Mexico, Andrés Manuel López Obrador, attracted global interest for letters sent to the Spanish king and the pope. In them, he entreated the recipients to apologize to the indigenous peoples of Mexico for the atrocities committed during the Conquest of Mexico five hundred years earlier. The letters' contents spread like wildfire across social media and sparked outrage in Spain. The crown swiftly rebuffed him, pointing out that the events of that time could not be judged by today's standards. It also maintained that the Spanish and Mexican people had always known how to "interpret our common past without anger and with a constructive attitude."[1]

Although the controversy over the conquest is many centuries old, it is still very much alive, and not just in the Spanish-speaking world. The fall in 1519 of Tenochtitlan, the capital of the Mexica or Aztec Empire, as it was later called, laid the foundation for the Spanish empire on the North American mainland.[2] It was the first time that Europeans had subjugated a highly organized state outside the world they had hitherto known. In the process, they created the basis for the first global colonial empires. By the sixteenth century, Spanish chroniclers and historians regarded their country as the legitimate successor to the Roman Empire, which they claimed Spain would even surpass.[3] This resulted in the fundamental assumption of the superiority of Christian Europeans and the inferiority of other ethnic groups, which was characterized as a quasi-natural order of things.

These aspects were always in the foreground in European historiography, though the original triumphalist attitude would reverse course in the twentieth century. The events of that era were celebrated hundreds of times over in popular stories, novels, poems, songs, and operas, and scrutinized in scholarly papers. The academic literature alone fills libraries. The conquest of Tenochtitlan between 1519 and 1521 was certainly an unprecedented event. The urban center was probably one of the largest cities in the world and the capital of a sprawling and, for Europeans, totally alien empire.[4] On the other hand, it was a devastating blow for the losers, the Mexica, who had been expanding their rule in Mesoamerica for decades.

For Renaissance Europeans, who prized first-hand testimony and personal experience and no longer exclusively relied on classical authorities, information from the New World had garnered great interest since 1492. The sensation of the Columbus voyage had already faded by 1519, by which point the Genoese had been dead for over a decade. But in Mexico, new discoveries emerged—things that had never been heard of before in Europe. Even the Bible was unaware of these lands.[5]

At first, the news mainly spread through Hernán Cortés's letters. The leader of the Spanish conquistadors described with wonder all the things that were new and strange to him. His depictions of the rituals, art, cuisine, and jewelry of the Mexica captured the public imagination. Significantly, he put the social hierarchy of Mexican society on par with that of the Spanish by alluding to important Mexica as *señores, vasallos,* and *señorios.* The Latin translation of his reports even uses the capitalized term "Don" for the ruler of the Mexica, Moctezuma II Xocoyotzin.[6] Cortés's emphasis on the discipline and remarkable social order in Mexican society starkly contrasts with the earlier experiences of Columbus. His first report of 1519 gave the impression that negotiations with a foreign ruler were carried out on an equal footing, just as the Catholic monarchs of Spain had expected when they sent Columbus on his journey in 1492.[7] But Columbus had failed to discover any states or powerful kings in the Caribbean. What Cortés described was much closer to the original vision, and Emperor Charles V therefore instructed him to treat the new subjects as well as he would vassals in Europe.[8]

For the people of Mesoamerica, the impact of the encounter was no less novel or surprising. The sight of the Spaniards opened up a new world for them, too. Everything was strange to them, from their light skin, occasionally fair hair, and body hair to their clothes and hats, tools, and food and drink. They were particularly struck by the design of their ships and their animals, as horses and dogs were unheard of in Mesoamerica. They were also curious about the armaments, flags, and Christian symbolism, especially the ever-present cross. They depicted these novelties in their historical records in the form of glyphs, a pictorial language that was the counterpart of the written language of the Spanish.[9]

The parties met each other with astonishment, but at eye level, even if both sides felt superior to the other. Indeed, until the end of the eighteenth century, the global dominance of the Europeans was hardly a given. At this time, around 80% of the world's gross national product was still being generated in Asia; Europeans had extensive colonial possessions only in America, and elsewhere they had established only trading stations.[10] Furthermore, in the early modern period, imperial expansion was not exceptional. In this era, the Ottoman, Chinese, Russian, and Songhay empires in West Africa greatly expanded their dominions, as did the Inca and Mexica empires until the arrival of the Europeans.[11] But these were land empires, whereas the Europeans were opening up utterly new horizons far away from home, across the ocean. The new insights and the knowledge they brought back with them figured prominently in the Renaissance conceptions of the world, which were imbued with humanistic ideals.[12]

The contact between cultures did not take place in a spirit of harmony, but under the banner of warlike conquest. In self-portraits, the conquistadors stressed the fact that, like the heroes of the medieval chivalric novels that were very popular at the time, they had defeated a large empire with just a negligible force. This myth has been passed down from generation to generation in modern schoolbooks.[13] Over and over again, authors have asked how a few hundred men under the command of the explorer Cortés could capture Tenochtitlan. This question, however, is based on assumptions that are highly suspect. Was it really merely a small band of bold Spaniards who triumphed in heroic battle against an enemy with superior numbers? Didn't other factors come into play?

This book describes the worlds the conquistadors created in the course of their mostly bloody encounters with the foreigners. In the process, it attempts to do justice to recent demands to pay more attention to the actors who were actually responsible for creating social spaces.[14] After all, the violent destruction and redefinition of these social and ethnic spaces affected all those involved, winners and losers alike. The book examines the perspectives of these individual actors, who reflect the ideas of the world at a particular point in time. It is therefore necessary to assess their scope for action and ability to shape the future.[15] Rather than attempting to address the usual biographical interest in an individual, *Conquistadors and Aztecs* attempts to decenter the protagonists as much as possible. On the one hand, research on biographical writing has shown that the central figures try to create the impression of coherence through their written testimonies.[16] On the other hand, contemporary witnesses and subsequent generations do not simply describe a life, but consciously and unconsciously construct it in the act of writing. One of the starting points of this book, then, is to question the manner in which the contemporary witnesses and later historians constructed and represented their subjects.

Those who took part in the battle of Tenochtitlan or reported on it as eyewitnesses also created worlds. By translating the chaos of the event into reports and images, they combined new and highly diverse entities. Depending on the circumstances, these worlds were constantly changing in response to current events. The pictures, objects, and people that Cortés sent to Europe and later took with him provided a material basis for this worldmaking, even on the other side of the ocean. Like Cortés and his men, the indigenous groups also tried to recognize the relevance and value of the new and to arrange it hierarchically.

Consequently, they eliminated certain factors from their experience, while adding, transforming, and rectifying others. Their concern was with restoring or inventing schemes that could be presented in reports, theories, maps, and drawings.[17] The actors succeeded in creating these worlds to varying degrees. *Conquistadors and Aztecs* is not only about the world of Hernán Cortés, which has been the focus of most previous studies, but also about the many versions of the world that competed with each other, a competition that went far beyond the battlefields.

The historiography on the subject is difficult to pin down. Traditionally, there are extreme appraisals, in which mostly Cortés and the Spaniards are the focal point, either as heroes or as monsters. The first interpretation is one of glorious conquest. Poets of the Golden Age, both in the Indies and on the Iberian Peninsula, glorified Cortés as a "new Mars."[18] Mythical and historical elements intermingled, contributing to the creation of a coherent version of the conquest in text and image. The conquistadors were portrayed as brave soldiers of a royal army fighting against savages. At the helm, according to this interpretation, was the heroic Cortés. It was thanks to him that the Mexica were delivered from superstition and then forgiven their sins. In turn, this paved the way for the construction of a new Christian Mexico. American historian William H. Prescott represents the more modern variant of this interpretation with his work, written in the Romantic vein and first published in 1843.[19] This tendency is further reflected in the twentieth century in the two classic, if hagiographic, Cortés biographies by the Spaniard Salvador de Madariaga and the Mexican Carlos Pereyra, both works published in 1942. Influential Mexican education minister and intellectual José Vasconcelos followed with his own contribution that presented Cortés as the founder of his country's nationality. In keeping with the spirit of the 1940s, he believed Mexican nationality was rooted in the mixture of European and indigenous "blood."[20]

In fact, Mexicans time and again questioned the origin of the nation in the evaluation of the actors and events around the Fall of Tenochtitlan.[21] The so-called black legend in particular took the events as evidence of the supposedly extraordinary brutality of the Spanish colonial rule.[22] After independence from Spain was gained in the nineteenth century, Cortés was for some time persona non grata in the nascent Mexican historiography. Descendants of the first Spanish conquistadors and settlers, the so-called Creoles who had lived in Mexico for many generations, appropriated the Aztec past, now revered as the glorious, ancient history of the new nation. The parallels to European Romanticism were unmistakable. The Mexica were thus reinterpreted as founding fathers, although there was little interest in the real situation of their indigenous descendants. According to this reading, Cortés became the antihero and destroyer of a great culture.[23] Attempts to build a monument for Cortés in Mexico repeatedly failed due to the resistance of the population, and in 2010 even the statue of him in his birthplace of Medellín, Spain, was no longer safe from vandalism. At least anniversaries like the conqueror's 500th birthday in 1985 and the 450th anniversary of his death in 1997 inspired new research that is more balanced in analysis. Overall, a more sober attitude now prevails, although the judgments of European and Mexican authors can still differ widely in some cases.[24]

If Cortés's role has not been considered dominant for some time, the same cannot be said of the negative assessment of his rival Moctezuma. As a rule, European sources said that God made the triumph of Cortés possible and punished the wicked character of the Mexican prince. Although moral condemnation is absent in modern interpretations, they nevertheless often assume that the Spanish were rational and civilized and therefore superior to the superstitious Moctezuma. However, this overlooks the fact that the late medieval Spaniards were anything but purely rational actors.[25] Even though historians have repeatedly pointed out the mythical quality of the sources on Moctezuma, the literature on the conquest tends to take it at face value, at least in part.[26]

Something that also has not changed over the years is the notion of the victorious Spanish and the defeated indigenous. The literature gives a variety of reasons for the former's success and the latter's failure. To begin with, explanations are offered for the dominance of the Spanish. The chroniclers and contemporary witnesses mention, among other things, the character of Cortés and his men; their superior weaponry, technology, and tactics; and ultimately even their cultural, religious, and psychological supremacy.[27] As for the decline of the Mexica, historians have cited their mental and ideological collapse and referred to their inept and wasteful way of combat as well as to deficiencies in their political system. Particularly intractable is the well-worn thesis that the Mexica viewed the Spanish as returning gods and were therefore utterly paralyzed. Typically, historians have conflated biological, psychological, military, and structural factors.[28] Added to this is an aspect highlighted by modern research: the impact of epidemics, especially smallpox, introduced by the Spaniards.[29]

According to a thesis popularized by cultural studies scholar Tzvetan Todorov, the inferiority of the indigenous peoples was due to cultural determinism. From this perspective, the demise of Tenochtitlan was sealed by a cyclical world view as well as by dire prophecies and the resulting indigenous fatalism. According to Todorov, the scales were tipped by Western civilization's superior powers of communication.[30] As critiques have made clear, however, the arguments supporting this thesis are untenable. In fact, pronounced differentiations and creative approaches to dealing with natural and cultural challenges can be discerned within Mexica society.[31] Another problem with the determinism thesis is that its adherents relied heavily on the Spanish reports and therefore assumed that Cortés always fully understood the Mexica and was therefore

capable of manipulating them. In light of more recent sources, the role of the
Spanish is far less impressive.[32] Particularly when it comes to the actions of the
indigenous people, we must investigate whether these were in many cases actually fictitious events. Such fabrications could have been accepted at some point
along the way as historical fact and conveniently integrated into the tradition
because they made the seemingly incomprehensible comprehensible.

At present, the conquistador myth, which reduces events to the clash of the
two great men, Cortés and Moctezuma, is obsolete.[33] The reality, we now know,
was much more complicated. The Spaniards not only used indigenous "helpers,"
but they also had allies of different ethnic groups. These groups had their own
objectives, which they were also able to achieve. The new Europeanized society
by no means fully superseded the old one. In other words, there was no complete conquest. The indigenous people, for example, adopted Christianity and
incorporated it into their own divine world. They treated the Spanish military
heroes the same way. They, too, were incorporated into the native world, where
war and conquest were also of central importance. In the historiography of the
Nahuatl-speaking peoples of the sixteenth century, the supposed conquest is
even a nonevent. The foreign word "conquest" did not in fact exist, and, while
"conquistador" was in use, it referred to Spanish and indigenous people alike.
The Nahua annals continued as if nothing had happened. Viewed from this perspective, the Spanish conquest no longer seems spectacular or unique. The period after the Fall of Tenochtitlan in Mesoamerica rather appears as a politically
necessary phase of reorganization to fill a power vacuum.[34]

Studies that paved the way for this new interpretive direction, by highlighting
the nuances of conquest and departing from the usual reductive framework, were
already emerging in the 1980s.[35] Notably, there was abundant material about the
history of the Mayan peoples of Yucatan, who were able to maintain their independence after their superficial conquest and essentially governed themselves.
Ethno-historical research over the last two decades, which has consistently included indigenous sources in its analysis, has shown that the pre-Hispanic expansion of the Mexica followed similar patterns to that of the Spanish. Cities
were attacked with the aid of troops from the newly conquered territories, local
conflicts and threatening gestures were exploited, and people offered themselves
opportunistically to one side or the other.

The Spaniards not only used the same strategies, but the indigenous people
also accepted them because they were familiar with this approach. This mattered,
especially in the early years after their arrival, because the Spanish were dependent on this acceptance. Indigenous sources, above all, reveal that what the
Spanish chronicles portray as a glorious conquest was actually a complex process of alliances and negotiations. There was a high degree of continuity in a region where wars were as commonplace as the rise and fall of city-states and their

gods. Cortés and the countless historians after him, who for centuries shaped the master narrative of the Conquest, either downplayed the role of the indigenous people or did not even mention them, as this would have diminished their own fame.[36]

Some historians now claim that events as the Spaniards portrayed them never happened. Consequently, they argue, there can be no talk of a Spanish Conquest; one should rather refer to "indigenous conquerors" who had co-opted a handful of Spaniards.[37] Nonetheless, this inversion of the interpretation does not break with the division of victor and vanquished any more than the traditional one and therefore fails to be convincing. Moreover, this cannot explain why the former Mexican Empire and large parts of Mesoamerica would later become part of a Spanish colonial empire that lasted three hundred years. This book, therefore, argues that the concept of the Conquest is still justified, even if one focuses on the short- and medium-term effects. At the same time, the autonomy and sovereignty of indigenous actors must be taken much more seriously than has previously been the case.

As this is an early modern development, the sources on this topic are relatively abundant. In addition, many of the reports themselves have already been extensively discussed in the scholarship. Still, the sources are characterized by contradictions, inaccuracies, and a lack of verifiability. Moreover, most of the sources were written retrospectively and often do not provide reliable interpretations of what unfolded.[38]

Eyewitness accounts are few and far between. First and foremost, Cortés himself should be mentioned in this context. His life is very well documented, especially because of the many court proceedings in which he was involved. His youth and family life, however, are less well known.[39] Above all, the letters to Charles V, the Spanish king who was to become king in Germany and emperor of the Holy Roman Empire, which Cortés wrote between 1519 and 1526, are regarded as essential sources, as they are the most detailed eyewitness accounts of what transpired.[40] Nevertheless, these so-called *cartas de relación* are rather problematic, as the nobleman was under great pressure to justify his actions. Cortés was familiar with the norms of legal correspondence, having studied the fundamentals of law and served as a secretary to a governor. He also wrote reports in which he repeatedly based his version of events on well-known classical heroic deeds and popular chivalric novels such as *Amadís de Gaula* and *Tirant lo Blanc*. Cortés bore in mind here the reports' appeal at court, but also their publication in Europe and his posthumous fame. In his account, the Spanish conquerors were the chosen instruments of God who brought the peace and justice of Christianity to a world without salvation.[41]

Detailed reports from Cortés's companions are rare. The most famous, undoubtedly, was written by Bernal Díaz del Castillo around 1568, though it remains unclear whether he dictated his memoirs to a ghost writer or penned them himself.[42] Díaz del Castillo is of limited value as an eyewitness, however. He began writing his memoirs only after the passage of many decades, relying heavily on the letters of Cortés as well as chronicles, especially those of Francisco López de Gómara, which he sought to distance himself from. His work, which was not published until 1632, almost fifty years after his death, is permeated by outright inventions and erroneous depictions.[43] Even so, Díaz del Castillo gives insight into the emotions, the prejudices, and the everyday lives of the conquistadors.[44] Also astonishing are the introspection and self-confidence of the author, who wrote at the end of his report: "Of the great heroic deeds of Cortés, I also deserve my due, for I was among the first in all his battles . . ."[45]

Francisco de Aguilar, another member of the expedition, became wealthy through the Conquest, but then joined the Dominican order in 1529. In 1565, at an advanced age, he dictated his *Relación breve de la Conquest de Nueva España*, a short chronicle in eight chapters, in which he describes the bravery and heroic deeds of the conquistadors.[46] Andrés de Tapia also served as a captain in Cortés's troops and was one of his most loyal followers. In his *relación* (account) from about 1539, he took pains to stress the bravura of his leader and was handsomely rewarded for doing so. The work, however, was not published until 1866. It influenced the contributions of many subsequent chroniclers, but describes only the initial phase of the venture.[47] The report of another unit commander, Bernardino Vázquez de Tapia, first published in 1939, also refers to the Conquest. Vázquez de Tapia, who held the position of mayor of the newly founded city of Mexico in 1524 and 1526 and then remained a member of the city council, focused on his own achievements to prevent the loss of his privileges under the new laws.[48] Finally, the report of an anonymous conquistador must be mentioned. Although it does not deal with what took place, it nonetheless gives a detailed account of nature, culture, religion, and life in ancient Mexico in general.[49]

Other important sources include the historical works of authors who, while they did not take part in the events themselves, were nevertheless able to draw on their own conversations with conquistadors. Some of these works contain information that cannot be found in the eyewitness reports. In terms of genre history, they belong to the category of chronicles, which in the Spanish-speaking countries of the sixteenth century includes writings that had terms such as *historia* and *relación* in their titles.[50] These sources are no less biased than the eyewitness accounts. Their authors constructed triumphant versions of the Conquest from different motives, but with the same basic intention of glorifying God and king. They, too, are characterized by exaggerations, falsifications, and inconsistencies.[51]

The Italian humanist at the Spanish court Pietro Martire d'Anghiera is of particular importance. He received only secondhand information but could rely on conversations, letters, and petitions that conquistadors and descendants of the indigenous rulers, the Tlatoque, sent to the crown shortly after the Conquest in order to claim inheritance.[52] From 1493 until his death in 1526, Anghiera was the first to continuously maintain a Latin chronicle of the discoveries and conquests, which was first published in full in 1530 and subsequently in many editions.[53] One of Anghiera's successors in the office of court chronicler was Gonzalo Fernández de Oviedo y Valdés, who had previously travelled to America and held high administrative offices there. His *Historia general y natural de las Indias* was written in the 1530s and was the most comprehensive work on the history of America during this period.[54] Due to a ban on printing, however, Fernández de Oviedo was able to publish only the first part of his chronicle, which extended to the year 1520. As was reflected in their works, both chroniclers primarily represented the interests of the crown.[55]

No less important is the contribution of Francisco López de Gómara, who, like Anghiera and Fernández de Oviedo, cultivated a close proximity to many contemporary witnesses. He is said to have been Cortés's court chaplain. More recent scholarship takes the view that he was more than simply Cortés's apologist, as Bernal Díaz del Castillo, for example, portrayed him in his work. Nonetheless, he was keen to legitimize the conquest and to emphasize the heroic deeds of the Spaniards involved, not least in the spread of Christianity.[56] In a similarly heroizing manner, the humanist and, after 1535, court chronicler and educator of Prince Philip, Juan Ginés de Sepúlveda, portrayed events up to 1521 in his *historia* in Latin. The text was based largely on the work of Fernández de Oviedo, but also partly on discussions with Cortés himself, among others. As Sepúlveda saw it, the violent intervention was necessary to ending the barbarism and, above all, the human sacrifices that took place among the Mexica.[57]

The great rival of Sepúlveda was Bartolomé de las Casas. He had first participated in campaigns of conquest in Cuba, but, later, as a priest and Dominican friar, he was the most influential critic of the exploitation of the indigenous peoples by the Spanish colonizers. He expressed his views in his numerous texts, especially his multivolume *Historia de Las Indias*, which he began writing in 1527 to cover the period up to 1520. The work draws on his own experiences, a large collection of original sources, and the testimony of many eyewitnesses. Las Casas also knew Cortés and Bernal personally. He strongly criticized the conquerors and portrayed the indigenous people as children in need of protection. Because of his great influence at the court, he also succeeded in imposing printing bans on the works of other authors, such as Fernández de Oviedo.[58]

Besides Las Casas, Franciscan friars and nuns, in particular, passed down accounts from the period after the conquest. They disseminated the notion of a God-given Christian triumph over the Mexican Empire, which they believed was dominated by the devil. Particularly important is the work of Toribio de Benavente, who called himself Motolinía, "the poor man" in Nahuatl. One of the earliest missionaries in New Spain, Motolonía wrote the *Memoriales* and the *Historia de los Indios*, which cover the period up to 1541 and are the oldest Spanish language chronicles written in New Spain. He worked with many Mexican nobles and even with Cortés's interpreter, Malinche.[59] His fellow friar Gerónimo de Mendieta lived in Mexico from 1554 on, where he served with Motolinía. He wrote his five-volume *Historia eclesiástica indiana* between 1573 and 1596; it was not published until 1870. Both friars still enjoyed access to eyewitnesses and to sources that were later lost.[60]

Like Mendieta, other historians did not come to New Spain until around the middle of the sixteenth century, decades after the Fall of Tenochtitlan. Some, however, still could talk to contemporary witnesses. Belonging to this group is the jurist Alonso de Zorita, who wrote *Relación de la Nueva España*. His work, first published in 1935, denounced, among other things, the abuses of colonial rule.[61] There was also the humanist and rector of the newly founded university in Mexico, Francisco Cervantes de Salazar, with his *Crónica de la Nueva España* (1903). From Cervantes's standpoint, the Conquest was a divinely inspired act of heroism in response to the cruelty of the Mexican people. In this effort, Cortés particularly stood out.[62]

The circumstances of the indigenous sources are similarly heterogeneous and are complicated by the history of their reception. Over the centuries, chroniclers and historians simply disregarded the perspectives of the many different ethnic groups that lived in Mesoamerica before the arrival of the Spanish. Only Cortés quoted Moctezuma's speech, though he paraphrased the dialogue he reproduced.[63] The indigenous people had already written numerous books— codices—in the sixteenth century, reflecting the events of the Conquest from their perspective. Under Spanish rule, however, the texts were often burned or kept under lock and key. It was not until the twentieth century that historians began to systematically examine those that survived. Yet the publication of these sources—the so-called *View of the Vanquished*, as the title of the best-known collection put it—one-sidedly presented the indigenous groups as passive victims.[64]

Indigenous eyewitness accounts were for some time thought to be available. For instance, a number of the ninety-one poems known as "Mexican songs," *cantares mexicanos,* were believed to have been written as early as the middle of the 1520s and could be regarded as the oldest written accounts of the historical events. Some of these songs described the defeat of the Mexica as the greatest sacrifice ever offered to the gods.[65] Research also assumed a very early origin for the Annals of Tlatelolco, dated 1528. Tlatelolco was the closely connected neighboring city of Tenochtitlan; both cities shared the island on Lake Texcoco. This chronicle, consisting of five independent documents, focused on the courage of the inhabitants of Tlatelolco who, unlike their neighbors in Tenochtitlan, did not give up hope of victory over the Spanish.[66] In the case of both sources it remained unclear who the authors were or how they could have mastered the Latin alphabet so soon after the end of the war. Today, many historians have concluded that the earliest indigenous testimonies may not have been written before the 1540s, several decades after the events they describe.[67]

When dating the indigenous sources to the second half of the sixteenth century, a basic problem emerges. At that time, there had already been many cross-cultural interactions, not least due to the transcription of the Nahua languages into the Roman script. Undoubtedly, these transcriptions into the alphabet resulted in shifts of meaning and omissions, which were further intensified by the time elapsed since the events they describe and by the self-censorship of indigenous authors.[68] For a long time, colonial indigenous sources were held in low esteem because they were supposedly already completely "westernized."[69]

In addition, the authors of the documents were often mestizos, which means they had Spanish fathers. These mestizo authors acted as cultural mediators, but also as social actors with specific interests in a dynamically changing context. Their texts emphasize affiliation with individual ethnic groups with which the authors identified for various reasons. Recent research has rediscovered these chronicles and stressed their importance for understanding early colonial society.[70]

Among the important mestizo authors of this period is Diego Muñoz Camargo (1529–1599), the illegitimate son of an indigenous noblewoman and a conquistador. He received a Spanish education, but also spoke Nahuatl. A successful livestock farmer, he served as a translator and held various public offices in the city of Tlaxcala, the great adversary of Tenochtitlan and ally of the Spaniards. His *Historia de Tlaxcala* of 1592 mainly represented the interests of the *cabildo* (city council) of his hometown. At the same time, he also condemned what he considered to be pagan cults of the past.[71]

The first generation of mestizos also included Don Hernando de Alvarado Tezozomoc (ca. 1525-ca. 1610), a grandson of Moctezuma, whose father was a *tlatoani* (ruler) and governor of Ecatepec. His *Crónica mexicana*, which was published in Spanish in 1598, along with the part of the *Crónica mexicayotl* in Nahuatl that is attributed to him, are among the most important sources of pre-Hispanic Mexica history. Little is known about Tezozomoc himself. Having grown up with the oral traditions of the ancients upon which his texts are based, he is considered the most important chronicler of the Tenochca, the inhabitants of Tenochtitlan.[72]

If Tezozomoc is considered the voice of Tenochtitlan, the mestizo Fernando de Alva Ixtlilxochitl (ca. 1578–1650) must be regarded as the most important spokesman of the neighboring town of Texcoco, which was a member of the Triple Alliance that included also the city states of Tenochtitlan and Tlacopan. His mother was a mestiza descended from the princes of Texcoco, and his father a Spaniard. Alva Ixtlilxochitl worked as a judge, civil servant, and translator. He drew on many indigenous sources for his *Sumaria relación* and his *Historia de los señores chichimecas*. He used the honorary title Don to signify his membership in the indigenous nobility.[73] Recently rediscovered, Alva Ixtlilxochitl is considered one of the most influential indigenous authors of the New Spanish colonial period.[74]

Domingo Francisco de San Antón Muñón Chimalpahin Cuatlehuanitzin (1579–1660) was a contemporary of Alva Ixtlilxochitl. Born in Chalco Amaquemecan into the indigenous provincial nobility, he moved at a young age to Mexico City and afterward worked as a chaplain in the church of San Antonio Abad in Xoloco. In contrast to Alva and Tezozomoc, he did not hold public office, but nevertheless produced an extensive body of writing.[75] Like the other authors, Chimalpahin wanted to write a history from an indigenous perspective and for the indigenous people of his homeland. Unlike them, he wrote his chronicles in Nahuatl and dealt with the entire former dominion of Tenochtitlan. His work is proof of the survival of indigenous cultural traditions and indigenous knowledge well after the Fall of Tenochtitlan. It is also the only example of a colonial Spanish text, that of López de Gómara, being appropriated and modified by an indigenous person. By contrast, there were many instances of the reverse.[76]

Much of what we know today about the Mesoamerican societies of the precolonial and early colonial periods has been handed down by missionaries. The Franciscans, who were the first in Mesoamerica to spread the Christian faith, were especially committed to changing the mindsets and lifestyle of the new Christians. Already in the first half of the sixteenth century, they made outstanding contributions to the textualization of Nahuatl. These early New Spanish chroniclers preferred indigenous oral traditions to the sparse written sources, which they were unable to understand. Of course, their goal was not to preserve the indigenous cultures but to learn more about them in order to destroy their religious beliefs and convert the population to Catholicism. While the ethnographic value of these sources is limited, it is not surprising that they reflect the influence of Franciscan translators, writers, and editors.[77]

In addition to Motolinía's work, Bernardino de Sahagún's *Historia general de las cosas de Nueva España* is undoubtedly the most famous collection of Mesoamerican voices from this period. It depicts the events in Nahuatl from the indigenous point of view, albeit through European eyes.[78] This collection, which was supplemented over many years from the 1550s onwards, was the result of Sahagún's collaboration with innumerable unnamed indigenous students, writers, and interlocutors, whose accounts, oral and written, the Franciscans had collected and transcribed. It is likely that he also added his own interpretations, for the account contains many echoes of Franciscan apocalyptic ideas. The Spanish translation of the text deviates from the version in the Nahuatl at crucial points, for example regarding the massacre of Alvarado and the death of Moctezuma.[79] Well-known in its illustrated version as the Florentine Codex, this work (especially its Book XII) offers a detailed depiction of the Fall of Tenochtitlan. Despite Sahagún's considerable experience, however, it is full of misunderstandings and distortions.[80]

The *Codex Ramírez*, or *Codex Tovar* after the Jesuit Juan de Tovar, can be considered the same type of text. Tovar himself had indigenous ancestors on his mother's side and spoke several Mesoamerican languages. He is thought to have compiled the manuscript around the middle of the sixteenth century based it on oral traditions of indigenous contemporary witnesses.[81] For the indigenous people, codices like these could have had the effect of strengthening an indigenous identity. Recognizing this, the rulers sensed that they might be a threat, potentially triggering a relapse into old beliefs. As a preventative measure, the Crown prohibited the distribution of ethnographic reports by the missionaries and confiscated the works from 1577 onward. The ban would remain in force until the end of the colonial era, leaving researchers to rediscover and edit these important sources in the nineteenth century.[82]

Visual sources are especially valuable for understanding the indigenous view of the Fall of Tenochtitlan. Pictograms and glyphs were the indigenous form of literacy and remained widespread in the sixteenth century.[83] To be sure, the interpretation of these sources is a special challenge, since the intention behind certain gestures, poses, and other details can often only be guessed at. The indigenous pictorial sources in particular, whose dating is often unclear, must be understood as dynamic products. Depending on whether they were read synchronously by different groups of the colonial society or diachronically at various points in time, they could be interpreted quite differently.[84] The large illustrations of the conquest on painted canvases such as the *Lienzo de Tlaxcala*, the *Lienzo de Quauhquechollan*, and the *Lienzo de Analco* can be highly illuminating in their depictions of events. On the other hand, the visual sources are equally compelling because of what they conceal. Thus, in their *lienzo*, the Tlaxcaltecs neither indicate their initial resistance to the Spaniards nor the contribution of other allies to the victory over Tenochtitlan. This official document, which was to be sent to the Emperor in Spain, is remarkably self-assured. The Tlaxcaltecs sought to establish their claim to certain privileges by highlighting their own contribution to the conquest as well as to Christianization.[85]

This book draws on these and many other sources, following a structure that is based on both chronological and thematic factors. The first chapter focuses on Cortés's youth and describes the initial situation of the Spanish possessions in the Caribbean until the exploratory expeditions of Francisco Hernández de Córdoba and Juan de Grijalva in 1517 and 1518, respectively. The following chapters examine the beginnings of the campaign (*hueste*) of Cortés and the events in the Mayan lands, as well as the origins and social composition of the conquistadors. The empire of the Mexica constitutes the primary focus of the next section, which looks at the origins of this ethnic group and its political, economic, social, and cultural world until the reign of Moctezuma II. Chapter 4 analyzes the arrival of the Spaniards in Totonacapan and their march inland as well as the Quetzalcoatl myth. Cortés's first reports to the emperor are also presented here. Chapter 5 centers on the events in Tlaxcala and its special role as the most valuable ally of the Spanish. The two subsequent chapters describe events from the arrival of the Spaniards and their allies in Tenochtitlan, to the capture of Moctezuma and the "sad night" (*noche triste*), to the siege and the fall of the city. The continuation of the war and the expansion into the peripheral areas as well as Cortés's personal consolidation of power are the subject of chapter 7. Finally, there is a chapter on the legacy of the Conquest, the construction of a new capital, the introduction of new systems of rule, Christianization, and daily life in New Spain.

Five hundred years have passed since the Fall of Tenochtitlan and the struggle to interpret what happened during this world-historical event fills entire libraries. Still, just as the story has never been completely told, there will never be and can never be a "definitive" retelling of events. In recent decades, new research has emerged and new interpretations have prevailed over long-established knowledge. Today, we know that Hernán Cortés was not the all-conquering hero he made himself out to be in his written reports to the emperor and as the many later chroniclers reverentially described him. But neither was he the devil who more or less single-handedly destroyed a flourishing culture. One of the aims of this book is to dispel such myths. Its focus will not just be on the conquistador Cortés, but on the conquistadors generally. They included the Spaniards who accompanied Cortés as well as people from the numerous ethnic groups of Mesoamerica. They had different motives for wanting to overthrow the mighty Tenochtitlan. The actual story, however, cannot be told without either Cortés or his men, for they would lay the foundation of a colonial empire that would last some three hundred years.

Setting Off for the New World

By the time Christopher Columbus died in Valladolid, Spain, on May 20, 1506, the euphoria about his westward voyage and the newly discovered territories in the Indies had turned to disillusionment. Since 1492, hopes for the discovery of the sea route to mythical gold-producing countries of the East had not been realized. The Caribbean islands, whose riches Columbus had once described in such florid terms, did not produce the hoped-for bounty. While Portuguese rivals opened the sea route to India as early as 1498, Spain's own settlers, above all the family of Columbus, caused so much trouble for the Crown that it had to repeatedly intervene—this, in spite of the fact that politics in Europe was actually much more important. It was also difficult to reconcile the humane treatment of the indigenous population with the pursuit of economic gain. From the point of view of the Spanish colonizers, the people they generically and pejoratively called "Indians" were of little value. They were hardly suitable as slaves, because they died quickly from overwork and from the diseases introduced by the Europeans, which the Spaniards believed explained why the population decline on the Caribbean islands was so dramatic. The appeal of the New World had faded. In order to revive the impulse for discovery, a new incentive was needed.

A Teenager in Extremadura

Hernán Cortés was a young man during this era. He was probably born in 1485 in Medellín, in the Spanish province of Extremadura, far from the centers of power. It was a time when the late medieval world was on the verge of a far-reaching period of change. Most of Spain was ruled by Ferdinand of Aragon and Isabella of Castile, who had married in Valladolid in 1469. During their reign, the country experienced a process of consolidation and expansion against a backdrop of debilitating plague and internal conflicts. The war against the Islamic realm of Granada ended with the city's conquest in 1492, a development that also heralded the start of Columbus's journey. Even though Spain was anything but a unitary state at that time—it consisted of numerous subkingdoms, some of which were linked in personal unions—Ferdinand and Isabella had nevertheless made progress toward centralization. Religious tensions were quelled by the Inquisition launched in 1478, and with the conclusion of the Reconquest, financial means became available in no small measure by the persecuted Jewish and Muslim minorities.[1]

Little is actually known about Cortés's life at this time, which only stoked legends early on. For example, Lucio Marineo Sículo, the Sicilian-born humanist at the Spanish court who wrote the first biography of the conquistador in 1530, claimed that Cortés came from the Eternal City, Rome.[2] Other Spanish chroniclers later claimed that Cortés was born in 1483, the same year as Martin Luther, the "terrible and cruel monster against the Church," and was thus the reformer's orthodox counterpart. This assertion was false too, however.[3]

Abundant biographical research has revealed that Cortés's father, Martín, was born around the middle of the fifteenth century and lived in Medellín as a member of the lower nobility, the *hidalgos*. His military achievements in the numerous bloody conflicts that shook the region at the time, as well as in the Reconquest, brought him certain recognition and privileges. His personal possessions remained modest, although according to some chroniclers the family probably was not poor. He married Catalina Pizarro, who herself came from an hidalgo family from the neighboring town of Trujillo.[4] The part of Extremadura where the family lived was fertile, but only a few owned land. Medellín thus was ruled by the counts of Portocarrero. There were few prospects for the lower nobility after the war, which may explain the high number of migrants to the New World from this region. They included illustrious names such as the Pizarro brothers, who conquered the Inca Empire, Nicolás de Ovando, the governor of Hispaniola, and Cortés.[5]

According to historian López de Gómara, Cortés was a sickly child who only narrowly escaped death.[6] As his family's only heir, he developed a close relationship with his father, which would be consequential for his life's path. His father probably taught him the military and riding skills that were de rigueur for a young nobleman.[7] Cortés learned to read and write at a time when Spanish culture was flourishing. In 1492, the scholar Antonio de Nebrija presented the first grammar of the Castilian language, having realized that "the language was always the companion of the empire."[8] Young Cortés, like many of his contemporaries, probably took a liking to the popular chivalric romances, such as the Amadís de Gaula collection by Garci Rodríguez de Montalvo (1508), printed in Seville by the publishing house of Jacob Cromberger, a native of Nuremberg.[9] Cortés's interest in distant lands may also have been aroused by the partly fictitious travelogues of Jean de Mandeville and Marco Polo, which circulated in the form of popular chapbooks.[10]

Cortés was probably sent as a fourteen- or fifteen-year old by his father to Salamanca to further his education. His stepsister Inés Gómez de Paz lived there with her husband, the scribe Francisco Núñez de Valera. It remains uncertain whether Cortés actually studied at the university without obtaining an academic degree, which was common at the time, or whether he merely learned the rudiments of Latin grammar and law as preparation for his continued academic training. Most important, he acquired valuable skills during these two to three years and became quite proficient with the written word, even Latin. He also learned how to argue on his own behalf with legal finesse. In his correspondence, he liked to bolster his words by quoting from the classics, which he encountered in the popular collections of aphorisms of the time. These skills would prove highly useful to him in the New World.[11]

After this apprenticeship period, Cortés hatched a plan to prove his courage and strength by taking part in military adventures. Despite his erudition, the depth of which can only be guessed at, despite his frequent boasting, he appears to have been more inclined to military service and gambling.[12] Numerous locations were well suited to these particular interests. He was probably first attracted to the Spanish campaigns in Italy, but then decided to join Nicolás de Ovando's fleet, which brought the young Spaniard Bartolomé de las Casas, who would later become the famous defender of the indigenous, among others, to the Indies. According to López de Gomara, Cortés returned to Medellín before his departure to obtain his parents' blessing and money for the journey.[13] Sources also mention that he moved to Seville, where he suffered an accident during an amorous affair and consequently missed his departure.[14] On the one hand, the patchy and rather contradictory lore about the early phase of Cortés's life suggests that he had less-than-promising prospects for the future. On the other hand, as a young hidalgo, he had sufficient social capital and kinship relations to take full advantage of opportunities that arose. If these were not to be found on the Iberian Peninsula, then the Indies probably seemed like a good bet. Indeed, Ovando's undertaking—the creation of a settlement in the New World—held out the promise of a new beginning.

The Lure of the Indies

There seems to be wide agreement among chroniclers that Hernán Cortés began his grand voyage in 1504, around the age of nineteen. According to López de Gomara, he sailed on a carrack (*nao* in Spanish) captained by Alonso Quintero from Palos de la Frontera via the Canary Island of La Gomera to Santo Domingo on the island of Hispaniola, the heart of Spanish rule in the Caribbean.[15] This was where Columbus had founded the first settlement of La Navidad and also the location of the governor's seat. In 1492, the population of the Greater and Lesser Antilles was estimated to have been around one million, but this number declined rapidly after the arrival of the Spanish. Any notions of peaceful coexistence must have dissipated quickly, as, starting with the destruction of La Navidad by the Taino in 1493, there had been an endless series of bloody reprisals, exploitation, and oppression. The massacre of the first settlers was most likely induced by the Spaniards, who brutally assaulted and sought to subdue the indigenous population.[16]

The inhabitants of the Caribbean at that time had a long history. As early as the fourth millennium BCE, hunters and gatherers from the Yucatán Peninsula had arrived on the islands of the Antilles. Two millennia later, settled groups from the region of Saladero in what is now Venezuela followed; they had already mastered pottery and practiced agriculture. These Saladoids dominated the indigenous population and intermingled with them. In the first millennium CE, the number of settlements exploded, and previously uninhabited islands were colonized. During this period, complex social hierarchies arose, such as that of the Taino, who were divided into subgroups and inhabited, among other places, the islands of the Greater Antilles: Haiti (Hispaniola), Cuba (Fernandina), and Boriquén (Puerto Rico).[17] The Taino lived off of agriculture—especially cassava—and fishing. Exotic fruits and plants, such as pineapple and tobacco, would later fascinate the Europeans. Clothing was hardly necessary given the climate, but the Taino made hammocks and other items. They built shelters, large huts made of wood and straw, that accommodated many people. Their weapons were the clublike macanas, but also spears and bows and arrows. The Taino were excellent sailors. Their canoes, though unimpressive at first sight, were seaworthy vessels and used for conducting trade between the islands. There were even dominions spanning several islands, the core of which were formed by villages that sometimes had over a thousand inhabitants.

That religion pervaded the lives of the Taino could be seen in their art and their rituals, among them a ball game that was likely adopted from Mesoamerica. Faced with frequent natural disasters, such as hurricanes and floods, their religious practices were a means of serving the common good. They also formed a link to the realm of the dead, who were venerated in a prominent ancestor cult.[18]

Apart from a few exceptions, the Tainos' early interactions with the Spanish ranged between cautious and generally friendly. But peace did not last long. The Spaniards' second attempt to found a settlement, La Isabela on the north coast of Hispaniola, failed. After 1494, the initially harmonious relations with the surrounding villages deteriorated rapidly after Taino chiefs (*caciques*) found out that the Europeans wanted to stay permanently and were eager to exploit their resources. Additional tensions were triggered by Spanish forays into the interior in search of gold and the construction of Fort Santo Tomás. The Spaniards demanded food from the locals and brutally punished any resistance from them; armed conflict proved inevitable. The settlement was moved again, this time to the south of the island. In 1502, after yet another move, it was named Santo Domingo.[19]

Having failed to find the anticipated riches, from 1495 the Spaniards began enslaving the native people and shipping them to Europe. While their motives were purely economic, they were legitimized by a professed missionary interest. Nonetheless, the Spanish crown banned this practice in 1500, not least because the enslaved locals usually perished in Europe under the unfamiliar living conditions. An exception, the enslavement of the supposedly cannibalistic Carib Indians—a neighboring population to the Taino—was permitted, though this often led to abuse. Generally speaking, the claim of cannibalism effectively allowed the conflict to be reclassified as a "just war." The Spaniards' harsh conduct and the diseases they carried with them caused the population of Hispaniola to drastically shrink, which, in turn, led to a shortage of manpower. The Spaniards responded by enslaving the inhabitants of the neighboring islands. From 1505 onward, they also imported slaves from Africa.[20]

This did nothing, however, to curtail the massive population loss. Uprisings became more and more frequent, and the Spaniards brutally suppressed them. Governor Ovando, who had been in power since 1502 and whose fleet Cortés had missed, was notorious for his so-called pacification measures.[21] Under his leadership, however, the settlements were successfully expanded and new towns were created. When a smallpox epidemic raged in 1518 and 1519, hopes of long-term settlement on the island on the basis of indigenous forced labor evaporated. The massive die-off of the population was due mostly to the cruel drudgery and violence of the Spaniards. In addition, there were infectious diseases such as measles, mumps, smallpox, typhoid, and flu, against which the locals lacked any immunity. As royal chronicler Pietro Martire d'Anghiera stated in 1530, "The number of the ill-fated inhabitants has greatly decreased."[22] In 1570, his successor Juan López de Velasco noted that, of the once large Taino population, only two villages had survived.[23]

The details about Cortes's early years in the Caribbean are sketchy. Sources indicate that he introduced himself to Governor Ovando, who was also from Extremadura, early on. He probably brought with him letters of recommendation from relatives in the region.[24] It is possible, however, that it was difficult for the young man to get a foothold in colonial society, even if gold mining was flourishing again between 1502 and 1508 due to the brutal exploitation of the labor force and the import of slaves from Africa under Ovando. The older, established conquistadors divided the profits among themselves.[25]

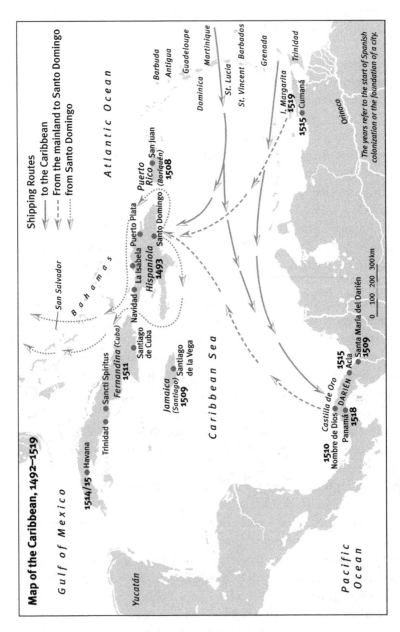

Fig. 1.1 Map of the Caribbean, 1492–1519

Cortés most likely first went in search of gold, and subsequently tried his hand at farming. Like Las Casas, he also participated in the fighting against the Taino, which was led by Diego Velázquez on Ovando's behalf. Cortés made a name for himself in the campaigns against the towns of Baoruco, Aniguayagua, and Higüey. In return for their services, the soldiers were assigned indigenous laborers.[26] Ovando had introduced this system of allocation (*repartimiento*) or—more euphemistically—entrustment (*encomienda*) of the indigenous population in order to avoid open slavery. Under this arrangement, the conquerors and later the settlers were allocated a certain number of indigenous people who were compelled to work for them. In return, the owners of an *encomienda*, the *encomenderos*, were responsible for the education and Christianization of the native peoples entrusted to them. In practice, however, things were different. Wanting to get rich quickly, the Spaniards saw the indigenous people as cheap slaves to be exploited at their whim. They accepted their decimation because they considered the locals to be pagans and barbarians.[27]

Along with the encomienda, Cortés was rewarded with the position of scribe in the small town of Azua. Chronicler Cervantes de Salazar affirms that he carried out his work to the full satisfaction of the area's few inhabitants. It remains uncertain, as Cervantes de Salazar further suggests, whether Cortés in fact had difficulties due to various love affairs. We can at least assume Cortés's fondness for women, given the frequent references in the sources. By this point, the hopes of fame and fortune that had motivated him to make the risky crossing to the Indies had not been fulfilled; his living conditions were quite meager. He therefore sought to cultivate personal ties with Velázquez, among others, which would be important for his advancement.[28]

A turn of good fortune finally seemed at hand with Diego de Nicuesa's campaign to the mainland in the Gulf of Darién at the end of 1509. The troops ended up waiting for Cortés for a long time, but illness prevented him from making the journey; Cervantes de Salazar tells us that Cortés suffered from syphilis.[29] He therefore had to wait for the expedition that set out in 1511 to conquer the neighboring island of Cuba. By this time, however, the balance of power on Hispaniola had shifted. After a long legal battle, the crown confirmed upon Diego Colón, son of Columbus, the privileges of his father. When Colón arrived in Santo Domingo in 1509, he replaced Ovando. Accompanied by his family, the new admiral and viceroy went about expanding his rule in the Caribbean. He benefited from the efforts of Ovando, who in 1508 had sent Sebastián de Ocampo and Juan Ponce de León to explore the islands of Cuba and Boriquén.[30]

Diego Velázquez, who came from a respected noble family, was commissioned by Diego Colón to conquer Cuba in the 1511 expedition. Velázquez had accompanied Columbus on his second voyage and had been in the Indies since 1493; Ovando had made him his deputy, and after more than fifteen years on the ground, Velázquez had gained significant knowledge and had made excellent connections. He had also accumulated great wealth. Above all, he was an experienced and ruthless commander in the fight against the indigenous inhabitants, which he demonstrated during the Jaragua massacre of 1503.[31] Cortés was not about to let this opportunity pass and jumped at the chance to join the expedition. His relations with Velázquez at this time were on solid ground because he knew how to ingratiate himself. Many impoverished and indebted Spaniards, for whom Cuba represented a fresh colonial start, also learned this skill. The expedition set sail in August with four ships and about three hundred men, among them men who would become well known: Cortés, Las Casas, Bernal Díaz del Castillo, Juan de Grijalva, Pedro de Alvarado, and Diego de Ordás.[32]

Their arrival and early days in the southeast of Cuba went smoothly. Taino lived here as well, but compared to Hispaniola the island was only sparsely populated. Velázquez founded Nuestra Señora de la Asunción de Baracoa in mid-August and made it the first capital. This was followed by the founding of more cities. The indigenous population resisted, but the Spaniards violently brought them under control; those who weren't killed were enslaved. Las Casas, who was ordained a priest in Rome in 1507 during a trip to Europe and participated in the war campaigns as chaplain, later reported extensively on the brutality of Spanish warfare on this once fertile and rich island. He wrote that they had "reduced it throughout to a desert and a wasteland."[33] What happened to the cacique Hatuey, from Hispaniola, who had fled to Cuba from the Spaniards and became a leader of the resistance, is notorious: after he was captured and tied to the stake, he refused baptism because he did not want to end up in the Christian heaven.[34]

Unlike Las Casas, Cortés had no pangs of conscience. On the contrary, the fighting, which always gave him pleasure, afforded him new opportunities to distinguish himself. He also made himself indispensable as a competent secretary for Velázquez. Nonetheless, as Las Casas reports in his *Historia de las Indias*, it was not Cortés but Captain Pánfilo de Narváez, Velázquez's closest confidant, who became second in command of the new government. Narváez had come to Cuba with several soldiers from Jamaica, where he had served under the conquistador Juan de Esquivel. He had met Velázquez in Spain.[35] Cortés, for his part, was given a generous encomienda and appointed scribe of the new capital, Santiago. In the period that followed, he had the Taino entrusted to him search for gold and profitably raised livestock. He was thus able to achieve a certain degree of prosperity and ascend to the upper stratum of the colonizers.[36]

According to López de Gomara, Cortés's modest rise aroused envy in a group of Velázquez's cohort. Apparently, they plotted against him and succeeded;

after a few years, he lost favor with the governor. Las Casas further relates that Cortés joined a conspiracy in 1514 against the governor to denounce him before a group of newly arrived judges. López de Gomara, conversely, describes how Cortés attracted the wrath of others because he refused to marry Catalina Suárez, whom he had courted. The encomendero Juan Suárez de Ávila had brought his sister, Catalina, to Cuba with his other siblings and his mother, María de Marcayda; they were among the first Spanish women to live in Cuba. Velázquez supposedly took the matter to heart, because he himself had had an affair with one of the sisters. In short, he imprisoned Cortés and even hoped to see him hanged. Cortés, however, took flight and then successfully sought the governor's mercy with a rather risky act of his obedience. He ultimately married Catalina Suárez, but it proved an unfavorable match, since she was not very well-to-do. Before her marriage, she had served as a maid to María de Cuellar, whom Velázquez had married. Eventually, the governor appointed Cortés *alcalde* (mayor) of Santiago de Baracoa. Later, he became the godfather of Cortés's first child.[37]

The Leap to Yucatán

The mainland, the Province of Tierra Firme, was no longer a blank slate for the Spaniards at that time. Still, they did not know much about it, either. Columbus had discovered the South American mainland on his third voyage (1498–1500) near the Orinoco estuary and sailed on his fourth and last voyage (1502–1504) along the Central American coast to Panama, where he founded the city of Portobelo. Yet the continental character of these regions remained a mystery. From as early as 1499, other seafarers had also explored the coasts of South America as far north as Florida and carried out raids. The Gulf of Darién and the land bridge between Central and South America, today Panama, were preferred destinations. In 1513, Vasco Núñez de Balboa, who had founded the city of Santa María la Antigua del Darién in 1510, crossed the isthmus of Panama and discovered the Pacific Ocean.[38]

Despite these undertakings, it took some time before the Yucatán peninsula, located further to the north, caught the Spaniards' attention. Although the Strait of Yucatán, which connects the Gulf of Mexico with the Caribbean Sea, is only about 125 miles wide at its narrowest point, the leap to get there from western Cuba was not an easy task, not least because of the prevailing ocean currents.[39] Moreover, the island had been settled eastward, and the city of Havana, as the center of the west, was not moved to its present location until 1519. Cuba also initially offered the conquerors sufficient spoils and income. But this would change after a few years.

Interest in the unknown countries to the west was first sparked when Columbus accidentally came across a large trading canoe on his fourth voyage off the Honduran coast in 1502. His son Fernando reported long after the Fall of Tenochtitlán that the boat was pushed through the water by numerous paddlers and that there were also several lavishly dressed men among the crew. The traders had loaded the boats with sundry items that were unknown to the Europeans and were carefully protected with palm leaves against the inclement weather. The Spaniards marveled at the exquisite and finely crafted garments, the weapons with "stone blades" (probably made of obsidian), metal axes, and crucibles. For provisions, the strangers had vegetables and grain, as well as "wine made from corn," or *pulque*. The Spaniards also believed that they saw almonds, which were used as money. In fact, they were cocoa beans.[40] The Europeans were obviously dealing with people of a different culture than the Taino of the Caribbean. They dressed elaborately and their commodities indicated a high level of technical know-how. Columbus and his men exhibited a keen interest and even exchanged a number of goods. It seems, however, that they did not succeed in eliciting information whence they came from the leader, since Columbus finally decided to continue his journey to the south.[41]

For many years, this was the only direct contact between the Spaniards and representatives of the culture they knew nothing about. It was not until 1508 that Vicente Yáñez Pinzón, who had commanded the Niña in 1492 and who, in 1500, was the first European to see the Brazilian coast, joined the seasoned navigator Juan Díaz de Solís on a voyage into the foreign waters. In searching for the sea route to the Spice Islands, they sailed westward from the Gulf of Paria and then northward across the Gulf of Darién to Honduras and Guatemala; from there, they reached the Yucatán Peninsula, which they also circumnavigated. We do not know how far they got in the process, though they may have reached the area of the Tabasco River and perhaps even the dominion of the Mexica. In 1509, however, the two abandoned their journey because they failed to find the passage to Asia. Once they were back in Spain, they were unable to report any contacts with the local population.[42]

Two years later, shipwrecked Spaniards actually found their way to Yucatán. They had been caught in a heavy storm on the journey from Darién to Santo Domingo and saved themselves only with considerable difficulty.[43] After they reached land, they were attacked by Maya, who enslaved the survivors. According to Cervantes de Salazar, friar Gerónimo de Aguilar, who witnessed the events, later reported that most of his shipmates were either sacrificed or died from the privations of slave labor. Only Aguilar and some companions, among them Gonzalo Guerrero, managed to escape. This small group was captured, though, by another cacique and again forced to do slave labor. According to this account, only Aguilar and Guerrero survived in the end.[44]

The Journey of Hernández de Córdoba, 1517

The Spaniards undertook a preliminary expedition to Yucatán at the beginning of 1517. It is not known whether it concerned a planned voyage of discovery in search of new lands or was just one of the usual campaigns to capture slaves on the neighboring islands. Indeed, it was likely a little of both. One of the participants was Bernal Díaz del Castillo, who reported on the excursion in his *Historia verdadera*. After a short stay in the Darién, where he had arrived with the fleet of the new governor of Tierra Firme, Pedro Arias de Ávila, he sailed on to Cuba with some comrades whose services on the mainland were no longer required. Here, Velázquez pledged to them "the next available Indians." However, as had happened on Hispaniola earlier, the privileges had already been allocated in Cuba and, despite the constant slave hunts on the neighboring islands, indigenous workers were scarce.[45]

Thus, after three years of waiting, Díaz joined together with over one hundred dissatisfied compatriots to form a *hueste*, a privately financed war enterprise approved and supported, directly or indirectly, by the king or his regent. They chose the wealthy hidalgo Francisco Hernández de Córdoba as their captain and bought two ships and provisions from their last savings. A third ship was provided by Governor Velázquez, who had granted approval for the venture. In addition to Hernández de Córdoba, Lope Ochoa de Caicedo and Cristóbal Morante shared in the financing and leadership. As was customary, a priest and a royal inspector were also present. Antonio de Alaminos, from Palos, in Andalusia, was chosen as captain. He knew the waters of the Caribbean better than anyone and had discovered the Gulf Stream on one of the Ponce de León voyages. On February 8, 1517, the fleet departed from Havana.[46]

Alaminos led the ship on a perilous journey to the hitherto-unknown coast of Yucatán. Diego de Landa, later the bishop of the peninsula, wrote in his chronicle (published in 1566) that the voyagers came across land near the upstream Isla Mujeres. Hernández baptized the island with this name because the Spanish discovered statues of half-dressed goddesses there, which seem to have impressed them as much as the stone dwellings. The latter were previously unknown in the Caribbean islands.[47] Hernandez, of course, did not fail to officially take possession of the island in the name of the Spanish crown and have the act notarized.[48]

The cultures that the Spanish first encountered here were certainly very different from those of the Taino and other ethnic groups in the Caribbean. They consisted of the heterogeneous Maya cultures that spread from the southwest of present-day Mexico to present-day El Salvador and Honduras. The Yucatán Peninsula, whose coastline runs along the Gulf of Mexico and the Caribbean Sea, was an important hub. The north, which the Spaniards circumnavigated, is a lowland region with limestone soil where water-filled sinkholes, called *cenotes*, are found.[49] This region was divided into numerous different political entities, some of which were at war with each other. Initially, Hernández de Córdoba and his men encountered the Ecab, and later they passed through the territories of Ah Kin Chel, Chikinchel, Ah Canul, and other groups whose settlement areas were close to waterholes.[50]

The Maya were able to look back on thousands of years of history. They reached their classical phase between 250 and 900 CE. During the third century, the population grew rapidly and urban centers with monumental structures were built. Many of the typical Mayan pyramids date from this period. Empires such as Tikal and Calakmul were ruled by god-kings who maintained magnificent courts. While the king was the mediator between the divine and the human realms, a caste of priests dispensed precise astronomical knowledge. Furthermore, in the classical period the Maya developed a hieroglyphic script, which was recorded on steles and in books made of bark paper. This writing permits the reconstruction of an eventful history. Presumably due to the interaction of ecological crises, overpopulation, wars, famine, social conflicts, epidemic diseases, and natural disasters, the decay of the large city-states began around the year 900.[51] New centers Chichen Itzá and then Mayapan coalesced in the period that followed, but the tide had already turned in the fifteenth century. When the Spaniards arrived, Sotuta and Tutul Xiue, together with the capital Maní, were the most significant of the numerous small towns that were connected through trade exchanges and cultural similarities.[52]

The astronomical knowledge of the Maya was paramount, as it was necessary for the creation of the ritual calendar used to predict fateful events. Every day had certain unavoidable attributes that determined, for example, the character of newborns or the right time to sow. The calendar priests who possessed this knowledge had the important task of positively influencing the future through ritual acts. For this purpose, they made regular astronomical observations of the course of the stars.[53] They were also responsible for forecasting the future. Thus, it could be read in the Chilam Balam prophecies that there would be an invasion of bearded strangers who might be emissaries of the cultural hero Kukulkaan, the feathered snake.[54]

The first Spanish efforts to communicate with the Maya were disappointing. According to Pietro Martire, they shouted in their language: "Ma c'ubab than" ("We do not understand your words"). The Spanish invaders thus turned their words into "Yucatán" and christened the area with this name.[55] They eventually continued their journey along the coast to Cape Catoche in the northeast of the peninsula, where Maya people approached them in large canoes. Hernández entertained them on board, and there was a peaceful exchange of gifts. The Europeans noticed the Maya's "civilized" clothing. When a land visit was arranged for the next day, the cacique proposed picking up his guests with canoes. The Spanish distrusted the peace, so they went ashore, heavily armed, on their own boats. They were, in fact, ambushed. Fifteen men were injured by the attackers' hail of arrows. In hand-to-hand combat, though, the Spanish weapons proved to be superior.[56]

Like all Mayan peoples, the Ecab were disciplined and experienced fighters. After all, warfare in the Yucatán was common, even before the arrival of the Spanish. While they did not have standing armies at their disposal, when necessary they could call to arms all able men under the command of their war leaders. The chief aim was not to destroy the enemy, but rather to capture them for enslavement or sacrifice. The Maya fought with bow and arrow, obsidian swords, lances, and stones and protected themselves with cotton armor. They entered battle with war paint, decorated coats of arms and standards, and terrifying sounds.[57] The armed conflict with Hernández de Córdoba shows that the Maya's favored ambush strategy was hard-hitting and that their psychological warfare was also effective. By all appearances, the indigenous population was not in awe of the Spaniards. The news of the unscrupulous Europeans had undoubtedly already spread, and the Maya had drawn their conclusions. Faced with superior firepower, they responded with a versatile strategy of ostensibly friendly concessions, threatening gestures, and military strikes whenever the opportunity arose.

During their further explorations, the Spaniards discovered stone temples with golden jewelry. Bernal Díaz described the joy at this sight, even if the "devil's grimaces" and the seemingly sodomitic imagery of the Maya provoked his disgust. These examples of cultural creativity fueled the Spaniards' dreams of riches. When they were invited to a city they called Cairo because of its size and the pyramids, the impression of abundance was only reinforced. There they witnessed large dwellings and temples, cobbled streets and marketplaces, and clean and well-kept corn fields. The Ecab hosted the Spanish; once again gifts were exchanged. But the Ecab were not as impressed by the Spaniards' glass pearls and bells as the Taino had been earlier. Expedition members later reported to Pietro Martire that the women there dressed "modestly" and that all the inhabitants eagerly paid homage to their "idols." They even observed crosses there, which undoubtedly fed speculation.[58]

While Europeans such as the Franciscan missionary de Landa constantly sought parallels to Christianity, the religious beliefs of the Maya could hardly have been more different. They worshipped a pantheon of gods, in particular the god of corn; deceased members of the ruling dynasties could also mutate into gods, which served to stabilize their rule. Blood sacrifices had to be offered to these gods to facilitate their rebirth, since they went through the same cycle of birth, life, and death as humans. Human sacrifices were not absolutely necessary, however. Drops of blood from priests and nobles or animal blood mixed with fragrant resin also sufficed.[59]

The marketplaces and farmland, which stunned the Spanish chroniclers, bore witness to the Maya's thriving economic activity. As in Europe, there was a focus on agriculture, which was dominated by maize cultivation. Beans, sweet potatoes, pumpkins, chilies, avocados, and cotton were also planted. The cocoa plantations and the salt flats near the sea were prized, in particular. Additional food was supplied by hunting for jaguars, deer, turtles, snakes, and monkeys, and by fishing. Trade was conducted both by land and sea, for example with cocoa, salt, baskets, ceramics, and textiles. Merchants exchanged goods with other Mayan communities, but also with other ethnic groups, such as the Mexica. Key import goods were obsidian, copper, gold, and feathers for weapons and the manufacture of luxury goods.[60]

As the Spaniards continued their voyage westward along the coast, they remained convinced that the land they saw was an island. But the longer the journey dragged on, the more they doubted this. They were astounded by the huge temple buildings, while the Maya gathering along the beach were captivated by the large ships. After a fortnight, the Spaniards came to the town of Campeche, which they christened in honor of the day's saint, Lázaro. Their barrels nearly empty of water, they had to go ashore to refill them. To win respect in advance, they unleashed a salvo of their ship's guns.

The leader of the Maya hosted them in royal style with exotic poultry and game. In Pietro Martire's account, the animals of the feast were transformed into partridges, deer, lions, and tigers. The locals, meanwhile, showed the Europeans their temples, which were stained with fresh blood. Their priests covered the visitors in incense. This may have served more than a ritual purpose, such as the masking of the unpleasant odors of the Europeans, who had different notions of personal hygiene. The Spanish were also deeply impressed by the reliefs and sculptures showing unknown deities and bloody carnage. When the menacing sounds of the shell trumpets and drums began, Hernández understood the signal. He therefore ordered his men to immediately march back to the ships in military order. They took with them two more captives, nicknamed Melchorejo and Julianillo, and all kinds of golden objects. They then continued on their journey.[61]

The two captives belonged to a society that was structured hierarchically and based on the division of labor. At the top was a small hereditary aristocratic class that held the leading political and religious offices. Even the largest economic enterprises—the plantations and salt works—belonged to the nobility. Beneath them was the group of free common people, who made up the largest part of the population. It had its own internal structure and included rich merchants as well as farmers. At the bottom of the hierarchy were the slaves, who were either prisoners or criminals.[62]

Due to unfavorable winds, the ships advanced only slowly. As a result, the men had to go ashore again near the present-day town of Champotón to replenish their water supply. Upon arrival, they were immediately attacked. The Maya, heavily armed and wearing war paint, and playing threatening military music and sounding war cries, surrounded the visitors. The Spaniards managed only to escape to their ships with heavy losses. In the end, more than half of the men were dead, while another five succumbed to serious injuries during the return voyage. Captain Hernández de Córdoba had also suffered numerous injuries.[63]

The Spaniards' defeat to an indigenous force was an entirely new experience. Until then, they had only known victory. As they had to sacrifice the smallest of the three ships, continuing the journey was unthinkable. Bernal relates that the return trip was especially miserable because there was no water on board. Due to the inclement weather, Alaminos took the remaining ships to Florida, of which he had firsthand knowledge. But when they tried to obtain water on land, the locals assaulted them and claimed more victims. Two months later, mercifully, the ship's few survivors reached the port of Havana.[64]

Hernández de Córdoba then made his report to the governor in Santiago. Word spread quickly of the discovery of marvelous new lands with sizeable populations and unknown riches. Francisco de los Cobos, the influential secretary of state of the king, learned of the promising news through a letter from the settler Bernardino de Santa Clara in October 1517.[65] Meanwhile, Velázquez shrewdly advertised that the trip was his own undertaking. Hernández de Córdoba could no longer defend himself, for he died just ten days after returning to his estates. The remaining men from his troops had gone their separate ways and were no better off than before.[66]

The Journey of Grijalva, 1518

As it turned out, the gold in Yucatán was an imported commodity. Still, the prisoners Hernández de Córdoba had kidnapped and who were interrogated by Velázquez swore that there was also gold in their country. Encouraged by this news, the governor immediately started to assemble another fleet. He bought two more ships, equipping them and the two that had returned from Yucatán with all the necessities. Velázquez entrusted the high command to his young nephew Juan de Grijalva; as commanders of the other ships, he appointed the *hidalgos* Francisco de Montejo, Alonso de Ávila, and Pedro de Alvarado. They

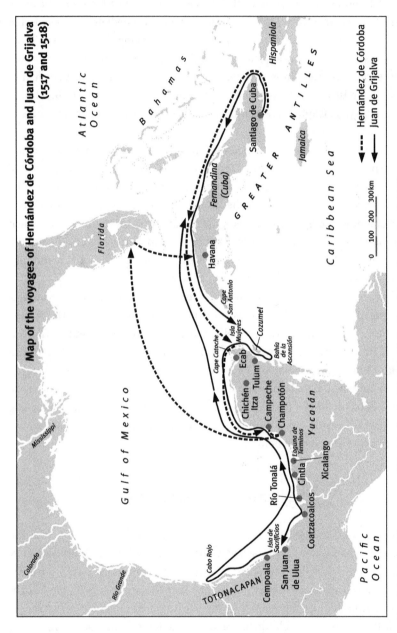

Fig. 1.2 Map of the voyages of Hernández de Córdoba (1517) and Juan de Grijalva (1518)

had to pay for their own provisions. Alvarado, who was about the same age as Cortés, also came from Extremadura, and the two were friends.[67] Getting the troops together was not difficult; before long, more than enough adventurers who were willing to undertake risks to escape poverty in Cuba were found. Once again, the crew included Antonio de Alaminos as pilot, Julianillo as interpreter, and also Bernal Díaz. Francisco de Peñalosa took on the role of royal overseer, while Juan Díaz from Seville accompanied the expedition as a priest. The latter would leave for posterity an account published first in 1520; it was reprinted multiple times and hastily translated into Italian and German.[68] Unlike his namesake, the soldier Díaz, the priest put pen to paper immediately after the experience. It must therefore be regarded as the most significant source used by later chroniclers such as Pietro Martire and Gonzalo Fernández de Oviedo.

The fleet first reached the island of Cozumel, which was spotted on the holiday of the Holy Cross on May 3, 1518, and from then on was called Santa Cruz. The Ecab approached the Spanish with great caution, as news of the encounter with Hernández de Córdoba had spread quickly among the Maya. Peering from their ships, the Spaniards once again witnessed sophisticated architecture and intensively cultivated land. By the time they went ashore on May 6, the Ecab had already fled. Thus, Grijalva immediately held a worship service and officially took possession of the island for the crown. According to the priest Díaz, several Ecab clerics approached them, bringing food and incense, only to leave again. Juan Díaz described the dwellings and streets in utter amazement. They almost looked "as if they had been built by Spaniards."[69] While several gold objects were also discovered, the hoped-for gold deposits were still not to be found. Consequently, they promptly left Cozumel and headed for Yucatán.[70]

The ships followed the Yucatecan coast southward, their commanders expecting to find the continent soon. The magnificent structures that the men saw from the ship probably belonged to the city of Tulum, which Juan Díaz thought was as large as Seville.[71] According to Pietro Martire, they turned back at the Bahía de la Ascensión because bluffs and sandbars impeded further progress. They then followed the familiar route northward and landed once again at Cozumel to fetch water.[72] The men discovered a pyramid on a cape which, as Díaz noted, was supposedly inhabited only by women who "belonged to the tribe of the Amazons."[73] The captain, however, was not willing to allow the voyage to be interrupted. A few days later, the fleet reached Champoton, which was still a bitter memory for the members of the previous expedition. Due to the lack of water on board—the crew had drunk only wine for three days—shore leave was imperative.[74]

Heavily armed and outfitted, Grijalva and most of his men cautiously drew close to the Maya, whose smoke signals and drums could already be seen and heard from the ship. The Spaniards did not realize that these natives were the

Putún of the region called Chakan Putum, or Champoton. The initial contacts were tentative and peaceable. After the interpreter helped to mediate, some Putún even brought the strangers food. The Maya reacted coldly, however, when Grijalva asked for gold in exchange for the goods they had brought. They ultimately sent a brother and a son of their leader to demand that the Spanish leave. Grijalva refused, and fighting commenced the next day. The Spanish guns and crossbows undoubtedly made an impression, but the arrows and lances of the Maya were also effective. There were dead and injured on both sides, including Grijalva himself. The soldier Díaz del Castillo vividly reports of a plague of locusts that made fighting difficult for the Spaniards; the priest Díaz was also convinced that the Europeans would have fared much worse without artillery.[75]

Grijalva recognized the seriousness of the threat. He commanded his revenge-thirsty men to return to the ships and to continue on with their journey. They finally found a safe port at the Laguna de Términos, where the crew rested ashore for almost two weeks and overhauled their ships. There was enough drinking water and fish to sustain them. Grijalva further took advantage of the lively canoe traffic to take captives. On June 8, after their rest period, the Spanish discovered a major river, the Tabasco, which they christened Río Grijalva. Here, they were immediately caught up in sea battles with the Chontal-Maya of the central village Potonchan. The locals were caught off guard by the power of the ship's guns and proceeded to hold negotiations the next day. Gifts were then exchanged in a process that Juan Díaz described as follows:

> The next morning the cacique, or master, came in a canoe and asked the captain to get into the boat. When he followed the request, the cacique instructed one of his Indians to dress the captain. The Indian then put on him armor and bracelets of gold, and he placed a crown of gold, or rather of finely worked gold leaf, on his head; the captain then ordered his men to dress the cacique as well. They then put on him a doublet of green velvet, pink stockings, a tunic, and canvas shoes, and placed a velvet cap on his head.[76]

This act of exchanging gifts, initiated by the ruler of Potonchan, had great symbolism. It is unlikely that the cacique was offering a tribute.[77] Probably, the reciprocal gift was seen as having lesser value, which triggered an asymmetry in the relationship between the two leaders. This is implied by the ruler's demand that Grijalva should give him one of the captured Maya. If an attempt was made to pay a ransom, the Spaniard rejected it. Though his men would have preferred to locate the source of the gold, Grijalva ordered the journey to continue.[78] This decision, though, may also have been prompted by an episode that Bernal Díaz recalled decades later. The Mayans, accordingly, had responded to the Spanish desire for more gold with the cry "Culúa, Culúa, México, México" and pointed to the west.[79] Undoubtedly, they wanted to get rid of the powerful strangers, with their unquenchable thirst for the precious metal, as quickly as possible.

After resuming their journey along the coast, the Spaniards once again thought that they spied gold glittering in the sun on Mayan shields, bracelets, and robes. Juan Díaz also saw women among the Maya. During this part of the journey, tensions arose for the first time between Grijalva and one of his officers. Pedro de Alvarado had left the fleet without permission to explore the course of a river. In response, the supreme commander severely reprimanded him, but the voyage continued.[80]

Some seventy-five nautical miles further west, near the present-day city of Coatzacoalcos, the coastline of the Gulf of Mexico gradually turns northward. After another 120 nautical miles, the Spaniards happened upon an island where they had a shocking encounter. Juan Díaz tells of their seeing massive buildings on high stone pedestals, decorated with alien sculptures, apparently made of marble. Before them was a stone basin full of blood. The men discovered a sacrificial stone and the bodies of some recently sacrificed people as well as a structure with skulls and bones, a *tzompantli*. They were flabbergasted. Grijalva had one of the prisoners fetched from the ships to explain the ritual to him. This is how the Europeans learned about the bloody sacrificial rite: that the priests tore out the hearts of enemies captured in war and made burnt offerings of them, cut off their heads, and later consumed their arms and legs. Fittingly, the Spanish christened the island Isla de los Sacrificios.[81]

The people who practiced these ritual sacrifices were unlike the Maya the Spanish had already encountered. Because the people here spoke a different language, their translators were at pains to make themselves understood. This population, the Totonaks, had settled in eastern Mexico around 1100, principally in the present-day state of Veracruz. The Mexica called the region Totonacapan. Similar to the Maya, the Totonaks lacked a central state, but rather had numerous urban centers. Among the most important were Papantla in the north and Cempoala and Xalapa in the south. Archaeologists assume that the Totonaks also inhabited the already deserted city of El Tajín, with its famous Pyramid of the Niches. Beyond the usual agricultural products of Mesoamerica, the Totonaks' land was known for its cotton and vanilla cultivation. Their weaving was especially prized in the barter trade.[82]

By the time Grijalva dropped anchor off the Isla de los Sacrificios, the Totonakian cities were already paying tribute to the Mexica. King Moctezuma I had subjugated them in the fifteenth century. The Mexica maintained numerous garrisons in the region. In fact, it was their emissaries who sent the signal to Grijalva to come ashore. After the advance guard under Francisco de Montejo (to which Bernal Díaz belonged) had been warmly welcomed, Grijalva made the crossing with the rest of his crew to the village of Chalchicueyacan, near the is-land of Kulua, which the Spanish christened San Juan de Ulúa. Tendile, the gov-ernor of Moctezuma, greeted them deferentially with a ritual involving incense. The Spanish once again took possession of the land for the crown and made it clear in their sign language that they wanted nothing more than to exchange for gold. During their ten-day stay on the coast, Mexica emissaries brought var-ious objects made of gold. Juan Díaz reported that the indigenous people even explained to them how they had melted the gold. In general, they were treated with great courtesy, cared for, and showered with gifts, which included a sump-tuously garbed woman for the supreme commander. The region seemed to be so abundant and the inhabitants so friendly that the priest lamented having to continue his journey. Indeed, Grijalva ordered the voyage to proceed despite the desires of many of his men and officers to stay and establish a settlement.[83] By now, however, it was clear that this was not just another island; it was a mainland area that would require significantly more men to settle.[84]

Many crew members shared Juan Díaz's disappointment and irritation. Grijalva justified his decision by noting the orders from Governor Velázquez, although they had left some latitude. Grijalva, nonetheless, decided to send as an advance guard Alvarado and the fastest ship of the fleet to Cuba with the treasure and the wounded. The rest of the convoy, however, did not travel much farther north. The city of Nautla reminded the Spaniards from afar of Almería. About one hundred nautical miles further on, they again encountered hostile locals who engaged them in a sea battle. At Cabo Rojo, not far from the present-day town of Tuxpan, adverse winds and sea currents stalled their journey. Due to the poor condition of the ships, the lack of provisions, and the men's exhaus-tion, the ship's council voted to turn back. The return voyage was not without its difficulties. The crew had to take a longer rest period at the mouth of the Río Tonalá for maintenance of one of the ships. They then needed another forty-five days before arriving again in Santiago de Cuba.[85]

In Cuba, meanwhile, Velázquez was growing anxious about the expedition. He sent Cristóbal de Olid to find the fleet, but he was unsuccessful. When Alvarado reached his home port just a short time later, he boasted about the rich lands he had seen and showed the gold and the luxurious feather robes. In honor of this, there was a big celebration that lasted days. In mid-November, Grijalva finally arrived in Santiago after a period of rest in western Cuba.[86] Rather than thanking him for faithfully following his orders, Velázquez reproached him for not founding a settlement, as his men had encouraged. Grijalva later bemoaned his suffering to Las Casas, who described his fall from grace Grijalva sought good fortune in Central America and later died in Nicaragua.[87]

The priest Juan Díaz, who had eloquently expressed both his astonishment at and admiration for the newly discovered lands and peoples, could not conclude his account without attempting to restore the biblical view of the world, even if only in a roundabout way. Thus, he wrote that the native inhabitants the Spaniards met along the way were all circumcised and that, not far from the furthest reaches of their voyage, there lived Arabs and Jews. He also noted that the population worshipped a large white marble cross with a golden crown upon which someone had died and who was brighter and more radiant than the sun.[88] Starting with Columbus, the Europeans did not want to trust what their senses told them about the new world. Instead, they preferred to see the foreign as conforming with their own patterns of tradition.

The Expedition Begins

By the age of 34, in early 1519, Hernán Cortés had already had an eventful life. He was a typical representative of the social class of hidalgos who headed to the New World to make their fortune because of limited opportunities for social advancement in Spain. Moreover, despite adverse circumstances, he managed to successfully establish himself in the Indies. These conquistadors of the New World were usually born too late to participate in the Reconquest. The conquest of the Canary Islands was also over, while forays into Africa were reserved for the Portuguese. Like many members of this generation, Cortés was obsequious and shrewd in his dealings with the higher-ups, unscrupulous in interactions with his peers, and brutal and ruthless in his engagement with the indigenous population. Among the conquistadors, his willingness to take risks, fueled by a hunger for fame and fortune, was not exceptional. As Cortés is said to have predicted, one day he would either "dine to the sound of the fanfares or die on the gallows."[1] His moment was still to come.

Preparations for the Third Expedition

Even before Grijalva had returned, Velázquez rightly feared that other rulers in the Spanish Caribbean, for example from Central America or Hispaniola, could preempt his plans. Word of the glorious prospects on the mainland spread quickly. He thus became feverishly active; he had already sent his treasurer Gonzálo Guzmán to Spain to obtain for him the title of *adelantado* of Yucatán. This would have given him both the military and political supreme command and he would no longer have been subordinate to the governor in Santo Domingo. To obtain permission to settle in Yucatán, the governor also sent his envoy, Juan de Saucedo, to the three Hieronymite friars in Santo Domingo. On behalf of Cardinal Cisneros, King Charles's regent in Spain, the friars had in the meantime replaced Diego Colón as governor of the Indies. In addition, Velázquez sent his confessor Benito Martín to Spain to secure the supreme command of all the newly discovered territories, which he had reason to hope would turn out to be vast. A key role in this process would be played by the president of the Indian Council, Juan Rodríguez de Fonseca, Bishop of Burgos and confidant of the governor. Velázquez did not neglect to provide his emissaries with valuable items from the Mayas and Totonaks as gifts for the king and his influential advisers.[2]

Even before the authorizations arrived, Velázquez was preparing for another, much larger expedition—this time with ten ships. It was nevertheless unclear who should receive the supreme command. According to Díaz del Castillo, several names were mentioned, including relatives of the governor and even Grijalva, whom the soldiers favored. In the end, however, Hernán Cortés prevailed. By this point, Cortés had achieved prosperity and prestige in Cuba. As he later observed, in the province of Baracoa he had the best hacienda on the entire island.[3] Moreover, he had succeeded in forging an alliance with two of Velázquez's most influential advisors, his private secretary Andrés de Duero and the royal financial supervisor, Amador de Lares. Together, they were able to convince the governor that no one other than Cortés, courageous, loyal, and the mayor of Santiago, should take command.[4]

On October 23, 1518, Andrés de Duero put the governor's instructions in writing, with much goodwill toward Cortés, as Díaz del Castillo noted. They were very detailed, for the partners were well aware of the scope of the undertaking. The soldiers were strictly forbidden from blasphemy, concubinage, dice, and card games; Cortés, moreover, was obliged to prevent his men from assaulting the locals. To this end, he was granted full judicial authority. As with similar ventures, the focus was to be on Christianization. Cortés was called upon to investigate the news of the crosses among the Maya and to discover whether Christians had already been there. Provisions and equipment were meticulously documented. Cortés's tasks also included the mapping of the newly discovered areas as well as the documenting of all foreign plants, animals, and—not least— the monsters and the Amazons. A further item on the agenda was to search for the shipwrecked Spaniards. Cortés, of course, was also to look for gold deposits and take possession of the areas in the name of the king. Finally, he was charged with sending news to the governor as soon as possible. While the settlement of the new lands was not addressed in the instructions, it was also not explicitly forbidden. This would subsequently become a major bone of contention.[5]

The missionary pretense aside, the expedition was primarily an economic endeavor, and its emphasis was on finding gold and hunting for slaves. Duero, Lares, and Cortés used their own resources to finance the operation, which, again, was essentially a private enterprise. They approached the local trade circles, among others groups, requesting loans in exchange for future returns. According to his

Fig. 2.1 Hernán Cortés depicted by Christoph Weiditz in 1529. This is one of the few pictorial representations of Cortés that was created during his lifetime. The image is taken from the book of traditional costumes by the German artist Christoph Weiditz, who stayed in Spain in 1528 and 1529 and saw the conquistador there. The inscription reads: "Don Fernando Cortés 1529 in his forty-second year. He has won for his Imperial Majesty, Charles V, all of the Indies." From "Trachtenbuch" des Christoph Weiditz, Germanisches Nationalmuseum Nürnberg, Hs. 22474. Bl. 77–78. Wikimedia Commons.

own testimonial, Cortés went into considerable debt. The governor also made a substantial contribution to the high costs incurred in equipping and preparing the large expedition. The question about who paid exactly how much would later become relevant in court.[6]

Because there was a constant danger that competitors might get a head start on them, everyone involved, especially Velázquez, rushed to prepare. According to Las Casas, Velázquez and a large entourage rode to the port each day to check on the fleet's progress.[7] Nevertheless, after the instructions were written down, it took over three months before the ships could finally depart. Cortés put together the largest expedition fleet for his conquest that the Caribbean had ever seen. He ordered massive amounts of artillery, ammunition, tools, horses, and supplies. Cassava bread, corn, pork, bacon, chicken, sugar, vegetables, wine, and vinegar were loaded in vast quantities. He even had his own standard made with the motto: "Friends, let us follow the Cross; and under this sign, if we have true faith, we shall win."[8]

Along with the two hundred or so veterans from the Grijalva expedition, other soldiers and sailors had to be recruited. However, this was not difficult due to the prospect of riches. The recruits, in turn, sold their possessions to buy weapons and equipment. As all sources point out, Cortés soon had an army that recognized him as a caudillo because he managed to strike the right tone in his speeches.[9] His drive and his exploits, however, began to make Velázquez uncomfortable. It was obvious that Cortés was heavily in debt; indeed, he invested all his wealth into the venture. According to Las Casas, he increasingly displayed a haughty demeanor and purposely dressed in a flamboyant manner. Rumors of Cortés's lack of loyalty, which were exacerbated by the governor's jealous entourage, awakened memories in Velázquez of his earlier problems with his subordinate. He thus became more and more convinced that it would be better to relieve Cortés of his command. Yet, Cortés was well informed about the intrigues by his confidant Andrés de Duero. When the hesitant governor finally decided to transfer command to Luis de Medina, the messenger who was to take the news to Medina was murdered. Cortés had left the killer, his brother-in-law Juan Suárez de Ávila, behind as a liaison and protector for his wife. Suárez immediately informed Cortés, who decided to leave Santiago straight away in order to evade the governor's grasp.[10]

The fleet set sail on November 18, 1518, with about three hundred men, headed first to Trinidad on the south coast of Cuba. There, Cortés procured more equipment, recruited farriers, and bought additional horses and all the crossbows and arquebuses he could get. According to Las Casas, this provisioning was not achieved without the use of force.[11] In addition, more than a hundred veterans joined from the Grijalva expedition. They included the brothers Pedro, Gonzalo, and Jorge de Alvarado. Pedro de Alvarado, a trusted confidant of Cortés, was thus given a second chance to satisfy his thirst for adventure, which he had been denied under Grijalva. The supreme commander also succeeded in recruiting for his expedition other hidalgos with illustrious names such as Alonso de Ávila, Alonso Hernández Portocarrero, and Gonzalo de Sandoval. Finally, Juan Sedeño from Havana more or less volunteered to join the fleet with his own ship, which was loaded with food and intended to sail to Santiago.[12]

Velázquez did not relent, however. He sent two envoys with letters to Trinidad, in which the mayor of the city, Francisco Verdugo, a brother-in-law of Velázquez, and some of the officers particularly close to the governor, such as Diego de Ordás and Francisco de Morla, were asked to stop Cortés. But Cortés used his considerable powers of persuasion to once again thwart his superior's scheme. First, he ensured the absolute loyalty of his men. He convinced the officers to follow him no matter what. They, in turn, induced the mayor to remain silent. Cortés, however, considered the situation to be precarious, so he immediately embarked with the entire fleet to San Cristóbal de la Habana (Havana). At that time, the city was still located at the south coast of the island; it assumed its present location shortly afterward. Under the command of Pedro de Alvarado, Cortés directed a number of his soldiers—including Bernal Díaz—to take the overland route to pick up more recruits along the way.[13]

In Havana, Velázquez tried one last time to halt the expedition. His confidant Gaspar de Garnica carried letters to his followers Diego de Ordás, his cousin Velázquez de León, and the Mercedarian priest Bartolomé de Olmedo that begged them to block the fleet's departure. Cortés himself also received a letter from the governor, asking him to hold off. Diego de Ordás went so far as to set a trap for—a trap that Cortés did not fall far. Ordás tried to lure Cortés onto his ship for a banquet in order to kidnap him and take him back to Santiago. But because Cortés's men were loyal to him and because others, including Juan de Cuéllar and Andrés de Tapia took his side as well, Velázquez's followers did not dare overthrow him by force. Even Ordás, who had already invested considerably in the project and equipped his own ship, finally yielded.[14]

What was still unknown in Cuba at this time was that in Spain Bishop Fonseca had complied with the governor's wishes on November 13, 1518, and officially granted him the authority to conquer and colonize the foreign lands. The rules of the Treaty of Tordesillas of 1494, which determined the division of the world along a fictitious line about 1100 miles west of the Cape Verde Islands into a Spanish portion and a Portuguese portion, were to be followed, as were provisions regarding the fair treatment of the "Indians." To avoid depopulating the Caribbean, it was suggested that no more than two hundred Spaniards depart at once. Velázquez was not only awarded the coveted adelantado title, but also promised generous compensation. Besides a guaranteed annual salary, he received the hereditary right to a share of the taxes of the territories conquered on his behalf. In addition, the agreements granted tax concessions to the new settlements for the initial period.[15] If the Cuban governor's new far-reaching powers had become known in due time, many men would undoubtedly have turned away from Cortés. With word of these events months away, the fleet was able to leave for Cozumel on February 10, 1519, with a total of eleven ships.[16]

Conquistadors

Cortés had repeatedly demonstrated his organizing talent and powers of persuasion. Again and again, he had displayed the charisma that enabled him to assert his strength and secure the loyalty of his men. This loyalty was desperately needed, for the challenges facing his army proved far greater than anyone in Cuba could have anticipated. Before crossing the Yucatán Strait, Cortés paraded his troops at Cape Corrientes. There were probably around five hundred men, including 32 crossbowmen, 13 musketeers, and 50 sailors, whom he divided into eleven companies according to the number of ships at his command. He placed them under the control of captains Alonso de Ávila, Alonso Hernández Portocarrero, Diego de Ordás, Francisco de Montejo, Francisco de Morla, Francisco de Salcedo, Juan de Escalante, Juan Velázquez de León, Cristóbal de Olid, and Alonso de Escobar, and Cortés took charge of one of these ships himself. Two hundred Cuban Taino and some African slaves also needed to travel with them. Melchorejo was present again as interpreter, alongside the Nahuatl-speaking Francisquillo, who had been abducted by Grijalva, and the position of chief pilot was held by Alaminos, a member of the two previous expeditions. The troops also had sixteen horses, several bloodhound mastiffs—a race used for war purposes since the Middle Ages—and ten cannons, four of which were light falconets.[17]

There has been extensive research on the origins and social composition of the crew, a difficult task, given that more than half of the conquistadors died without a will or other written record. The regional origins of the men stretched from central Spain to Andalusia. Cities such as Seville, Huelva, Badajoz, Cáceres, Valladolid, Salamanca, Toledo, Zamora, Burgos, and Segovia were especially well represented. The sailors often came from Andalusia, especially from Sevilla and Huelva. Despite the royal prohibition, some foreigners even took part in the hueste. The actual proportion of hidalgos among the men was significantly lower than their own portrayals suggest.[18] Apart from a few exceptions, the men around Cortés were between twenty and forty years of age. While they all came from a society experienced in warfare, there were actually very few professional soldiers among them. Nevertheless, a good number of them had taken part in the conquests on Santo Domingo, Cuba, and Puerto Rico, and later in the slave hunts on the Taino, where they had cut their teeth.[19]

As in the case of Hernández de Córdoba and Grijalva, the operation was a hueste. This meant that the king was entitled to a share of the profits and sovereignty over the conquered territories. Nominally, then, the hueste operated in the name of the king, who himself, however, did not take any risk in case of failure, since the conquerors had to organize the entire enterprise on their own. Everyone involved contributed their own resources of materiel, equipment, labor, and fighting power to achieve the common goal. In theory, this meant that, as investors, they each had a vote in the decision-making process. While the sailors could expect to be paid their wages, the soldiers were entitled to a share of the loot; how much of a share depended on their investment in the company. Even though they had voluntarily joined the company, leaving the force was considered desertion and punishable by death. Since 1503, the crown had required huestes to take a priest with them. In this case, Juan Díaz, who had already participated in Grijalva's expedition, and the Mercedarian Bartolomé de Olmedo were responsible for pastoral care. Cortés was the leader, chosen and recognized by all. He had invested more than the others in the venture and was therefore entitled to most of the spoils.[20]

For those participating in such a hueste, the term "conquistador," conqueror, was adopted. The term originated in the Spanish Middle Ages and was used in the thirteenth century as an honorary title for King James I of Aragon.[21] Just how strongly the Spaniards felt connected to the Reconquest tradition is demonstrated by the fact that chroniclers such as López de Gómara repeatedly emphasized the long history of the fight against the infidels, the *moros*, which was now being continued in the New World. Even Bernal Díaz later thought he heard "Alala" as the battle cry of the Mexica, as had been the battle cry of the Muslims in the wars of the Reconquest; Cortés and other eyewitnesses wrote of *mesquitas* (mosques) in their letters to designate the temples of the indigenous people.[22] In order to put his own achievements in the proper perspective for European readers, in his writings Cortés compared his successes with the glorious struggle of the Reconquest. This was only somewhat effective, however, since in Europe the war against Islam undoubtedly received far greater recognition than the war against the supposedly "naked savages" of the Indies.[23]

The term conquistador, however, not only signified the successful, but above all the legitimate conqueror who fought for the right cause, namely for Spain and the Christian Church.[24] Indeed, it was always important to the Spaniards that they waged a *bellum iustum*, a "just war." In the Indies, this claim was based on the missionary mandate given by the bulls of Pope Alexander VI, which the conquistadors could invoke. In view of the rapid population loss in the conquered territories, missionaries and legal experts in Spain discussed the lawfulness of the acquisition of territory and especially the treatment of indigenous peoples. Provisions for their protection were first introduced in the so-called Laws of Burgos of 1512 and 1513. One contributor to the discussions, the crown jurist Juan López de Palacios Rubios, wrote the *requerimiento* (demand) on behalf of the government. In this text, the "Indians" were asked to convert to Christianity and submit to the Spanish crown. The requerimiento was to be read aloud, regardless of whether those addressed could understand the language or content. Military action against them was permitted if they did not comply with the demand, that is, if they proved to be "unreasonable," according to the standards of the Spaniards.[25]

The requerimiento was undeniably a farce, but it served the purpose of soothing the conquistadors' conscience. To most of them, the Christian faith, as reflected in the use of the cross as a war symbol and in the veneration of St.

Jacob the Moor slayer (*matamoros*), was very important. It even justified the massacres of peaceful indigenous people that repeatedly occurred during the Conquest. For the conquistadors, the intermingling of Christian ideas with dubious superstitions and miraculous beliefs was by no means a contradiction in terms.[26] Aided by the speeches of Cortés, they were able to cultivate an image of themselves as missionaries of the sword, even though, in reality, this was only a cover for their true motivation.[27]

To be sure, the actual motives of the conquistadors were far more profane than the narratives in the chronicles, with the exception of that of Bartolomé de las Casas, would suggest. For the soldiers, a hueste offered a chance to escape social subordination and impoverishment. Most of the men who joined Cortés had failed in their existential quest for honor and social recognition. Like the ancient heroes of Troy or the Punic Wars cited by Bernal Díaz, they wanted to distinguish themselves through their military achievements. Even though probably only about 6 percent of them were hidalgos, the hidalgo culture nevertheless shaped the entire group.[28] Warfare was an attractive activity for them since it promised the fame they were striving for. Hand in hand with this went the craving for material prosperity—gold and riches—that every newly discovered region seemed to portend. In return, these soldiers of fortune and comrades in arms were prepared to risk everything, physically and financially. As the historical record shows, however, the vast majority of conquistadors had at best a very small stake in the promise of the New World. Very often, they lost their livelihoods or even their lives.[29]

In the Land of the Maya

Like the fleets before his, Cortés's ships were initially headed for Cozumel. Contrary to what had been agreed, however, Pedro de Alvarado's ship, which carried Bernal Díaz, had sailed ahead of the convoy and arrived on the island two days earlier than the others. Most of the Ecab had fled and were in hiding, but some were dragged along by Alvarado and his men, who had gone on a looting expedition. When Cortés arrived with the rest of the fleet, he was furious with his captain and severely reprimanded him. He even put the pilot, who had defied orders, temporarily in chains. He released the captured Ecab and returned their possessions.[30] Cortés desired to send a signal of his peaceful intentions to the Maya. He also did not want to prematurely exhaust his soldiers in battle. Instead, he sought to reach the unknown empire in the west, which had much greater appeal than the inhospitable coasts of Yucatán.

The stopover in Cozumel was intended only for obtaining drinking water. But for Cortés and many of his men who had not participated in the expeditions

of Hernández de Córdoba or Grijalva, it was also their first experience of the
Mayan culture. The encounter proved to be extraordinary and unlike what they
already knew about the Taino. Like their predecessors, they were struck by the
dwellings, clothing, trade, agriculture, and, above all, religion. Pietro Martire
d'Anghiera, who addressed this part of his chronicle directly to Pope Leo X, wrote
in astonishment: "[The Spaniards] even discovered—marvel, Holy Father!—
numerous books."[31] Later, he continued: "Wonderful things are also said about
the splendor, the size and the tasteful furnishing of the rural properties, which
are arranged in the countryside as places for relaxation; the buildings have sun
terraces, inner courtyards and several floors, like we know in Spain."[32] Wanting to
establish contact with the local population, Cortés asked one of the freed Ecab
women (upon whom he had already bestowed lavish gifts) to bring her people
back to him. The Ecab accepted Cortés's proposal of peace, and so there was a
meeting and an exchange of gifts.[33] Since Cozumel at that time was a place of pil-
grimage for the Maya, the inhabitants were used to seeing strangers. Ultimately,
they accepted the Spaniards, too, without conflict and even supplied them with
food throughout their stay.[34]

Following orders, Cortés investigated the whereabouts of the shipwrecked
Spaniards who had gone missing in the Yucatán years earlier. With the help of
the interpreter Melchorejo, he made his request intelligible. As it turned out,
the people of Cozumel were aware of the situation. The supreme commander
learned from them that two Spaniards were living as slaves near Cape Catoche.
Cortés immediately sent a search expedition under Diego de Ordás with the
order to purchase the prisoners' freedom, while at the same time indigenous
messengers carried a letter to the prisoners. The captain's interest here was not
entirely altruistic. Not only was he concerned about the fate of the Christians,
as he later wrote, but also about their knowledge of the country, the people,
and, above all, the local language, which could have great value to him in his
endeavor. Although the search party returned to no avail after a week, one of
the shipwrecked men managed to join the fleet in Cozumel shortly thereafter,
having actually received the letter. His name was Gerónimo de Aguilar.[35]

Aguilar was incredibly fortunate to reach his compatriots. Cortés had already
sailed on to Isla Mujeres, but turned back because of a leak in Juan de Escalante's
ship. Having lived as a slave among the Maya for eight years, Aguilar knew their
customs and traditions and therefore had a lot to say. He told the men details
about the sacrificial rites and ritual cannibalism of the Maya, to which most
of his comrades had fallen prey. Meanwhile, the only other Spaniard still alive,
Gonzalo Guerrero, did not want to come back. He had married the daughter of
Na Chan Can, a leader of the Ecab, started a family, and had even been promoted
to war chief. He also displayed the tattoos and facial decoration that were

Map of the Voyage of Cortés to Potonchán

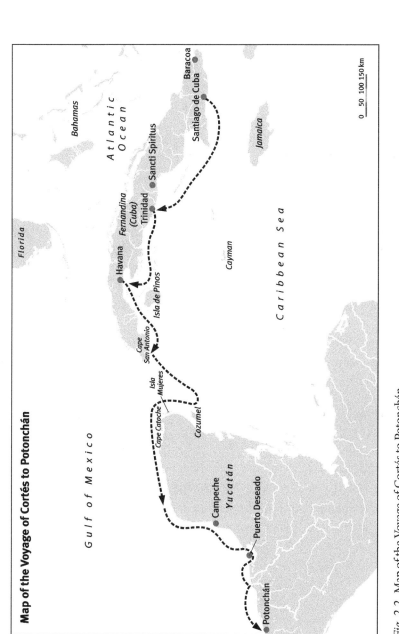

Fig. 2.2 Map of the Voyage of Cortés to Potonchán

common among the Maya and considered extremely repulsive by the Spanish. It is said that Guerrero even took the Maya into battle against the Spaniards.[36]

On Cozumel, Cortés fulfilled another part of his mission by trying to Christianize the Maya. In his own letters, he emphasized this aspect of his activities to justify his endeavor. Other eyewitnesses, such as Díaz del Castillo, also reported that Cortés interrupted a Mayan religious celebration, for which many Mayan pilgrims had gathered, to hold a mass. With Melchorejo's help as translator, Cortés himself preached about the Christian God and called on the Ecab to renounce their deities. He exhorted them in particular to stop making human sacrifices. Afterward, the Spanish destroyed the Mayan idols and replaced them with an altar, a statue of the Virgin Mary, and a large wooden cross on one of the platforms, while the clergy instructed the indigenous people on the Gospel. López de Gómara, who was quite disposed to Cortés, wrote that the inhabitants of Cozumel had even happily participated in the destruction of their own idols. Bernal, on the other hand, remarked that the Maya by no means went along with this decision quietly. Instead, they prophesied that their gods would take revenge on the Spaniards.[37] Still, in the face of the Spaniards' superior strength, the locals did not actively resist, either.

The journey was resumed at the beginning of March. Without making lengthy stops along the Yucatán Coast, the fleet followed the route of the two previous expeditions. When they reached the waters near Champotón, the men urged their leader to go ashore to avenge their dead comrades from the Grijalva expedition. However, at the urgent advice of Alaminos, who had identified shoals, Cortés abandoned the idea. As Escobar's ship had drifted away from the fleet for some time, they began to search for it. They found the vessel together with its crew safe and sound in a place that Cortés called Puerto Escondido. About ten days after their departure from Cozumel, they reached the mouth of the Río Grijalva, which the Maya called Tabasco. There, Grijalva had been richly rewarded after the Chontal-Maya had been defeated in battle. Cortés had some of his troops board the lighter brigantines and dinghies and head toward the shore in the direction of the village of Potonchán. He was lured by the prospect of gold.[38]

From the boats, the men could see that there were plenty of armed Maya on land and that they were also being approached by war canoes. Cortés tried to negotiate by making use of Aguilar's interpreting skills. He promised that they came in peace; they only wanted to replenish their water and supplies—and to pay for everything, he told them. The Maya subsequently brought bread, fruit, and turkeys to the ships—though only in small quantities—but also made it clear to the Spaniards that they should leave. When Cortés requested more provisions, the Chontal agreed to come back the next day. They used the night, however, to take their women and children to safety and to prepare for battle. For their part, the Spaniards took precautions; a division of ninety men was sent out under Alonso de Ávila and Pedro de Alvarado with the order to encircle the area. Not surprisingly, negotiations the next day failed. We learn from the Conquistador Bernardino Vázquez de Tapia that Cortés repeatedly warned the Chontal, had the requerimiento read out, and then had his actions notarized in order to fulfill his duty to the king. The Maya simply laughed in his face and mocked him: "They said to the Marqués [Cortés] that, like women, he spoke too much; instead of words, he should, like a man, let his actions speak for themselves."[39]

In the evening, the Spaniards attacked the port city of Potonchán, which had been heavily fortified by the Chontal.[40] Potonchán at that time was a capital to which the neighboring villages had to pay tribute. Tributary payments were first imposed in 1512, when their leader defeated the rival neighboring town of Xicalango. Once again, Cortés had the requerimiento read aloud, but the Maya responded with a hail of arrows, stones, and other projectiles. They also used their spear-throwers, called *atlatls*, and attacked from their canoes. The battle was fiercely contested on both sides. Vázquez de Tapia, who was already a tested warrior, vividly reported on the danger the Spaniards faced, given the superior strength of the enemy. Twenty men were wounded. Yet, in the end, they managed to overcome the barricades and enter the city victoriously, not least thanks to the use of artillery. Cortés proceeded to take official possession of the country in the name of the king of Spain, which he symbolically represented with three notches in a ceiba tree and which the scribe notarized. Then, just as Cortés had warned the Maya, the troops stayed overnight in the city center. Melchorejo, the interpreter, used the opportunity to defect. According to Díaz del Castillo, Melchorejo subsequently counselled the Chontal in their struggle against the Spaniards.[41]

The Spanish did not suffer heavily after the confrontation. They had no dead to mourn, though they still had to bear the losses of several wounded. The number of fallen warriors was higher on the Chontal side. The Spanish finally prevailed, in large measure, because of the shock and awe inspired by their guns and the advantage of their steel swords. There was no doubt, however, that they had overcome a mighty force—a fact that steeled the men's resolve.[42]

In any event, the battle was not over yet. The next morning the captains Pedro de Alvarado and Francisco de Lugo were sent out, each with one hundred men as scouting parties. Lugo was ambushed and rescued only with great difficulty and by using all available means. Two Spaniards were killed in combat, but the troops managed to take three prisoners, whom they interrogated with the help of Aguilar. The Spaniards found out that the Chontal were mobilizing reinforcements from surrounding villages and organizing further assaults. After the interrogation, Cortés allegedly sent out two of the prisoners with a renewed peace offer. He conveyed that if their leader came in person talk to him, he would forgive him for his belligerent activities.[43]

Concurrently, however, Cortés had additional support and the horses sent from the ships. His aim, once again, was to use the element of surprise. He assigned most of the officers and the best riders to the cavalry, which he commanded himself. Diego de Ordás, who was not among this group, was given command of the infantry. Early in the morning, the Spaniards celebrated a mass and prepared themselves for the impending battle. As for the Chontal, they too had armed themselves and would make a formidable impression on the Spaniards. Díaz del Castillo described the beginning of the battle, which took place near the village of Centla, as follows:

> With large feather decorations, trumpets and drums, with faces painted red, white and black, with large bows and arrows, with lances and shields, with swords that could be wielded with both hands, with slings and clubs hardened in fire, and with their cotton body armor, they lunged at us from all sides like wild dogs, and there were large regiments covering the entire plain . . .[44]

Seventy people were injured in the first wave of attacks. But the crossbows and above all the artillery also caused substantial losses on the Maya side. They were horrified when Cortés and his cavalry suddenly attacked them from the rear. The Maya had never seen mounted horses before and were shocked by the sight of the animals galloping towards them. Bernal would later write that the Maya first thought that the mounted men were centaurs. In any event, the intended effect was achieved, and the enemies fled in panic. The Spaniards counted more than eight hundred dead and half-dead Maya on the battlefield, whereas no one from their side had fallen. Only sixty were injured. To treat their wounds, the Spaniards slit open the corpses and rubbed the fat from them on themselves and the injured horses. In gratitude for their victory, they christened the town Santa María de la Victoria.[45]

It was reported afterward that the appearance of an unknown fighter on a white steed had turned the tide of the battle. Many Spaniards believed that this was none other than St. James, who had come to their aid in their fight against the infidels. Indeed, he is said to have done so repeatedly during the Reconquest. This anecdote, which was handed down in eyewitness accounts and chronicles, reinforced the Spaniards' belief in their divine election and their just cause. In contrast, Bernal Díaz took a more sober view. He not only wrote that he did not see a saint, but also added, not without irony, that he might not have enjoyed this privilege because of his many sins.

The conquistadors also reported that they had defeated a superior force of forty thousand warriors with only four hundred men. This figure has also often been questioned, and rightly so. The number helped to mythologize the conquistadors' achievements, which were equated with those of ancient heroes such as Caesar or Themistocles. There is little doubt, however, that the deployment of the mounted troops and above all the firepower of the artillery were decisive in the Spaniards' victory.[46]

The Chontals' will to resist was broken. At the prompting of the translator Aguilar, Cortés sent several captured leaders, whom he had earlier bestowed with glass beads, with a message to their people. He asked their commanders to meet with him unarmed to negotiate peace. The Chontal first tried to trick the Spaniards by sending slaves in disguise, but Aguilar immediately saw through the deception. A delegation of high-ranking Chontal then arrived the following day, bearing food. They asked for permission to burn and bury their dead, because, as Bernal remarked, "they would otherwise start to smell or be eaten by tigers or lions." The delegation said that the leaders would appear in person the next day for the peace negotiations.[47]

Cortés proved once again his keen understanding of psychological warfare. The leader and about forty commanders arrived around noon, bringing with them valuable gifts and food. The incense ritual was repeated. Meanwhile, Cortés had had a stallion tethered in close proximity to a mare, so that the stallion would become restless. The horse snorted and neighed wildly and then spun out and reared up directly in front of the Chontal nobles. Cortés chided the Chontal leaders and declared that the Spanish artillery was also dangerous, whereupon, his men fired off one of the cannons. With this gambit, the Spaniards managed to scare the Maya into negotiating. Indeed, the Maya seemed to respond to Cortés's demands. They behaved submissively, and when they returned the next day, they brought more gifts that were even more lavish. As Cortés had desired, the inhabitants of Potonchán then returned to their homes. The Spaniard instructed them about the Christian faith; he also urged them to destroy their idols, to stop human sacrifices, and to profess their faith in Jesus Christ. Finally, he directed them to submit to the Spanish king as vassals.[48]

The Chontal appeared to consent to the demands enthusiastically. The royal notary public was thus, once again, able to perform his office and register the new subjects in writing. The Chontal even allowed the Spanish to destroy some statues and to install in their place an altar to Mary and a cross. It is unlikely, however, that the Maya understood the implications of what had transpired, that they actually deliberately converted to the Christian faith, or, for that matter, that they regarded themselves as vassals of the Spanish king. Instead, they probably made a series of tactical concessions, realizing that a victory against the Spaniards was doubtful or only possible with heavy losses. Even if they could have triumphed, their sacrifice would probably have been so massive that they would have been left defenseless against their many enemies. Besides, the Chontal were able to employ a ruse that had already been tested. Recognizing the Spaniards' lust for gold, they impressed upon Cortés the wealth of their neighboring countries. First and foremost, they described the great empire of Mexica, "Colhúa and México," which had an abundance of all the treasures not to be found in their own country.[49]

Malinche

Among the gifts that the Mayan nobles brought to the Spaniards were twenty female slaves. Cortés divided them among his officers. First, however, they had to be baptized. This was a precondition for assignment to the captains, who were only allowed to have relations with Christian women. The baptized women became the first new Christians in this region, and all twenty received Christian names. Among them was a woman renamed Marina who, according to eyewitnesses, was strikingly beautiful and stood out from the others. This may explain why Cortés gave her as a gift to Portocarrero, who, as the cousin of the count of Medellín, his native city, was especially important to him. Marina would play a vital role later on in the Conquest.[50]

Marina, or Malinche or Malintzin, as she was also called, especially in the indigenous sources, was clearly special—something that Bernal Díaz recognized early on and so dedicated a separate chapter of his chronicle to her origins. Given the concentration on the deeds of men in the sources of that time, this was a notable exception. Women were generally used in the Conquest as provisioners, slaves, and, above all, as concubines. But they are hardly mentioned in the chronicles, and when they are, they remain nameless, except for Doña Marina, as Bernal reverently called her.[51] She was probably born into a Nahua family around 1500 in Painala, near Coatzacoalcos, in the region of the Isthmus of Tehuantepec, the border area between Nahua and Maya. As the daughter of a nobleman, a *pilli*, she initially enjoyed high esteem, but her fate changed after the death of her father and the remarriage of her mother. According to Bernal, Marina was sold into slavery around 1510, first to the merchants of Xicalango and from there to Potonchán. According to Sepúlveda, however, whom Alva Ixtlilxóchitl followed, the girl was kidnapped during the war.[52]

Thus the child, whose mother tongue was Nahuatl, the language of Central Mexico, learned Chontal Maya and Yucatec Maya. After she was given to Cortés, her language skills became crucial to her future existence. The more the Spaniards moved away from the Mayan territories, the clearer it became that Aguilar's translation abilities were no longer adequate. It was then discovered that Malinche could speak the unknown language. At first, she translated from Nahuatl into Mayan, while Aguilar continued to interpret into Spanish. But Malinche's gift for languages was undeniable. She was also young and keen to learn. Due to her unfortunate childhood, she did not have close ties to her community and so was able to relate to the Spaniards, which made her a particularly suitable translator. Under Aguilar's guidance, she quickly learned the language of the Europeans and soon understood not only individual words but also difficult contexts. Over time, Aguilar's role as an interpreter became superfluous.[53]

Language and translation were of enormous importance to the Conquest.[54] Conquistadors such as Bernal Díaz correctly understood the great value of Malinche's services. Years later, Gonzalo Rodriguez de Ocaño, a conquistador and contemporary of Malinche, testified in court that "Doña Marina, after God, played the greatest part in winning New Spain."[55] In Cortés's reports, however, Malinche is rarely mentioned. When he does refer to her, he calls her only the *lengua*, the translator. Nevertheless, it is known that after arriving in the land of Mexica, Cortés's trust in her grew. He even took her as a concubine for himself only a month after leaving Potonchán and assigned another woman to Portocarrero. After the conquest of Tenochtitlan in 1522, Malinche gave birth to Cortés's son Martín. But in October 1524, at the behest of Cortés, she had to marry the officer Juan Jaramillo de Salvatierra, for whom she bore their daughter María. After this, traces of her fade. She probably died in the 1530s.[56]

The indigenous sources speak with reverence of Malinche, to whom they invariably ascribe aristocratic origins. She is frequently depicted in the illuminated manuscripts and mostly at the side of Cortés.[57] For the indigenous population, Malinche was the medium of Cortés—the "one who speaks." This gave the translator not only considerable practical import but also symbolic relevance.[58] From the perspective of the Mexica envoys, it was as if the Spanish existed only in their relationship with and through Malinche. For them, she was the spokeswoman, the *lingua* ("tongue"), whom they reverently called Malintzin.[59] In the Franciscan Sahagún's collection of stories of the Mexica and in the Lienzo of Tlaxcala, Malinche was even depicted as a supernatural being through whom God would speak. Based on the Mexica beliefs, she could also be portrayed as a "woman of strife," who often appeared at historical turning points and played an active part in them.[60]

Following the baptism of Malinche and the other women who shared her fate, Cortés organized a large celebratory mass on Palm Sunday, April 17, 1519. With great pageantry and wearing their finest garments, the Spaniards formed the procession with palm branches in an effort to impress the Chontal. In the run-up to the event, an unusually large wooden cross had been erected. The mass was important as symbolic proof of the Mayas' conversion to the new faith, even if they had not yet been baptized. In his letter-reports, Cortés also emphasized how enthusiastically the Chontals had accompanied the mass celebration and the Spaniards' departure.[61]

From his perspective, Cortés had made great strides. After an intense battle, he had finally won the first vassals for his king, more or less peacefully. This was an important point, because the crown demanded the good and just treatment of the new subjects in the Indies. Yet the Chontal people must also have participated in the farewell celebrations with genuine joy, even if there was little enthusiasm for the Christian message of salvation. Indeed, their leaders grasped the danger that these strangers posed, and so they sent the Spaniards off to the lands where the gold they craved came from. Their sense of relief must have outweighed the fact that others now had to deal with the threat. The more perceptive among the Maya, however, no doubt realized that this would not be their last encounter with the intruders.

The World of the Mexica

The western territory to which the Maya sent the Spaniards was home to the Mexica—a recently established empire with diverse origins. Their precursors in this region of Mesoamerica had formed a world that dated back centuries and was considerably older than the Christian and Muslim kingdoms of the Spanish Middle Ages, and older still than the Visigoth kingdom on the Iberian Peninsula. Similarly to Spain at the time of the Reconquest, the Mexica heartland had also undergone a lengthy period of violent state formation. What were the origins of the empire that would pose a completely new challenge for the Spanish invaders? What was the context that created it and what were its defining characteristics?

The Origins

Geographically, the world of the Mexica was concentrated primarily in the so-called Valley of Mexico. This plateau, situated at an altitude of almost a mile and a half, is surrounded to the east, west, and south by mountains, some of which are just over three miles high. Located in its southern center was the salt-lake region, often referred to as Lake Texcoco, which has since largely dried up. The territory that encompassed the empire at its apogee is located in the tropics, but is sharply divided due to the considerable differences in altitude and rainfall, from the mountainous *tierra fría* to the temperate *tierra templada* and the hot *tierra caliente*. In addition to high, snow-covered volcanic mountains, there are fertile plains, lakeland areas, rainforests, swamps, and coastal landscapes.[1]

The Valley of Mexico was the cradle of Mesoamerican civilization, as Mesopotamia was for Europe and Asia, albeit at a much earlier time. The region of the southern Gulf Coast in today's Tabasco and Veracruz had already experienced the flowering of the Olmec culture from 1500 BCE to about 400 BCE. There are also traces of settlements in the Valley of Mexico from 1500 BC that point to a sedentary society that came about after thousands of years of hunter-gatherer cultures. This formative phase came to an end around 100 CE. With the rise of Teotihuacan, the first urban center in the northeastern part of the high valley emerged in the so-called classical period. The city with its monumental architecture, which probably had between one hundred thousand and two hundred thousand inhabitants, dominated the region for more than half a millennium. It set the standard for supplying a large and densely packed population and for the integration of heterogeneous ethnic groups. Different trades and professions satisfied the needs of the inhabitants as well as the demands of the powerful, who oversaw and continually expanded the military. The city-state was marked by a hierarchically structured society and intensive agriculture. Teotihuacan also distinguished itself through its centralization of power, which polytheistic religion played an important role in preserving. It did not leave behind the courts on which the sacred ball games so typical of later periods were played or monumental sculptures that glorified the deeds of the rulers.[2]

Teotihuacan would play a formative role in the development of the world of the Mexica, as did Tula (or Tollan), the capital of the Toltecs, which was founded around the year 950. This much smaller city with its approximately fifty thousand inhabitants, whose golden age ended around 1175, is only forty miles northwest of Teotihuacan. But while Teotihuacan had been uninhabited since around the year 750, Tula remained settled until the arrival of the Spanish. Both cities were important reference points in the process of identity construction, as the ruling elites of Mexica considered them venerable cultural sites significant to their origins. In particular, the myth of Quetzalcoatl, the last priest-king of the Toltecs who was forced to flee around 1168, had a lasting influence on the Mexica's religious beliefs. After the decline of Tula, numerous patchwork dominions emerged in the region, often only a few miles apart, all of which laid claim to the Toltec heritage.[3]

One among these "heirs" of the mythically transfigured Tollan was the ethnic group of the Mexica. According to linguistic studies, their origins can be traced back to nomadic peoples who migrated south from the areas of what is now northern Mexico and the southwestern United States about two millennia ago. They were in search of better living conditions, not least due to climatic factors. There are numerous sources for the history of these migratory movements. Some were written before the arrival of the Spaniards, others after the fall of the Mexica Empire in the form of illustrated manuscripts, so-called codices, and chronicles from the pens of the conquerors, the conquered, and their descendants. According to the beliefs that can be reconstructed from these sources, the Mexicas' place of origin was either Chicomoztoc, the site of seven mythical caves, each of which produced a Mexica tribe, or it was the island of Aztlan, from which the name "Aztec" was later derived.

The tribal god Huitzilopochtli, who is said to have spoken to his people during the migrations and to have given them instructions, was already interpreted by some chroniclers of the sixteenth century as a former human leader who later acquired divine status. When the Mexica finally reached the Valley of Mexico, they encountered there a heterogeneous world of multiple city-states. Until the early fifteenth century, they oscillated between the poles of strong fragmentation and centralization via empire-building.[4]

Around 1200, numerous sources agree, the Mexica reached the hill of Chapultepec with its freshwater springs, where they drove off the Chichimeca. Some forty years later, however, they were defeated and subjugated by the city-state Colhuacan. Afterward, they married into their masters' families and provided them with military services. There is no doubt that these early Mexica had adopted cultural elements of the Chichimeca and Toltecs whom they had encountered on their centuries-long migrations. Like them, the Mexica had an affinity for luxurious clothing, cocoa, and precious stones such as jade, along with monumental buildings. They also spoke the same language, Nahuatl. Like their neighbors and rivals, they worshipped an array of gods, relied on the guidance of priests, and played their ritual ball game. They did not simply adopt the practices and ideas of other ethnic groups, but transformed them. In doing so, they developed their own distinctive identity, which set them apart from their neighbors. At the same time, they also maintained their cultural proximity and kinship with the other tribes. They were therefore well suited for permanent settlement in the Valley of Mexico even at this early stage.[5]

The Mexicas' coexistence with their neighbors was by no means entirely harmonious. Indeed, in 1299, the Mexica had to flee when the Colhuacans retaliated for their having killed the daughter of the local ruler and ritually flayed her during festivities for the god Xipe Totec. They subsequently remained south of Lake Texcoco. Most sources agree that in 1325 the Mexica chose an inhospitable island in the lake, which belonged to the city-state of Azcapotzalco, as the seat of their new city. According to legend, they saw there an eagle sitting on a prickly pear cactus and fighting a snake, as their tribal god Huitzilopochtli had prophesied to them. This city was called Tenochtitlan by the Mexica, meaning roughly "near the prickly pear cactus on the stones." They almost certainly encountered and then pushed out the previous inhabitants. They shared the island with the Tlatelolca, with whom they had a kinship but also a strained relationship.[6]

The founding of the city was by no means the beginning of a linear success story, despite that Mexica sources often attempted to convey this impression. The Mexica soon fell under the rule of the closely related Tepanecs in nearby Azcapotzalco. During the period of the city's foundation, the Mexica dynasty commenced with the first *tlatoani*, or ruler, Acamapichtli, whose reputation

Fig. 3.1 The foundation of Tenochtitlan according to the Codex Mendoza. According to Mexica sources, Tenochtitlan was founded where an eagle was seen on a prickly pear cactus—here without the snake in its beak—at the crossing of two bodies of water in a marshy area. The figures depicted in the four triangles, which symbolize the four quarters of the city, represent the city's ten founding fathers. The Codex Mendoza was probably created around 1541. It contained a description of the history as well as important information about the administration and organization of the empire of the Mexica. It also reflected the self-image of the Mexica, who saw themselves as superior to other peoples and as inhabiting the center of the world. Bodleian Libraries, University of Oxford.

was based on his kinship with Colhuacan and his Toltec heritage. Nonetheless, Tepanec domination would continue until 1428.[7]

That year, several smaller city-states led by Tenochtitlan rose up against Azcapotzalco when the death of the longtime tlatoani Tezozomoc in 1426 triggered a succession conflict. To quash the vassals' resistance, the disputed pretender to the throne of Azcapotzalco, Maxtla, ordered the killing of the leaders of Tenochtitlan, Chimalpopoca, and Tlatelolco, Tlacateotl. The subsequent uprising was later joined by the city-states of Tlacopan and Texcoco. In Texcoco, however, the situation was rather ambiguous, and Nezahualcoyotl, who sought the throne, had to fight against the camp of the Tepanec supporters. Together, Tenochtitlan (with Tlatelolco), Tlacopan, and Texcoco formed a triple alliance that won the decisive battle in 1430. According to sources, the new ruler of Tenochtitlan, Itzcoatl, stood out in particular. The triple alliance then took control of the tribute payments that had previously gone to Azcapotzalco, which was subjected to the victors' wrath and degraded to a central slave market as punishment. Moreover, with the involvement of the local rulers, a reorganization of the Valley of Mexico took place. Thus, the levies were divided and the border lines were precisely drawn and recorded on *lienzos*, or linen maps, in order to prevent conflicts. The triple alliance would dominate the Valley of Mexico for about ninety years, until the arrival of the Spanish.[8]

The City

The city of Tenochtitlan rose to become the leading member within the alliance. In the fifteenth century, several hundred thousand inhabitants lived on an area of about eight and a half square miles, which was divided into large districts: Moyotlan in the southwest, Teopan in the southeast, Atzaqualco in the northeast, and Cuepopan in the northwest, and the special district Tlatelolco in the north. This made Tenochtitlan one of the ten largest cities in the world at that time. Based on the calculation of the possible population density in relation to the island's available surface area, which was severely restricted by the numerous uninhabited and sparsely populated ritual districts, it is estimated that the inhabitants of the entire Valley of Mexico numbered between one and two and a half million.[9]

Around 1500, the Valley of Mexico experienced a long period of abundant moisture. As a result, the population growth, as recent archaeological research has shown, was quite strong. At the end of the fifteenth century, the population density was likely higher than at any other time in Mesoamerican history, and in any case much higher than on the Iberian Peninsula. This circumstance, however, gave rise to conflicts and wars. Periods of peace were based on a fragile

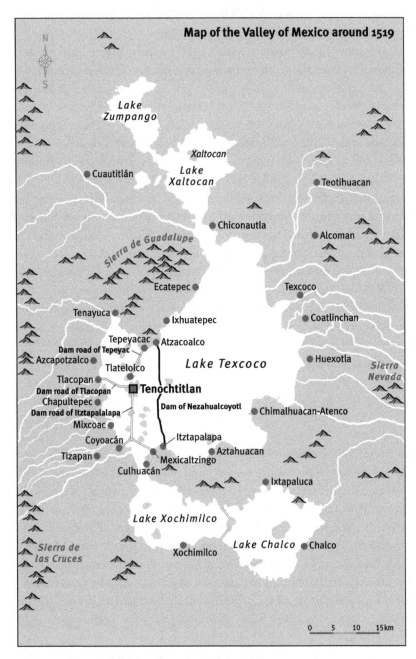

Map of the Valley of Mexico around 1519

Lake
Zumpango

Xaltocan

Lake
Xaltocan

● Cuautitlán

● Teotihuacan

● Chiconautla

● Alcoman

Sierra de Guadalupe

● Ecatepec

Texcoco ●

Tenayuca ●

● Ixhuatepec

● Coatlinchan

Tepeyacac ● Atzacoalco

Lake Texcoco

Dam road of Tepeyac

Azcapotzalco ●

Tlatelolco

● Huexotla

Sierra
Nevada

Tlacopan ●

Dam road of Tlacopan

■ Tenochtitlan

Chapultepec ●

Dam road of Itztapalalapa

Dam of Nezahualcoyotl

● Chimalhuacan-Atenco

Mixcoac ●

● Itztapalapa

Coyoacán ●

● Aztahuacan

Tizapan ●

Mexicaltzingo

Culhuacán ●

● Ixtapaluca

Lake Xochimilco

Lake Chalco ● Chalco

Sierra de
las Cruces

Xochimilco ●

0   5   10   15km

Fig. 3.2 Map of the Valley of Mexico around 1519

equilibrium prone to disruption. The balance was finally destroyed by the Spaniards.[10]

Dams, aqueducts, and irrigation systems bear witness to the urban development skills of the Mexica. A five-mile-long water pipeline provided the town of Tenochtitlan, whose location on an island in a brackish lake meant that drinking water wasn't easily accessible. In order to bring fresh water to the urban area, the inhabitants had to clear land from the lake, create artificial islands, and connect them with bridges and canals. Under the direction of the tlatoani of Texcoco, Nezahualcoyotl, the Mexica built in the middle of the fifteenth century the large dam between Itztapalapa and Atzacoalco to protect the city from floods. In addition, shipping canals that could be closed for defensive purposes were constructed. In the south of the lake system, the Chalco and Xochimilco Lakes provided fresh water. Here, too, there was a risk of flooding, which the dam road from Itztapalapa to Coyoacán was intended to alleviate.[11]

However, as archaeologist Michael E. Smith has pointed out, Tenochtitlan represented an exception in the urban landscape. Much more widespread were the smaller towns that had been established in the early days of the Mexica's arrival in the region. From the preceding cultures, the Mexica adopted certain architectural norms for public spaces, such as stone pyramids, ball playgrounds, altars, and ceremonial sites. Atop the pyramids were one or more temples dedicated to different deities and containing sculptures and paintings. The altars also served various purposes, ranging from the performance of fertility rites to the display of skulls of the sacrificed to the worship of various gods. In addition, each city had its own ruler's palace, where the tlatoani lived with his family. Architecturally, these buildings followed the same pattern despite displaying many differences in their details. They had a large inner courtyard with an altar and adjoining chambers for the ruling family and members of the government. Other public buildings included the schools for the children of the nobility (*calmecac*) and for those of common freemen (*telpochcalli*). The leading warriors gathered in so-called eagle houses.[12]

On the oval island where Tenochtitlan was located, the Great Temple, with its demarcated district, formed the city center. It had been repeatedly extended and enlarged under the different *tlatoque* (rulers; plural of tlatoani). When Cortés first encountered it, he was astonished:

> . . . among the temples there is one which is the main temple and for whose size and characteristics there are no words. Because it is so large that one could very well build a place for five hundred inhabitants on its plot, which is completely surrounded by a high wall . . . There are easily forty towers there, all of which are so high that in the case of the largest one must climb fifty steps to even reach the base. The main temple is

taller than the cathedral of Seville. They are so well-built of both stone
and wood that it could not be improved upon anywhere . . .[13]

On the west side, a double staircase led up to the two sanctuaries at the top
of the pyramid, which was dedicated to the rain god Tlaloc in the west and
Huitzilopochtli in the south. In front of it, there was an altar on which human
sacrifices were offered. There were more than seventy ritual structures in the
temple district, including a skull rack (*tzompantli*), a ball playground, and a
round temple dedicated to Quetzalcoatl. There was also a place for statues of the
gods of subjugated peoples.[14]

The splendor of the palaces, with their gardens, libraries, and even a zoo
impressed the Spanish conquerors as much as the general cleanliness of the
streets, which according to Cervantes de Salazar were cleaned daily by a thousand
men. The stench typical of European cities was less pronounced in Tenochtitlan,
with the exception of the temple district, where the smells of human sacrifice
took the Europeans' breath away. To suppress this odor, nobles carried fragrant
flowers with them. Overall, the hygienic conditions contrasted positively with
those of the European cities they knew, not least because the Mexica attached
great importance to physical hygiene. If the Europeans had understood the

Fig. 3.3 The main temple of Tenochtitlan. Model of the great temple of Tenochtitlan
from the National Museum of Anthropology in Mexico. Wikimedia Commons.

symbolic language of the urban landscape, they would have noticed that it just as consciously made references to the idealized Tula as they did themselves in their own cities to Rome or Jerusalem.[15]

Beginning in the second half of the fifteenth century, the wealth of Mexica grew by leaps and bounds. Evidence of this can be seen in the public buildings and the impressive parklike garden landscapes, which became increasingly monumental. The Chapultepec complex, also designed by Nezahualcoyotl, was a precursor of the botanical gardens of modern times. The visible and external center of power of each city-state was the palace, the *tecpan*. Since Tenochtitlan was the capital of the empire, the *tecpan* of Moctezuma, which was rebuilt only in 1502, after a disastrous flood, outshone all others in size and splendor. According to López de Gómara, it had three courtyards, each with a graceful fountain, and more than one hundred rooms, all with private bathrooms. The walls—artistically painted—were made of alabaster, jasper, and a crystallized rock called porphyry, and the floors were covered with furs, cotton, and feather carpets. The ground floor was used by administrative officials and craftsmen of all kinds, while the rulers lived above. At night, the fires from large coal pits illuminated the palace, as candles were still unknown.[16]

The great majority of the city's inhabitants did not live in palaces, but in the simple dwellings of the common people, which were built of adobe bricks. In Tenochtitlan and the Valley of Mexico, these dwellings often had several rooms, while in the more remote provinces they usually consisted of a single room. In the capital, the single-story houses with their flat roofs were placed around a courtyard, where the inhabitants shared a communal kitchen, water and corn containers, and a steam bath. Within the cities, the common people lived in clearly defined settlement associations or districts called *calpultin* (sing. *calpulli*). In Tenochtitlan, more than one hundred *calpultin* were spread out among city's four districts. Together the inhabitants farmed the land that belonged to a nobleman. A calpulli usually had a school and a market. The likeness of the respective protective deity was housed in its own temple. The inhabitants of different calpultin came together at the markets, for religious feasts, and for community work. Thus, everyone had to alternate between either providing certain services to the tlatoani or assigning workers to the major infrastructure projects.[17]

The cities fulfilled political, religious, and economic functions. First of all, they were the center of an *altepetl* (pl. *altepeme*), a political unit or city-state whose seat of power was the residence of the tlatoani. The centers of the *altepetl* were distinguished from other city states by the existence of a legitimate dynasty, domination over the land and its people, a foundation myth, and their own protective deity. The rulers legitimized their power through supernatural forces. Religious rituals, which were performed in the city at sacred sites, were directed at the entire altepetl, and the participants came from all across the empire. The balance of power of the city-states in the Valley of Mexico was anything but stable. On the contrary, it was continuously shaken by rivalries and wars. When one was conquered by another, it resulted in a redistribution of tributes and land ownership.

Each city was the heart of its region's economic life. Markets were held weekly in most, and in Tenochtitlan and Tlatelolco, daily. Varieties of craft production differed from town to town. While some specialized in obsidian processing or ceramics, others remained in the production of textiles from agave fibers.[18]

Economic Foundations

As in Europe, the economic mainstay of the society was farming, and the vast majority of the population lived from the cultivation of land. Given the distinct natural conditions of Mesoamerica, with its great disparities in altitude and rainfall, different strategies were adopted to feed the hundreds of thousands of people who lived in the cities. The farmers had precise knowledge of weather patterns, land use, and water management, which were passed down from generation to generation orally, but also in writing in books. However, recurring natural disasters such as earthquakes, plagues of locusts, volcanic eruptions, frost, hail, dry periods, and, above all, flooding could not be avoided. Arable land was a greatly disputed commodity, and its products were considered the currency of tribute payments that farmers had to make to local landowners and the rulers of the empire.[19]

Depending on the circumstances, the available soil was used in many different ways. Terrace farming was widespread. In addition, sophisticated irrigation methods were used to make prudent use of land and to distribute precious water. Occasionally, there was little or no water available for a long time, until it was again, in torrential overabundance. Water was carried to the farmland from rivers and lakes via channels and dams. This system was used on a small scale for irrigating nearby fields as well as for large-scale infrastructure measures and even for diverting an entire river bed. One of the skills of the engineers and countless workers included the drainage of marshes and fields with high groundwater levels to gain new areas of cultivation. No doubt what the Europeans called "floating gardens," the *chinampas*, were particularly impressive. These were created on shoals, especially in Lake Texcoco, by means of raising earth and mud from the bottom of the lake and securing it with stakes and reeds. It was probably a state-ordered, coordinated infrastructure measure to provide for the steadily growing urban population in the fifteenth century. In the *chinampas*, four to seven harvests per year were possible. To achieve this, farmers planted seedbeds, used sophisticated crop rotation, and applied natural fertilizers.[20]

Given the large number of inhabitants and the island location of Tenochtitlan, the chinampas could only feed a small part of the urban population, however. The capital relied on deliveries of tributes from subjects and dependent city-states,. In this way, the non-noble population also profited from the tributes of the subjugated peoples. Most food and even, as mentioned earlier, drinking water had to be procured from the mainland. During its heyday in the fifteenth century, there were no shortages, as the long lists of tributes that have been preserved, particularly in the Codex Mendoza, show. The tributes were calculated for the individual provinces of the empire, whereby those regions close to the capital mainly supplied food and those further away, more luxurious goods and valuable raw materials. Officers of the ruler oversaw the timely receipt of the levies in the provinces. In addition to the payments for the capital, levies were also due to the respective landlords, who generally had to be paid more frequently.[21]

The granary of the empire was located in the Valley of Mexico, where corn, the high-carbohydrate staple food, yielded rich harvests. Beans provided protein; pumpkins and chilies supplied the people with vitamins and minerals. Amaranth and chia, and various fruits, including avocados, prickly pears, and tomatoes rounded out the inhabitants' diet. The range of available flavor enhancers included vanilla, agave syrup, honey, salt, flowers, and chili. In comparison, relatively little meat was consumed, even though domestic animals such as turkeys and dogs, as well as deer, rabbits, fish, salamanders, ducks, and insects supplemented the food supply. The popular drink *pulque* was made from the maguey cactus, while cocoa and chocolate were reserved for nobles.[22]

Agricultural work was intimately connected with Mexica worldview. Plants fulfilled spiritual purposes for the home, the calpulli, and the state. There were specific beliefs regarding the sacredness of certain landscapes and, above all, of religious ceremonies and rituals tied to the seasons and agricultural work. According to Mexica beliefs, work originated in the creation of the first workers by the gods; men were assigned to cultivate the land and women to spin fiber and weave textiles. The idea of reciprocity was important. It was the basis of all actions, including those between humans and gods. Like the gods, humans had a certain role to play in the cosmic cycle to guarantee the fertility of the soil and thus survival. For this purpose, human sacrifices were necessary as a kind of advance payment to the holy mountain, the source of life. It was viewed as the origin of the water that filled the rivers, lakes and seas, and the fertility that made seeds sprout and grow. This is why sacrificial rituals—some of which were ordered and directed by the state, some of which were smaller, decentralized rituals—regularly took place to ask for rain. Such rituals, which included child sacrifices, were not meant as thanks for the received benefits, but rather were oriented toward the future.[23]

Agricultural goods and other commodities were traded in the markets. However, as the Mexica neither used farm animals nor the wheel in transport, the flow of commerce was restricted. Porters had to transport goods over long distances. While small producers hauled their products to market themselves, noblemen and big merchants had professional carriers and slaves at their disposal, who would also render important services to the Spanish invaders. A lively trading activity therefore developed, even over long distances, as no Mexica household was completely self-sufficient. Among the daily markets in the urban centers, Tlatelolco's stood apart. The largest market in America at that time, it greatly impressed the Spaniards. Smaller markets also took place at varying intervals. The requirement that goods be exchanged in these places was regulated by law, and guards were employed to oversee the marketplaces.[24]

Farmers were the most numerous vendors, selling parts of their surplus production of food or textiles. There were also the craftspeople, most of whom practiced their craft as a part-time occupation. A select group of craftspeople produced luxury items for the nobility. Some of the craftspeople did not go to the markets themselves, but instead sold their products to merchants, who either had fixed stalls at the large markets or peddled their wares in the countryside. A small but privileged and well-organized group were the wealthy long-distance traders, the *pochteca*, who had their own calpulli.[25]

The exchange of goods made it possible to create a society based on the division of labor. This enabled the craftsmanship of a wide range of products to achieve a high degree of perfection and specialization. In earlier times, luxury goods were mainly produced for the nobility and priests from sumptuous feathers, precious metals and stones, shells, and exquisite fabrics. In general, the common people were deprived of these luxury goods and works of art. In the course of the fifteenth century, however, the craftsmen of Mexica produced ever more luxury goods, even for the broad strata of the population. This demonstrates the increasing prosperity of the Mexica, and above all that of the inhabitants of Tenochtitlan. Metal handicrafts, stone work, and pottery were widespread. A common daily craft was the production of textiles, which women and girls sometimes made in excess of their own needs for market sale.[26]

Because of its proximity to raw material deposits, Otumba, for example, became a hub for obsidian processing, while pulque production flourished especially in the highlands, where maguey grew in large quantities. Some city-states and ethnic groups were famous for certain products and skills, such as Xochimilco for precious stones, Texcoco for polychrome pottery, and Coyoacán for its masonry. On the other hand, the Mixtec people in Oaxaca, far south of the Valley of Mexico, proved to be experts in processing the commodity most coveted by the Spaniards, gold, due their proximity to the deposits. The goods were produced either directly at the market or in the households of highly specialized professionals who passed on their knowledge and tools over generations. Often a calpulli concentrated on a particular craft, such as the famous feather craftsmen from Amantlan in Tlatelolco, or particularly skilled craftsmen were settled in their own calpullis, such as the gem cutters from Xochimilco in Tenochtitlan. Moreover, noblemen and rulers had their own privileged and highly respected craftsmen who produced elaborate luxury items from rare and particularly precious materials directly in the palaces where they lived. The manufacture of some of these luxury products and the processing of cotton also required a division of labor.[27]

As a general rule, textiles were central to economic life, because they served, among other things, as a means of payment. The luxurious cotton garments had a higher value than the simple ones made of agave fibers, as the raw material cotton had to be imported into the valley from the warmer region of tierra caliente. There, it was further processed in the individual households.; it became loincloths and shoulder capes for men and blouses and long, belted skirts for women. Although these standard items of clothing were found throughout Mexica, strict dress codes regulated their every detail. For example, it was possible to detect the social status from the different lengths or ways of carrying the shoulder cloak. Additionally, there were especially splendid robes for high-ranking warriors and, of course, for the ruler and his court. So important were the attire that the work that went into its creation was highly regarded. Weaving and spinning were women's work, and their tools of the trade were considered "weapons" that, according to the ideals of the Mexica, were equal to those of the male warriors.[28]

The Society

The standing of a Mexica in society was determined by birth. Social ancestry, gender, and astrological signs determined one's course in life. Either one was born a member of the common people or the nobility. This fundamental difference likewise shaped early modern European societies. Within these two social strata, however, there were great disparities that could be traced back to different distributions of wealth, freedom, power, and lifestyle. Class differences were linked to religious ideas and political realities. For instance, religion served to legitimize social inequalities, which were interpreted as given by the gods and necessary to maintain the world order. Political authority was responsible for maintaining this arrangement.[29]

The basis of social inequality was the control over land, work, and the power to govern, which were in the hands of the nobility. The number of nobles was in the tens of thousands, likely representing about two percent of the population.

Nobles' privileged position was based on their descent from the Toltec kings in Tula and from the creator deity Quetzalcoatl. They did not consider themselves to be ordinary mortals, which is why non-nobles could not ascend to this class. There was indeed at certain times a kind of merit nobility, but it was not equal to the birth aristocracy and was abolished by Moctezuma II. The nobility enjoyed privileges that distinguished them from the common people, even externally. Certain foods (such as meat), jewelry, and clothing (especially that made of cotton) were reserved for this social class. Of course, the nobility also revealed their power through the size of their palaces.[30]

There were also gradations among the nobility. Most *pipiltin* (sing.: *pilli*) did not have any particular wealth and influence. They occupied the lower offices as civil servants, teachers, scribes, officers, or priests. Higher up were the *teteuctin* (sing.: *teuctli*), who, for example, possessed extensive estates as judges, ambassadors, and governors and were heads of the large houses to which pipiltin also belonged. The more important the offices and the closer the proximity to the tlatoani, the higher the standing. The tlatoani was perched at the top of the pyramid as ruler of a city-state and was only surpassed by the *huey tlatoque*, the rulers of the triple alliance. While the nobles were privileged in every respect, they also had to follow a strict code of honor. For behavior that was not exemplary, they could be severely punished. Manual labor was beneath them, but they were responsible for security, religious rites, social peace, and warfare.[31]

The privileged life of the nobility was enabled by the common freemen who were obligated to pay tribute and to work. Their name in Nahuatl—*macehualtin* (sing.: *macehualli*)—means not only "common freeman," but also "subject." What is more, they constituted the overwhelming majority of the population. Many farmers lived in the cities and worked their fields there and elsewhere. In the Valley of Mexico, they lived in the calpulli and delivered their tributes in kind or as pieces of work according to their profession. They were also required to perform public duties on a rotational basis. These included, for example, cultivating the land of the tlatoani; work for the temple, the army, or for canal and dam construction; and as military service. In addition, there were also communities directly subordinate to noble houses, which were not subject to the public duty to work, but neither did they belong to any calpulli. There were some similarities to European serfs, but a crucial difference was that unlike a serf, a farmer could change to another lord and calpulli if they accepted him.[32]

The prosperity and degree of personal freedom among the common people varied and depended on the quality and size of the cultivated land. Though commoners were not allowed to own the land, belonging to the calpulli had its advantages. Indeed, the calpulli determined for itself the distribution and use of the land that had been placed at its disposal by a nobleman, who normally did not reside locally. In some respects, the lifestyle of the craftsmen and merchants, who were also non-nobles, differed considerably from that of simple farmers. The pochteca and the highly specialized craftsmen sometimes accumulated so much wealth that they surrounded their houses with high walls to avoid arousing the envy of less wealthy nobles. There were also limited opportunities for advancement in the priesthood and through warfare, as well as among lower civil servants, such as the tribute collectors in provincial cities.[33]

At the lowest end of the social scale of Mesoamerica were the slaves. In contrast to European forms of slavery, in Mesoamerica this status was not hereditary. Slaves retained the right to marry, and their children were born free. A person became a slave when, for example, in distress, he sold himself into slavery and received protection in return. Debt or misdeeds such as theft could also lead to slavery. Some tributary cities also had to deliver a certain number of slaves to their leaders. Female and male slaves were often called upon to perform a variety of tasks as domestic servants. Owners could give them away or have them offered as human sacrifices. Furthermore, they were among the commodities that the pochteca brought to the markets over long distances.[34]

Another category of social inequality determined by birth was gender. The Mexica Empire presented itself to the outside world as a warrior society dominated by men. Internally, gender relations were more balanced than they might appear at first glance. These corresponded to the sacred principle of complementarity, which played a central role in the religious ideas of the Mexica. Men and women, accordingly, performed different tasks and fulfilled different roles in separate spheres, but they were fundamentally equivalent and both essential for the functioning of society as a whole. Thus a woman who died in labor was considered equal to a warrior who lost his life in battle. The contribution of women to military success by giving birth to warriors, provisioning troops with supplies, and offering prayers was considered just as important as the contributions of the men fighting on the battlefield. Newborn boys were given toy weapons; newborn girls, a broom and weaving tools. While men held the highest positions of political, economic, and military power, women held sway in medical, social, and administrative areas. Both sexes were entitled to receive inheritances. Women had the same rights as men, could dispose of individual property, and could divorce.[35]

The Valley of Mexico also had a large number of ethnic groups. Only about half of the population belonged to the Nahua-speaking peoples; the other half was part of the Otomí linguistic family, which in turn branched into numerous subgroups. The Otomí lived mainly in the mountains and the country's more arid zones and were considered to be peasants. Their settlements were much smaller and their dwellings simpler than those of the Mexica. Otomí society was less stratified. The Nahua-speaking Mexica, who mostly lived in cities, looked down on them; in fact, "Otomí" was understood as a curse word. Nevertheless, they respected their neighbors for their martial skills.[36]

In child rearing, the strict separation of the gender spheres was reinforced by fathers who devoted themselves mainly to boys, mothers to girls. As the children grew, they took on more tasks and responsibilities in the family. There was a highly developed school system for boys, which was divided into education for warriors and for priests. Girls, by contrast, continued to learn their tasks at home. Only in adolescence did the young people come together in the so-called singing houses, where they learned together to assume certain responsibilities during public ceremonies. With the exception of celibate priests, the Mexica entered into arranged marriages. The unions were negotiated by the families, and wives were adopted into their husbands' households. Young couples were integrated into the calpullis and pursued their gender-specific duties, although there were certainly overlaps in market activities and trade. Monogamy was the rule. Only the high nobility could afford polygamous relationships and often kept numerous concubines in addition to various legitimate wives.[37]

Households were generally shared by several generations, although there were also nuclear families and single households. On average, between five and fifteen people were likely to live in a common house, the number varying considerably depending on ethnic group, social status, and geographical location. The household played an identity-forming role in the daily life of Mexica. It was also there that the ethical values that bound society were communicated. But not all Mexica adhered to them. Antisocial behavior such as crime and dishonesty were met with draconian punishments, which were often carried out in the market square to deter others. The death penalty was often implemented, for example, for the mortal sin of drunkenness.

The morals of the Mexica were strict, and the containment of strong emotions, such as anger, was considered important for maintaining physical health. An exception was intense crying and wailing to express mourning or sorrow. There were rigid rules about sex. In contrast to some other ethnic groups in Mesoamerica, the Mexica dress code required the preservation of modesty of men and women. Nudity and sexuality were largely absent from Mexica art. Divergent sexual behavior was allowed only among tolerated, socially ostracized groups such as prostitutes and transvestites, who served as a negative example for the mainstream society. Otherwise, marital infidelity or promiscuity were severely penalized. Nobles were expected to lead particularly exemplary sexual lives. The sexual mores of Mexica thus resembled those of their early modern European counterparts in some respects, though in others they were more restrictive.[38]

The everyday life of the city inhabitants was tightly regulated by the penetrating sounds of the great drums at the main temple. In the morning, the city was filled with bustling activity. People congregated in the public squares, markets, and especially in the community building of the calpulli. Here, they not only worked and prayed together, but they also laughed, played, celebrated, and danced. They took care of widows, orphans, and impoverished families, and arbitrated disputes. Individual transgressions were covered up so that the calpulli would not be disgraced. There was an ideology of equality that condemned personal ambition. When the drums beat in the evening, all business activities were suspended and people retired for the night. When the flutes and percussion instruments played in the temples by the novice priests could be heard, a curfew went into effect, if it hadn't already. For reasons of security, curfew was closely enforced, and the still of the night was disturbed only by major public celebrations. But public monitoring had its limitations; instance, there were certainly people from marginalized groups, such as the homeless, alcoholics, and criminals, who were out in the city overnight.[39]

Religion and Culture

As with the spheres of politics and economics, the everyday lives of the Mexica were intimately connected also to religious ideas and practices. These were not limited to the spiritual elite, but affected all people. There was no separation between the spiritual and the worldly sphere. The highly evolved religious dimension of Mexica culture produced monumental temples, a diversified priesthood, and a faith with centuries-old roots that was spread throughout the Mesoamerican region. This was not an orthodoxy, but rather symbols and rites that had manifested themselves in different ways in different places over the course of time. Beliefs were characterized by principles such as the duality of complementary opposites, the never-ending struggle of the gods, and the cosmic cycles.[40]

The Mexica imagined their world as a space in-between, a kind of a flat disk between the supernatural underworld and heaven. The disk was accordingly believed to be a crocodile or caiman, an earth monster surrounded by water. They thought that heaven was held up by gods who had been transformed into trees, which allowed the earth to remain in contact with it. Heaven consisted of thirteen layers and the underworld of nine. The underworld also remained connected to the earth, especially by means of caves. There was no moral distinction between the upperworld and the underworld, as in Christian concepts of heaven and hell. The points of the compass had a symbolic meaning. The capital Tenochtitlan with its main temple was considered a cosmic center, a holy place and world axis where the energy of heaven and earth were concentrated.[41]

Concepts of time also followed the idea of cosmic cycles. According to the Mexica, their epoch, their "sun," began with the self-sacrifice of the gods, which had set the sun in motion for the first time. This particular era had already been preceded by four other eras, each of which the gods had destroyed through various natural disasters. Their own sun was the sun of the earthquake, which was similarly doomed to perish if the people failed to ensure its duration through their blood sacrifices.[42]

Mexica calendars were widespread throughout Mesoamerica. Thus the annual calendar that counts 365 days for the solar year followed a fifty-two-year cycle. It was used to structure everyday life, for example by determining the market day of the five-day week and the day of the larger fairs once every twenty days of the month. The 260-day cycle of the divination year ran parallel and in a complementary manner to this. Each day and each year had its own name and its own meaning, which was interpreted by the soothsayers, who played an extremely important role in the daily life of the Mexica. Soothsayers were consulted when it came to determining the right time to sow or harvest, to travel or marry, to build a house or choose a ruler. The belief prevailed that the day of birth influenced people's personalities and destinies and that impending dangers could be averted through certain types of behavior, such as self-mortification, which was also practiced in Europe. Ultimately, the aim was to influence and satisfy the gods in order to obtain security from life's constant dangers.[43]

Also serving this end were the numerous public celebrations and rituals, which probably even surpassed the celebrations in Catholic Spain in number and scope. They were celebrated with processions, combat exhibitions, dances, songs, banquets, and sacrificial ceremonies. The calendars fixed the holidays as well as work, according to the season. For instance, a festival was celebrated in each of the eighteen months of the calendar year under a particular motto, such as a natural phenomenon ("sprouting maize") or a ritual ("sweeping the path"). The natural sequence of growing cycles, the harvest season, and the beginning of the rainy season were also celebrated. Apart from the monthly festivals, there were also festivals that did not take place every year. The most important festival was that of the "new fire drilling" at the end of a fifty-two-year cycle, which was last celebrated in 1507. After extinguishing all the fires across the land and other ritual acts, the high priest on a mountain near Itztapalapa lit a new fire on the body of a person to be sacrificed. The flame was then passed on from there to the temples and then on to households. In contrast, the celebrations around the divination calendar were simpler and only held by certain occupational groups. As a rule, the festive rituals not only took place in public spaces, but were also prepared and continued in individual households, for example through the making of sacrifices and singing.[44]

Certain gods dominated over thirteen-day periods of the divination calendar, during which they were worshipped with special reverence. Altogether, there were a multitude of gods in the pantheon of the Mexica who commanded the three spatial dimensions of the cosmos. The Mexica believed that the deities could assume different guises and forms and fulfill different roles and functions. They imagined their gods in anthropomorphic form and attributed to them human qualities such as reason, passion, and volition. The gods were venerated with sacred bundles filled with relics, decorated figures, and idols. The gods were "neither infallible nor omnipotent, nor, for that matter, moral role models."[45] Humans and gods existed in a state of mutual dependence. The concept of complementary duality also applied to those deities for whom female and male qualities supplemented each other. Objects or people could temporarily be considered divine or divinely inspired.[46]

Research classifies the deities of Mexica according to their main functions: creation and protection, rain and agricultural fertility, war and sacrifice. The first category includes the god Tezcatlipoca, the "Smoking Mirror," who was thought to have great influence on everyday life. Due to the vulnerability of agriculture to crises, the Mexica dedicated most of their festivals to their countless fertility deities. The rain god Tlaloc was especially prominent. As with Tezcatlipoca, the influence of Tlaloc could be positive or negative. The war deities, on the other hand, made substantial claims on people, demanding sacrifices for the renewal of the sun and moon, day and night. The sun deities Tonatiuh and Huitzilopochtli were highly important to the Mexica. The god Quetzalcoatl deserves a category of his own because of his numerous connections to all three dimensions; he was regarded as a benevolent deity who was open to humans. The center of the Quetzalcoatl cult was the city of Cholula. Certain gods were venerated by the different ethnic or occupational groups with great zeal. Moreover, the world of the gods was by no means fixed. New deities were incorporated into it with every conquest.[47]

Alongside the gods, there were also supernatural forces in the Mexica imagination that did not assume the guise of human beings or animals. The cosmos mirrored the exchange between the natural world and the gods and supernatural forces. The latter had the task of guaranteeing the cyclical return of the course of the year, of day and night, and of heaven and earth, and thus providing people with the basic means for their survival. However, humans likewise had to contribute to this through their sacrifices and celebrations and therefore shared responsibility for the functioning of the cosmic whole. In return for their services, people could expect divine compensation. At the same time, there was no concept of a reward or punishment in the hereafter for one's particular way of life. To preserve the world, life had to be lived in an appropriate way. The interpretation of what was good and right from a religious point of view was the responsibility of a hierarchically ordered priestly caste: men and women were trained for their service in special schools from their youth onward and lived off of government tributes. They had a wide range of tasks to perform, from cleaning the temples to overseeing daily prayers and sacrifices to the organization of the major ceremonies.[48]

High and experienced priests also performed the ritual of human sacrifice. In the process, they opened up the chests of the chosen individuals with a sharp obsidian blade and ripped out their hearts. The Spanish conquistadors were shocked by this practice, which they seized on to validate, among other things, their conviction of waging a just war. Human sacrifice had been common in Mesoamerica for thousands of years. From the Mexica point of view, it was crucial for preserving the cosmos; it was also closely associated with the myth of the creation of the sun and moon through the self-sacrifice of two gods. The Mexica believed that this act alone was responsible for the movement of the sun and the only way that night and day could alternate. People were thus instructed to repeat this sacrifice by offering their bodies and their holy blood in order to maintain the cosmic order. The individual gods also demanded human sacrifices for their services at their high feasts. The sun god Huitzilopochtli, for example, needed the blood of the sacrificed as food in order to successfully wage his daily struggle against the night.[49]

Victims could also be offered up in connection with solemn oaths by groups or individuals or for political purposes. Sacrifice was part of elaborate rituals that varied according to the occasion. Some gods demanded children or virgins. The more the empire expanded, the higher the number of human sacrifices. Mexica warfare was in fact geared toward taking prisoners for sacrifice. Though this now seems unlikely, according to Diego Durán in his 1579 accounting, more than 80,400 people were sacrificed at the dedication of the great temple.[50] In any event, the mass sacrifice of prisoners of war was a demonstration of political power that required the rulers of the tributary city-states to participate, whether they wanted to or not. The eating of body parts of the sacrificed—including arm and leg meat—was a fixed component of the sacrificial rituals, which themselves were an integral part of the countless public ceremonies.[51]

A central element in the beliefs that the Mexica ritualistically affirmed was their treatment of history, which was constructed to legitimize their present world. To achieve cosmic legitimacy, they combined circular and linear concepts of time and dated historical events. Although they could have easily dated past events according to their calendar, historical accuracy did not actually interest them. The history they transmitted was a manifestation of their world view in narrative form. Like the celebrations, it thus served to explain the origin and continued functioning of the cosmos.[52] This history was passed on performatively in songs, speeches, hymns, and prayers. In addition, the Mexica produced books, whose artistry inspired the humanist Pietro Martire d'Anghiera. The Spaniards were stunned by this, for they had not suspected such a level of cultural achievement.[53] Until then, the Indies had been largely perceived as barbaric.

The importance of these books to the Mexica is shown by the fact that after the consolidation of power between 1428 and 1440, the tlatoani Itzcoatl had the pictorial traditions both of the subjugated peoples and his own burned in order to invent a story that corresponded to a greater claim to authority. Like the Europeans of the Renaissance with their references to antiquity, the Mexica constructed an imperial past that seemed all the more significant the further back it went. Their integration of elements of the historical tradition of conquered peoples into their own was consistent with the general approach to the achievements of other ethnic groups. As a result, they could legitimize their political claims to power and ambitions. The reference to the prestige and fame of Teotihuacan and Tula served to establish a historical continuity with these past city-states, which were highly venerated in Mesoamerica. Nevertheless, the Mexica did not forget their nomadic and Chichimeca origins.[54]

War and Imperial Expansion

In their books, the Mexica scribes were able to record many glorious military deeds. The empire, after all, had been expanding almost continuously since the 1430s. At the height of their power, the Mexica's territory extended to the present border between Mexico and Guatemala. Their political rise was accompanied by the ascendency of their own language, Nahuatl, as the lingua franca. Their conquests were intended to assert the Mexica's sovereignty throughout Mesoamerica. In this way, they followed in the footsteps of previous empires; war and expansion had long been an integral part of the Mesoamerican world. The Mexica had already proven themselves an especially belligerent people during the domination of the Tepaneca. As successors of the glorious ancestors, they were thus able to legitimately invoke the time-honored tradition and felt obliged to do so: conquests were a task given by the gods. This idea was further validated by the religious necessity to preserve the cosmos through the sacrifice of people and objects collected as tributes from militarily subjugated peoples.[55]

There was also a more profane reason for the tremendous military drive of the Mexica Empire, namely that rulers and nobles depended on success in war to secure and demonstrate their prestige and the legitimacy of their rule. The more the empire expanded, however, the more the threat of revolts grew, especially in the provinces far away from Tenochtitlan. The constant war campaigns thus also served as a deterrent against rebellion. The wars of conquest had an economic importance as well for the Mexica, as they involved plunder and the securing of tributes. Finally, successful wars gave rulers the opportunity to reduce internal political tensions resulting from disgruntled nobles.[56]

Since the ruler had no standing army, he had to mobilize his troops when a campaign was close at hand. The war council—the general staff of the army, which included the tlatoani and many other high dignitaries—organized provisioning and deployment. It is estimated that Tenochtitlan could mobilize up to twenty thousand warriors, and the whole triple alliance up to sixty thousand. Allied and tributary cities provided auxiliary troops, especially porters. Normally the army was led into the field by the ruler himself or, in his absence, by the supreme general of the war council, the *tlacatecatl*. In the combat units, macehualtin from a calpulli served together. They could be recognized by their luminous pennants, which served to identify warriors to each other in the turmoil of battle. Whenever their bearers fell in battle, it caused great confusion in the unit, a situation that the Spaniards would later use to their advantage.[57]

Battles usually began at sunrise. If the fighting did not conclude within a day, the parties would withdraw at sunset to continue the conflict the next morning. Smaller night raids were not uncommon, however. During large troop deployments, smoke signals served as a means of communication, and the sounds of drums and trumpets launched the frontal attacks. Subcommanders meanwhile urged on their units with inspirational speeches. The combatants went at each other armed with bows and arrows and slingshots, which were mainly used at the beginning of the battle, and with clubs, wooden swords, and spears with obsidian blades. The warriors of higher social standing wielded the swords. By contrast, the bows and slings, which were also used for hunting and did not require extensive training, were used by those of lower status. To protect themselves, the soldiers wore cotton armor, which the Spaniards would adopt for themselves later. The higher the warrior's status, the easier it was to recognize him by means of his fine garments and precious jewelry. This was all the more true of the elite units of the eagle and jaguar warriors, who enjoyed the honor of being the first to engage in hand-to-hand combat.[58]

Because the campaigns served in large part to take prisoners for sacrifice, the warfare was conceived with this goal in mind. The greatest glory went to those warriors who captured the most enemies. Nevertheless, countless fighters also lost their lives in the battles, especially in the wars of conquest, in which the military calculus involved capturing the marketplace of the attacked city-state, destroying its temples, and literally taking away its deities, that is statues. The wars of enthronement in particular combined two important aspects for the throne claimant: fame and prestige, along with evidence of an ability to govern. War was a highly ritualized affair and was prepared for and followed by sacred dances, sacrifices, and fasting exercises. It was also officially declared with symbolic gifts to the enemy. War was a sacred act among equals that revealed which tribal god was the strongest. As a result, the opponents needed to be of roughly equal strength, since there was no honor in defeating a clearly inferior enemy.[59]

In contrast, the so-called "flower wars" had a special function. Invented by the Mexica, this type of warfare involved the capture of enemy warriors for sacrificial purposes, though many of their own warriors died in action. Flower wars were not waged with the aim of seizing the defeated enemy's city. In this case, the battlefield and the number of fighters involved were negotiated in advance, and the side that captured the most enemies declared itself the victor. Flower wars were also held for military training purposes. On the other hand, they could also turn into wars of conquest, as with the capture of Chalco. At the beginning of the sixteenth century, the cities of the Valley of Tlaxcala—despite being partners in the flower wars—increasingly felt the pressure of their larger neighbor. It was probably only a matter of time before the triple alliance changed the rules of the game. With the arrival of the Spaniards, the situation for the city-states of Tlaxcala, Huexotzinco, and Cholula would change drastically.[60]

In general, the Mexica went to war to defend themselves against attacks. But this occurred with less frequency in the course of the fifteenth century. The battle with the neighboring Tlatelolco in 1473 was portrayed as a retaliatory strike against its ruler Moquihuix, who had abused his wife, a daughter of the tlatoani of Tenochtitlan, Axayacatl. The conflict ended with the triumph of Axayacatl, who killed his adversary himself. From that point on, Tenochtitlan appointed the two governors of the neighboring city. Even assaults on envoys or the long-distance merchants of the Mexica, who often fulfilled military espionage duties, were considered grounds for war. Support for allies or the suppression of insurrections also often led to military interventions, and refusals of bribes and blackmail justified declarations of war; refusing an invitation to a high feast—an insult to the host city-state—could also bring about armed conflict. Even bored warriors itching for the thrill of fighting could escalate a small interaction into an actual war.[61]

In Mexica society, the individual's success in battle was central to his social standing. Limited social advancement was possible through military achievements, although the most important positions in the army were reserved for the nobility. While the vast majority of warriors worked as farmers in peacetime, war offered them an opportunity to realize their personal ambitions. Young people were systematically prepared for military service and at first went to the battlefields as porters and observers. War was seen as a test, and reward belonged to those who brought home the most captives. The higher the military or noble rank of a soldier, the more that was expected of him in battle to maintain his privileges. Combat itself was highly individualistic, for all the warriors competed with each other for prisoners. Once the war conch sounded, everyone fought for himself, albeit without straying from the order of battle. The individual warriors would seek out enemies of equal or higher-rank in order to prove their worth. Occasionally, warlike violence spilled over into everyday life in peacetime, such as when proud young warriors would harass and mistreat free merchants or farmers. Such behavior, however, could be met with severe punishment.[62]

After the victory against Azcapotzalco, the triple alliance waged—mostly victoriously—numerous larger and smaller wars. The campaign against the Tarascans in today's Michoacán around 1471 was an exception. The Mexica's strategy involved a springboard tactic: they exploited the resources and troops from the conquered cities to enter into the next battle even stronger. Through this approach, which was later successfully emulated by the Spanish conquerors, the Mexica effectively expanded the area that had to pay tribute to them. In the newly subjugated lands, sovereignty was secured by the stationing of garrisons, which were not intended to be permanent, and by appointing governors. Given the oppressive tributes and the burden of provisioning the occupiers, rebellions by the subjugated peoples were by no means rare.[63]

The Mexica organized the conquered territories into provinces consisting of various city-states subordinated to a capital city. Sometimes they adopted a government structure that had already existed before the conquest, putting themselves at its head. The provincial division was designed to make the collection of tributes more efficient. Each triple-alliance partner had a preferred sphere of influence. The form of rule was not direct but hegemonic, with local elites, tolerated by the Mexica rulers, controlling the fate of their cities. When necessary, the invaders reinstated the rulers deemed sympathetic to them. A permanent military presence was not required in most cases; as a rule, the threat of force alone was sufficient to achieve obedience. Still, power had to be repeatedly demonstrated, which is why the need for warfare was constant. This form of sovereignty worked well so long as there were no serious competitors, which remained the case until the Spanish arrived in 1519.[64]

The triple alliance retained its heterogeneity. This fact attested to the reality that the Mexica of Tenochtitlan did not fully control the entire Valley of Mexico, despite their superiority.[65] Although the alliance was held together by a complex web of marital relations, diplomatic agreements, gift exchanges, and joint celebrations, the three city-states each had their own spheres of influence and local autonomy. At the beginning of the sixteenth century, there was no imperial unity, along European lines, in the sense of a shared consciousness in the territories conquered by the Mexica. The historically still quite recent and ethnically heterogeneous entity, which was constantly expanding into new territories, lacked the power to integrate. In particular, far-flung peoples outside the Valley of Mexico who had only recently been subjugated tended to seek out allies with whom to break free from the yoke of the tributary rulers. Given these

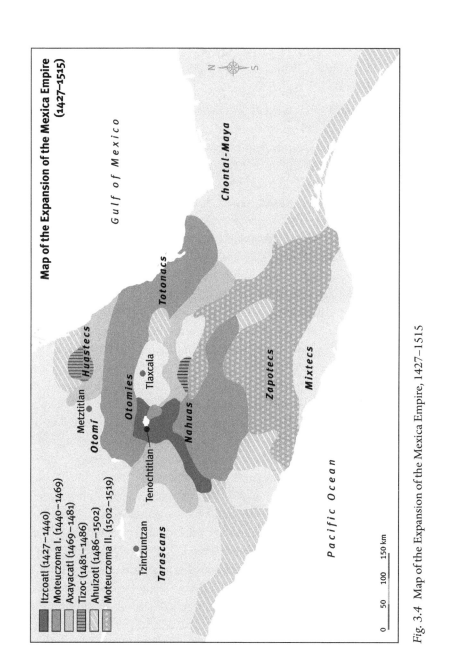

Fig. 3.4 Map of the Expansion of the Mexica Empire, 1427–1515

reservations the European concept of empire is misleading, especially as the Mexica themselves were not familiar with it.[66]

The Tlatoani Moctezuma II

War was declared by the tlatoani, who presided over the ruling dynasty and guaranteed the status of his altepetl on the basis of his prestige and that of his dynasty. There is historical evidence of nine tlatoques of the Mexica, who ruled between 1372 and 1520 and were in charge of the state system. They were responsible for warfare and diplomatic foreign relations as well as the religious sphere, in which they assisted in important ceremonies that included human sacrifices. Ideally, they earned the respect of their subjects every day through their exemplary bearing and conduct, military successes, and leadership—although by no means were all occupants of the throne up to the task.[67]

The empire was an electoral kingdom. The choice of ruler was limited to close—and with few exceptions—adult male relatives of the previous sovereign. In the ideal scenario, the mother of the future throne holder was the predecessor's most distinguished wife. The continuity of the dynasty, indeed, played a central role in the ideas of the Mexica, and there was a strong interest in preserving it. Only altepeme who had lost their independence in war were likely to have to deal with genealogical interruptions. On the other hand, there was no primogeniture. What mattered most was proof of military prowess, which the candidate would have repeatedly demonstrated in campaigns and as a member of the war council. Frequently, the tlatoani recommended a successor, but this was not binding. Consequently, several men were usually considered at once. The right to vote was granted to high noblemen and priests of Tenochtitlan as well as the rulers of the other cities of the triple alliance.[68]

Moctezuma—the second tlatoani with this name, hence the sobriquet Xocoyotzin, "the Younger"—perfectly fulfilled the requirements for an heir apparent. He was born in 1467 as the child of the prince and later ruler Axacayatl and a princess from Texcoco. His great-grandfather, Moctezuma I, had consolidated and considerably expanded the empire during his reign from 1440 to 1469. In 1469, his grandson Axacayatl followed him as sovereign; he was then followed in 1481 by his brother Tizoc, who, in turn, was followed by another brother, Ahuizotl, in 1486. Before Moctezuma II was chosen in 1502, he passed through the stages of a prince of royal lineage. He graduated from the nobility training of the calmecac and became high priest of the temple of Huitzilopochtli. Under Ahuizotl, he was given an office on the war council, and soon his success on the battlefield was signaled by taking captives.[69]

It was therefore not surprising that, at the moment of his election, Moctezuma was on a campaign against Tolocan in the west of the country to crush a rebellion. The investiture of a new ruler was an elaborate process that lasted several days and was accompanied by numerous religious rituals. He was transformed from one prince among many into a singular ruler and demigod, endowed with special powers that needed to be handled with great care. At his coronation, he was bestowed with a turquoise-colored cloak; ear, nose, and lip plugs; and a crown made of turquoise. Turquoise established proximity to the fire god Xiuhtecuhtli and assured the transfer of the divine qualities to the ruler. In addition, the tlatoani wore precious arm and calf bands and magnificent feathers. The throne consisted of a mat of woven reeds, which was located in a huge, bustling palace built especially for him. With the new building, he followed in the footsteps of his predecessors: they, too, built new palaces whose majesty trumped that of the other existing stately homes. Next to the ruler's chambers there were numerous rooms for the court and visitors, provisions, craftsmen, and attendees of meetings. The tlatoani had landscaped gardens and a zoo where wild animals were kept. There was also a wing of his palace where people with physical deformities lived.[70]

Court etiquette was regulated down to the smallest detail. Physical contact with the tlatoani was kept to a minimum. One did not look him in the eyes and, if one addressed him at all, it was with a subdued voice. When welcoming audiences and visitors, Moctezuma appeared remote and austere. His eating habits were transformed, for the ruler had to take care of his strength and maintain his body. The sumptuous meals served by young nobles, with countless courses and exquisite dishes, were consumed by the tlatoani in a solemn ritual in which he ate and drank alone. The remaining food was then distributed among the palace residents.[71]

The tlatoani wielded ultimate power and made decisions about life and death, war and peace. This authority, however, had been granted to him for the good of his people. To earn the obedience of his subjects, he therefore had to exercise it scrupulously. The tlatoani had complete responsibility for the welfare of the state, and his duties extended to the supervision of the religious realm. He took care of the priests and the holy sites, had new temples built, and expanded the great temple. He presided over countless public religious celebrations, some of which required him to dance in the costume of a god. In cases of natural disasters, it was up to him to appease the gods through pilgrimages or self-sacrifice. He was thus a mediator between earth and heaven and a speaker of the gods. His responsibilities also included state visits to foreign rulers and, of course, the supreme military command. A powerful ruler had to display his wealth, which was exemplary for that of his people, in celebrations and banquets that could last for

Fig. 3.5 Moteuczoma in Codex Ramírez. The Tovar Codex (or Ramírez Codex) originated in Mexico in the second half of the sixteenth century as a manuscript entitled *Relación del origen de los indios que habitan esta Nueva España según sus historias*. The work is attributed to the Jesuit Juan de Tovar and is based on the chronicle of the Dominican Diego Durán, who in turn drew upon an older indigenous source. The more than fifty full-page illustrations are based on precolonial representations. Courtesy of the John Carter Brown Library.

days. He further demonstrated his might through the bestowal of gifts. These, too, were fundamental to ensuring order and legitimacy.[72]

Militarily, Moctezuma followed his predecessor and waged numerous wars of conquest that extended the empire far to the southeast to what are now the states of Chiapas and Soconusco, up to the border with Guatemala. Nonetheless, the troops did not manage to end the resistance of the locals everywhere. Where they deployed garrisons far from the capital, the embers of resistance often continued to smolder beneath the surface. In other cases, wars could not be successfully concluded, for instance, because of rugged mountain terrain.[73]

Starting in 1508, Moctezuma relaunched the flower wars against Huexotzinco and Atlixco, which resulted in heavy losses for the Mexica. Several brothers of the tlatoani fell, including Macuilmalinaltzin, who had been a leading candidate to the throne in 1502. In the end, it was Nezahualpilli, the ruler of Texcoco, who tipped the scales in Moctezuma's favor with his vote. After that, the passed-over sibling represented a threat to the new ruler. According to Alva

Ixtlilxochitl, Moctezuma had his brother and his entourage murdered during the 1508 campaign against Atlixco. He also arranged for a purge of the highest state offices occupied by his predecessor's cohort and then filled them with loyalists. Furthermore, he excluded from power the merit nobility, who had ascended under his predecessors, in favor of the hereditary nobility.[74]

The conflicts that Moctezuma aroused at different societal levels through his crackdown had a disastrous impact on the triple alliance. Nezahualpilli was angry about the death of his son-in-law Macuilmalinaltzin and refused to simply accept the increasingly flagrant claim to supremacy of the tlatoani of Tenochtitlan. During a flower war, he ordered Texcoco's troops to withdraw, whereupon Moctezuma prohibited the Texcoco tributary towns in the Valley of Mexico from continuing to meet their payment obligations. When Nezahualpilli died in 1515, Moctezuma pushed through his nephew Cacama as successor against opposition in Texcoco. The still young prince Ixtlilxochitl, one of the legitimate sons of Nezahualpili, then openly rebelled against the new tlatoani and was able to capture various cities or win them over to his side.[75]

The image of Moctezuma II passed down to us is undoubtedly somewhat muddled. In the sources, all of which date back to the time after the fall of Tenochtitlan, the tlatoani is blamed for the Mexica's demise because he had failed to appease the wrath of the gods and restore the world order. Nonetheless, however harshly one may judge the part played by Moctezuma, the world of the Mexica had already fallen into disarray. Divisions at home had emerged, and although the empire had reached a remarkable size in geopolitical terms, it was also overstretched militarily. In many places, an intense hatred of the conquerors persisted. With the Spanish arrival in 1519, the dissatisfied tributaries found the opportunity they had been waiting for.

Totonacapan

The Spaniards had already heard of the Mexica Empire in the west when they left the Mayan country in April 1519. But they did not yet have a clear idea of its extension and assumed that they were still exploring an island. The further they traveled, the greater the diversity was among the ethnic groups they encountered. Their next destination, the land of the Totonacs, held another surprise in store for them. As even the rank-and-file soldiers surely had recognized, the cultural heterogeneity of this region was far greater than anything that had ever been witnessed before in the Indies. This learning process, however, was not limited to the Europeans. When the Totonacs and the Mexica envoys came to meet them, they devised various incentives and activities of their own to integrate the strangers into their world in their own particular way.

The Envoys of Moctezuma

The Spaniards left Potonchán on Palm Sunday, and the fleet reached the natural harbor of the island of San Juan de Ulúa on Maundy Thursday, April 21, where Grijalva had been a year earlier. To welcome them, a group of indigenous people appeared in two large canoes at the captain's ship. They identified themselves as envoys of Moctezuma and wanted to know the reason for the strangers' visit. Cortés invited the envoys aboard, hosted them in a friendly manner, and explained to them that he wanted to go ashore the next day. The envoys cautiously tasted the food that was presented to them and asked for some samples to take to their governor, Tendile. Tendile had his headquarters in Cuetlaxtlan and was commissioned by Moctezuma to collect the tributes in the province of Totonacapan. Communication was difficult, however, because Aguilar, the translator, did not understand the language.[1]

The Spaniards went ashore on Good Friday morning near the Totonac village of Chalchiuhcuecan, where they set up camp. Cortés arranged for all his men, the artillery, and also the horses to be brought to the settlement while the Taino slaves from Cuba built huts. On Easter Saturday, curious inhabitants from the village appeared. They were sent on behalf of the Mexica to help set up the Spanish camp. Lively bartering then took place, with the Totonacs showing great interest in the foreign objects—glass beads, mirrors, scissors, and knives. The Europeans, for their part, were grateful for the offered food, and their enthusiasm grew considerably when the Totonacs started to bring gold objects to trade. Cortés tried to keep his men's avarice in check. He ordered them not to exchange gold for cheap baubles and, above all, not to reveal their lust for the gold.[2]

On Easter Sunday, Tendile himself came to visit, unarmed, with a large entourage in splendid robes and copious gifts for the Spaniards. Following Mexica custom, he paid tribute to Cortés with incense and wooden sticks, which he handed to the captain general after dipping them in his own blood. For Malinche, this was a momentous occasion: she would demonstrate for the first time her interpreting skills in collaboration with Aguilar. Cortés was delighted. He had heard her life story and promised her "more than freedom" should she satisfactorily complete her task.[3]

After a joint mass and banquet, the two military commanders withdrew with the interpreters and a few confidants for a more intimate discussion. Different versions exist of this first conversation between Cortés and a high-ranking Mexica. According to a source influenced by Cortés, the captain general told Tendile that he and his men would henceforth be vassals of the king of Spain, the powerful ruler of "the greatest part of the world," serving him as all subjects did and surrendering all their land and possessions. Supposedly Tendile was entirely pleased with this opportunity and assured Cortés of his willingness to serve such a powerful majesty. To his great satisfaction, Cortés then dressed him in noble garments. The following day, Tendile presented Cortés with lavish gifts, including gold jewelry.[4] López de Gómara's version reads quite differently, however. In his telling, Tendile replied politely but firmly that he was pleased to learn of the greatness and benevolence of the foreign monarch, but that his own master Moctezuma was no less great and benevolent. Tendile apparently intended to inform his master that there was another ruler as great as he was and then wait to see his reaction to the news.[5]

Cortés gave Tendile numerous gifts intended for Moctezuma. These included pieces of jewelry, an elaborately crafted armchair, and a red cap decorated with a Saint George medal. The Spanish supreme commander expressed his wish that Moctezuma should sit on this armchair and wear one of the chains when he met him, a request to which Tendile reacted with reluctance. Cortés again displayed his military might, Cannons were fired, and the riders held an exhibition fight in which the horses were chased at full gallop over the sandy ground.

All of this impressed the Mexica envoys, who were to report on what they saw to their ruler. Tendile had brought along illustrators to capture the events visually; they depicted in particular the clothing and beards of the Spaniards, their ships, horses, dogs, armor, and weapons. A partially gold-plated helmet of one of the Spaniards caught Tendile's fancy, because it reminded him of the headgear of his war god Huitzilopochtli. Cortés then handed him the helmet with the request that Tendile bring it back filled with gold dust. According to López de Gómara, Cortés justified this demand by saying that his comrades "suffered from a disease of the heart that could be cured with gold."[6]

Tendile eventually departed, but left a representative and a large number of servants with the Spaniards to look after them. Word of the meeting between Tendile and Cortés reached Moctezuma quickly, thanks to a highly efficient messenger system. The governor, too, sent gifts to Tenochtitlan along the fastest route. A source from the highlands of Tlaxcala related some of these impressions:

> When the Spanish were seen . . . they (the scouts) said to Moctezuma: "Ruler! We went to the shore to see them there. The fire that they emit is very frightening . . . . And they travel swiftly on their deer . . . . And the dress of the warrior is made entirely of iron. Everyone carries a house on his head . . . . When they breathe fire, it terrifies you. If you heard it, you would scream."[7]

The news from the coast was unexpected and caused anxiety in the tlatoani's palace in Tenochtitlan. However, Moctezuma had learned in the previous year about Grijalva's expedition, which seemed to him to have been undertaken for commercial purposes. The ruler still dressed himself in the costly blankets the messengers had brought to him then. Furthermore, in his conversations with Cortés, Tendile claimed that Moctezuma had known about the activities of the new fleet for some time, indicating that news had reached Tenochtitlan from Yucatán. The Mexica therefore were not entirely unprepared.[8] Moctezuma's immediate response was to send another delegation bearing gifts; as messenger, he appointed the nobleman Teoctlamacazqui.[9]

At the end of April, about a week after Tendile's visit, the Mexica delegation advanced toward the leader of the Europeans in a highly sophisticated welcoming ceremony. Cortés had been on board his flagship and, dressed in his festive attire, sat down on a thronelike chair. The delegation presented him with even more impressive gifts: a golden disk, the size of a wagon wheel, that represented the sun; an even larger silver disk that was a symbol of the moon; and, finally, the Spanish helmet filled with tiny nuggets of gold. They also placed upon him precious garments of symbolic import. For instance, they adorned him with a jaguar head, wrapped him with a precious feather cape, and decorated him with gold and silver jewelry. According to the Codex Mexicanus, which was written around 1590, Cortés was given, among other things, a cape, two feather headdresses, two feather coats, five disks with turquoise mosaics, a tunic, and two shields. Finally, they served him elaborately prepared food. Cortés refused, however, when the delegation wanted also to offer him their own blood. The indigenous chronicler of the Annals of Tlatelolco describes the scene:

> In year 1 Reed, the Spaniards appeared in Tecpan Tlayacac. Then the captain came. When he arrived in Tecpan Tlayacac, the Huaxtecs greeted him by giving him a golden sun, one golden and one silver, a cross mirror and golden helmets, golden vessels in the shape of snails, which were worn on his head, and the green feather ornaments of the people from the coast and shields of shells. Before the captain, they made a sacrifice. He was enraged when he was handed the blood in an eagle bowl. And with the sword the captain personally killed the one who gave him the blood. As a result, those who had greeted him became utterly agitated. But it was the will of Moctezuma that the captain be given so many things just so that he, the captain, would return home. The Huaxtec had acted on his orders.[10]

Fig. 4.1 The Tlillancalqui, Cortés, and Malinche (Codex Durán). The Codex Durán of the Dominican Diego Durán was created in the second half of the century. The scene shows the meeting of Cortés, known as the *marqués*, with the Tlillancalqui, Lord of the House of Darkness, and the interpreter Marina/Malinche, dressed in Spanish garments. The scene on the left shows the ships, the "moving houses" of the Spaniards, which particularly impressed the Mexica. From Fray Diego Durán, *Historia de las Indias de Nueva-España y islas de Tierra Firme*, 1581. Biblioteca Digital Hispánica, España Biblioteca Nacional de España.

It cannot be conclusively determined whether this version, or that of the many Spanish eyewitnesses who stated that Cortés had returned the gifts and courtesies, is correct. We do know that he expressed his desire to visit Moctezuma in his palace—an idea that the Mexica envoys rejected. The journey there was too dangerous; enemies of the Mexica could be lying in wait for the Spaniards in order to kill the ruler's friends. Cortés, though, was not put off by these warnings. On the contrary, he again ordered his artillery be fired. And to frighten the envoys, whom he had previously shackled, he also displayed their sharp iron weapons.[11]

The intricate and extended communication through the exchange of gifts did not end there. When Tendile again appeared in the Spanish camp about ten days later, the gifts he brought were less impressive. His demands, however, were as plain as could be: Moctezuma let it be known that the Spanish should board their ships and leave right away, for a visit to Tenochtitlan was impossible. With this the sovereign sought to test whether the Spaniards would finally bow to his will. When Cortés insisted on visiting Tenochtitlan, thereby underscoring his own claim to superiority, Tendile ended the dialogue. At the same time, the large number of servants who until then had made life easier for the Spaniards also departed. Cortés now awaited an attack and ordered his troops to prepare themselves. But nothing happened. When the Spaniards' supplies ran out after a few days, they realized they needed to reassess their situation.[12]

The Return of Quetzalcoatl?

So how did the ruler of the Mexica react to the news of the Spanish? According to the Florentine Codex, there had been worrying omens in Moctezuma's empire even before their arrival. Ten years earlier, it is said that the dawn painted threatening images in the sky at night in the east, which seemed to herald a new era. Then, the temple of the god Huitzilopochtli was set on fire and could not be extinguished with water. The third omen was a lightning bolt that struck the temple of the god of fire Xiuhtecuhtli without thunder. A comet also appeared in the sky, which caused a shower of sparks. Afterward, there was catastrophic flooding at Lake Mexico, even though there was no storm. The sixth omen is said to have been a woman who was heard at night mourning the fall of the city. The seventh, that a fishermen caught a strange bird with a mirror between its head feathers, in which Moctezuma could see a battlefield and warriors riding on deer. The eighth omen was to do with disfigured individuals who vanished when the ruler desired to view them in prison. According to Muñoz Camargo, who mentioned the same omens, the people of Mexico understood all of these as signs of the end of the world and the arrival of new peoples on earth.[13]

Supposedly Moctezuma had been preparing for the return of the god Quetzalcoatl since the news of Grijalva's arrival.[14] Díaz del Castillo reported that the moment the ruler saw the golden helmet sent by Tendile, he was convinced that it was the same as that of Huitzilopochtli and that the Spaniards were among those who, according to the prophecies of the Mexica ancestors, would one day come to rule his country.[15] As Dominican Diego Durán writes, drawing on an unknown Mexican codex from the time shortly after the Conquest, Moctezuma was stunned and at first even speechless. He proceeded to have his craftsmen produce precious gifts, while imposing the strictest secrecy.[16]

The gifts that Moctezuma entrusted to Teoctlamacazqui are said to have had high symbolic value, representing the clothing and food of different gods. The choice of messenger was also carefully considered: at court, Teoctlamacazqui had held the office of *tlillancalqui*, master of *tlillancalco* (the house of darkness), which was especially dedicated to the cult of the gods Cihuacoatl and Quetzalcoatl. Moctezuma allegedly further instructed him to greet the Spaniards like returning gods to a land that was rightfully theirs. In addition, Teoctlamacazqui was to pay close attention to whether the foreigners' leader ate the offered food and drink. If he did, it would be certain that he was Quetzalcoatl.[17] The eyewitness Juan Álvarez, who testified as early as 1521 in a preliminary investigation initiated by Velázquez and who attended the gift-giving ceremony, confirmed that the Mexica had called the Spanish officers *teule* or *teotl* in Nahuatl, that is, divine beings. Among them, the Mexica also counted Malinche.[18]

According to the Florentine Codex and Alvarado Tezozomoc, Moctezuma was restless and apprehensive during his envoys' absence. When Teoctlamacazqui returned, he received a special welcome: The ruler had prisoners sacrificed, and the envoys were sprinkled with their blood. After hearing the report about the terrifying weapons, horses, and dogs, and the strange appearance of the Spanish and their black slaves, Moctezuma was supposedly seized with fear. As Sahagún tells us, he sent his magicians to the Spaniards disguised as craftsmen, but they could do nothing against the ostensible gods. Other sources—for example, the chronicle of Chimalpahin—also relate that the troubling news spread among the population, causing great fear and sadness. Above all, the Spaniards' beards, their light skin, and long hair, along with the riders on horseback, are said to have convinced the subjects that the strangers were magicians.[19] Moctezuma presumably tried to take flight to the cave of Cincalco, near Chapultepec. This would not have been surprising given the importance that Mexica attached to the influence of their gods in daily life and the extraordinary challenge posed by the arrival of the strangers. While Moctezuma eventually returned to his duties as sovereign, he remained in constant contact with his soothsayers and magicians.[20]

That the Mexica perceived the Spanish as gods can be found in most colonial chronicles, both in those written by Spanish and indigenous or mestizo authors.

According to this narrative, this apotheosis gave the Spaniards a decisive psychological advantage and ultimately contributed to Tenochtitlan's downfall. The mostly ecclesiastical chroniclers of European origin took the story at face value because they were able to read a salvific dimension into the act of conquest. Hence, the devilish Mexica religion was brought down almost without effort by the Spanish, which in the end could only be due to the providence of the Christian God. The notion of "white gods" whose return drove the indigenous people to despair can also be found in indigenous traditions, though most of these have passed through the hands of colonial translators or scribes. For contemporary witnesses from the indigenous population who dictated their memories of the events to Christian missionaries (as in the case of Sahagún and Motolinía), the narratives supposedly served the retrospective purpose of explaining the seemingly inexplicable collapse of the powerful Mexica Empire. Here, the predetermination of events explains the lack of will to resist, indeed the fatalism of the Mexica. This could also be conveniently reconciled with the faith teachings of the indigenous New Christians, even if the subtext of this interpretation still derives from pre-Hispanic religious ideas. Moreover, by pointing to the failures of the tlatoani Moctezuma, it was possible to identify the culprit whose misconduct disrupted the order of the cosmos and who could therefore be scapegoated for the defeat and the subsequent catastrophes.[21]

Historians and ethnohistorians have long debated about the authenticity of this interpretation. Conventional studies assume that the confusion of the Spanish with gods was the most prominent reason for the rapid collapse of the Mexica Empire.[22] In contrast, ethnohistorical literature of the late twentieth century often dismisses the prophecies and the return of the gods as myths essentially invented by Christian chroniclers out of a colonialist impulse or reinterpreted ex post facto into their own and indigenous narratives to legitimize the Conquest, the resulting Spanish rule, and Christianization.[23] Franciscans in particular would have played a large part in this, since this story fits perfectly into the chiliastic thinking of the friars of that time. For a historian such as Motolinía, for example, the prophecies were especially appealing because they could be understood as harbingers of Christianity. The story of the return of the gods, on the other hand, could be read to mean that many years ago there was a Christian saint in Mesoamerica who now came back and fought against the devil Huitzilopochtli. The work of Sahagún, which for the first time brought the components of the narrative together in full, was thus nothing more than a form of mythologizing the Conquest. By embellishing the past, the conquest could be transformed into a narrative adapted from the Nahua calendar. For the indigenous people who "wrote" this narrative, it meant neither a renunciation of their identity nor a nostalgic look at the past, but rather a way to look into the future.[24]

Fig. 4.2 Gifts for the *teotl* (according to Sahagún). The Florentine Codex provides a pictorial representation of the bestowal of gifts on the captain's ship. The lavish pieces of clothing and jewelry that the Mexica presented to Cortés, who is sitting on an armchair with Malinche on his left, can be seen. *General History of the Things of New Spain by Fray Bernardino de Sahagún: The Florentine Codex. Book XII: The Conquest of Mexico* (1577). Library of Congress, https://www.loc.gov/item/2021667857/.

These interpretations offer important insights. For instance, the notion of superstitious Mexica with their traditions and cyclical history is obsolete. We cannot answer with absolute certainty the question of whether they really considered the Spaniards to be gods incarnate. As the indigenous sources show, the experiences with the strangers quickly destroyed this belief, if it had ever existed. What's more, the ancient Mexica view of history was familiar with the repeated conquest of foreigners who brought their new gods with them. The arrival of the Spanish was therefore not radically new.[25]

Nevertheless, the often-told prophecies and stories of the return of the gods cannot simply be dismissed as ahistorical inventions of colonialist Europeans, especially since they appear again and again in pictorial representations by indigenous artists. Critics who argue that the narrative did not appear until long after the Conquest ignore, for example, the significance of Álvarez's statements, which were written as early as 1521.[26] This and further evidence suggest that the Mexica and the other Mesoamericans whom the Spanish encountered had problems categorizing the Europeans. The repeated incense rituals and offerings of various divine foods can be attributed to their uncertainty about who they were dealing with. The notion of the return of the ruler and god Quetzalcoatl must therefore be viewed as an authentic Mesoamerican tradition.[27]

Still, it is important to remember that the worldview of the Mexica people was very different from the Europeans'. Thus, there was no separation between the worldly and divine spheres in the beliefs of the Mexica. Without having to be incarnated deities, the Spaniards could still appear at certain moments and in certain places as their embodiment; in Nahuatl *teixiptlahuan*. In this respect, a proper interpretation of the sequence of events involves a translation problem, which requires not only the correct literal translation of the term teotl into Spanish, but also an understanding of the meaning of the concept behind it.[28] The gifts that Moctezuma brought to the Spaniards were not the usual welcome gifts, but things with which the tlatoani, as the highest priest of his people, fulfilled his religious duties toward the teotl. At the moment of his first contact, Cortés was (or at least could have been or could have become) the local embodiment of a god in the eyes of the Mexica, especially once he donned the symbolic garments he was given.[29]

Cempoala, Capital of the Totonacs

During the first contact with the Mexica in Tabasco, it was already apparent that there were other ethnic groups living in the region. After the departure of Moctezuma's subjects, the Spaniards were visited by a delegation of the Totonac ruler of Cempoala, Chicomecatl, whom they would later call the "fat cacique." As the Spanish eyewitnesses noted, these men were taller than the Mexica and wore what they considered to be particularly disfiguring facial jewelry, which involved a piercing that pulled the lower lip down to the chin.[30]

At that time, Cempoala, located in the mountain ranges of the Sierra Madre Oriental and the coastal zones of the state of Veracruz in what is now eastern Mexico, was one of the capitals of the Totonac province of the Mexica Empire. It had a population of around thirty thousand. Still, this region, which the Mexica called Totonacapan, had not been part of the empire for long. It had only paid tribute to Tenochtitlan since Moctezuma's father Axayacatl subjugated the territory in the middle of the fifteenth century. Since it has historically been subject to strong external influences, Toltec and Chichimeca elements, for instance, can be detected. The society showed a clear hierarchical structure and was characterized by its multiethnic character. Diverse cultural influences can be seen in its iconography. This region therefore was very much accustomed to the mobility of people and the exchange of ideas and technology. Totonacapan was, in a manner of speaking, the laboratory for the increasing integration of Mesoamerica in the late postclassic period, from about 1200 on.[31]

From the Mexica point of view, the Totonacs were barbarians. In fact, they were hardly inferior to their tribute masters. The influences of the Maya cultures are noteworthy. The weaving art of the Totonac women immediately caught the attention of the Spaniards. In the late postclassic period, similar developments had occurred here as in other parts of Mesoamerica. The ritual ball game was as widespread as human sacrifice and the Mesoamerican calendar, with its astrological significance for the individual, the community, and the cosmos. Since this time, new architectural styles and technical innovations, for example in the processing of obsidian, also became established. The Totonacs were engaged in irrigation management and built canals. Among other things, they grew cotton. They benefited from the great diversity of ecosystems, the fertile soils in their region, and the abundant supply of water. Additionally, there was a lively trade between Cempoala and its neighbors.[32]

The city of Cempoala had an administrative center, where both secular and spiritual authorities lived. Above them stood the ruler and high priest. Monumental structures with sculptures of equal grandeur dominated the urban landscape. The temple pyramids and platforms with their symbolic imagery gave expression to the power of the gods and their worldly representatives. The highly organized caste of priests, who attracted the attention of the Spaniards with their long, blood-stained hair and dark clothes, enjoyed special esteem. Dignitaries, who were in part responsible for the accurate collection and accounting of the tributes, also lived in the districts assigned to them, in prominent buildings, though these were not comparable to those in the center. Numerous walls and courtyards were built, perhaps to protect against tropical storms and floods, but perhaps also to delineate certain sacred areas. By the time the Spanish arrived, the city was already under the powerful influence of the Mexica. Nahuatl was the lingua franca in Totonacapan; even the name "Cempoala" came from this language. The influence could also be seen in the architecture, which the Mexica deliberately used to emphasize their claims to power in the subjugated regions.[33]

The great majority of the people in this city, which was large even by European standards, lived in simple huts, however. They were mostly built on raised platforms to protect against the seasonal floods and only had enough space for the extended family. As the colonial-era sources noted, the Spaniards noticed the numerous gardens with their own ponds. Distribution of water through pipes, which also served for drainage during floods, had reached a high level of sophistication. Among other benefits the pipe system made possible, it provided the craftsmen, whose work was essential to meeting Mexica's tribute demands, with sufficient water.[34]

Cempoala was in no way satisfied with the heavy burden of its vassal status vis-à-vis Tenochtitlan. Along with considerable payments in kind, the Totonacs were repeatedly forced to hand over their sons and daughters for sacrifice. The Mexica punished their subordinates' complaints and insurrections in draconian fashion. For Cortés, this was good news. He realized that the powerful Mexica had enemies who did not dare to openly show their hostility for fear of retaliation. These Totonacs were potential allies.[35]

The Foundation of Villa Rica de Vera Cruz

However, the Spaniards were also keen to improve their own position. Cortés accordingly sent out two of his ships, under the command of Montejo and Rodrigo Alvarez and with Alaminos as helmsman, to continue exploring the coast further northward. They headed towards Pánuco, as had the Grijalva expedition before them. They were nearly shipwrecked but managed to save themselves. Before the ships returned, Cortés also sent a reconnaissance squad under the command of Pedro de Alvarado into the interior, where the men encountered an apparently abandoned village and stole food. There, again, they found clear signs of human sacrifice.[36]

Not all members of the Spanish expedition welcomed these activities. From the very beginning, there had been tensions between Velázquez's followers and those of Cortés. They came to a head because of the food shortage and the demands of some men to return to Cuba. As Díaz del Castillo observed, these included first and foremost the well-off, who longed to return to their estates. They probably assessed the risk as being too high, not least because of the looming threat of indigenous groups with their sacrificial cult. Velázquez's closest associates, including his relative Velázquez de León, Diego de Ordás, Montejo, Juan Escudero, and the priest Juan Díaz, became the spokesmen for this faction. They argued that the governor's written instructions did not provide for a longer stay. In addition, the expedition had already obtained enough information and treasure to be able to deliver a report in Cuba. They also complained about the rampant bartering. This brought large quantities of gold into the possession of the soldiers, whence it went to the sailors, who supplied them with fresh fish, all without the royal fifth being deducted. They asked Cortés to appoint an army treasurer, even though a royal treasurer, Alonso de Ávila, was already present. Cortés responded to the demands and made sure that his henchman, Gonzalo de Mejía, got the office.[37]

Cortés's own faction, including the brothers Alvarado, Portocarrero, Escalante, Olid, Lugo, Ávila, and Sandoval, opposed any return. They thus headed a sizeable group of men who, like Bernal Díaz del Castillo, had nothing left to lose in Cuba. After the Spaniards had become convinced of the country's wealth, not least through the gifts of the Mexica, greed took hold with new intensity. The group asked Cortés to found a settlement, maintaining that their participation in the expedition in the first place was based on the understanding that this would occur. Furthermore, since the Mexica would surely not let the Spaniards return to ashore peacefully, a settlement ultimately would serve the interests of the Spanish crown. They noted that Grijalva was confronted with the same demands from his crew, which he had ignored at his own peril. They also made a point of reminding Cortés that Grijalva had been strongly rebuked by the governor just a few months earlier for this failure. In short, those who a wanted to return to Cuba should be allowed to do so.[38]

We do not know whether Cortés considered returning to Cuba before his men asked him to stay, or whether it was a set-up. The fact that Montejo, one of Velázquez's most important and loyal supporters, was still on an exploratory trip suggests the latter. According to the description in the letter of July 1519 from the city council (*cabildo*) to the monarch, the entire hueste met in mid-May and unanimously called upon the *caudillo* to establish a settlement.[39] Cortés made his decision a day later. He accepted the demand and explained that a cabildo was necessary to ensure a functional government. This meant that mayors (alcaldes), council members (*regidores*) and functionaries had to be nominated. All the members of the hueste would be citizens (*vecinos*) of the new town, which would be called Villa Rica de la Vera Cruz, in reference to the wealth of the country and the fact that they had gone ashore on Good Friday. According to the statements of Cortés's followers, an election of officials then took place. Candidates from Cortés's home region, Extremadura, predominated, including Portocarrero as one of the two magistrates (*alcalde mayor*), Alvarado as a council member, and Sandoval as chief constable (*alguacil*). There is no question that this election process was a farce or, as Las Casas put it, "malevolent and absurd."[40]

The notarized act practically created the town out of nothing. In fact, the camp near San Juan de Ulúa, on the sandy, mosquito-contaminated and malaria-prone beach, was scarcely suitable as a place for settlement. Nevertheless, the act of founding a city was not Cortés's invention. He had personally witnessed similar actions on several occasions in the conquest of Cuba under the command of Velázquez and, due to his basic legal education, knew what formalities to observe. What lent legitimacy to this venture was that it was not the decision of the supreme commander alone, but of the troops as a whole. Because the royal court was far away and there was no legitimate representative on-site, governmental power reverted, so to speak, to the community of the governed. For this reason, the act of assembly and the unanimous decision, which Cortés and his sympathizers emphasized in their reports, was accorded great importance.[41]

The advantages for the caudillo were obvious: The cabildo had the right to contact the monarch directly in writing and to appoint a supreme judge and military commander on a provisional basis. This allowed Cortés to free himself from his status as Velázquez's representative and to submit directly to his majesty's command. As a consequence, he was effectively subject to a higher law so that Velázquez's instructions lost their validity. In fact, one of the first official acts of the new city council was to declare the governor's instructions met, for Cortés supposedly had already satisfied all the requirements. The latter then resigned pro forma from his office, whereupon his men immediately elected him military supreme commander (*capitán general*) and supreme judge (*justicia mayor*). This enabled Cortés to gain the support of his men. Extending the logic of this outcome, whoever wanted to rebel against him would, in doing so, commit high treason. The expedition, which was originally designed only for trade, had become a political enterprise.[42]

But Cortés's "maneuver"—as even his sympathizer Sepúlveda called it—did not take place without resistance.[43] Some of Velázquez's supporters were angry and alluded to the instructions of the crown, which said nothing about settlement development. They most likely accused the commander of high treason; for their part, they could argue that Velázquez was the governor appointed by the monarch. Cortés nevertheless succeeded in silencing these voices with soothing words, as well as threats and bribery. A good example of this concerned Montejo: after returning from his reconnaissance, he learned that he had been appointed alcalde mayor, along with Portocarrero. As for his most tenacious opponents—including Velázquez de León and Diego de Ordás—Cortés had them put in chains for a short time and would later win them over with generous gifts of gold. In the end, he convincingly argued that, with Velázquez out of the picture, everyone's share of the spoils would increase significantly. At the same time, in a highly unusual measure, he had the cabildo guarantee him the fifth part of all profits, the same share that was due to the crown.[44]

The arbitrariness of Cortés's actions was by no means exceptional. Spanish officials repeatedly had to make decisions that the crown had not yet approved. Cortés became familiar with such practices during his time as mayor of Santiago de Cuba. With Spain so distant, the court's approval would have taken too long. The sea voyage from Mexico to Spain took about four and a half months, and that with favorable winds, between May and June. In the best-case scenario, an inquiry to the monarch and his response took at least a year. This gave the local officials relative autonomy. Cortés was aware of this, as was Velázquez. He had hesitated for so long in choosing his fleet captain, not least because he knew from his own experience the risk of a subordinate becoming independent.[45]

After the disagreements had been settled, captain general Cortés ordered that their location be moved about forty-three miles further north by land to a place that Alaminos had identified as auspicious. It was located near the Totonac village of Quiahuiztlan, which was situated on a hill near the sea. Provisions and heavy weapons were loaded onto the ships, while Cortés set off on foot with four hundred men. During their march, Totonacs supplied the men with food and prepared them a night's lodging in a village. After about thirty miles, the troops reached Cempoala, where Chicomecatl welcomed the Spaniards and gave them food and shelter. According to the Spanish sources, the Totonacs were utterly submissive and welcomed Cortés as their new master. The inhabitants of the city are said to have welcomed the Spaniards with flowers and the blare of trumpets. The Spaniards renamed the Totonac city New Seville because the houses reminded them of the palaces of the Andalusian capital. It was the largest city they had seen in the Indies up to that point, and they were profoundly impressed by it. The freshly whitewashed houses glistened so intensely in the sun that the mounted advance guard at first thought they were coated with silver.[46]

For Cortés, this arrangement proved to be a stroke of luck. The tensions with the Mexica certainly did not bode well; moreover, requesting supplies from Cuba was ruled out due to the problems with Velázquez. To escape isolation, then, the only alternative was to seek alliances with other indigenous groups. The self-assured captain general entered into negotiations with Chicomecatl. He tried to introduce the Totonac to the Christian religion, but did not consider it an opportune time to intervene against the human sacrifices, which were also frequently offered in Cempoala.[47]

Cortés stayed vigilant. He had the dwellings that had been provided for them closely guarded, day and night. Indeed, the friendly reception was not without ulterior motives. Nevertheless, Chicomecatl was hoping for an alliance with the powerful strangers, so there was no cause for concern. In their conversations, he lamented the oppression and cruelty of the Mexica and also gave Cortés important information about the expansion of Moctezuma's empire, the triple alliance, and the cities of Tlaxcala and Cholula. The captain general pledged the desired support against the Mexica, stressing that one of his monarch's missions was to bring peace and justice. In return, the Totonacs are said to have submitted to the Spanish crown. Chicomecatl appears to have been prepared to do anything to further the cause, and so even provided the Spaniards with servants and porters. In addition, he gave Cortés twenty young women from the Totonac nobility, accompanied by their servants.[48]

Around the beginning of June, after about a two-week stay in Cempoala, Cortés and his men moved on to the smaller Totonac village of Quiahuiztlan, near the site that the scouts had recommended the settlement be built. Although the journey was short, Chicomecatl placed four hundred porters at Cortés's disposal; they would accompany him on subsequent campaigns and provide important relief for the soldiers. After some initial hesitation, they also received a friendly welcome in Quiahuiztlan, where another incense ritual was performed. In Cortés's conversations with the local ruler, the latter also complained about the Mexica and may have asked for assistance. The veracity of these statements, which were spread by Spanish chronicles, is debatable, however. Cortés's attempt to connect the campaign with the Gallic Wars, in which Caesar was also called on for help by subjugated peoples, strains credulity.[49]

The "Rebellion" of the Totonacs

As luck would have it, Mexica emissaries arrived at this time to collect the tribute. This gave the captain general an early opportunity to demonstrate his resolve. The noble dignitaries allegedly displayed great arrogance, ignoring the Spaniards' presence and explaining to the Totonacs that their ruler Moctezuma would not tolerate their friendly behavior toward the strangers. As punishment, twenty men and twenty women, respectively, were to be made available for sacrifice to appease the gods. Cortés took the opportunity to intervene. According to Spanish accounts, he first had to persuade the initially hesitant and fearful Totonacs by referring to his friendship with Moctezuma; he then arrested the tribute collectors and placed them on the ships. In Bernal Díaz's retelling, this tactic greatly impressed his hosts, who considered the Spaniards all the more to be gods. Given the initial situation in Totonacapan, however, not much persuasion was required. The Totonacs were by no means the timid natives that the Spaniards wanted them to be; rather, they recognized the chance, with the help of the strangers and their powerful weapons, to liberate themselves from the relatively recent yoke of the Mexica. Evidence of this is found in the fact that Chicomecatl subsequently turned to neighboring towns for support.[50]

Yet another turn of events, also unanimously passed on by European sources, shows that the Spaniards were by no means sure of their dominance over the Totonacs. That very night, without their noticing, Cortés secretly released two of the Mexica. He sent them to Moctezuma to tell him that he was his friend, which was why he freed the nobles from the hands of the faithless Totonacs. He would also do everything possible to maintain their friendship in the future, the emissaries were meant to convey. With this ruse, the captain general sought to maintain his relationship with the Mexica, while exacerbating the discord between them and the Totonacs, who could no longer turn back. At the same time, Cortés formally welcomed the Totonacs as vassals of his monarch, though it can be assumed that they were unaware of the intended scope of this particular act.[51]

At last, the men around Cortés could begin to build their city on a plain a few hundred meters from Quiahuiztlan. The formal founding date was June

28, 1519. The central square, with a church, marketplace, public buildings—including the prison—and several other houses were built by the men with the active help of the Totonacs and the Taino slaves. They also built a fort near the harbor with palisades, embrasures, breastwork, watchtowers, and a castle gate. Only after the buildings were completed did Cortés have the ships completely unloaded. Villa Rica de la Vera Cruz developed into a valuable base camp for the Spanish. It also fulfilled another important function: with its foundation, the conquistadors were able to place themselves directly under the monarch and bypass the governor of Cuba and the *audiencia*, the court, in Santo Domingo.[52]

According to the Spanish chronicles, Moctezuma subsequently responded by sending another legation, consisting of two nephews of the ruler, four older advisors, and a large entourage, who, in turn, brought gifts. He let it be known, however, that he was displeased with the capture of his tribute collectors, while grateful for the release of two of them. He also complained about his renegade subjects, the Totonacs. In his reply, Cortés, who received the legation courteously and hosted it for a few days, reaffirmed his friendship with the Mexica, sent gifts in return, and even granted the other three prisoners their freedom. Finally, Cortés informed Moctezuma that the Totonacs were now vassals of his monarch, but that they would also follow the orders of the Mexica should the Spanish captain general order them to do so.[53] After his officials were arrested, the tlatoani must have interpreted this as yet another unfriendly act on the part of the strangers. They appeared to be questioning his supremacy in a fundamentally insecure border area.

While the Mexica legation was with the Spanish, Cortés also maintained contact with the Totonacs. In the meantime, the latter had informed their neighboring cities of the unheard-of activities of the powerful foreigners and had won additional allies. The alliance's first test came shortly thereafter, when Cempoala asked the Spaniards for support against the Mexica garrison town of Tizapantzinco, some twenty miles away. Its troops had destroyed the crops of the Totonac villages in retaliation for the vassals' rebellion. Cortés found himself in a double bind: On the one hand, he still did not want to risk an open war against the Mexica, but, on the other, he had to prove his loyalty to the alliance. Consequently, four thousand Totonacs and about four hundred Conquistadors went into battle together for the first time. As Bernal Díaz reports, however, no battle actually occurred, as the Mexica had withdrawn from the city. Other chroniclers, such as Cervantes de Salazar, mention a short battle that ended with the flight of the Mexica. Following this, the Spaniards would have seen with their own eyes for the first time how the Totonacs roasted and devoured fallen enemies. According to Bernal, Cortés accepted the remaining city dwellers as new vassals of the crown and ordered his allies to stop the traditional hostilities against Tizapantzinco. Obviously, the inhabitants of Cempoala had exploited the Spaniards in their fight against a neighboring city without the Europeans even realizing it.[54]

This first successful joint military action increased the willingness of the Totonacs to risk open insurrection. The Mesoamerican customs of that time were to stabilize interdynastic relations through marriages. Chicomecatl thus gave Cortés and his officers eight women of high nobility, including his niece. Although Cortés accepted the gift, he insisted on the women's baptism. On his return, he used the opportunity to have the idols of the Totonacs in Cempoala destroyed. An uprising almost took place when some Spaniards threw the statues from the steps of the highest temple pyramid. The conquistadors even had to take the "fat cacique" and his noblemen hostage to prevent fighting and successfully quash a surprise coup. However, this episode also shows that the Spanish position was by no means as uncontroversial as the Spanish sources suggest. Cortés then preached about the Christian faith and against human sacrifice and the Totonac idols. Apparently, he was able to get the interior of the temple freshly whitewashed and an altar with a statue of the Virgin Mary installed. According to the sources, the Spaniards also erected a high wooden cross. They left behind one of the conquistadors, an old invalid, as a guard. During a solemn mass in which the city's elite had to participate, the women were baptized and given Christian names. The Totonacs who took part in these ritual acts were probably not aware that the Spaniards expected the monarch's new vassals to renounce their own religion, at least in the medium term.[55]

Once again, Cortés's interest in proselytizing was not awakened until he was sure of his military purpose and could operate from a position of strength. This Christianization was undoubtedly only superficial, and even at the moment it had no great significance, since it was assumed even in church circles that the necessary religious fervor among the New Christians would come with time.[56] For Cortés, at any rate, it was important to be able to report to the monarch on his success in this area, if necessary. For the leaders of the Totonacs, on the other hand, the destruction of the statues of their gods caused them reputational damage among their own people. They also lost the support of their priests. As a consequence, they were even more dependent on the Spaniards. The dependency was by no means one-sided, however. Indeed, the importance of indigenous local knowledge, food supplies, and military support from the Totonacs had already been demonstrated in Cempoala.

The First Reports to Charles V

On their return to Veracruz, the Spaniards were delighted to see the arrival of another ship from Cuba under the command of Captain Francisco de Salcedo, called "El Pulido" (the handsome one) and a friend of Cortés. One of the crew was Luis Marín, who would later distinguish himself as a captain in the Conquest. The ship also brought ten additional warriors and two horses.[57] However, Salcedo had more than just good news to report. He had to inform Cortés that word of a royal *capitulación* (an agreement) had arrived in Cuba that granted Velázquez, at his own expense, the privilege of discovering, conquering, and colonizing new lands in Mesoamerica, at that time still called Santa María de los Remedios after the name chosen by Hernández de Córdoba. In return, Velázquez was to receive the profits of the expedition minus the royal fifth, which would be reduced in the initial years, and other economic privileges, some of which were even hereditary. Velázquez would also receive the title of adelantado for the discovered regions. This news must have come as a shock to Cortés.[58]

Suddenly, the ingenious construction of the captain general's claim to legitimacy, which had prevailed among the conquistadors only with luck, was null and void. From the capitulación, it was clear that he could now be charged with treason against a loyal governor. Cortés saw only one solution to this problem: he had to seek direct recognition from the monarch himself, which also meant that he had to prove that the success of the venture was solely his doing and that further success depended on his personal initiative. To this end, he had to present his view of things to the monarch in writing, which was only possible by means of sending his own legation to Europe. Moreover, Cortés was shrewd enough to know that without abundant gifts, little could be achieved at court.[59]

According to Bernal Díaz del Castillo, it was not Cortés himself who took the initiative, but his crew. The men are said to have asked Cortés not to abandon the march into the interior of the country, despite the new turn of events. Allegedly, they also proposed sending a report to the monarch, along with all the gold they had exchanged up to that point. Ordás and Montejo went to each member of the crew to obtain his consent. By contrast, López de Gómara wrote that Cortés dictated the plan and the conquistadors happily followed along. It is unclear whether the possibility of rejection even existed. No matter which version is historically accurate, the captain general arranged and oversaw the activities behind the scenes. Ultimately, the appearance of operating on behalf of the cabildo and his men lent a certain degree of legitimacy to his conduct. These events also had a cleansing effect on the hueste. Velázquez's supporters, who questioned Cortés's authority after the announcement of the mandate, once again saw themselves forced onto the defensive. Even though they could have rightfully protested and brought charges, the judges were a long ways away.[60]

The cabildo, on behalf of Cortés, therefore set about writing the instructions for the envoys who were to be sent on the long journey to Spain. Cortés carefully selected the men to be entrusted with this task. The two alcaldes mayores, Portocarrero and Montejo, seemed most suitable. On the one hand, they were of high-ranking nobility; on the other, they each represented one of the two factions of the hueste. So the cabildo officially informed the royal procurator Francisco Álvarez Chico, a confidant of Cortés from Extremadura, of the choice of the two, after which he informed the citizens of the city. The community of vecinos expressed their approval, called for their participation in the drafting of the instructions, and requested the confirmation of the supreme command of Cortés, who, because of his great merits, was also to be assured of a substantial share of the profits. Afterward, Cortés, as well as the officers and members of the crew, wrote a first "letter-report," while the city officials were busy preparing the gifts for the monarch. A third report was also written by the cabildo. This thoroughly oversubtle approach, which historian María del Carmen Martínez has reconstructed meticulously, can only be understood against the background of Cortés's legitimacy deficit and his desire to avoid any kind of formal error at all costs.[61]

A recently rediscovered document dated June 20, 1519, a petition by the cabildo, contains the most important points of the more detailed letter-report of July 10. In it, the representatives of the city government ask the majesties not to give Diego Velázquez any authority in the new regions, because he would otherwise persecute the members of the hueste who had broken away from him. They justified their defection from the governor by stating that they could better serve the royal interests under the leadership of Cortés. Moreover, they asked that the transfer of the captain general and chief magistrate's office to Cortés be confirmed because of the high risks and financial commitment that he had made. Finally, he was also to become governor after the conquest was completed.[62]

The detailed submission of the cabildo, which summarizes the history of the undertaking since the voyages of Hernández de Córdoba, has been known for some time. It questioned the legal basis of the claims Velázquez made, arguing that Cortés had contributed more than the governor from the start, including seven of the ten ships. What's more, the newly discovered land was not even Yucatán, but a previously uncharted territory. The letter-report portrayed Velázquez as a greedy and ruthless man who was not concerned for the interests of the crown or his subjects, but only his own advantage. Cortés, on the other hand, was described as a prudent and selfless leader, interested only in the crown's benefit, who respected the welfare of the indigenous people with whom he came into contact, but who at the same time took a tough stand against their "idolatry" and especially against human sacrifice. The report argues that the conquest and Christianization of these peoples is absolutely necessary to abolish this practice. Above all, the report emphasizes the tremendous wealth and highly developed culture of this new country, which, notwithstanding the bloody practices already described, could not be compared to anything that the Spanish had ever found in the Indies: "In our opinion, there are as many [treasures] in this country as in the country from which Solomon is said to have taken the gold for the temple." The report also included the version according to which the Mexica had voluntarily placed themselves under Spanish sovereignty. All this suggests that, even if Cortés did not write the letter himself, he influenced it significantly.[63]

The treasures were collected for everyone to see in the marketplace of Villa Rica. The value of the golden objects and precious stones was immense, whereas the value of the cotton clothing, feather work, and other works of art were beyond appraisal. Some of the mysterious illustrated books were also part of the shipment. They are among the few codices that survived the Conquest. The crown was to receive a treasure of enormous size, which was intended to create a sensation in Europe. Secretly, however, Cortés kept some of the spoils for himself, as the historian Henry Wagner pointed out in 1942.[64]

On July 26, Portocarrero and Montejo left for Spain on the ship Santa Maria de la Concepción, commanded by Alaminos, with the important documents, treasures, and six locals. Cortés also gave the pilot some personal letters for his parents, in which he asked his father to represent his interests and to support the intermediaries. Against the instructions of Cortés and the cabildo, the ship stopped in Havana, presumably because Montejo wanted to take provisions from one of his nearby estates. In truth, he wanted to warn Velázquez, with whom he was still in close contact. The governor immediately tried to prevent the ship from continuing its voyage, but it had already passed the Bahamas and could not be overtaken. Alaminos had seen through the subterfuge to sail away in time.[65]

At the beginning of November 1519 Cortés's procurators arrived in Seville but were hardly warmly welcomed. The accounting officer of the Casa de la Contratación, the highest authority for trade with the Indies, confiscated the Mexican gold treasure. Juan Rodríguez de Fonseca accused the envoys and their master, Cortés, of bypassing the royal governor and thus violating law and order. This accusation was due not least to the intervention of Velázquez's chaplain Benito Martín, who had won Fonseca's confidence. Cortés's procurators, his father, Martín and Portocarrero, nevertheless knew how to skillfully use the funds to establish a lobby for Cortés, especially in trade circles. An exhibition of the treasures of the Mexica in Seville at the end of 1519 played its part in reviving enthusiasm in Spain for the promise of the New World. While Fonseca did not spare the monarch the accusations against Cortés, the latter's supporters launched a series of counter-attacks. Francisco Núñez, an influential courtier and cousin of Hernán Cortés, was especially helpful. The monarch even wrote them an accommodating letter and summoned them to his court, where they arrived in early March 1520. There, the treasure and the Totonacs made a big impression. It was not until the end of April that the procurators, who used the occasion to hand over the various documents, were heard before the Crown Council, which was now in Santiago de Compostela. This was likewise the case

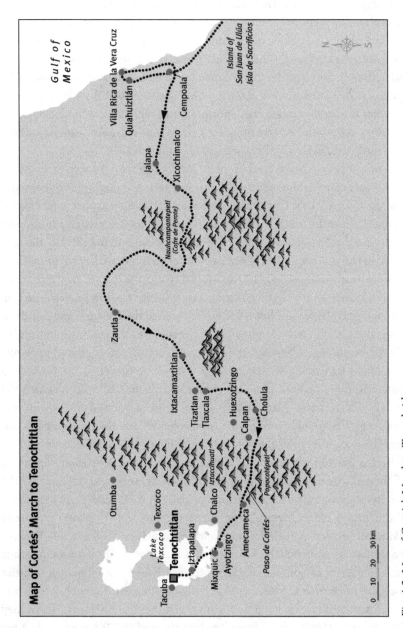

Fig. 4.3 Map of Cortés's March to Tenochtitlan

for Cortés's opponents. However, a decision on the status of Cortés was tabled and the proceedings were postponed. When the monarch sailed toward the German Empire, he took with him part of the Mexican gold treasure, which he would use to help alleviate his financial burdens.[66]

In Totonacapan, meanwhile, shortly after the ship's departure at the end of July 1519, renewed unrest broke out among the Spaniards. Some of Velázquez's followers saw the last opportunity to leave for Cuba before heading inland and planned to steal a ship. The scheme was exposed and Cortés imposed severe punishments. The two commanders, Pedro Escudero and Juan Cermeño, were hanged, and the helmsman Gonzalo de Umbría's toes were cut off. Cortés sentenced a number of ordinary sailors to two hundred lashes each. But recognizing the critical state of his troops, he did not discipline other suspects with the same severity, including Ordás and the priest Díaz. By the same token, he issued a ban on all attempts to return to Cuba under the threat of death.[67]

Beyond this, the preamble of the cabildo's petition to the monarch on July 10 already reported that Cortés had had some of his ships put aground to prevent mutinies or desertion. Thus, he had already noticed or suspected the activities of the disaffected men. After the escape attempt, he also ordered the other ships to be rendered unseaworthy. The valuable ship's instruments and equipment were safely stored in the town under the supervision of Juan de Escalante and the two new mayors, Alonso de Ávila and Alonso de Grado, all partisans of Cortés. The captain general reassigned the sailors as foot soldiers. Although this measure aroused the displeasure of parts of the crew, the men were left with no other choice. The march to Tenochtitlan could no longer be stopped.[68]

5

Tlaxcala

The time spent in Totonacapan revealed that interdependencies had developed between Europeans and the local population—with both sides wanting to exploit them to their own advantage. For the Spaniards, the alliances were crucial from the very start, since they did not have enough troops or attendants to make large inland marches on their own. For the Totonacs, the alliance with the Spaniards represented an opportunity to challenge the dominance of the Mexica. Due to his success in dealing with the Maya, Mexica, and Totonacs, Cortés tended to overestimate his own strength. He probably did not realize that the Totonacs had a far less powerful army than the Mexica. However, having burned all his bridges, he had no other option. He trusted the optimistic promises of his new allies, who pledged a hundred thousand warriors.[1] The expectations of the Totonacs were undoubtedly just as high. To them, the strangers represented a kind of surprise weapon, who might even have possessed, if only sporadically, supernatural attributes. Even so, the great risk of a move against Tenochtitlan could only be taken if the alliances could be expanded to include other partners. Tlaxcala would play a central role in this.

The Beginning of the *Entrada*

Before marching into the interior (the *entrada*), Cortés assembled his troops and gave a rousing speech to boost morale. He invoked ancient Roman role models and reminded the men of their responsibility before God and king. At the end, the captain general made it clear that there was no way back. In short, his glorious appeal was: conquer or die. According to Bernal Díaz, his army "answered him as if with a single voice that we would do what he commanded; the die was cast, as Caesar said on the Rubicon."[2] Afterward, Cortés directed the garrison's operations, whose forces were to occupy Vera Cruz. He chose his close confidant Escalante as supreme commander and placed 150 men at his disposal, consisting of the ill and less robust soldiers. Those who remained were awarded the same share of the plunder; as for Cortés, his share of one fifth of the spoils, which corresponded to the royal fifth, was also formally acknowledged. The garrison was to be a place of refuge for the Spaniards as well as a guard post against any expeditions sent by Velázquez. Thus, major artillery was also left behind. The role of the Totonacs remained critically important. They were not only supposed to secure the provisions for the settlement, but also to support the Spaniards militarily in case of an attack. For this purpose, up to twenty thousand warriors could be mobilized on short notice.[3]

Similar to the garrison, Cortés himself could not do without Totonacan support. The indigenous allies not only provided a large number of porters, but also warriors who set off together with the Spaniards. Cortés had already arrived in Cempoala when a message that necessitated his return to Vera Cruz reached him. An unknown Spanish ship had been sighted along the coast. It belonged to a small fleet under the command of Alonso Álvarez de Pineda, who had explored the North American coast from Florida to the mouth of the Mississippi. Several crew members, some of whom had been lured ashore, were taken prisoner. They stated that they were taking possession of the land around Pánuco, the final destination of Grijalva's journey. They had been commissioned by the vice-governor of Jamaica, Francisco de Garay, who was officially subordinate to Velázquez. In the end, Cortés did not succeed in capturing the ship, which departed from the coast again. He incorporated the prisoners into his own troop. Garay's objectives, which could not be determined at this point, were potentially a threat to the captain general.[4]

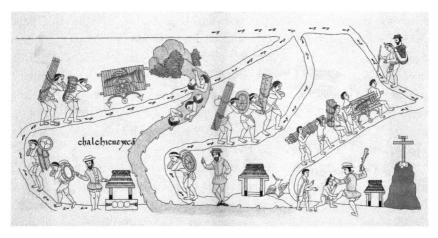

Fig. 5.1 The value of indigenous porters. This scene, originating from the Lienzo de Tlaxcala, shows indigenous porters. During the Conquest, the allies carried supplies, weapons, and even the wounded. Smithsonian Libraries and Archives. Internet Archive.

The entrada could finally begin in mid-August. The destination was the town of Tlaxcala. Its inhabitants were allies of the Totonacs and among the mortal enemies of the Mexica. A huge convoy embarked: about three hundred Spaniards, probably about forty thousand to fifty thousand Totonacs, and numerous porters, who were primarily responsible for transporting the heavy weapons. By way of Jalapa, Xicochimalco, they marched to Ixhuacan, where they were welcomed by the local Totonacs. They all identified themselves as vassals of the Moctezuma. South of the Cofre de Perote, they had to climb the arduous path over the pass of the Sierra Madre Oriental, which they called Nombre de Díos. Not only was the landscape inhospitable, but the climate also became increasingly harsh. The unaccustomed cold in the high mountains, which to the Spaniards seemed higher than any of the other native mountains, took its toll. Many of the Taino slaves, who were completely unprepared, froze to death or died of consumption.[5]

The subsequent march through the deserted plain was full of hardships, all the more so as they had to take a detour northward to avoid a saltwater lake. Supplies dwindled; the men are said to have gone hungry for three days. Before any fighting even began, Cortés thus had to cope with considerable illness-related losses among his crew due to the immense hardships, the inadequate supplies, and the changes in climate.[6] In fact, the Spaniards' adventure would have already come to a halt here were it not for their Totonac guides. They finally reached the next larger settlement, the town of Zautla, where they made a stopover. The local ruler Olintlece received them amicably and provided them with food and shelter. When Cortés asked him if he were a vassal of the Mexica ruler, Olintlece allegedly replied in astonishment: "Is there anyone who is not a slave or vassal of the Moctezuma?"[7] As Cortés pointed out, what he meant to say was that he considered the tlatoani of Tenochtitlan to be the ruler of the world. Olintlece explained to the captain general the extraordinary power of Moctezuma, who sacrificed twenty thousand people every year, and the greatness, splendor, and defensive strength of his capital Tenochtitlan. But Olintlece, too, impressed the Spaniards with his wealth. He had five thousand combat-ready warriors and countless servants and women at his disposal. He reacted negatively to the Spanish desire for gold, saying that he would only procure the precious metal for them with Moctezuma's approval.[8]

It was clear that Cortés could not display the same level of aggression here as in Cempoala. True, he preached to the ruler about the Christian God and tried to explain to him the power of his own monarch. But after consulting with Father Olmedo, he refrained from another act of iconoclasm as in Cempoala. He did not even erect a cross, for he could not be sure that it wouldn't be desecrated after his departure. The fact that the inhabitants had no interest in conversion was demonstrated in no small measure by the enormous size of the tzompantli,

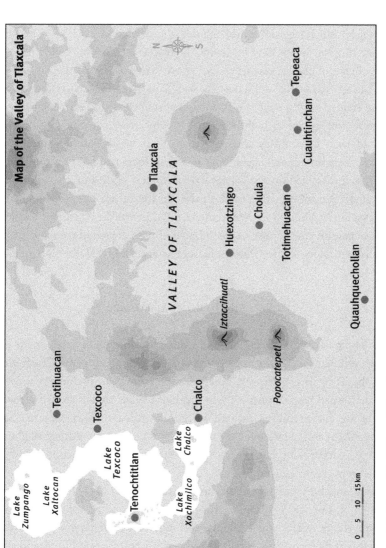

Fig. 5.2 Map of the Valley of Tlaxcala

the skull rack, which terrified the Spaniards. Bernal claims to have counted a hundred thousand skulls. Cortés therefore preferred to make preparations for the continued march and sent messengers with gifts to Tlaxcala to announce his arrival. Allegedly Olintlece and some leaders from neighboring villages recommended that the Spaniards head directly to Cholula instead of Tlaxcala. But the Totonacs, who were familiar with the strength of the Mexica garrison there, categorically rejected this idea and finally prevailed.[9]

After resting for several days in Zautla, the troops marched on to the heavily fortified village of Ixtacamaxtitlan. The impressive bastion of the city again stunned the Spaniards. Although this city also had to pay tribute to Tenochtitlan, they were treated very hospitably. It finally became clear that Moctezuma was using a new strategy: by letting the Spaniards come closer, he could also better understand their capabilities and, above all, their weaknesses. Without any word from their own messengers, however, they soon marched on until they came across a massive border wall several kilometers wide and several meters high, stretching from one side of the valley to the other. The inhabitants of Ixtacamaxtitlan had built it to defend themselves against the Tlaxcalans, whose territory began on the opposite side. Tlaxcala was a dangerous enemy of the Mexica, their masters, so they were more or less permanently at war with them.[10]

The Special Role of Tlaxcala

When the Spanish arrived, Tlaxcala was a small federal military state made up of various ethnic groups who spoke Nahuatl and belonged to the Chichimec culture. The Tlaxcalans interpreted their descent from the Chichimeca and especially their warrior spirit positively. In the divine order, first and foremost was the god of war and hunting, Camaxtli. With the Mexica, they shared ritualized human sacrifices and ideas about the cosmos.[11] Located at an altitude of about one and a quarter mile, large stretches of the territory were mountainous. The settlements were concentrated in three valleys. Although the region was only about one hundred kilometers from Tenochtitlan and was completely surrounded by the Mexica Empire, the group was able to repeatedly assert itself against the powerful triple alliance and maintain its independence. More recent research assumes that, at that time, between one hundred thousand and two hundred thousand people lived in the territory of Tlaxcala, which did not extend over more than one and a half square miles.[12]

The city of Cacaxtla, which was initially overshadowed by the large ceremonial centers in Teotihuacan and Cholula, was founded in the south of the region toward the end of the first millennium CE and inhabited by members of the newly immigrated Olmeca-Xicalanca culture. During this period, the Otomí settled in the northern part of the territory. While Toltec-Chichimeca groups ousted the Olmecs around the year 1000, the Otomí were able to retain their relative autonomy. A political landscape developed that was divided into many small spheres of influence of individual *caciques*. Since the thirteenth century, the four major centers—Tepeticpac, Ocotelulco, Tizatlán, and Quiahuiztlán—had developed in the fertile region along the Zahuapan River, which maintained friendly relations with the Otomí people in the north. In the northwest, the area bordered the Central Valley of Mexico, in the south the cities of Huexotzinco and Cholula. While migrations by other groups remained commonplace and led to wars, they also resulted in the merging of different ethnic groups. Despite being enemies of its neighbors to the northwest and south, Tlaxcala experienced a period of prosperity in the fourteenth and fifteenth centuries, which is reflected in, among other things, its growing long-distance trade.[13]

With the expansion of the triple alliance, the Tlaxcalans were increasingly put on the defensive. They lost tributary territories and were cut off from their trade routes. The Mexica were concerned with the control of the traffic routes to the Gulf of Mexico, which led through Tlaxcala. They also regarded Tlaxcala as a repository for their human sacrifices and as terrain for their military maneuvers. This was the reason they introduced the flower wars.[14]

The pressure on Tlaxcala grew in the later fifteenth century, when the Huexotzinco peoples became a tributary of the triple alliance. For example, there were supply bottlenecks for salt and sugar. At the beginning of the sixteenth century under Moctezuma II, the Mexica led several conquest campaigns against the Tlaxcalans. Despite their numerical superiority, however, they did not prevail. Meanwhile, the constant threat and the military clashes led to the impoverishment of the resource-poor Tlaxcala and the development of a siege mentality, which was reflected in the costly expansion of the border fortifications with trenches and walls.[15]

Alliances between cities, which were quickly formed and just as quickly dissolved for special defense or conquest purposes, were not uncommon in pre-Hispanic Mesoamerica. Often the occasion was an uprising against the tyrannical rule of other cities.[16] In the case of Tlaxcala, however, the alliance persisted for a considerable time and created the basis for state-formation. Recent research has found that the changes in the political system of this state were responsible for Tlaxcala's remarkable perseverance. In the face of external pressure, the Tlaxcalans concentrated the highest executive power in a government council consisting of up to one hundred members. This council was empowered to decide on war and peace, the formation of alliances, and the removal of officials. Public office was opened up to all social classes. After a harsh initiation ritual, even common people could rise to the rank of nobility. Advancement was likewise possible due to special achievements in war, religion, or trade. Land ownership was attached to the office, which could be revoked in the event of failure. The pomp of the aristocracy seen in other Mesoamerican communities was far less pronounced in Tlaxcala.[17]

The stronger emphasis on the cult around Tezcatlipoca, the god of the night, gave rise to a meritocratic and relatively egalitarian ideology. This ideology was further underpinned by the redistribution of state festival and ritual practices, the effective establishment of public internal and external security, equal treatment, and the expansion of infrastructure. What's more, new ethnic groups were increasingly integrated. The foundation of a ceremonial capital, Tizatlan (later to become the city of Tlaxcala), on neutral ground also served to reinforce cohesion. By providing the heads of small villages far from the centers with access to the supreme council, the readiness to fight for the common welfare grew there as well. This was particularly evident with the Otomí in the north. As a result

Fig. 5.3 Malinche in the Lienzo de Tlaxcala. Otomí messengers welcome Spaniards with provisions on arrival. According to the Spanish sources, however, fierce battles were initially fought. This image clearly shows the veneration for Malinche, from whose lips Cortés spoke. Smithsonian Libraries and Archives. Internet Archive.

of this transformation, the state of Tlaxcala—despite high taxes and service requirements for inhabitants from different social classes and ethnic groups—was able to achieve an exceptionally high level of acceptance and successfully defend its own independence.[18]

When the Spaniards appeared at the Tlaxcala border in early September 1519, they were faced with the question of how to react to the strangers. At that time, Maxixcatzin ruled in Ocotelulco, Xicotencatl in Tizatlan, Tlehuexolotzin in Tepectipac, and Citlapopoca in Quiahuiztlan. They greeted Cortés's messengers from Cempoala in the government council and listened to what the Spaniards wanted from them. The captain general announced that he had come in the name of the true God and wanted to help the Tlaxcalans in their fight against Moctezuma. In subsequent consultations, different views were expressed. Thus, where Maxixcatzin demanded that the offer of peace be accepted, Xicotencatl's son of the same name, an important military commander, favored war. Tlehuexolotzin, meanwhile, advocated a more flexible strategy. The Otomís should first draw the intruders into combat. If they won, the problem would be settled; if not, the others could still negotiate and blame the Otomís for the hostilities.[19]

From Enmity to Alliance

The sources contain different versions of the first meeting between the Spaniards and the Tlaxcalans in September 1519. According to the Tlaxcalan accounts, the inhabitants received the Europeans in a friendly manner. However, these sources emerged after the conclusion of the Conquest, when the Tlaxcalans sought to secure their privileged special position as allies of the Spaniards.[20] Therefore, they tended to keep quiet about the initial bloody conflicts, which the Spanish chronicles and reports told in detail. One reason for the initially guarded stance was the fact that the Spaniards had been warmly received in many cities that paid tribute to Moctezuma, their mortal enemy, and even had some of their warriors in their ranks.[21]

At first, the Totonacs and Spaniards dealt only with a vanguard of the Tlaxcalans. The efforts of the captain general to persuade them to negotiate failed and were probably not even understood. The Tlaxcalans consequently lured the strangers into an ambush. Although the Spanish riders certainly shocked them, they did not shrink at this challenge and instead killed two horses. As Bernal Díaz noted, the Tlaxcalan army, with its war-painted fighters and terrifying war cries, was undeniably fearsome. An intense battle ensued, in which the use of artillery finally tipped the scales in the Europeans' favor. They camped on a plain and cared for their wounded. Bernal Díaz described the methods of wound healing that were common at that time: "We treated the wounds with the fat of a corpulent Indian whom we had killed there and slit open."[22]

The supposed ally the Totonacs had promised the Spaniards turned out to be a formidable adversary who joined in battle again the following day. Once again, the Spaniards and their indigenous allies had to defend themselves against a superior Tlaxcalan force that trapped them in an ambush. As Bernal Díaz emphasized, Cortés again had their requerimiento read aloud and had made every other attempt to bring his opponents to the negotiating table—albeit without success. These words were, of course, written primarily with a view to their effect at court and to justify the legality of the Spanish actions against the Tlaxcalans. According to Bernal, Cortés himself had also taken precautions in this respect, having instructed the royal scribe Diego de Godoy to write everything down in precise detail.[23]

Despite the great danger they faced, the Europeans and their allies were able to prevail, not least because of the superiority of their iron weapons, cavalry, crossbows, and cannons. A mountaintop temple was converted into a base camp, although this would cause supply problems. The Spanish soldiers were to take turns recuperating there, while the indigenous troops were not allowed any rest. Otherwise, European sources are silent about the deployment of indigenous allies, who outnumbered the Spanish. In the days that followed, Cortés and his troops plundered, pillaged, and murdered in a campaign of terror in order to demoralize the enemy. He had fifty prisoners' hands cut off and sent them back to their people with the threat of killing them all if they did not start negotiations.[24]

Even these atrocities did not break the Tlaxcalans' will to fight. They went on with their attacks, both day and night. In between, they repeatedly sent delegations allegedly bearing gifts, but their real purpose was to spy, since the people of Tlaxcala remained unsure of just who they were dealing with. This tactic also revealed the continuing disagreement in the Tlaxcalan camp over the correct course of action against the Spaniards, which explains, at least in part, the mixed strategy of attacks and tidings of peace. Although their own magicians and priests had assured them that the Spaniards were ordinary mortals, the Tlaxcalans' furious assaults were never successful. Even a large-scale attack at night advocated by the clergy proved to be in vain.[25]

The warriors were helpless against the concentrated firepower of the Spaniards. Their method of attack in tight and closed formation made them welcome targets for the Spanish riflemen, leading to high losses. Even in hand-to-hand combat, they could achieve little with their obsidian swords, which broke quickly on impact with iron weapons. Although they inflicted painful wounds on the Spaniards with arrows and by throwing stones, which caused many conquistadors and horses to retreat, a decisive reversal was not in the cards. Despite the intense fighting, the Spaniards ultimately mourned relatively few deaths. Bernal Díaz noticed early on that the Tlaxcalans were not very disciplined fighters. Above all, there was a lack of coordination between the numerous armies, each with its own captain. Some of them competed with each other and, as in the case of the troops from Ocotelolco, even withdrew when they were dissatisfied with a decision by their supreme commander, Xicotencatl. The indigenous military lacked the necessary logistical know-how to come up with the obvious solution of laying siege to the Spaniards.[26]

On the other hand, the situation was also highly precarious for the allied Spaniards and Totonacs. To begin with, there were not endless supplies and ammunition. And, unlike all other indigenous armies that the Europeans had encountered up to that point, the Tlaxcalans showed no signs of giving up. For the first time, Cortés encountered a militarily strong indigenous opponent in Tlaxcala, which obviously took him by surprise. If he had done reconnaissance beforehand, he probably would not have taken the risk and instead have given the region a wide berth.

Yet, he could not go back, if only to avoid losing face before his indigenous allies. However, as the enemy's superiority seemed overwhelming and the intensity of the fighting increased day by day, resentment began to spread among his men. The supply situation had become critical, and the men were so tormented by the cold that the majority were sick if not wounded. A group of Velázquez supporters under the alcalde mayor Alonso de Grado, who had turned his back on Cortés, spoke out and demanded that they return to Vera Cruz to ask the governor for help. By a narrow margin, the captain general was able to prevent a mutiny. Under these circumstances, his plundering actions must be seen as procurement activities to provision his troops. It was moreover a strategy to keep the men employed and a way to send a signal that he was unbowed in the face of the enemy.[27]

The allies then had a turn of good fortune: The Tlaxcalans suddenly gave in. In their internal consultations in the governing council, those voices that assessed the Spaniards as an enemy that could only be surmounted with heavy losses prevailed. Thus, the faction headed by Maxixcatzin of Ocotelulco had won out over Xicotencatl the Younger of Tizatlan, who had urged that the war be continued. There were many reasons for this turn of events. First, in terms of their military strength, they had already suffered severe losses, which meant, second, that they were weakened in their ongoing fight against Mexica. Third, they realized that the Spaniards, because of their superior weapons, could prove to be valuable allies in waging a successful war against the Mexica. After all, Cortés had repeatedly suggested in his appeals for peace that the Spaniards would offer assistance against their oppressors. Although the Tlaxcalans did not believe that the strangers were gods, a suspicion that the Spaniards were temporarily embodied by gods may well have influenced their decision.[28]

According to Bernal Díaz, the Tlaxcalans only capitulated in the end because they did not realize how weakened the Spaniards and their allies were. In fact, almost all the Spaniards and most of the horses had been injured in the various battles. About fifty conquistadors had fallen, which was relatively few, considering the intensity of the fighting. The chronicler does not say anything about the number of dead among the Totonacs. It must have been significantly higher because the indigenous allies were not as well protected; they were also deliberately used by the supreme commander for riskier maneuvers.[29]

So when four Tlaxcalan negotiators first approached with a serious peace and alliance offer the sense of relief was palpable. According to Spanish sources, they explained that their resistance was based on the assumption that they were dealing with allies of their mortal enemies, the Mexica. They also shifted blame for the repeated attacks on the Otomí. Thanks to this reasoning, it was possible for both sides to save face. Cortés allegedly reacted harshly to the peace proposal and demanded to see the rulers themselves. Subsequently, a larger delegation arrived under Xicotencatl the Younger, who ultimately had to bow to the decision of the governing council. The Spanish sources portrayed this meeting as if the Tlaxcalans had thus formally submitted to the Spanish monarch and sworn allegiance to him as vassals.[30]

Cortés intended next to march on Tizatlan, but Mexica envoys, who had been with his troops during the fighting, asked him to hold off. About a week later, Cortés having used the time to recover from his own illness, they received a reply from Tenochtitlan. The Mexica messengers, who arrived with a large entourage, brought many gifts with them and tried to persuade the captain general not to visit the Tlaxcalans. Moctezuma and his advisors had recognized that an alliance between the strangers and their archenemies could pose a danger and wanted to prevent this from happening at all costs. Consequently, they offered the Spaniards military support against Tlaxcala. Allegedly, Moctezuma even had it communicated in this context that he was a loyal vassal of the Spanish crown and would pay the required tributes. Contradicting this, however, is the fact that he wanted to keep the Spanish hueste away from his city. Cortés suddenly found himself in an enviable situation, as he was being courted by both the Mexica and the Tlaxcalans. Taking advantage of this, he negotiated with both sides.[31]

Cortés turned to the Tlaxcalans, even though they had already been supplying his troops with food since the first peace offer. After a few days, the old leaders appeared with their court and Xicotencatl the Elder directly appealed to the captain general to accept the offered hospitality. They also offered him porters to carry his heavy guns. Cortés accepted the proposal and departed for Tlaxcala around September 20. In order to not completely sever contact with the Mexica, he asked for permission to visit in the company of several noble Mexica, with the others returning to report to Moctezuma. The Spaniards were impressed by the royal reception in the city of Tlaxcala. To further strengthen the alliance, they were given lavish gifts, and the daughters of nobles and slaves were presented to them. All in all, there are said to have been three hundred women, so that almost all the men were able to enjoy this "gift." The city itself also made a very strong impression. According to Cortés, it surpassed Granada in size and magnificence. He was especially taken aback by the political order, which proved the reasonableness of the inhabitants. The system reminded him of the aristocratic city-republics of Venice, Genoa, and Pisa. Nevertheless, he addressed Maxixcatzin as if he were the absolute ruler, consequently elevating him.[32]

The religious question was less easy to resolve, however. According to the Spanish sources, Cortés admonished the Tlaxcalans to renounce their faith and accept Christianity. Above all, they needed to end human sacrifice and ritual cannibalism. Though the acceptance of a new god was by no means unthinkable for the polytheistic Tlaxcalans, they were unwilling to renounce their own deities. Some members of the Tlaxcalan aristocracy, with whom the Spaniards negotiated, feared a popular uprising; others did not want to simply throw off their centuries-old traditions. Still others thought that they would only be able to accept the new religion after a period of familiarization and adaptation. Cortés promised he would send missionaries to them as soon as possible. In the meantime, they settled on a compromise. In view of the imminent journey to Tenochtitlan, forced Christianization was out of the question, even from the perspective of the priest Olmedo. Thus, the Christians were given their own purified temple where they could place the cross, the statue of the Virgin Mary, and the altar and celebrate their religious ceremonies. The daughters that had been given to the Spaniards as gifts were again first baptized before Cortés distributed them among his officers. He gave the noblest, a daughter of Xicotencatl, to his captain, Pedro de Alvarado.[33]

This supposed great triumph over the Tlaxcalans encouraged Cortés's basic tendency to underestimate the power of the Mexica. After all, instead of attacking the Spaniards, Moctezuma was still sending him gifts. From the Spanish point of view, this wait-and-see attitude was proof of his weakness, which was also evident from the fact that the Mexica had not yet been able to conquer Tlaxcala. Nevertheless, the practice of flower wars was as unknown to Cortés as the reality that the gifts were by no means a simple sign of submission. Rather they were proof of the enormous wealth and power of the Mexica. On the other hand, the captain general had at least learned from the fierce battles against the Tlaxcalans that he would need more indigenous support if he were to achieve his objectives. In contrast to his campaign against Tlaxcala, in which the number of Totonac allies was still relatively small, Cortés would go into future battles with armies comprised of no more than ten percent Spanish fighters.[34]

The Tlaxcalan view of their contact with the Spaniards, which would so de-cisively change their future existence, differed considerably from that of the Spaniards. It was not until after they formed an alliance with the Spaniards that Tlaxcalans spread the belief that the Spaniards were invincible gods. By doing so, they wanted to justify their own strategy, intimidate the Mexica, and attract new allies. The so-called Lienzo de Tlaxcala, whose no longer extant original was produced long after the Conquest, tells the story in pictures on a sixteen-by-six foot canvas. Here, the encounter with the Spaniards was described in chrono-logical sequence. The codex was a hybrid depiction, which demonstrates that the indigenous people were quite adept at taking the stories of the Spanish and presenting them in their own way and for their own benefit. No mention is made of the initial fighting. Instead, the source stresses the friendly reception of the Spaniards, who, in any event, were able to rest in their city for about three weeks; it also points to the early acceptance of Christianity with a view to presenting the Tlaxcalans as Christian conquistadors. Finally, it details the military services that Tlaxcala subsequently provided to the Spaniards.[35]

It is striking how often Malinche is depicted in the codex. Bernal Díaz re-ported that the Tlaxcalans addressed Cortés with the name Malintzin/Malinche. She was the tongue through which the Spaniard spoke to them and was there-fore held in high esteem.[36] Since the source was created after Christianization, it can probably be assumed that the Tlaxcalans associated Malinche, as body incarnate, with Mary, the mother of God, who assured victory in battle. Women in general—even those presented as gifts—were often seen in the early depictions of the Tlaxcalans. Giving away wives and daughters corresponded to a Mesoamerican tradition, which paralleled the aristocratic marriage politics in Europe of the time. With this, the Tlaxcalans wanted to symbolize the perma-nence of the bond to the Spaniards. At the same time, they were eager to docu-ment their own chosen status as nonsubjugated allies and to secure it for future generations through shared children.[37]

The continuity of indigenous political life, which was not interrupted by the appearance of the Spaniards, was not solely demonstrated by the giving away of the women. The form of alliance policy, which the "fat cacique" of Cempoala had already proposed in order to conquer Tenochtitlan, also followed this pattern. Thus, the alliances of the Spaniards with Cempoala, Tlaxcala, and later other city-states were concluded in rapid succession, which was typical for the whole of Mesoamerica. The Tlaxcalans' decision to request a treaty after they had failed to achieve a military victory was consistent with custom. Like the warriors from Cempoala, the Tlaxcalans were integrated into the alliance and went under their own supreme command. The springboard like advancement from city to city was conventional. Even in the following period, this tactic was to be used again and again in the conquest of Mesoamerica, with the only difference being that the foreigners took part in it. The Spaniards had thus become part of an indigenous world without even being aware of it.[38]

The nationalist historiography of the nineteenth and early twentieth centuries sometimes condemned the alliance of a state like Tlaxcala with the Spaniards as betrayal. Yet the rationale for this decision is put in a fundamentally different light when viewed in context. In fact, the dichotomy of Europeans and indigenous peoples recognized by the Spanish did not exist in the same form for the natives. Although they certainly recognized the big differences, their own world was anything but homogeneous. Rather, Mesoamerica consisted of many small competing entities, which themselves also exhibited internal ethnic differences. Thus, in a culturally heterogeneous world, alliances with foreign invaders were no exception and certainly no betrayal. Instead, they represented the norm, for in the end one's very survival was at stake.

The Bloodbath of Cholula

The alliance between Tlaxcalans, Spaniards, and Totonacs seemed to benefit all parties involved. They jointly formed a powerful army that could stand up to Tlaxcala's and Cempoala's worst enemy. From the Spanish point of view, the advantages could not have been clearer. Their indigenous counterparts were a welcome reinforcement not only as warriors, but also as attendants, cooks, bread makers, servants, scouts, spies, interpreters, and concubines. Without pack animals, their work as porters remained indispensable. The message runners were also very important. They permitted the Spaniards to more or less seamlessly adopt the Mexica's communication network. Bernal Díaz, moreover, could not help but rhapsodize about the enormous importance of the interpreters, especially Malinche, which was again impressively demonstrated in their dealings with the Tlaxcalans.[39]

Given the positive turn of events, there was no doubt that the road would lead to Tenochtitlan. Nevertheless, the Spaniards convened a war council beforehand with all participants in the hueste, which the captain general used as an opportunity to rally the troops behind him. The path they would take still had to be determined. When a new legation of Moctezuma arrived with valuable gifts, they also recommended the route via the city of Cholula, which was friendly toward the Mexica. The Tlaxcalans, however, advised against this precisely because of this friendship, for fear of being ambushed. Instead, they proposed travelling via the allied Huexotzinco. True to his strategy of maintaining a dialogue with both sides, Cortés chose Cholula. Not only was the march there less arduous, but he also hoped to make the city an ally in order to keep the supply line clear. In response, the Tlaxcalan leaders offered him a large protection force.[40]

While the army was preparing for the march, Cortés had his captains Pedro de Alvarado and Bernardino Vázquez de Tapia head to Tenochtitlan with part of the Mexica legation to get firsthand information. Because it was a precarious mission, they had to leave their horses behind and travel by foot. Vázquez de Tapia described the strenuous and harrowing route on which skirmishes were repeatedly fought. The Mexica urged their Spanish companions to make haste, and even dragged and carried them along. They thus made their way to Texcoco on the eastern shore of the lake of the same name, and from there they could see the mighty Tenochtitlan in the distance. Moctezuma had sent a delegation of seven high dignitaries, including his son Chimalpopoca and his brother Cuitlahuac, to meet them. Alvarado and Vázquez presented gifts and made it clear that their captain general wanted to meet Moctezuma. But the Mexica made it equally clear to the two Spaniards that they would not be allowed to see Moctezuma or even enter the city. They had no choice, then, but to turn back. The excursion, in any event, at least brought knowledge of the routes into the Valley of Mexico.[41]

The allies took an aggressive stance toward Cholula. When they were sent only unimportant envoys to Tlaxcala after demanding a delegation of high dignitaries, they increased the pressure. They gave an ultimatum that the rulers of the city appear within three days, or else Cholula would be considered openly rebellious and punished. Meanwhile, the Tlaxcalan leaders continued to plot against the neighboring city, spreading a rumor that an ambush was in the works. According to López de Gómara, Cortés even had a Tlaxcalan captain who had made common cause with Cholula strangled. It was in this climate of suspicion that the delegation of high dignitaries arrived in Tlaxcala. They explained that they had not appeared earlier for fear of being attacked. We learn from Cortés that they even willingly submitted to the Spanish crown as vassals, which was immediately confirmed by a notary. They also invited the Spanish to visit to their city.[42]

After leaving a majority of their allies outside the city gates at the request of their hosts, the Spaniards received a festive public reception in Cholula in mid-October. As always, it was accompanied by a ritual of incense. The city at the foot of the Popocatépetl and Iztaccíhuatl volcanoes could boast a thousand years of history and was already an important spiritual center for the entire region in the era of Teotihuacan. Nobles from surrounding city-states traveled there to receive symbols of their rightful rule. For this reason, Spanish chroniclers compare the city with Rome or Mecca. Besides a large number of temples, there was the great pyramid dedicated to the god Quetzalcoatl, which was the world's largest in terms of its dimensions. The conquistador Andrés de Tapia later reported that Quetzalcoatl was the mythical founder of the city, who once banned human sacrifice and whose return was anticipated. It is disputed whether Cholula was actually a tributary of Tenochtitlan or whether this was deliberately false information from the hostile Tlaxcalans. If this was true, then it had probably only been the case since the second half of the fifteenth century.[43]

According to the Spanish and Tlaxcalan sources, however, the initial impressions faded quickly. After two days in the city, the provisioning of the guests supposedly decreased significantly and then stopped completely. Those in charge blamed this on the lack of supplies. Observers, including Alvarado, who had already passed through the city on his march to Tenochtitlan, detected signs of an ambush. Moctezuma, we are told, sent large units of troops that gathered near the city to wipe out the strangers. In the city, barricades are said to have been installed, and projectiles placed on the roofs of houses. In addition, well-meaning Cholultecas supposedly warned the Spaniards of the impending attack through Malinche. This was confirmed by the high-ranking hostages who were subsequently captured, but claimed to have acted on Moctezuma's orders.[44]

In any case, the Spaniards and their allies decided in favor of a preemptive strike. In Cholula's main square, which had previously been barricaded, Cortés called together the city officials, who arrived unarmed. A massacre lasting several hours ensued, during which women and children were not spared. Several thousand people reportedly died. Not only did the summoned Tlaxcalans take part in the bloody slaughter, but they appear to have continued murdering in the days that followed. The Spaniards, for their part, went on plundering the city and burning its temples. The massacre was concentrated mainly in the districts where the nobility and high priests lived, as well as in the Mexica colonies. In contrast, other districts went unharmed, which suggests that the city was divided into different camps, as Cervantes de Salazar reported. The camp that had sympathized with the Mexica and ruled the city was ruthlessly slaughtered. The opposition, which had determined the city's fate before its subjugation by Moctezuma and were related and in league with the Tlaxcalans, offered itself as a new ally. Cortés, in fact, let these nobles live and graciously accepted their submission to the Spanish monarch. In his own, though not very credible, words: "After the fifteen or twenty days I spent there, (the city) was again as peaceful and inhabited as if no one had been lost."[45]

Researchers do not entirely agree on whether the conspiracy of the Cholultecas and the Mexica really happened this way. Historian Ross Hassig is not convinced; he considers this version to be a legend invented by Cortés to justify his subsequent brutality. As in Tlaxcala, Cortés's strategy may have been to set an example through terror in order to induce the neighboring towns to submit without resistance. Spanish eyewitness reports, on the other hand, confirm the version of the indigenous plot. One supporting argument is that, given the dangerous situation in Cholula, the Spaniards could not really have been interested in a military conflict. Ultimately, they wanted to take the fastest possible route to Tenochtitlan and act as liberators. There is no doubt that Cortés was also convinced that his actions corresponded to a "just war" against insurgents who refused to recognize Spanish sovereignty.[46]

In the end, the outcome of the massacre mainly served the interests of the Tlaxcalans. The Spaniards had proved to be reliable allies. Maxixcatzin's wish came true, namely that the old ruling family, to whom he was related, would regain power in Cholula. Thus, after taking revenge on their enemies and also capturing many prisoners for sacrificial purposes, the Tlaxcalans were able to win back a strategically important ally. It is therefore at least plausible that the Tlaxcalans either triggered the massacre themselves or incited the Spaniards to do so.[47]

The March over the Mountains

When Moctezuma learned of the massacre from his envoys who had witnessed the killing in Cholula, he appears to have become despondent. Cortés informed him that the Cholultecas had accused him of being the instigator of the conspiracy. Undoubtedly, Moctezuma felt threatened by Cortés's desire to come to Tenochtitlan to meet with him face to face. Straight away the tlatoani sent messengers back to the Spanish with ample gold, clothing, and food. He also begged for forgiveness, as his local commanders had made common cause with the Cholultecas. In addition, the messengers on Moctezuma's behalf tried to dissuade the Spaniards from marching on to Tenochtitlan because the city was suffering. In return, the ruler promised to supply the Spaniards from afar. Moctezuma finally gave in when Cortés, with the help of another messenger, announced that he would not disobey the instructions of his royal patron. The compliance of the Mexica was most certainly due to the great pressure they felt in the face of developments in their provinces. Nevertheless, it soon became clear that the invitation was by no means entirely sincere.[48]

While they were still in Cholula, Cortés dispatched some men under the command of Ordás to explore the ascent to Popocatepetl. Though they did not quite reach the summit, they could admire the active volcano and see the high Valley of Mexico on the other side of the mountains. Ordás thought he had glimpsed "another new world."[49] The captain general had already set off with the rest of the troops at the end of October or the beginning of November and chosen the difficult route between Popocatepetl and Iztaccíhuatl. They crossed the pass at an altitude of about twelve thousand feet, which today bears his name, Paso de Cortés. The Tlaxcalans had recommended this route, as the northern route led directly into the Texcoco area, where Moctezuma was backed unreservedly. In contrast, in the south was the city-state of Chalco, which was only conquered in the 1460s after lengthy flower wars. Although it was ruled by Mexica governors, they were very displeased with the arrangement. The overall importance of the approximately one thousand Tlaxcalan allies, supplemented by men from Cholula, had grown since the Totonacs had left for their homeland. Their departure came after the grueling marches, for which they were, however, richly rewarded by Cortés.[50]

The allies first reached Calpan. Envoys from Huexotzinco, who were friends with the Tlaxcalans, showed up there. They likewise assigned troops to Cortés's march and offered advice on their route. When they came to a fork, the troops were advised to take the overgrown pathway to avoid a Mexica trap. Supposedly, the latter lay in wait for them along the seemingly easily passable path. The expedition heeded the warning. They exercised particular caution on the march through the icy and snow-covered high mountains and during the rest breaks, since an attack could be expected at any time. Eventually, they reached the territory of Chalco, where they listened to the already familiar complaints about the Mexica yoke and the harsh tribute demands.[51]

Moctezuma, in the meantime, had sent a legation with a large retinue—among them several magicians—under the leadership of the high prince Tziuacpopocatzin to try to talk the strangers out of their plans. Among the precious gifts they brought with them were a gold banner, a banner made of quetzal feathers, and a gold necklace. The moment when the treasures were handed over to the Spaniards is described in the Florentine Codex:

> And when they had given them these, they appeared to smile; they were greatly contented, gladdened. As if they were monkeys they seized upon the gold. It was as if there their hearts were satisfied, brightened, calmed. For in truth they thirsted mightily for gold; they stuffed themselves with it; they starved for it; they lusted for it like pigs. And they went about lifting on high the golden banners; they went moving them back and forth; they went taking them to themselves. It was as if they babbled. What they said was gibberish.[52]

Tziuacpopocatzin had put on magnificent robes to convince the Spaniards that he was Moctezuma. But Cortés, who had been enlightened by his indigenous allies, was not fooled. As the Florentine Codex reports, the Spanish mocked the envoy and sent him on this way with the threat that Moctezuma could no longer hide from them.[53]

Not even Moctezuma's magicians could restrain the Spaniards. Upon their return, they told the tlatoani of a vision: they allegedly encountered a drunken man who denounced the ruler and said, "Why in vain have you come walking here? Nevermore will there be a Mexico; it is already [gone] forever."[54] When they looked around, they reportedly saw all the temples and houses in Mexico on fire. Although it cannot be said whether this actually transpired, according to Sahagún the failed deception attempt caused great alarm in the capital.[55]

The Spaniards and Tlaxcalans would not be stopped. After their descent from the mountains, they reached the town of Amacameca, where they were treated hospitably and remained for several days. In his report, Cortés nevertheless explains that he had to be on his guard, since they were in enemy territory. A relative of Moctezuma governed the area, and spies lurked everywhere. But even there the inhabitants allegedly complained about the tribute collectors from Tenochtitlan. The army then continued on to the city of Chalco, which was situated right on the lakeshore. The complaints were repeated here, too, whereupon Cortés once again promised to help.[56]

According to Sahagún, the prevailing mood in Tenochtitlan deteriorated rapidly. The inhabitants were scared; the city streets were completely deserted. Members of the crown council are said to have advocated military action, which Moctezuma rejected. It is hard to say to what extent the narrative seeks to retrospectively portray the tlatoani as a dithering scapegoat who alone was to blame for the fall of the empire. The ruler tried yet again to prevent the allies from marching into the capital with a mixture of promises and threats. Allegedly Moctezuma even promised the strangers he would make tribute payments if they just stayed away. The allies, unimpressed, continued their advance. As they approached Tenochtitlan via Ayotzingo, another delegation, led by Cacama, the ruler of Texcoco and nephew of Moctezuma, met them to serve as escorts. They arrived in Culhuacan by way of the small village of Mixquic. Now accompanied by hundreds of Mexica dignitaries and onlookers, the army's last leg of the journey led them to Itztapalapa, where they were received by the city ruler, Moctezuma's brother Cuitlahuac, and other nobles. Cortés and his captains were housed in sumptuous palaces and marveled at the architecture of their hosts. They were to rest there for one night and then move on to Tenochtitlan. They had almost reached their destination.[57]

The Spaniards had learned quickly. They were able to penetrate a world of alliances as a foreign, but perfectly assimilable element, where supremacy and subordination were constantly being fought anew. They became part of this world by forging coalitions. Totonacs and Tlaxcalans joined the Spaniards because they found them useful in pursuing their own goals. We find evidence of this, not least, in the massacre of Cholula. For Cortés, the end justified the means. If we are to believe the Spanish sources, he used standard methods of the era's statecraft in order to achieve his objectives. So far, his strategy of keeping the enemy in the dark, playing hostile indigenous groups against each other, and then reconciling and rallying behind them had worked. Though the individual

Fig. 5.4 The messengers of Moctezuma from Sahagún. The drawings from Sahagún's *Historia General* show Moctezuma's futile attempt to thwart the Spaniards through a deception. *General History of the Things of New Spain by Fray Bernardino de Sahagún: The Florentine Codex. Book XII: The Conquest of Mexico* (1577). Library of Congress, https://www.loc.gov/item/2021667857/.

Fig. 5.5 The Spaniards' procession. The Codex Azcatitlan, whose name refers to the mythical place of origin of the Mexica, Aztlan, probably originated around the middle of the sixteenth century. The picture once again underscores the important role of the Malinche, who even precedes the troops here. An African slave is also depicted for the first time in the ranks of the Spanish. At the center, however, is the red flag with Christian symbolism, signifying the arrival of the new religion. *Codex Azcatitlan* (1530). Library of Congress, https://www.loc.gov/item/2021668122/.

circumstances could differ greatly, the Spaniards were always able to exploit the festering ethnic conflicts to their advantage. Luck was also on their side. They safeguarded their profits by leveraging traditional sources of legitimacy, specifically by ostensibly forging bonds with noble indigenous women and appointing submissive rulers. The most difficult test, however, was yet to come.

6

Tenochtitlan

From the beginning of the Spanish entrada, the attitude of the Mexica and its ruler was anything but unambiguous. On this point, both the European and the indigenous sources (the latter often influenced by the former), agree. The tactics of Moctezuma and his crown council oscillated between threats and welcome gifts, ambush and escort. Undoubtedly, this fickleness was due to the uncertainty created by the news of the steadily advancing strangers and their indigenous allies. The Mexica had not much to fear from the Tlaxcalans, Cholula, Huexotzinca, and Totonac. The Spanish, on the other hand, were a source of consternation, an element that raised questions about the order of the cosmos. Thanks to spies and their well-functioning message system, the rulers in Tenochtitlan were always up to date. They had to decide how to deal with these strangers—a foreign force who could unleash unprecedented military might with their powerful weapons and animals, who could not be dissuaded from their plans with kind words or magic, and who were now standing at their gates.

Cortés Meets Moctezuma

If we are to believe the sources, the tlatoani made a decision at this critical moment, which, in retrospect, would prove to be a fatal mistake. Specifically, he allowed the army to enter the city on November 8, 1519, unmolested. The Florentine Codex contains so much detail about this arrival that we can assume that the Mexica interviewed by Sahagún personally witnessed the event. Four riders and their heavily panting dogs formed the head of the procession. The banner bearer followed, waving his flag. Spanish infantrymen then followed with drawn iron swords gleaming in the sun. More mounted men followed in full armor on neighing, salivating, and noisily trampling horses. Behind them were the crossbowmen and arquebusiers each with shouldered weapons. Cortés and his highest officers concluded the Spanish part of the procession, arriving on horseback. The last to appear were the indigenous allies, uttering wild war cries. Some were armed; others were carrying loads or pulling cannons.[1]

The convoy traveled westward from Itztapalapa over the elaborately designed "two-spear-length"-wide dam in the middle of the lake. Before reaching the cities of Huitzilopochco and Coyoacán, they switched to the much wider large dam

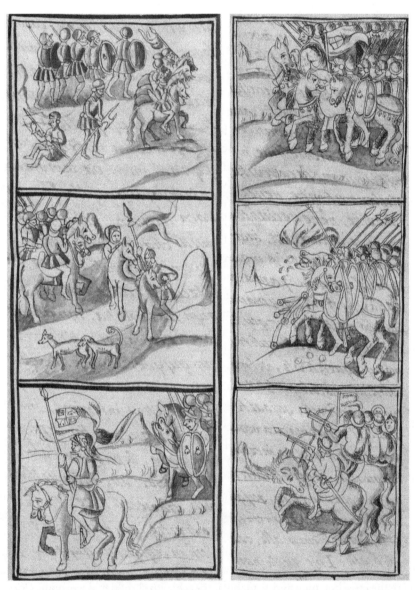

Fig. 6.1 Marching into Tenochtitlan according to Sahagún. *General History of the Things of New Spain by Fray Bernardino de Sahagún: The Florentine Codex. Book XII: The Conquest of Mexico* (1577). Library of Congress, https://www.loc.gov/item/2021667857/.

secured with drawbridges, following it northward all the way to Tenochtitlan. As Cortés wanted to make a positive impression, he forbade his men from breaking ranks under threat of severe punishment. Thousands crowded the streets, temples, and towers of the city or were in canoes on the lake. Everyone wanted to see the strangers. The sight of the huge city and the other villages around and in the lake surpassed anything that the Europeans had seen up to date. While these brilliant scenes did not fail to impress the Spaniards, they did not only arouse their exuberance. Their allies, after all, had strongly warned them of the dangers awaiting them there. Bernal Díaz thus remarked: "Interested readers should take a moment to ponder what I'm writing here. Were there ever men in all the world who took such a risk?"[2]

A large delegation of high nobility in festive robes approached them on the dam. The usual welcoming ceremony followed, during which the Mexica touched and kissed the ground with their hands. Due to the large number of dignitaries, the ritual dragged on. Only then did the Spaniards meet another delegation of nobility in whose midst was the ruler, carried on a sedan with baldachin and dressed festively for the occasion. When the strangers reached the actual city of Tenochtitlan, he climbed down from his armchair. He then proceeded to the captain general of the Spaniards under a magnificent canopy, led by his highest nobles, the princes of Texcoco, Tlacopan, and Tlatelolco, and was held aloft under his arms. The group's splendid clothing aroused the admiration of the European observers. Except for the four princes, no Mexica dared to look at the tlatoani. His entourage spread out cloths before him so that his feet, in elaborate shoes, did not have to touch the bare ground.[3]

Cortés approached him on foot, removing his hat. The moment of the encounter was depicted in the eyewitness accounts with minor differences. According to Cortés's retelling, he wanted to embrace Moctezuma but was not allowed to touch the body of the tlatoani and was therefore prevented by the ruler's attendants from doing so. The captain general then put his jewel-studded necklace around Moctezuma's neck, whereupon an Aztec servant placed a precious necklace with golden lobster-shaped pendants on Cortés. The two leaders exchanged greetings with the help of the translators Malinche and Aguilar. Moctezuma then led his guest into the city and assigned the strangers to the palace of his late father, Axayacatl. There, the Mexica gave Cortés precious gold jewelry and textiles as gifts and even provided the ordinary Spanish soldiers with lavish items. According to Bernal Díaz, the palace housed a secret treasury and numerous religious paintings and statues, which supported the conquistador in his belief that the Spaniards were regarded as gods. The building was made of solid stone and thus also served as an excellent fortress. The Spaniards quickly brought their guns into position and remained vigilant. Only then did they devote themselves to the feast that the Mexica served them.[4]

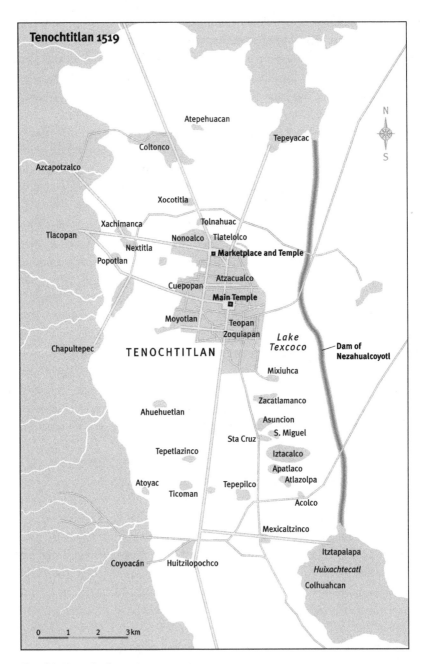

Fig. 6.2 Tenochtitlan, 1519

The course of the events that followed is highly debated in the research. According to Cortés and most of the eyewitness accounts and chronicles, Moctezuma gave a speech at the first, longer meeting of the two leaders, in which he apologized for his ambivalence. He referred to the immense fear that the news of the arrival of the strangers in Tenochtitlan provoked. Allegedly he then mentioned the myth of the return of a ruler—there was no mention of Quetzalcoatl—and how he took Cortés as his messenger, for he had come "from the sunrise." The mighty monarch in Europe apparently could have been none other than this ruler, who was reclaiming his rightful dominion. As Cortés reports, Moctezuma said:

> Be assured, therefore, that we obey you and recognize you as representatives of the great ruler you have told us about. And no fault or deceit will be found in this. And you shall command in all the land under my dominion according to your will, and your orders shall be obeyed and carried out. And you shall dispose of all that we possess at your pleasure.[5]

Based on his own letter-report, Cortés reinforced Moctezuma's belief. He replied that he had indeed come by order of the omnipotent ruler Charles to visit the Mexica Empire, which was already familiar to him, and to proclaim here the true Christian faith. The chroniclers López de Gómara, Sepúlveda, and Cervantes de Salazar updated Cortés's version of events with slight changes. The other eyewitnesses, Bernal Díaz, Aguilar (who even mentions a notarial certification of submission), and Tapia, also report in varying detail about Moctezuma's speech, although they date it differently. This similarly applies to the indigenous sources and especially to Sahagún, whose sources predate the speech to the reception on the dam.[6]

Despite the seemingly unambiguous source material, researchers have expressed considerable doubts about the authenticity of the account for many decades. In order to justify the illegal enterprise, Moctezuma's voluntary act of submission and the accompanying transfer of rule to the king of Spain, for whom the captain general served as proxy, was of central importance to Cortés. Nothing less than the legitimacy of his hueste hung in the balance. Critics have noted that the tale of Tenochtitlan's acquiescence perfectly matched the myth of the return of the gods and, for this reason, they call it a fiction. In his second letter-report, which forms the basis of this account, Cortés is not only the protagonist of the plot, but he also seeks to mythologize himself: He is a humble subject who asserts the claims of his monarch and his god, not his own, and by persuasion, not by force.[7]

Certainly, the captain general tended to twist and exaggerate the truth in his letter-reports. The highly ritualized courtesies with which Moctezuma greeted his guest, as well as the translation problems, could also have led Cortés to report what corresponded to his own wishful thinking—namely, that the tlatoani had actually surrendered. In addition, according to the Mexica's concept of history, past events were made comprehensible (by today's Western standards, ahistorically) by embedding them in ancient stories. Such tales traversed the boundary between myth and history and also included fortune telling and dream interpretation. Thus, from the Mexica perspective, Cortés was, or could become, at the moment of the encounter a local embodiment of a deity.[8]

This interpretation can provide answers to other open questions. For instance, Moctezuma's decision against defending the capital militarily is easier to grasp in this light. There had been worrying news about the entrada for some time, which in Tenochtitlan had given rise to repeated meetings between the ruler and his advisers and priests. Uncertainty about the identity of the Spaniards persisted, especially since they supposedly came with peaceful intentions. Furthermore, the correspondence with the calendar also played a role: the strangers came in the year "1 Reed," which was associated with the Quetzalcoatl myth. There were likewise pragmatic considerations, since November was not the time for military campaigns. This meant there was a lack of supplies and of porters, who were still doing agricultural work. The standing elite force could not face the army on its own. An easy victory without high losses was not to be expected. At the same time, the army's attenuated state would have increased the likelihood of rebellion among the subjugated peoples. Finally, Moctezuma did not want to incite further internal political discord over his rule, which might upset the balance of power in the Valley of Mexico.[9]

Conversely, we must also ask why Cortés and his troops ventured into the lion's den. Certainly the boost to the Spaniards' self-confidence after their successes in dealing with the Totonac and in the fight against the Tlaxcaltecs played a decisive role. Because of this and because of their strong belief in what they saw as the only true God, Europeans felt naturally superior to the indigenous people. Undoubtedly, they also underestimated the power of the Mexica and the size of their capital. Once they descended into the Valley of Mexico, there was no turning back. They were too dependent on the support of their allies, which, in turn, was only secure as long as they were viewed as powerful collaborators who offered effective protection against Mexica retaliation.[10]

Already the day after their arrival, Cortés, accompanied by Velázquez de León, Ordás, Alvarado, Sandoval, and some soldiers, including Bernal, visited the tlatoani. During the meeting, the captain general tried to enlighten the ruler on the merits of Christianity. In concise terms, he explained the Christian belief

Fig. 6.3 Conversation between Moctezuma and Cortés/Malinche. Lienzo de Tlaxcala. Smithsonian Libraries and Archives. Internet Archive.

system and the history of creation. The Spaniard specifically asked Moctezuma to stop sacrificing human beings and tried to convince him of the meaningless-ness of his "idols." He also announced that missionaries would soon be sent there to teach the Mexica the Christian faith. In his response, Moctezuma was polite but evasive. He said he believed that the Christian god was good, but that his gods were also good and that he did not intend to forsake them. When bidding farewell, the tlatoani offered the Spaniards another lavish gift.[11]

In the city, the splendor of what they saw quickly whetted the newcomers' curiosity. After a few days in the palace, they began to discover their surroundings with the captain general and accompanied by Moctezuma and his advisors. Díaz del Castillo reported in great detail on this tour of the city. They first went to the marketplace of Tlatelolco. There the Europeans were amazed by the abundance of goods on offer, which included everything from gold and silver jewelry and slaves to coarse fabrics and all kinds of food. As much interest was aroused by the order maintained by a market court as by the money made from cocoa beans or grains of gold and the skill of the various craftsmen. Even the widely traveled conquistadors who had already seen Rome or Constantinople agreed that they had never seen such an enormous marketplace.[12]

The subsequent ascent to the main temple in Tenochtitlan was at once fascinating and frightening. At its top was a wide platform with numerous sacrificial stones. The temple loomed above the entire area. There were impressive causeways, wooden bridges, and sanctuaries of the city; the lively movements of the canoes on the lake and the sheer number of people at the market were also a sight to behold. At Cortés's request, Moctezuma showed them the inside of the temple. The images of gods and statues frightened the Spaniards. They were particularly nauseated by the stench, by the sight of fresh human blood everywhere, and by the bloodstained priests in their long black cloaks. According to Bernal Díaz, it was at this moment that the first confrontation between Cortés and Moctezuma occurred. The captain general asked to be allowed to place a cross and an altar with an image of the Virgin Mary on the pyramid, which the tlatoani indignantly refused.[13] We can conclude from the lively market activity that the presence of foreigners was no longer a surprise to the inhabitants of Tenochtitlan. They had been curious about the arrival of the Spaniards, and no doubt they also looked upon the conquistadors with great interest once they appeared in the city. So far, there seemed to have been no disruption to their daily life.

The Capture of Moctezuma

Once Cortés had arrived at the destination of his entrada, what was next? Did he have a plan for how to proceed? These and similar questions might have been asked by the conquistadors after they had rested in their palace. It is questionable whether the captain general himself knew what steps to take next. He had failed to convince Moctezuma to convert to Christianity. His more central plan to acquire fame and fortune had not yet succeeded to an extent that would have justified his unauthorized behavior toward Velázquez and the crown. The further development of this fundamentally open-ended situation was again determined by various factors that were out of the Europeans' control.

Since Cortés had not been able to impose his desire for a Christian altar on the great pyramid, he had a chapel built in the palace with Moctezuma's permission. In the process, the workers came across a treasure chamber whose contents—gold, precious stones, and feather work—made a profound impression on the Spaniards. The decision was made, however, to close the chamber for the time being. This was not the only reason for the unrest that broke out among the men. Viewed objectively, the situation was quite threatening: They were dependent on Mexica supplies; there was uncertainty regarding the

Mexica ruler's attitude toward strangers; and, with its fortifications, the city was imposing. The Tlaxcalans continued to warn of the cunning of their enemies, who were supposedly lying in wait to sacrifice them all to the gods. We learn from Bernal Díaz that a delegation of the troops under Ordás spoke to the captain general about their precarious situation: "We told him that he needed to realize in what kind of net and in what kind of trap we were in." They suggested taking Moctezuma prisoner in order to have a bargaining chip against the superior strength of the Mexica. According to Aguilar, Cortés at first rejected the request, as the tlatoani was already a vassal of the crown and had done nothing wrong. Bernal Díaz reported, however, that the captain general's hesitation was due more to the pragmatic consideration of how to pull off the capture and then defend the palace.[14]

Tlaxcalan messengers, however, then secretly delivered bad news from Villa Rica de Vera Cruz. There, the Totonac allies had refused to make further tribute payments to the Mexica. As a consequence, they faced attacks by troops under captain Qualpopoca, who allegedly acted on Moctezuma's behalf. Although Governor Escalante came to the aid of the Totonacs with his handful of combat-ready men, the battle near Nauhtla was lost. Escalante and several of his men were seriously wounded. A conquistador fell into the hands of the enemy while still alive, but soon died of his wounds. Qualpopoca then had his head sent to Moctezuma. A few days later, Cortés learned that Escalante had succumbed to his injuries and that the Totonacs were so scared that they would no longer provision the city or offer military support to the Spaniards. The strangers had proved to be vulnerable, and the belief in their invincibility began to crack. Moreover, it also turned out that there were leaders among the Mexica who wanted to, and were able to, prove that the Spanish were also only common mortals.[15]

The sources say that Cortés took these events as an excuse to capture Moctezuma. Along with his leading captains Alvarado, Sandoval, Velázquez de León, Lugo, and Ávila, and several soldiers, he requested a private audience in the ruler's palace. Once there, he severely reproached the tlatoani and explained that he had to move to the Spanish quarters to ensure their safety. A lengthy exchange ensued in which Moctezuma denied the accusations and declared that the culprit, who had acted without his knowledge, would be punished. He supposedly even offered up his children as hostages. But Cortés stuck to his demand and conveyed the impression that he was acting under the pressure of his men. After some back and forth, the heavily armed officers appear to have actually threatened Moctezuma with death—whereupon the tlatoani relented. Reportedly of his own volition, he moved to the palace of Axayacatl on his magnificent sedan, where he was immediately placed under strict guard. In response to his nobles and relatives, who soon came to express their consternation and ask the reason for this turn of events, Moctezuma professed his willing participation. Cortés sought to uphold this pretense and allowed him to take his servants and high officials with him. Nevertheless, the Spaniards' move spread terror throughout the city over the well-being of the protector and keeper of the universe.[16]

While the tlatoani continued to run the government over the following months, it was under Spanish supervision. As a first course of action, he ordered Governor Qualpopoca, his son, and fifteen noble captains to come to the capital to investigate the events of Nauhtla. The governor first testified that Moctezuma had not ordered the attack, but recanted later when Cortés announced that Qualpopoca and his men were to be burned alive at the stake. Although the captain general confronted Moctezuma with the confession and insisted on his guilt, Moctezuma continued to deny it. Cortés decided not to punish the tlatoani "out of friendship," but Moctezuma was still forced to attend the execution in chains, which took place in public in front of the large temple. As Cortés and López de Gómara stressed, there were no revolts. Nevertheless, the distress among the spectators must have been great. Their nobles, after all, were being burned on a pyre consisting of weapons from their own arsenals, and their godlike ruler had been shackled.[17]

In his report to the Charles V, the captain general tried to justify his brutality toward a ruler, who, by his own account, was a vassal of the monarch of Spain. Along with noting the overall precariousness of their circumstances, he also remarked that the subjects of the Mexica would more readily submit to the Spaniards with their tlatoani in his power. The conquistadors had used this process since the campaigns to conquer the Canary Islands and in the Caribbean, where they applied it with repeated success.[18] Indeed, the move came as such a surprise to the Mexica that they had no time to react. In this respect, the Spaniards' strategy had paid off. Nevertheless, the question remains as to why the Mexica did not resist their ruler's imprisonment.

After Moctezuma's public humiliation, life simply appeared to continue as normal. Cortés himself claimed to have offered freedom to the tlatoani, only to have the latter gratefully decline. While the veracity of this offer is doubtful, Moctezuma nevertheless sensed the gradual loss of his authority and feared an uprising. It was only with apparent freedom that the ruler went about his daily business, received his officials, advised on government affairs, and gave instructions that continued to be followed. Under guard, the Spaniards allowed him to pursue pleasures like hunting, visiting his zoo, and attending a ball game. He could also freely practice his faith, and, though the sources are silent on the subject, the Europeans even tolerated the continuing practice of human sacrifice. According to Bernal Díaz, Moctezuma was friendly in his daily interactions; he was moreover interested in the Europeans, chatting and joking with the ordinary soldiers. If these reports are to be believed, then the ruler very well may

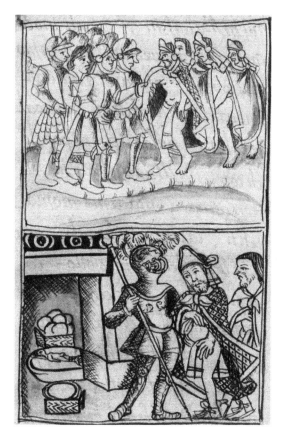

Fig. 6.4 Moctezuma's capture. According to the Florentine Codex, Moctezuma was captured by the Spaniards as soon as they entered the city. Though possibly true, the Spanish sources do not support this assertion. *General History of the Things of New Spain by Fray Bernardino de Sahagún: The Florentine Codex. Book XII: The Conquest of Mexico* (1577). Library of Congress, https://www.loc.gov/item/2021667857/.

have experienced a kind of liberation from the constraints of his life as a tlatoani while in captivity.[19]

For Cortés, the capture of Moctezuma proved beneficial in other respects as well. The siege of Villa Rica de la Vera Cruz was over and the Totonacs, who were likewise impressed by Qualpopoca's draconian punishment, resumed supplying the city. Cortés sent one of his rivals, Alonso de Grado, to the coast to replace Escalante. However, Grado's arrogance and pretentious lifestyle soon attracted unwelcome attention and stirred up resistance from his subordinates. Before long, the captain general, who had heard about the abuses, instructed his confidant Sandoval to replace Grado, who was ordered back to Tenochtitlan. The Spaniards used this respite to further explore their surroundings, especially Lake Texcoco. For this purpose, Cortés had his carpenters build three brigantines that made it possible toward the end of 1519 to navigate the lake system, which consisted of five interconnected bodies of water.[20]

In addition to these strategic military measures, the conquistadors returned to their original goal: the exploration of gold and wealth. Until then, the Mexica had delivered the treasures to them without any special effort on their part. However, the finds in Tenochtitlan stirred new cravings. At Cortés's request, Moctezuma agreed to show the Europeans the way to the precious metal deposits. Then, in early 1520, the captain general sent delegations of Mexica and Spanish officers to different parts of the country. Thus, the helmsman Gonzalo de Umbria set off for Zacatula in present-day Oaxaca, where the Mixtec people lived. They were subjugated by the Mexica and famous for their gold trade. Captain Diego Pizarro, a relative of the captain general, travelled to Pánuco in the northwest. During this period, Moctezuma also displayed a map of his empire, which piqued Cortés's interest in settlement opportunities. He accordingly sent Ordás to Coatzacoalcos in Veracruz, a region already known to the Spanish. Gonzalo de Umbria and Pizarro returned with abundant gold, and Ordás reported on the warm welcome from the inhabitants. All three of them also reported on the borders of the Mexica Empire, the hostile neighbors, and the complaints of the tributaries.[21]

In the meantime, the Europeans were keen to collect as much gold as possible in the form of levies. Officially on behalf of Moctezuma, his officials called on the provinces to once again pay the same amount of tribute that they had already paid that year. Moctezuma himself is said to have set a good example by giving his father's entire treasure, which the Spaniards had previously discovered, to the monarch in distant Europe as a gift. Allegedly, he did this with reference to the old prophecy, according to which the treasures were entitled to the foreign ruler. Afterward all kinds of treasures reached the capital. As Cortés himself reported, he had them marked to prevent any theft. The valuable gold handicrafts were then melted down into bars.[22] What the European reports portrayed as an act of voluntary donation or as legitimate levies was interpreted otherwise in the indigenous sources:

> And when [the Spaniards] were well settled, they thereupon inquired Moctezuma as to all the city's treasure, the devices, the shields. Much did they importune him; with great zeal they sought gold. . . . And when they reached the storehouse, a place called Teocalco, thereupon were brought forth all the brilliant things; the quetzal feather head fan, the devices, the shields, the golden discs, the devils' necklaces, the golden nose crescents, the golden leg bands, the golden arm bands, the golden forehead bands. Thereupon was detached the gold which was in the shields and which was in all the devices. And as all the gold

was detached, at once they ignited, set fire to, applied fire to all the various precious things [which remained]. They all burned. And the gold the Spaniards formed into separate bars. And the green stone, as much as they saw to be good they took. But the rest of the green stone the Tlaxcallans just stole. And the Spaniards walked everywhere taking to pieces the hiding places, storehouses, storage places. They took all, all that they saw which they saw to be good.[23]

The spoils were divided among the conquistadors, although, as Bernal Díaz reported, this was by no means without conflict. The royal fifth was deducted, as well as the agreed fifth for Cortés. The captain general then subtracted the expenses for ships and equipment, the cost of the envoys' journey to Spain, the value of the horses killed, and the share of the garrison in Vera Cruz. The remainder was distributed to the troops, but there were incremental differences. The two priests, the captains, and the horse owners, as well as the arquebusiers and crossbowmen, each received double shares. After that, there was hardly anything left for the crews who had accepted severe privations and whose entire existence depended on these spoils. It is therefore unsurprising that they felt deceived and grew restless. When it became known that some leaders, including Velázquez de León, had stolen parts of the treasure, violent clashes broke out. Cortés had to go to great lengths to soothe his men with speeches, gifts, and assurances.[24]

Tensions arose not only within their own troops, but also in their relations with the Mexica. Cacama, the ruler of Texcoco, headed a group of discontented nobles who renounced the tlatoani because his captivity increasingly deteriorated the sacred foundation of his legitimacy. According to Cervantes de Salazar, the stumbling block was Cacama's reluctance to pay the tributes demanded by Cortés. The Mestizo historian Alva Ixtlilxochitl also stressed this factor in his account. He moreover mentioned that the captain general had threatened to hang one of Cacama's younger brothers, which was averted only by Moctezuma's intervention. Following this account, it was another brother, the former rival to the throne Ixtlilxochitl, who ambushed Cacama and handed him over to Cortés. In this way, he was able to avenge himself for the fact that Moctezuma had brought his brother to power after the death of his father Nezahualpilli, despite internal resistance.[25]

Bernal Díaz del Castillo tells that Cacama had been plotting to destroy the Spanish and overthrow Moctezuma. For his cause, he had won the tlatoque of Toluca, Coyoacan, Tacuba, Itztapalapa, and Matalcingo. However, the conspirators could not agree on a successor for Moctezuma. When Cacama claimed this honor for himself, the ruler of Matalcingo felt slighted. He, in turn, informed Moctezuma, who then alerted Cortés. Moctezuma rejected the captain general's suggestion of attacking Texcoco with military support from Tenochtitlan. He preferred to summon Cacama in order to persuade him to reconsider. The latter finally refused the meeting and severely rebuked his uncle. Among other things, he blamed him for having brought "shame and disgrace" to the empire under the evil influence of the European magicians. He also promised that he would destroy the Spaniards. Moctezuma then had Cacama abducted from Texcoco and handed him over to Cortés, who immediately deposed him. Cortés appointed a submissive relative in his place as ruler of the city. The other conspirators were likewise captured and put in chains.[26]

López de Gómara described this moment in his chronicle: "Cortés made kings and commanded with as much authority as if he had already conquered the entire Mexica Empire."[27] The situation was indeed favorable for Cortés, and he took advantage of it to take a step that was considered far-reaching from the Spanish point of view. He instructed Moctezuma to officially take the oath of allegiance to the Spanish monarch before the nobility and the allied rulers for the entire empire and all his subjects. A gathering was convened for this purpose and was attended by all the empire's leading figures, Cortés, the royal notary, the officers, and numerous soldiers. In this setting, Moctezuma is said to have repeated the legend of the return of the mythical ruler from the East, who came to reclaim his land. The time had now come to submit to him again. Moctezuma, supposedly with profuse tears, took the oath, which was immediately notarized. The attending Mexica then followed their tlatoani's lead.[28]

Seemingly having reached the height of his power, Cortés returned to the thorny issue of religion. The captain general had repeatedly raised the subject in talks with Moctezuma—albeit unsuccessfully. Friar Olmedo, in whom Cortés placed particular trust, was instructed to sway the ruler. Once again, the tlatoani refused the attempts at conversion and emphasized that his subjects were likely to resist any attack on their gods. However, the Spaniards were emboldened by their strengthened position and convinced that they could overcome resistance even in this sensitive matter. After consulting with his men, the captain general allegedly decided to have all the paintings and sculptures in the main temple replaced or destroyed. Conquistadors Bernal Díaz and Andrés de Tapia had a different take on the events, however. According to Díaz, Cortés and Moctezuma agreed on a compromise. Here, the Spanish were allowed to place two altars with the image of the Virgin Mary and the cross in a hall of the great temple next to the images of the gods of the Mexica. Tapia tells us that Cortés and several soldiers personally destroyed various sculptures, dropping them from atop the temple to the depths below. Cervantes de Salazar, on the other hand, was informed by another Conquistador, Alonso de Ojeda, that the priests undertook a large-scale rescue operation. After salvaging their idols with the utmost care, they then hid them from the Spaniards.[29]

Whichever version came closest to reality, the upshot was that Christian symbols were placed in the main temple. The Spaniards seized on this fresh victory to celebrate a triumphant mass, which, according to Cervantes de Salazar, the Mexicans endured in silence. The Christian altar was subsequently to be maintained and cleaned by the Mexica priests. What's more, they were supervised by an elderly soldier to make sure that this actually happened. If we are to believe Cortés, there were no more human sacrifices in Tenochtitlan from that day forward. At least, he did not see any.[30]

Nevertheless, the captain general must have noticed that the Mexica were showing less respect with each passing day toward Moctezuma, who no longer performed his religious duties. As a result, the captive increasingly lost his importance. In a rebellious moment, the tlatoani is said to have summoned Cortés during the spring to tell him that there would be an uprising against the Spaniards by order of the gods. This, he asserted, could only be averted if they immediately returned to their homeland. Moctezuma even offered large amounts of gold to Cortés if he would give the order to return. Most likely, the tlatoani was responding to the mounting pressure from his own people, especially the powerful caste of priests, whose patience had run out after the sacrilege of the Spaniards. He may also have been responding to the burden of having to provision several thousand visitors. In the meantime, the Mexica made military preparations against the foreigners and mobilized their tributary cities. Cortés then sent some men to Vera Cruz to start building ships, presumably to create a diversion and gain time. It is doubtful that the captain general actually considered the possibility of leaving. In any event, he must have made it clear to Moctezuma that, if this happened, he would take the ruler hostage. There is no doubt, however, that the situation of the Spaniards took a turn for the worse with the destruction of the idols. They were conscious of this, and their fear of falling victim to human sacrifice intensified.[31]

The Punitive Expedition of Narváez

In the meantime, another battleline had opened up for Cortés. Soon after his departure from Cuba, Governor Velázquez complained about him to his superiors. First he turned to the Hieronymites in Santo Domingo, but they replied that Cortés and his men were innocent. They even sent the judge Alonso de Zuazo to investigate the governor. According to Díaz del Castillo, Velázquez was so distressed about this that he became very ill: "Whereas he was previously very fat, in those days he was utterly emaciated."[32] In October 1519, Velázquez sent a letter to Bishop Fonseca in Spain, summarizing the complaints about his subject's breach of trust and demanding harsh punishment. He further announced that he would send Pánfilo de Narváez with all of the ships available in Cuba to arrest Cortés.[33]

Narváez was a long-time henchman of the governor who had gained military experience in the conquests of Jamaica and Cuba. Since 1518, he had occupied a public post and developed a reputation for brutality. Bernal Díaz tells us that Narváez set sail in March 1520 with a fleet of nineteen ships and fourteen hundred men, including many battle-hardened Conquistadors, twenty guns, eighty horsemen, ninety crossbowmen, and seventy musketeers. An unknown number of indigenous and African slaves were also on board. This was the largest armada that America had witnessed up to that time. Numerous men voluntarily joined the company, with some coming especially from Santo Domingo with an expectation of easy spoils. By contrast, the professional soldiers needed to be coerced because Velázquez did not want to pay them. The sheer magnitude of the expedition resulted in a virtual depopulation of the Caribbean island, which was also hit by the first smallpox epidemic that claimed many Taino victims. The army would take the disease with them into the Mexica Empire.[34]

Word of the preparations for the massive undertaking spread across the Caribbean. It also reached the interim governor in Santo Domingo, Rodrigo de Figueroa, who sent the auditor Lucas Vázquez de Ayllón from the audiencia to Cuba to prevent a clash between the Spaniards. As Ayllón did not manage to dissuade Velázquez and Narváez from their plan, he decided to accompany the fleet with his own ships to mediate between the conquistadors. Due to the stormy weather, the punitive expedition did not reach San Juan de Ulúa until mid-April; Ayllón had arrived a few days earlier. Ayllón and Narváez received critical information from Francisco Serrantes about developments and the current state of affairs. Serrantes was part of Cortés's troops, but had defected from Diego Pizarro's reconnaissance team. Narváez decided to emulate Cortés's approach: he founded the city of San Salvador near San Juan de Ulúa and had the Totonacs supply him with food; at the same time, he stirred up opposition to Cortés. This heightened tensions with Ayllón, whom Narváez finally had arrested and sent back to Cuba on his ship, along with several other supporters of Cortés. Using threats, Ayllón was able to persuade the captain to transport him to Santo Domingo. There, he immediately wrote a letter to the crown in which he bitterly criticized Velázquez and Narváez.[35]

Meanwhile, the nearby Villa Rica got wind of the new arrivals, whereupon garrison commander Sandoval had them immediately spied on. He and his men began to prepare for a siege. For the sake of deterrence, he had gallows erected to prevent any desertion plans. Soon, he had to deal with a legation from Narváez led by the priest Antonio de Guevara, who, by order of the governor of Cuba, asked Sandoval to submit. Sandoval remained faithful to his master, however, and even arrested the envoys who reproached him. They were bound and transported to Tenochtitlan under the command of Pedro de Solís. He also dispatched express messengers to warn Cortés.[36]

In the interim, Cortés had learned of the arrival of the Spanish fleet through other channels, but did not know whose command it was under. He therefore decided to send several scouts to the coast. Spanish sources claim that Moctezuma also received news of Narváez's arrival, unbeknownst to the captain general. Indeed, they were supposedly in communication with each other, whereby Narváez assured the tlatoani that he had come to set him free and to punish Cortés. Moctezuma would therefore have had his people supply the new expedition behind Cortés's back and hoped to pit the rivals against each other. It is hard to say with certainty whether this really happened or whether it was an attempt by the chroniclers to show Moctezuma and Narváez in a negative light. After some time, the tlatoani probably decided to disclose what he knew to Cortés and showed him the pictographs that his scouts had recorded on a cloth. He wanted to convince the captain general to leave with his ships while he still had a chance. However, Cortés decided to turn to his trusted friends and so sent Andrés de Tapia to Sandoval and Friar Olmedo to Narváez. The priest was charged with investigating what the new arrivals were up to.[37]

When Solís arrived in Tenochtitlan shortly thereafter with Sandoval's prisoners, the captain general received the group respectfully and apologized to Guevara for the rough treatment by his subordinates. The priest and his escorts were impressed by this hospitable reception and even more by the size and splendor of the capital. They also admired the enormous amount of influence that Cortés and his allies had amassed. The captain general wanted to enlist Narváez's envoys to his side, which, according to Bernal Díaz, he managed to do very quickly:

> They had been with us for less than two days when Cortés had already flattered them with promises and greased their palms with gold bars and golden jewels . . . so that those who arrived as ferocious lions returned very tame and wished to serve Cortés.[38]

Cortés sent the emissaries back to the coast with a letter and handed them plenty of gold. Once they arrived there, Guevara told them about the magnificence of the country and the wealth and beauty of Tenochtitlan. The expedition members urged Narváez to seek a compromise with Cortés, as the country held enough riches for everyone. Meanwhile, Cortés's followers distributed the gold to Narváez's soldiers to win them over to the captain general. With men like Cortes's longtime backer Andrés de Duero, they had an easy time of it. Their success overall was due to the fact that Narváez's stinginess had made him unpopular with the troops. In the face of an imminent shift in the mood in San Salvador, Velázquez's protégé remained firm and furiously dismissed his emissaries. He rejected the offer of collaboration in Cortés's letter. Aware of his own numerical superiority, Narváez intended to persuade Cortés to leave for the coast unarmed and to submit to his orders.[39]

The situation had become critical for the man from Medellín. While his soldiers were initially pleased with the news of the arrival of Spanish ships, as they had been hoping to get reinforcements, Cortés must have suspected from the start that the newcomers were acting under the orders of Velázquez. The intelligence about the behavior of the Totonacs—even Chicomecatl had switched to Narváez's side—did not bode well. Cortés first reacted to the threat by forging closer ties with his men and giving them gold from his own treasure. When it was clear that Narváez had no interest in compromise, Cortés held a war council. There he called upon the troops to prepare for the imminent battle against their own countrymen. As captain general and supreme judge of New Spain, Cortés appeared to have the law on his side. After all, the newcomers did not have a royal mandate for their actions.[40]

He planned to take almost half of the men on his march to the coast. Along the way, near Cholula, he wanted to unite his troops with those of Velázquez de León and Rodrigo Rangel, whom he had sent to explore Coatzacoalcos and Chinantla, respectively, before Narváez arrived. In total, he had about three hundred soldiers under his command. The remainder, about one hundred and twenty men, were left under the command of Alvarado to guard Moctezuma and the accumulated treasures in Tenochtitlan. Since these men included many real and presumed sympathizers of Velázquez, such as the priest Juan Díaz, they had to swear an oath of allegiance to Alvarado. Cortés's request for military assistance proved unsuccessful with the Tlaxcalans, because they did not want to fight against the Spaniards. Nonetheless, they supported the force with supplies of provisions. Cortés declined the escort offered by Moctezuma, doubting its reliability.[41]

After uniting the troops in Cholula, the captain general headed toward Totonacapan. They were soon joined there by Sandoval with the combat-ready men from Vera Cruz and several deserters from Narváez's camp. On the way, he encountered Olmedo and his men, who reported on their unsuccessful mission and the clandestine arrangements between Moctezuma and Narváez. This confirmed Cortés's skepticism toward the tlatoani. A little later, emissaries from San Salvador under the scribe Alonso de Mata arrived and repeated the demands made by Narváez, who had since left for Cempoala. Cortés was not about to relent, but he treated the envoys well and sent them back to Cempoala unharmed. Both sides subsequently continued with this fruitless exchange over long distances. Thus, Cortés sent his captain Rodrigo Álvarez Chico with the notary Pero Hernández, and Friar Olmedo, and later Velázquez de León, while Narváez dispatched Andrés de Duero twice to the other side, with no change of heart. On the contrary, Cortés finally sent an ultimatum that he would attack should Narváez refuse to leave the country. In turn, the latter put out a bounty on Cortés. Ultimately, the quarrel was about the respective sides justifying their actions to the crown. It was also conducted with a view to the expected future legal dispute. Cortés consequently covered this matter in great detail in his report.[42]

Just an hour-long march from Cempoala, Cortés drew up his audacious battle plan. He did not fail to make his men pledge their loyalty with impassioned speeches. He then prepared a surprise nighttime attack. The first company under Diego Pizarro was to take out the artillery; the second company under Sandoval was to eliminate the commander Narváez, for whom Cortés also offered a bounty; the third and fourth companies under Velázquez de León and Ordás were to overpower the most important enemy captains; and, finally, the fifth company under the captain general himself was to form the rear guard and intervene where necessary. The heavy rain, which had persisted for days, had weakened the vigilance of Narváez's camp. Certain of victory, he did not count on an attack by his opponent. Moreover, Narváez underestimated the effect of the bribes that Cortés had made through his emissaries to Narváez's men. By this point, Cortés's go-betweens had considerably undermined the morale of Narváez's troop.[43]

Cortés's surprise attack on the night of Pentecost, on May 28, 1520, went off as planned. Narváez, who lost an eye in the melee and finally had to surrender, was hunted down by Sandoval on the great temple pyramid. The resistance of his men then quickly collapsed. The casualties were kept to a minimum: all in all, the short battle claimed thirteen lives and injured several more. According to Cortés, Narváez's men were relieved to have gotten off so lightly. Once they heard his take on the situation, they all allegedly willingly and enthusiastically agreed to follow him. Afterward, they got their weapons back, which caused a slight uproar among the victorious conquistadors, who had counted on some spoils. Even some of the women who had come with Narváez joined the army. Only Narváez himself and his highest officers, Gerónimo Martínez Salvatierra and the younger Diego Velázquez, a nephew of the governor, were transported to the prison in Vera Cruz. Cortés took over the fleet and brought ashore the supplies, sails, rudder, compass, and the captured treasures. The ships themselves were made unseaworthy. Buoyed by their victory, the captain general sent two expeditions under Velázquez de León and Ordás to establish settlements in the provinces of Pánuco and

Fig. 6.5 Cortés versus Narváez. Lienzo de Tlaxcala. The surprise attack was successful in no small part due to the opponents' lack of vigilance. The scene in the bottom left corner shows the arrest of Narváez. The Tlaxcalans also proudly point out their own role in the victory. Smithsonian Libraries and Archives. Internet Archive.

Coatzacoalcos. For this purpose, Cortés mostly delegated Narváez's men, who were still considered unreliable.[44]

Judging from the Spanish sources, Cortés once again scored a brilliant victory. The reasons for his success were numerous. Undoubtedly, Narváez felt too comfortable, behaved too passively, and left the initiative to his rival. Although they did not provide him with military support, Cortés benefited in many ways from the local knowledge and various services of his indigenous allies. He also knew how to win over the conquistadors on both sides with bribery. Also important was that the captain general, unlike Narváez, managed to maintain the loyalty of his men even in times of crisis. To this end, upholding an iron discipline and imposing severe punishments for violations were just as important as the fact that Cortés knew how to address his people in the right way and to set a good example. Unlike commanders of Narváez's type, the captain general was not ashamed to share in the everyday rigors with his men.

Alvarado's Massacre

Cortés did not have time to enjoy his triumph, however. While still in Cempoala, he received news from Tenochtitlan through messengers from Alvarado and Moctezuma that the Mexica had revolted. The palace that served as the Spaniards' quarters was under siege.[45] The events that led to this reversal are reported at length almost exclusively by indigenous sources. Spanish accounts are mostly silent about it, as it was by no means a glorious page in the history of the Conquest. Only the records of Pedro de Alvarado's *residencia*, an official review procedure required by Spanish law at the end of a term of office, provide details from the perspective of Spanish eyewitnesses.[46]

The Mexica's festival calendar included the important festival of Toxcatl in May, at the end of the dry season. Moctezuma had obtained permission from Cortés, and after his departure also from Alvarado, to celebrate this festival as usual. The climax of the multiday celebrations in honor of the god Tezcatlipoca was the sacrifice of a young prisoner who had attracted attention because of his beauty, physical prowess, and intellectual abilities. As a so-called *ixiptla*, he had previously embodied the god for a year, learned to play the flute, put on fragrances, speak reverently, and dress nobly. He was also clad with precious stones and flower garlands. Twenty days before the feast, his clothes were replaced and he was given four virgins as brides, who in turn embodied goddesses. Then he received the accoutrements of a high warrior. Five days before the actual feast, he was worshipped like a god, which included a large banquet attended by all the nobles except the tlatoani. He then voluntarily walked up the steps to the great temple for the solemn sacrifice and broke flutes along the way. Afterward, the young prisoner's lifeless body was not thrown down the temple stairs and ritually eaten as was customary. Instead, his head was placed on a tzompantli and the flesh was distributed to the high nobility.[47]

The ceremony itself was not problematic, even though Alvarado had reportedly prohibited human sacrifice. There were, however, already signs in the run-up to the event that pointed to a change in the Mexicas' attitude and heightened the anxiety of the Spaniards. For instance, the supply of food slowed down without warning. The Tlaxcalans moreover told Alvarado that the Mexica wanted to attack and sacrifice the allies after the celebration. It turned out that that moment was auspicious, for ritual and strategic reasons, for liberating their tlatoani following Cortés's departure. According to Alva Ixtlilxochitl, the Tlaxcalans spread this rumor in order to take revenge on the Mexica for having repeatedly sacrificed untold numbers of Tlaxcalan prisoners at the Toxcatl festival. Allegedly, Narváez's announcement that he would liberate Moctezuma also fueled the Mexica's willingness to fight the enemy's depleted army. On the

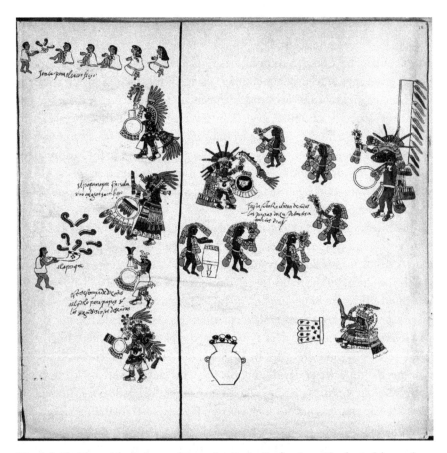

Fig. 6.6 The Toxcatl festival according to the Codex Borbonicus. The festival focused on the *ixiptla* of the four gods Tezcatlipoca, Huitzilopochtli, Cihuacoatl, and Atlahua. Bibliothéque Du Palais Bourbon—Codex Borbonicus. From Foundation for the Advancement of Mesoamerican Studies.

Spanish side, however, their own vulnerability and insecurity about the outcome of the conflict with Narváez reinforced the perception of being under threat.[48]

The preparations for the festival included the making of a large statue of Huitzilopochtli, which consisted of a dough of seeds decorated with the insignia of the god. On the feast day, the statue was unveiled. However, it was not brought to the great temple, as might have been expected before the Spaniards' arrival. Supposedly, Alvarado learned from a Mexica prisoner that the statue would soon be placed back in its intended location—specifically, where the Christian altar and the statue of the Virgin Mary were located. According to the later testimony of Bernardino Vázquez de Tapia, a rival of Alvarado, the captain then decided to interrogate several prisoners intended for sacrifice and two members of Moctezuma's family. Under torture, they confirmed what the captain wanted to hear: an attack was imminent. In order to justify his actions, Alvarado made a whole series of claims—true or invented—to give the impression that a preemptive strike was necessary to save the lives of the Spaniards. He also stressed, among other things, that the Mexica had defiled the Christian altar when trying to remove it.[49]

Alvarado thus resolved to leave half of his men in the palace to guard Moctezuma and the nobles and to go with the other half and numerous Tlaxcalans to the square in front of the great temple, where several hundred magnificently adorned male nobles danced to the sound of big drums in front of several thousand spectators. In the center the Macehualiztli snake dance, in which both dancers and spectators were being transported into an ecstatic state, was being performed. This ritual group dance accompanied by chanting was a form of prayer, and the priests kept strict watch to ensure that discipline was maintained and that no one left without permission. Alvarado stationed his heavily armed men at the exits of the square and encircled the Mexica. He then commanded his men to attack the defenseless revelers.[50] The Codex Durán describes in impressive detail what came next:

> . . . these preachers of the gospel of Jesus Christ, or rather these disciples of wickedness, stepped unhesitatingly into the midst of the unfortunate souls, who, except for a cotton cloak, were all but naked and held nothing in their hands but roses and feathers with which to dance, and they killed them all. When the others saw this, they rushed to the gates, where the guards killed them. They tried to hide in the vaults to escape from these emissaries of the devil, but they did not succeed and were all murdered. The square was full of blood, entrails, and severed heads, hands and feet of these wretches. For others, their guts were spilling out of their slashed bellies, and this was the most lamentable sight imaginable, especially because of the painful whimpering and screaming that could be heard in that square, with no one to help or do anything about it.[51]

The Spaniards were caught off guard by the Mexicas' reaction. Led by the surviving nobles and Calputin leaders, they took up arms and went on the attack. Caught up in fierce melees, the Spaniards retreated to their palace fortress, yet suffered seven dead and many injured. For the time being, they were able to halt the attackers with artillery fire. The Mexica then formed a blockade around the building, burned the brigantines to deprive the Spaniards of their means of escape, and continued their assault. Alvarado managed to smuggle out two Tlaxcalans, who informed Cortés of the shocking events. The furious attacks of the warriors dragged on for several days and brought the Spaniards to the brink of defeat. After they had weathered the storm, some believed they had found the reason for this in a Marian apparition and the aid of St. Jacob. More decisive, though, was the intervention of Moctezuma. Together with his brother Cuitlahuac and Itzquauhtzin, the governor of Tlatelolco, he had survived the massacre that the Spanish guards had perpetrated against the princes who were imprisoned in the palace. Reportedly put in chains and threatened by Alvarado with death, Moctezuma and Itzquauhtzin called upon their people from the roof of the building to restrain themselves. This noticeably diminished their fighting spirit as much as the news of Narváez's defeat. Moctezuma acted out of an instinct of self-preservation, but also lost status among his people. As we learn from Vázquez de Tapia, the ruler's speech ultimately prevented the Spaniards from being killed in a highly perilous situation.[52]

Cortés responded immediately to the call for help. He entrusted Rodrigo Rangel with the command of Vera Cruz, where the sick and injured as well as the prisoners were left behind. He then recalled the two expeditions under Velázquez de León and Ordás. In Tlaxcala, he conducted a military review, which showed that he had thirteen hundred Spanish soldiers, ninety-six horsemen, eighty crossbowmen, and eighty arquebusiers at his disposal. The Tlaxcalans provided another two thousand warriors. The army returned to Mexico along the speediest route. This time, they were not warmly welcomed by the villages along the

Fig. 6.7 Alvarado's massacre. The massacre ushered a turning point in the relations between the Spaniards and the Mexica. The picture expresses the horror that this event caused. It would remain deeply ingrained in the collective memory of the Mexica. From Fray Diego Durán, *Historia de las Indias de Nueva-España y islas de Tierra Firme*, 1581. Biblioteca Digital Hispánica, España Biblioteca Nacional de España.

way, nor did they receive any supplies. Nevertheless, the captain general was able to return unmolested to the palace fortress on St. John's Day, June 24, 1520, in the deadly silent and seemingly deserted city.[53]

Even those actively involved in the events at the time were well aware of the magnitude of what transpired. Alvarado's massacre was a watershed moment from which there was no turning back. Naturally, the question of guilt also arose right away. Cortés, accordingly, interrogated Alvarado, who noted the allegedly imminent attack by the Mexica. Rather than accepting this explanation, the captain general accused his captain of having made a serious mistake. He refrained from any punishment, however, and later placed the blame on Narváez, whose appearance had provoked Mexica's willingness to resist. Despite his blatant and momentous breach of the law, Alvarado escaped judgment. Later Spanish and indigenous chroniclers more or less agreed that Alvarado was responsible for the massacre, which they nonetheless assessed differently. In his letter-report, Cortés was silent about the subject, while others only touched upon it briefly.[54]

As per the indigenous sources of Sahagún and the Codex Durán, the Spanish nobles were dancing at Cortés's special request. In fact, according to Durán, the captain general was even present during the massacre, although this assertion is only found in this source. These statements have caused researchers to suspect that Cortés may have ordered the assassination of the Mexica elite to decisively weaken his opponent, following the example of the Cholula massacre. Given the parallels between the two bloody deeds, the idea is by no means absurd. Nonetheless, it can only be found as conjecture in the Codex Ramírez and otherwise cannot be further substantiated.[55]

No doubt both fear and the example of Cholula, where a massacre had already been carried out once under the ruling class, were contributing factors to the Spanish atrocity. There is also no question that Alvarado was responsible for this as commander on the ground, while Cortés's role remains uncertain. Finally, the crime was counterproductive, for it put an end, once and for all, to the Mexicas' support for Moctezuma. From that moment on, the Spaniards' hostages were worthless. This outcome, together with the fierce battle that the soldiers had waged against their Spanish enemies, allows for only one conclusion about Alvarado's bloodbath: the political cost was too high.

The Death of Moctezuma and the "The Sad Night"

We can only speculate why the Mexica let Cortés and his men back into the city without a fight. Was it because they thought they could better combat the Spaniards there? Or because they were still mourning their dead? Neither of these hypotheses is entirely convincing, however, and the sources do not

provide any answers. The details in the Anales de Tlatelolco and Sahagún suggest that there may still have been a great deal of respect for Cortés and that the
Mexica were perhaps still willing to negotiate.[56] Of course, Cortés had significantly increased the number of fighters among his men, but they could hardly
rest easy. While they occasionally managed to get messengers through the
blockade, the supply situation was becoming more critical by the day, despite
the discovery of a brackish water source in the inner courtyard. During the siege,
which lasted a good three weeks, the Mexica raised the dam bridges and attacked
the Spaniards whenever they ventured out of their fortress. Cortés ordered several advances, once with self-made "towers" to protect the soldiers. During the
day, the Spaniards managed to occupy houses in the surrounding area and once
even the palace of Moctezuma. But the Mexica retook the buildings at night
when the Spaniards retreated to their palace. Apart from casualties and injuries,
the attacks yielded nothing. According to Bernal Díaz, the horsemen had a particularly harrowing experience in the alleys and canals of the city. Within a short
time, almost all horses were injured.[57]

The Mexica demonstrated their full fighting power only the day after Cortés's
return, "when we were attacked." The Spaniards were again taken by surprise.[58]
The Mexica attacked the palace, set fires, and threw stones and spears at the
trapped enemies from neighboring buildings, which proved to be the most effective method of combat. The major temples in particular were used as bases
for these attacks. Cortés then successfully stormed one of the pyramids, though
without managing to hold the structure. The Mexica were not intimidated by the
heavy losses they had sustained under the Spanish artillery and gunners. For the
Spaniards, it appeared as if, for every warrior they killed, two new ones would
emerge on to the battlefield. Yet the Mexica also adapted their fighting style to
reduce the losses. And so they strategically retreated, attacking from cover and
hindering the Spanish repair work on the palace fortress. They also learned to
stay out of the way of the Spanish firearms. Psychological warfare also played
an important role: the Mexica deliberately made war cries at night to scare their
enemies and rob them of sleep, while issuing targeted verbal abuse and threats.
They also consulted their priests about auspicious omens and prayed to their
gods. The Mexicas' greatest advantage was their high numerical superiority,
which was heightened by the mobilization of the surrounding tributary cities.
Díaz del Castillo, who admired the bravery of his enemies, aptly remarked: "and
even ten thousand Trojan Hectors, and as many more Rolands, could not have
killed them all."[59]

In the meantime, the morale among Cortés's men, especially the new recruits
from Narváez's army, had visibly deteriorated. Cortés felt compelled to renego-
tiate. In fact, he had already made an attempt a few days earlier, and even released
one of his most important hostages, Cuitlahuac, the ruler of Itztapalapa, probably

Fig. 6.8 The siege. The Mexica siege caused great distress among the Spaniards. The picture shows the considerable differences in armament and equipment between the unequal adversaries. From Fray Diego Durán, *Historia de las Indias de Nueva-España y islas de Tierra Firme*, 1581. Biblioteca Digital Hispánica, España Biblioteca Nacional de España.

in exchange for provisions. This move, however, did not appease the Mexica. The brother of Moctezuma, who had already advocated a hard line against the Spaniards, organized the great council, which transferred power to him without yet enthroning him. He was thus made the new supreme commander of the Mexica army. In this predicament, Moctezuma was Cortés's last bargaining chip. And yet, since his return, the captain general had avoided contact with the tlatoani and had also insulted him for his alleged betrayal. At this moment, he ordered him to address his subjects from the roof of the palace to urge them to call a ceasefire and to negotiate.[60]

Spanish sources report that the prince, along with some other noble prisoners, commanded his warriors to stand down. According to some accounts, a moment of silence set in, and they listened to him. Other chronicles, however, claim that the ruler's presence, surrounded by Spanish shields, was not even noticed in the turmoil of battle. In the first version, the tlatoani ordered his subjects to stop fighting because the Spaniards wanted to immediately withdraw. The Mexica, however, rejected the idea—in tears, in the retelling of Díaz del Castillo, and by issuing a series of profanities and curses against Moctezuma, in that of Cervantes de Salazar. It is reported that they attacked at once, injuring the poorly protected tlatoani so severely with their projectiles that he soon—some sources speak of a period of several days—succumbed to his injuries. We are told by Díaz del Castillo that Cortés released several priests and also handed over the body to Mexica. But they were still not ready to give in.[61]

Moctezuma's death is described differently in some of the sources, which are based on indigenous contemporary witnesses. Here, too, the depiction is inconsistent. According to Sahagún and the Codex Ramírez, however, the Mexica discovered the body outside the gates of the palace and concluded that he had been murdered on Cortés's orders. Both versions can be reconciled insofar as the Mexica did not know that the tlatoani had fallen victim as an unintended target.[62] The handling of the corpse is also disputed. While some claim that the Mexica did not shed any tears for their tlatoani because he had lost his legitimacy and was despised by the people, other eyewitnesses and Sahagún's interlocutors report that the subjects honored their deceased ruler with magnificent ceremonies and cremated and mourned him according to ancient custom.[63]

The Mexica formally designated Cuitlahuac as the tlatoani of Tenochtitlan. Cortés, mindful of European inheritance law, then released a prisoner to tell his compatriots that either the sons or the nephew of Moctezuma, who were also in Spanish custody, were the rightful successors. But the Mexica ignored this desperate ploy and continued their assault. Frustrated by his failure to negotiate, the captain general and his officers agreed to kill all the other hostages—except for Chimalpopoca and two daughters of Moctezuma, who were in Spanish hands— and to toss their bodies outside the palace. Among them were illustrious figures, such as Itzquauhtzin and Cacama.[64] Aguilar, an eyewitness to the events, vividly described what happened next:

Fig. 6.9 The handling of Moctezuma's body, after Sahagún. It is debated whether Moctezuma was actually mourned by his subjects as shown here and his corpse honorably cremated. *General History of the Things of New Spain by Fray Bernardino de Sahagún: The Florentine Codex. Book XII: The Conquest of Mexico* (1577). Library of Congress, https://www.loc.gov/item/2021667857/.

The bodies were carried out by a few of the Indians who had not been killed. At night, around ten o'clock, we then saw so many women with burning torches, braziers, and fires that we were quite terrified. They came to look for their husbands and relatives lying dead in the colonnade . . . and when the women recognized their relatives and loved ones (whom those of us standing guard on the roof could see very clearly), they threw themselves over the corpses, seized by deep sorrow and pain, and began to shout and wail so loudly that we felt overwhelmed with fear and terror . . .[65]

The situation became more and more hopeless for the conquistadors, which only intensified the pressure on the captain general. The men wanted to break out of the Mexica siege and flee Tenochtitlan. This notion, however, was highly repugnant to Cortés, who intended to hand the city over to his monarch. The Spaniards made further attempts to escape by fighting their way to the dam bridges. In the process, they demolished the adjoining houses and used the rubble to span the breaches created by the Mexica. Their efforts failed, however, as their opponents managed to reopen the breaches during the breaks in the fighting. When the supply situation became intolerable and ammunition scarce, Cortés resolved in consultation with his captains to take action. Without further delay, the Spaniards decided to break out, at midnight, from the trap that the palace of Axayacatl had become. With all their men, they would take the last passable causeway to Tlacopan, in the west. A conquistador, who claimed to be an astrologer and suggested his bona fides by mentioning that he was once in Rome, tipped the scales with his prophecy. The time of day also had a practical reason, for the Mexica did not usually fight at night. In preparation, the captain general had a movable makeshift bridge built. The force was split up: Sandoval led the advance guard; Cortés headed the bulk of the army, which included the prisoners and clergy, in the middle; and Velázquez de León and Alvarado marched at the rear, while the heavily decimated Tlaxcalans rounded out the rest. At this moment, the most pressing concern for many of the Spaniards was how to take away the gold treasure amasses in Tenochtitlan. They loaded a mare with the monarch's share, which proved so massive that the animal could barely walk. The soldiers were then permitted to help themselves to the gold and stuff as many bars as possible beneath their armor. The Spaniards' great escape could now begin.[66]

From June 30 to July 1, 1520—some sources mention July 10—the Spaniards crept away from the capital in the dark of night and in fear, a good six months after having arrogantly and triumphantly marched into it. The weather favored their plan; it rained in torrents, which the eyewitnesses interpreted as divine providence. They were able to reach the city limits unnoticed and had already arrived at the causeway when a woman and a guard at one of the temples sounded the alarm. What happened next is one of Spain's blackest hours in the history of the conquest of the New World. Both on land and at sea, the Mexica ferociously attacked the conquistadors from all sides. The makeshift bridge they had used to cross the first canals collapsed when two horses were spooked by the slippery ground. The canal began to fill up with dead animals and men, who had been shoved into the water by the advancing soldiers. As a result of the bottleneck, the riders became powerless, and the shooters' guns were useless due to the moisture. The fighting order quickly dissolved, with everyone left to their own devices. Many Spaniards drowned when the weight of the gold they were carrying dragged them into the watery depths. Many Tlaxcalans, who had assumed the thankless role of rearguard, were almost completely wiped out. Numerous men fell into the hands of the Mexica, though the latter were no longer keen to take prisoners, but instead to kill their enemies wherever they could. The advance guard under Sandoval and the main army under Cortés reached the shore at Tlacopan with heavy losses. While Alvarado was able to escape on foot with serious injuries, Velázquez de León and most of the men under his command were killed, as were some of the hostages. Included among them was Chimalpopoca, Cortés's designated heir to the throne. Some members of the rearguard were forced to fight their way back to the palace fortress, where they were able to hold out for a few more days before being killed.[67]

For Spain, the outcome of this battle, which would go down in European history as "La Noche Triste" ("The Sad Night") and in Mexica history as the Battle of the Toltec Canal, was catastrophic. Cortés played down the number of the fallen in his report to the crown, but other eyewitnesses estimated that several hundred conquistadors and several thousand Tlaxcalans had perished. According to Aguilar and Vázquez de Tapia, casualties were around fifty percent. The loss of about forty-five horses and the entire artillery was also reported. Even worse, all the gold was lost. The Mexica and their allies certainly also lost a large number of warriors that night. On the other hand, despite the new tactics, they took many prisoners, whom they would later sacrifice. From their perspective, the night was a great success—they had finally managed to drive the enemies out of the city. If any of the indigenous people still held the conviction that the Europeans were immortal gods, the events of this night must have shattered it.[68]

The Spaniards' stay in Tenochtitlan from November 1519 to July 1520 raises many questions. The discrepancies between the numerous reports and chronicles are sizeable, and it is impossible to clearly distinguish between indigenous and European authors. In spite of the multitude of different versions of the events, some incidents cannot be explained. Nevertheless, the key points are beyond dispute and permit some inferences to be made. It is safe to assume, for instance, that conquistadors would not have survived their escape without the support of

Fig. 6.10 The "Noche Triste." The Lienzo de Tlaxcala shows the Mexica attack on the Spaniards and their allies from canoes and the continuation of the bloody battles in the water, on the so-called Toltec Canal. On the right side of the image, Cortés and some of the allies have already crossed the breach but are still under attack. Smithsonian Libraries and Archives. Internet Archive.

their indigenous allies. The Spaniards' room for maneuver was much less than they let on, though they were not always aware of this fact. In their actions they thus also followed the logic of the Mexica, in whose cosmos they had insinuated themselves. If we are to believe the Spanish account, the Spaniards gained the upper hand through lies and deceit, and especially through their surprise capture of the tlatoani. However, as the developments in the spring of 1520 showed, Moctezuma's power was not all-encompassing, and his person was not sacrosanct. In the tense atmosphere between April and June, each side trusted in a higher power; in the great Battle of the Toltec Canal, or the "The Sad Night," the Mexica recognized the workings of their gods. Whereas the Mexica honored them with victory celebrations, the Spaniards, who had just managed to save their own skin, mourned with prayer. The war, however, had only just begun.

War and Destruction

For the Mexica, the Battle of the Toltec Canal came at a high price. Parts of the city were devastated, and the basis of the state, the authority of the tlatoani, was utterly shaken. Although Cuitlahuac was a new tlatoani ready for battle, the shameful death of Moctezuma and many members of the elite was highly distressing. Moreover, numerous provinces had risen up against the Mexica. The switching of alliances was already commonplace in the highly structured city-state world of Mesoamerica in pre-Hispanic times, so the arrival of the Europeans was only a further catalyst. The Tlaxcalans and the numerous other city-states that joined the allies wanted to take advantage of this dynamic. For the Spanish conquistadors, the disaster was more than just a "sad night." Due to the enormous losses of men and materiel, the troops' morale had been dealt a severe blow. The majority wanted to swiftly return to Cuba. They were afraid of being slaughtered and sacrificed like their captured compatriots and allies by the seemingly immeasurable number of Mexica in Tenochtitlan. For Cortés, however, there was no turning back, since a vengeful Velázquez was waiting for him in Cuba. He was condemned to fight.

Return to Tlaxcala

While the battle was still raging, the Spanish vanguard had reached Popotlan, where it was again attacked by Mexica warriors and driven toward Tlacopan (Tacuba). Faced with a continuous onslaught, they were forced to leave behind many wounded, who fell into the hands of the enemy. For the time being, they retreated to the Otoncalpolco, a hill that was later called Nuestra Señora de los Remedios. The Tepaneca living in nearby Teucalhuiacan warmly received the half-starved and wounded men and provided them with urgently needed food. The fact that the Tepaneca did not heed the Mexicas' appeals for a joint struggle against the strangers shows how much Tenochtitlan's authority had already been eroded. According to the sources, Cortés was rather dejected at first because of the high losses, but he quickly recovered and declared Tlaxcala to be his destination. The surviving Tlaxcalans were to lead the decimated army on the northern route around the lake, since this would allow them to gain more distance from the capital and to move through less densely populated areas.[1]

After a military review that revealed the full extent of their losses, the Spaniards moved north via Tepotzotlan, Citlaltepec, and Xoloc, but continued to be attacked sporadically. The inhabitants of these villages had in fact abandoned their houses when the foreign soldiers appeared, but the structures offered shelter and provisions so that the exhausted Europeans could at least get some rest. During the march, they knew how to defend themselves effectively through their cavalry, especially since their opponents did not fight in large numbers. Nevertheless, the troops undoubtedly presented a miserable sight. As the seriously wounded were placed in the middle of the less seriously wounded, they determined the tempo of the march. Many men died from their wounds or from starvation, as the sparsely populated areas provided an inadequate food supply.[2]

At the beginning of July, near the village of Otumba, the Spaniards were confronted by a well-equipped army sent into the field by Cuitlahuac. Since it was outside the usual time of year for war, the Mexica troops had to be supplemented. They were therefore unable to immediately launch their pursuit. In addition, the vassals, who had used Tenochtitlan's period of weakness during the captivity of Moctezuma to loosen their ties, had to be brought into line. Finally, the political turmoil following the death of the tlatoani and large parts of the ruling class posed a serious challenge that took some time to resolve. Nonetheless, the Battle of Otumba lasted several hours, bringing the Spaniards and their allies to the brink of defeat. They had the advantage that the fighting was taking place on a single plain so that the cavalry could exert its full force. When the Spanish cavalry succeeded in locating and killing the Mexica supreme commander, who stood out from the mass of his warriors because of his conspicuous war attire with feather ornament and standard, the tide turned. Losing their banner was a particularly bad omen for the Mexica, because it signaled that the battle was lost. The army withdrew and therefore missed the golden opportunity to annihilate a severely battered enemy once and for all. Some Spaniards later claimed that they owed the miraculous rescue to the intervention of St. Jacob on his white horse.[3]

The Spaniards were greatly relieved when they returned to Tlaxcala a few days after Otumba. Díaz del Castillo recalled: "We were as happy as if we had arrived home." Cortés urged his men to stop looting and to refrain from any attacks on the population. The standing of the Europeans in the region had deteriorated. In the Tlaxcala village of Hueyutlipan, they received a friendly but fairly tepid welcome, and for the first time they had to pay for the Tlaxcalan food with gold.

After a few days, the Spaniards received a visit from a high-ranking delegation under Maxixcatzin. They assured Cortés of their support and their willingness to continue fighting, not least because they wanted to avenge their own dead. They also invited the Spaniards to rest in the capital to regain their strength. Toward mid-July, the worn out remnants of the once-proud army arrived in Tlaxcala, where they stayed for about three weeks to nurse their wounds. Due to the insufficient medical care, more men died from their injuries. The survivors were well aware that they would have been lost without the help of the Tlaxcalans.[4]

The question of how to deal with the Spaniards had previously led to a dispute among the leaders in Tlaxcala. Xicotencatl the Younger, who had spearheaded the struggle against the foreigners at the first meeting, spoke out against any cooperation. In addition, the Mexica sent six high-ranking envoys to Tlaxcala to promote an alliance, which aroused interest among some members of the local elite. They sought to persuade their interlocutors with gifts and the argument that Tlaxcalans and Mexica were related and worshipped the same gods, while the greedy Spaniards sought to rule the entire country. This issue is said to have been the subject of violent disputes within the supreme council of the Tlaxcalans, with the Cortés's friendly party around Maxixcatzin winning the day. It was decided that the assurances of the Mexica could not be trusted, while their revenge was famously brutal. Nevertheless, the Tlaxcalans managed to secure large concessions from the Spaniards for their continued support. Thus, they claimed permanent exemption from the tribute to Tenochtitlan, a fortress of their own in the capital of the Mexica, a share in the spoils of war, rule over Cholula, and tributes from Huexotzinco and Tepeyaca.[5]

Given Tlaxcala's importance, Cortés had no choice but to agree to the demands. During his stay in Tlaxcala, the captain general collected all the gold that the conquistadors had been able to salvage from Tenochtitlan. Naturally, this stirred up resentment among the troops, but the captain general thought it was necessary to replenish the war chest of the hueste. In any case, many of the men were hardly ecstatic about the announcement to continue the war. Indeed, they did not feel safe even in Tlaxcala, for, as López de Gómara noted, "friendship between persons of different religions, clothing, and languages never lasts long."[6] A number of the conquistadors who had only arrived with Narváez were particularly anxious to return to Cuba. Under the leadership of Narváez's former close confidant Andrés de Duero, they persuaded Cortés to allow them to depart at the earliest opportunity. Meanwhile, the captain general sent messengers to Veracruz to assess the situation and urge the commander there to not allow any ship to leave for Cuba. Since the routes had become unsafe during the fighting against the Mexica, he wanted the envoys to keep their distance. While Cortés had been in Tenochtitlan, a whole regiment of forty-five men and five horsemen under Juan de Alcántara and several hundred Tlaxcalans, who were supposed to fetch supplies in Vera Cruz and bring parts of the treasure left behind in Tlaxcala for safety, had fallen into a Mexica trap and perished. The news that came from the coast was mixed: the region remained peaceful, but since few men were available in the garrison, the hoped-for supplies failed to materialize.[7]

Nevertheless, Cortés was already planning the next campaign, partly to keep his disgruntled men busy. It was clear to him that he had to secure the supply lines to Veracruz if he wanted to triumph in the intended final battle. Moreover, he realized that the cohesion within the Mexica Empire was fragile. As a rule, a demonstration of power was sufficient to coax the tributary cities to change sides. Cortés chose to attack the cities of the region allied with Tenochtitlan in an effort to weaken the Mexica, gain new allies, and show the Tlaxcalans proof of regained strength. About a month after fleeing Tenochtitlan, his troops—no doubt partly at the behest of his hosts—attacked the nearby town of Tepeyaca, which was of great strategic value due to its location along the road to the coast.

Tepeyaca was a tributary to Tenochtitlan and many Mexica lived there. Allegedly, warriors of the city and neighboring villages had killed several Spaniards, which Cortés interpreted as a rebellion against the crown. In a particularly cruel punitive action lasting about three weeks, the Spaniards and their allies conquered the entire province. Those who did not submit voluntarily as well as many others were enslaved and branded with a G for *guerra* (war). Countless prisoners of war were sacrificed by the Tlaxcalans. In his report to the monarch, Cortés cited cannibalism as one of the reasons for his brutality, a factor he had so far deliberately overlooked and continued to overlook among his allies. In truth, his main purpose in enslaving the prisoners of war and their wives and children was to gain porters, since he needed the Tlaxcalans as warriors. Besides, by assigning slaves to his men, he could compensate them somewhat for the loss of gold. Finally, Cortés's violent approach was intended to make the inhabitants of the region submissive and to dissuade them from taking sides with the enemy again if given the chance. To secure their conquests, the Spaniards founded the garrison town of La Villa de Segura de la Frontera in Tepeyaca in early September. In this way, they were able to control the routes to the Caribbean coast, while having virtually destroyed the influence of Mexica in this region.[8]

Just as Cortés was setting up headquarters in the new city, seven Spanish ships arrived at Vera Cruz for different reasons. Pedro Barba, a messenger from Velázquez, assumed that Narváez was now in command and sought to have Cortés brought back to Cuba as a prisoner. Other ships from the Caribbean and even directly from Spain had no connection to those from Cuba. For instance, Francisco de Garay, the governor of Jamaica, sent a small flotilla under the command of Julián de Alderete, with about one hundred and fifty Spaniards and eighty horses, to explore Pánuco. After one ship sank, Alderete's troops reached Vera Cruz badly decimated. The crews were sent to Cortés in Segura de la Frontera as reinforcements, sometimes under false pretenses. They brought important supplies of weapons and ammunition. Overall, the Spanish army grew by about 50 percent due to the new arrivals. The fifty horses were especially appreciated by the troops.[9]

The ships also brought news from Spain. Among other things, Cortés learned that his cause was faring better on the home front, as Bishop Rodríguez de Fonseca's position had become controversial. After losing all his papers and records, it was now time for Cortés to document the events of the past months in writing and to inform the crown. With the help of his notaries, the captain general had various letters drawn up, in which he gave an account of the whereabouts of the gold and the costs of the expedition. In addition, he wrote a detailed second letter-report to the monarch, which would become famous as one of the most important sources on the dramatic experiences of the hueste. Cortés's main concern was to justify his actions and to put the failure in Tenochtitlan in a softer light. Since he still could not be sure of his position, the captain general did not shy away from distorting the truth. First and foremost, he sought to discredit Governor Velázquez and Narváez. He commissioned his confidant Alonso de Mendoza to take the letters to Spain, but due to bad weather, the Mendoza could not depart until March 1521. Cortés also sent Alonso de Ávila and Francisco Álvarez Chico to Santo Domingo to buy weapons, ammunition, and horses, and to enlist the support of the audiencia there under Rodrigo de Figueroa. At the same time, he dispatched the still-seaworthy ships to obtain supplies in Jamaica, among other places. As for the disaffected crew members, most of whom belonged to the former Narváez troops, he kept his promise and allowed them to leave. Among them was his confidant Andrés de Duero, whom Cortés gave gold and letters for his wife and brother-in-law in Cuba.[10]

As the Spanish situation consolidated, the Mexica were unable to capitalize on their victory on the Toltec Canal. The celebrations, in which numerous Spanish and Tlaxcala prisoners were sacrificed, were followed by disillusionment on account of the fact that the Spaniards became entrenched in Tlaxcala. Additionally, diplomatic efforts to forge an alliance failed there, as well as with their northern neighbors, the Tarascans. Moctezuma had already begun negotiations with Zuangua, the *cazonci* (ruler) of the Tarascan Empire, which was located roughly within the territory of what are now the Mexican states of Michoacan and Jalisco. The Tarascans, whose empire represented the second strongest polity in Mesoamerica at that time, were feared as warriors. Like the Tlaxcalans, they distrusted the Mexica, which is why the cazonci decided to maintain neutrality. The diplomatic setbacks overshadowed the solemn enthronement of Cuitlahuac in September 1520. His position had not yet consolidated internally, either. He was unable to conduct the customary pseudowarfare by means of which a new ruler usually won victims for the coronation ceremony, proved his strength, and thus ensured the loyalty of his vassals. Civil war–like unrest between a peacemaking and a warring party undermined coexistence. While the former sought an alliance with the Spaniards in order to find a reprieve, the group of war supporters prevailed and eliminated all resistance. Accordingly, the new tlatoani had the damage to the Great Temple repaired and the statues of the gods restored. The fortifications were also repaired and new ones added; the armament was enhanced as well.[11]

Cuitlahuac also tried to block Spanish expansion in the provinces, sending troops to the heavily fortified Quauhquechollan and Itzyocan near Cholula to block the main pass into the Valley of Mexico. However, this strategically vital measure failed when the leaders of Quauhquechollan called on the Spaniards and Tlaxcalans for assistance against the occupying forces. An army consisting of a few hundred Spaniards and several thousand indigenous people joined the battle. The allies won the victory in no small part because the inhabitants of Quauhquechollan exposed the military positions of the Mexica and also attacked the hated occupiers. The army then launched a successful attack on Itzyocan. Both cities got new rulers and joined the allies. Here, as elsewhere, the alliance of Europeans and indigenous peoples pursued a policy that sought to achieve peace by appointing submissive new rulers. In the wake of these military successes, other places in the surrounding area spontaneously surrendered, so the region between Popocatépetl in the west and Orizaba in the east came under the control of the alliance. Increasingly, local rulers turned to Cortés for help in settling disputes and regulating succession to the throne. Resistance flared up only occasionally, and when it did, it could be crushed with smaller expeditionary corps as in the case of Xalatzinko and Ixtacamaxtitlan.[12]

With these victories, the captain general's self-confidence grew and he felt sufficiently strong to take a tougher stance among his own men again. He thus had the entire booty, including the slaves, collected for registration under threat of severe punishment. The royal fifth and the fifth part that Cortés claimed were deducted from it, which triggered unrest, especially among Narváez's men. Juan Bono de Quejo, who announced that he would take legal action against the captain general in Spain, served as spokesman. But even Cortés's most loyal followers were displeased, because, as Bernal Díaz wrote, the "good" female slaves were taken from them and instead "the old and ugly" ones redistributed. The gold that the men had risked their lives to secure in La Noche Triste was also confiscated, and only a third was to be returned to them. Nonetheless, when the crews refused to obey this order, the captain general was moved by the general discontent and announced that he would make the process of distributing human booty fairer in the future. Subsequently, he would no longer pursue the collection of gold.[13]

In mid-December 1520, the Spaniards moved back to Tlaxcala from Segura de la Frontera, where Cortés had a crew of only twenty mostly infirm men. Once there, Cortés learned of the death of his closest partisan, Maxixcaztzin. The Spaniards mourned the deceased in their own fashion. The captain general seized the opportunity to appoint Maxixcaztzin's underage son as the new ruler and had him baptized. Several Tlaxcala nobles, among them Xicotencatl the Elder and the young commander Chichimecatecle, followed suit and received Christian names. The baptism of their princes would later play an important role in the self-portrayal of the Tlaxcalans, as they presented themselves in their chronicles as loyal friends and pious Christians who had stood beside the Spaniards unwaveringly from the start. A more realistic depiction of the events was given by Juan Buenaventura Zapata y Mendoza, a noble Tlaxcala historian of the seventeenth century. He recorded that the Christian priests did not yet speak Nahuatl and instead pointed to heaven with the words "Dios" (God) and "Santa María, siempre verdadera virgen" ("Holy Mary, ever-true virgin") while administering the sacrament.[14]

The stay in Tlaxcala at the end of 1520 was used to plan the great campaign against Tenochtitlan for the coming year. Thus, the Tlaxcala warriors practiced military discipline while the Spaniards repaired their equipment. Since gunpowder was in short supply, Cortés sent two artillerymen to the craters of Popocatépetl to gather sulfur. In addition, on December 22, he issued strict disciplinary orders for his own troops, prohibiting cursing and gambling, assaults on indigenous people of any tribe, and theft of booty. That some basic military matters also appear in this document, such as mustering to the sound of the drumbeat, shows how much discipline in the troops had suffered. On December 26, Cortés and Chichimecatecle held a large troop parade. There were forty horsemen; five hundred and fifty infantrymen, including eighty crossbowmen and arquebusiers; ten small cannons, and about ten thousand indigenous warriors mainly from Tlaxcala, but also from Huexotzinco, Cholula, and Tepeyaca.[15]

The Spanish preparations were facilitated by a development in which the conquistadors were only indirectly involved. As early as 1518, a smallpox epidemic had spread from Hispaniola to the Caribbean, leading to horrendous death rates among the indigenous population, which lacked immunity. The epidemic reached Mesoamerica via Cuba in 1520, where it first devastated the Maya. The disease ran its course over several weeks. No symptoms were observed during the first twelve days. This was followed by three to five days of high fever, aching limbs, and nausea, which was then followed by a rash. This was the time of the highest risk of infection. The rash was accompanied by incrustations that fell off six days later, whereupon fever flared up again. Those who survived were immune to the disease like the Europeans, but most of those affected died. The Spanish

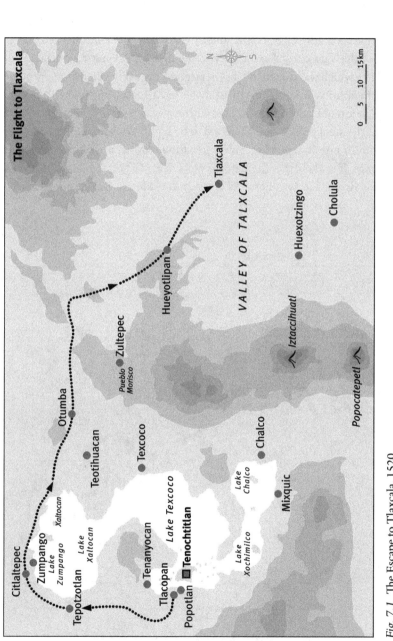

Fig. 7.1 The Escape to Tlaxcala, 1520

chroniclers blamed the outbreak on an African slave, Francisco de Eguía, who is said to have come with Narváez. Starting in Totonacapan around mid-year, the deadly epidemic soon reached central Mexico. The most prominent casualty was the tlatoani Cuitlahuac at the end of November or beginning of December, after he had ruled for only eighty days. The rulers of Tlacopan and Chalco and the cazonci of the Tarascans also fell prey to the disease. A famine associated with the malady, which was due to the loss of farmers, probably killed as many people as the epidemic itself. According to estimates by historians, around 40 percent of the population of Central Mexico died within a year.[16]

While the smallpox epidemic proved to be highly convenient for Cortés, enabling him to install dependent rulers in various towns, it was catastrophic for his enemies. It is likely that the tlatoani was unable to perform his duties weeks before his death due to illness. As a result, the Mexica lacked a leader when

Fig. 7.2 Baptism of the Tlaxcala rulers (Lienzo de Tlaxcala). The Lienzo de Tlaxcala for legitimation reasons claimed that the baptismal act of the Tlaxcala nobles depicted here had taken place several months prior to the actual date and presented it as if all four rulers had been baptized, which was not the case. Smithsonian Libraries and Archives. Internet Archive.

preparing for the next war, and many warriors were greatly debilitated by the outbreak. The Florentine Codex provides a striking description of the impact:

> But before the Spaniards had risen against us, first there came to be prevalent a great sickness, a plague. It was in [the month of] Tepeilhuitl [end of September] that it originated, that there spread over the people a great destruction of men. Some it indeed covered [with pustules]; they were spread everywhere.... No longer could they walk; they only lay in their adobes, in their beds. No longer could they move, ... And when they bestirred themselves, much did they cry out. There was much perishing. Like a covering, covering-like, were the pustules. Indeed, many people died of them, and many just died of hunger. There was death from hunger; there was no one to take care of another; there was no one to attend to another.... At this time this plague prevailed indeed sixty days—sixty day signs—when it ended, when it diminished; when it was realized, when there was reviving, the plague was already going toward Chalco.[17]

The Spanish allies also suffered from smallpox and counted high losses, but it did not lead to such an acute leadership problem for them as in Tenochtitlan. As successor, the Mexica chose Cuauhtemoc, the young nephew of his two predecessors and son of Ahuizotl. Cuauhtemoc was also the husband of Moctezuma's daughter Tecuichpo. The election was a concession to Tlatelolco, since Cuauhtemoc had been ruler of this triple alliance partner since 1515 and supreme commander of the Mexica military since 1520. In February 1521, the month of Izcalli, the new ruler was enthroned, which brought another interregnum that could have ended fatally, given the time pressure. As Bernal Díaz later learned, the new tlatoani was initially inclined to make peace with the Spaniards, but his priests and generals refused to do so because they considered coexistence impossible. Cuauhtemoc changed his mind and swore to fight to the death. Since his position had not yet been consolidated, as was the case with his predecessor, he had several of Cuitlahuac's sons killed to demonstrate his resolve. Like Cuitlahuac, he had the city fortified and stockpiled provisions in the event of a siege. In addition, he sent legations to the neighboring peoples and promised to suspend the payment of tributes if they fought alongside the Mexica. Failing this, he threatened them with complete annihilation. The strategic decision not to leave the Valley of Mexico made military sense, for only in their home region did the Mexica have a sufficiently large following to be able to supply their own troops. In battle on open fields they remained inferior to their enemies. On the causeways, on the other hand, the Europeans were vulnerable, as proved by the Battle of the Toltec Canal. Ultimately, the Mexica elites prepared themselves for the defense of Tenochtitlan and therefore had the rulers of neighboring cities brought to the capital.[18]

Campaigns in the Valley of Mexico

Undoubtedly, the Mexica blamed their gods for the epidemic, just as the Spaniards thanked their god and Saint Jacob for the unexpected aid. In a society like that of the Mexica, the proliferation of unfortunate events would have been interpreted as divine punishment, whereas the Europeans saw their Christianizing mission vindicated—something Cortés never tired of emphasizing in his addresses to the troops. He made it clear to his men that he was striving for the military res-olution in order, as he put it, not to betray God and king.[19] Since the Spaniards were scarcely informed about developments in Tenochtitlan, the captain ge-neral sought a grand alliance with the opponents and vassal states of the Mexica. Those who did not want to join voluntarily were to be coerced. Cortés's next destination was the Valley of Mexico, the heartland of the empire.

Even before Cortés headed there with his army in early 1521, he had already made a decision that showed that he had understood the lessons of La Noche Triste. In October 1520, he had commissioned master shipbuilder Martín López to build thirteen brigantines so that he could gain control of Lake Texcoco. From Veracruz, several hundred indigenous porters transported anchors, sails, and other equipment from the old ships to Tlaxcala. A blacksmith and sailors expe-rienced in shipbuilding followed. The construction of the ships was to be carried out outside the Valley of Mexico so as to surprise the enemies at the moment of the battle. Near Tlaxcala there was enough wood, workers, and, above all, protec-tion from Mexica attacks. The pitch for caulking was extracted from the Tlaxcala pine forests. Once again, the help of the indigenous people was crucial in all the work that needed to be done. The ships were tested on the Zahuapan River, which was dammed especially for this purpose. They were then dismantled for transport to the Valley of Mexico. The ships were about forty-two feet long and almost ten feet wide; the captain's ship measured seven feet longer. At the bow there was space for artillery and crossbows, as well as a reinforcement for ram-ming other watercraft. Half of the ships had one mast, the other half had two. In addition, they were outfitted with oars. The draft of the boats was minimal, allowing them to navigate the shallow waters of Lake Texcoco without risk.[20]

Before the work on the ships was completed, on December 28 Cortés and his army marched via Tetzmollocan into the Valley of Mexico. Their destination was Texcoco. Along the way, there were skirmishes with Mexica warriors who had barricaded the through roads and communicated with each other by smoke signals. In keeping with their new strategy, however, the Mexica avoided an open field battle. Although there were far fewer Spanish soldiers than in the first march over the mountains in 1519, they had many more indigenous allies, and not only Tlaxcalans. The city of Texcoco was a member of the triple alliance and a strategically important location for supplies to Tlaxcala and access to the lake. In the world of the Mexica, the city ranked second only to Tenochtitlan. Since the death of the ruler Nezahualpilli in 1515, a dispute over succession had been smoldering there; the Mexica had only partially resolved this. Moctezuma had succeeded in installing his nephew Cacama. After Cacama fell into the hands of the Spaniards and died in the Battle of the Toltec Canal, Coanacoch, a son of Nezahualpilli, took the reins of government in Texcoco.[21]

After a two-day march, the allied army reached Coatepec, near Texcoco. Shortly before moving into the deserted city, a delegation from Texcoco arrived to meet them; according to Alva Ixtlilxochitl, it included his ancestor Ixtlilxochitl.[22] The envoys offered the commanders peaceful entry and adequate food and lodging, and asked that the city be spared. They blamed the attacks of the previous days on the troops from Tenochtitlan. The allies thus decided to spend the night in Coatepec in order to march from there into Texcoco on New Year's Eve. The march went without incident, but the army once again entered a town where there were hardly any inhabitants. Although the Spaniards sensed an ambush, they took up quarters in the palace of Nezahualpilli. Then they set out to explore their surroundings. From the top platform of the main temple they could see that the population had fled with the tlatoani Coanacoch across the lake to Tenochtitlan. Furious about the alleged betrayal, the army burned and looted the magnificent city and killed or enslaved the residents who had not joined the escape. The royal palaces and the valuable archives of Nezahualpili also fell victim to the devastation. According to Alva Ixtlilxochitl, this was "one of the greatest losses that this country has suffered, because the memory of its history . . . has been lost forever."[23]

Thereafter, Texcoco proved to be an ideal base for further endeavors because of its central location and control of the traffic routes, even though some officers had initially advocated for Ayotzinco as a starting point. Another son of Nezahualpilli, Tecocol, was declared the new ruler; he died soon after, however, so in early February 1521 Ixtlilxochitl succeeded to the throne and was baptized with the Christian name Fernando. Here, as elsewhere, discontented rivals took advantage of the moment to seize power with the help of the Spaniards, while the previous rulers, who had fled to Tenochtitlan, lost all ties with their cities. Ixtlilxochitl, who brought his partisans in the region into the alliance, clearly understood the balance of power so that rivalries could be exploited in a targeted manner. After numerous neighboring towns had voluntarily submitted, the invaders controlled the region as far as Iztapalapa. Some of the new vassals brought with them captured Mexica messengers, whom Cortés released in hopes of encouraging negotiations with Cuauhtemoc, which the latter rejected. The tlatoani, for his part, was anxious to keep the princes of the surrounding city-states on the side of the Mexica and had sent the messengers for this reason.[24]

The strategically important city of Iztapalapa, located on a peninsula in the lake and known to the Spaniards from 1519, was the target of the next military action. With several noblemen from Texcoco and a large portion of the troops commanded on the Spanish side by Cortés, Olid, and Alvarado, the allies moved against the site defended by Mexica units. After the first clashes, the defenders made a tactical retreat, drawing their enemies into the city. The allies rejoiced in the victory, plundering and pillaging and taking quarters in the empty houses. At night, the Mexica flooded the site by opening sluices on the Nezahualcoyotl Dam. The Spaniards, who were tipped off by their new friends from Texcoco, barely managed to escape. Many indigenous warriors, however, drowned. When the battle commenced the next morning, the allies, having lost their gunpowder, had difficulty holding on and had to shamefully retreat to Texcoco. There they spent the next three months, until April 1521.[25]

Despite this victory, more and more villages broke away from the Mexica. These included Otumba and Mixquic, but above all were the important cities

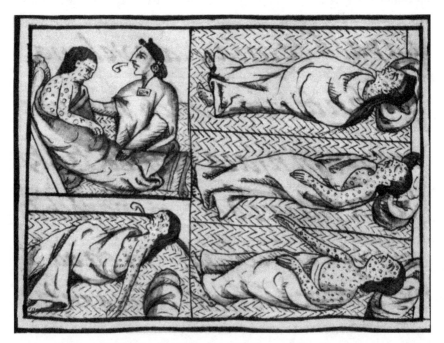

Fig. 7.3 Smallpox epidemic. *General History of the Things of New Spain by Fray Bernardino de Sahagún: The Florentine Codex. Book XII: The Conquest of Mexico* (1577). Library of Congress, https://www.loc.gov/item/2021667857/.

of Chalco and neighboring Tlalmanalco. Those responsible did not act out of conviction, but out of fear of possible retaliation for the past assaults on the Spaniards and their allies, or out of anger over the mistreatment by the Mexica. Cortés apparently accepted the apologies with generosity and declared the peoples vassals of the Spanish king, although the new subjects likely did not understand this status or the respective obligations. As much as the numerous offers of confederation in the allied camp may have been welcomed, they also entailed commitments, for the Mexica warriors took every opportunity to attack the traitors. Smaller villages found themselves caught between the two fronts and were alternately assailed by one side and the other. The allies did not have a sufficient number of men to defend all their besieged partner cities, so they concentrated on the most important ones, such as Chalco. Given that the ruler of the city had died of smallpox, Cortés had yet another occasion to arrange the succession. All of these developments show that Cuauhtemoc's alliance efforts in his own neighborhoods barely bore fruit, despite all of his assurances and threats. In view of Tenochtitlan's dependence on supplies from the surrounding territory, this was quite worrying.[26]

After nearly a month in Texcoco, the moment had arrived at the end of January for bringing the brigantines from Tlaxcala. Sandoval took command of the Spaniards, who were accompanied by numerous Tlaxcalans. En route, the Spaniards took retaliatory action in the town of Zultepec, which the Europeans called Pueblo Morisco: the previous year about fifty Spaniards had perished there and had been sacrificed, and their skulls and those of their horses could still be seen at the town's tzompantli. After the bloody punishment, the troops moved on in the direction of Tlaxcala. When they reached the halfway point, the army was met by Martín López and several thousand indigenous porters and warriors under the command of Chichimecatecles. They had transported the dismantled ships in a formation several miles long to Texcoco, where they were received with great jubilation. This logistical tour de force was followed by the assembly of the brigantines, which took many weeks. Meanwhile, work had already begun in Texcoco on a canal that would shorten the distance to the lake. The Mexica repeatedly failed in their attempts to destroy the ships.[27]

While the shipbuilding work proceeded according to plan, the allies launched their second major campaign, with Cortés himself at the helm. In this effort, he was responding to Chichimecatecle, who recognized the danger that the Mexica might regain the territory they had secured in the meantime, under heavy losses. This time it was decided to move north, first attacking Xaltocan, located on a lagoon in the lake of the same name, and from there go on to Tlacopan. The Spaniards mobilized about half of their men, and Sandoval commanded the garrison at Texcoco. Several thousand indigenous people formed the main contingent of the army. After a two-day march, during which they had to repeatedly defend themselves against attacks, they reached Xaltocan. The city's guardians showed no signs of surrendering, and instead destroyed the points of entry via the dam roads. After fierce fighting, the attackers prevailed and proceeded to plunder and destroy the city. Inhabitants of the village of Tepetzinco, which was the enemy of Xaltocan, had told the Spaniards the location of a ford through which they could gain entry to the city. Afterward, the army moved further south and came to Cuautitlan, whose population had already fled. Five days later, the troops reached the actual destination of the expedition, Tlacopan, by way of the towns of Tenayuca and Azcapotzalco, both of which had been abandoned.[28]

The Spaniards were already familiar with the city, where they had been heavily attacked after fleeing during La Noche Triste. Awaiting them now was a powerful army made up of warriors from Tenochtitlan and the surrounding cities. The grim battle that ensued dragged on for two days. When the allies gained the upper hand, Cuauhtemoc ordered a retreat. At the same time, he sent reinforcements to the dam road to ambush the attackers there; the Spaniards were caught flat footed, and Cortés himself, who was hunting down the runaways, found himself in desperate straits. The men were only able to save themselves with considerable difficulty and suffered heavy losses. Five Spaniards died and there were numerous critically injured. Nevertheless, the allies were victorious and stayed for six days in the conquered city, which they then plundered and destroyed. In their reports, Spanish eyewitnesses blamed their indigenous allies for the murderous rampage. It can be assumed, however, that the Europeans did not hold back either. After all, they were interested in exacting revenge and the spoils of war, which, according to European notions, were the personal property of the soldier who seized them. The Mexica did not stand by idly as their enemies ran riot in the triple-alliance city, but rather launched daily attacks. Reading between the lines, the withdrawal of the allies in mid-February hardly seems to have been glorious. In the end, they were lucky that the Mexica did not pursue them over long distances. In his third letter-report, Cortés claimed that he attacked Tlacopan primarily in an attempt to negotiate with Cuauhtemoc. But the Mexica responded with insults and combat. The time for negotiations was clearly over.[29]

Back in Texcoco, the Tlaxcalans left the Spaniards to take their spoils home. Probably due in no small part to the unsuccessful and costly second campaign, tensions that had boiled beneath the surface among the various interest groups during the fighting made themselves felt among the Spaniards. In the days that followed, Cortés uncovered a conspiracy targeted against him, personally. Antonio de Villafaña, a friend of Narváez and Governor Velázquez, had allegedly enlisted the support of up to three hundred Spaniards in an attempt to assassinate the captain general and his closest associates. Velázquez's brother-in-law, Francisco Verdugo, was to replace Cortés. For a bribe, Captain Diego Díaz intended to bring Narváez and some of the men back to Cuba. The plot was exposed, however, and the captain general, aided by his most loyal companions, arrested the conspirators. In the process, a long list was found; it bore the names of several hundred sympathizers. It was impossible to punish nearly half of one's own troops, let alone imprison them. Therefore, Cortés decided to make an example of Villafaña as a deterrent, but to refrain from persecuting those who knew about the conspiracy. As a warning, he publicly announced that he was aware of the list, which also included many names of those who knew nothing about the plot. Villafaña was condemned to death, and the sentence was quickly carried out. The sailor Díaz was also hanged, after the city council of Vera Cruz had ruled that he should die. From then on, Cortés was accompanied by a body-guard.[30] If the number of conspirators is even approximately correct, this shows how pronounced the fault lines were within the Spanish camp, even after many months of fighting together. The situation quieted down after the hangings, but only somewhat. Much discontent remained, and it was repeatedly inflamed by the distribution of the booty.

Nevertheless, the arrival of further reinforcements in Vera Cruz in early March brought some positive news to the Spanish camp. The recruitment efforts of Alonso de Ávila and Francisco Álvarez Chico had been successful. Conquistador and businessman Rodrigo de Bastidas brought back on two ships from Santo Domingo a large number of adventure-seeking soldiers and officers, weapons, gunpowder, and horses. In the meantime, those in the trading circles in Santo Domingo sensed a promising business opportunity, while, for the ordinary settlers, there was a strong incentive to move on, in view of the crisis triggered by the mass deaths of their indigenous slaves due to disease and mistreatment. Among the passengers was the Franciscan Pedro Melgarejo de Urrea, who carried with him papal bulls that allowed him to grant a special dispensation to the war veterans, and who, as Díaz del Castillo noted, later returned to Castile a rich man. Vázquez de Ayllón had personally outfitted another ship. Among others, Julián de Alderete, who was officially appointed treasurer by the audiencia, came to Texcoco. Thus, while Cortés's enterprise had not yet gained full royal legitimacy, it did acquire that of the highest royal authority in the Indies.[31]

In total, some two hundred new arrivals reinforced the Spanish conquistadors. They reported on the enthusiasm that the news of Cortés's successes had generated among the Spanish settlers in the Caribbean, even if they were few and far between. Cortés himself helped spread the news of his deeds. Finally, the ship was able to set sail for Spain with his letter-report to the monarch written in October, along with large sums of gold and countless gifts from previous spoils of war. In addition to Captain Alonso de Mendoza, Diego de Ordás and Alonso de Ávila, who were to represent Cortés's cause at court, were aboard. The dissatisfied former followers of Narváez were also on board; they were dropped off in Matanzas, Cuba. A stopover in Santo Domingo provided an opportunity to exhibit the valuable works of art, armor, weapons, and other curiosities from the land of the Mexica. Not all the gifts were intended for the imperial treasuries. Cortés not only sent important documents in which he justified his claims to the title of governor for the new countries, but also a large sum of money for his family. Moreover, he had earmarked considerable funds—exactly how much is not known—for bribing influential personalities in Santo Domingo and especially at courts in Spain.[32]

In mid-March, the allies sent a formation to Chalco, led by Sandoval, who was increasingly recognized as Cortés's first deputy. The city and its environs were of great importance because of their location along the strategically significant roads to Tlaxcala and Vera Cruz and because of their corn production. The longer the stay in Texcoco lasted, the more problematic the supply situation became there; the army of many thousands and the many slaves, whose number increased from campaign to campaign, made tremendous demands on the city's resources. The supply from Chalco was therefore all the more vital. But this was also true for Tenochtitlan, which made the conflicts with the Mexica there especially fierce. In March, the Spaniards repeatedly sent armies to the region, whereupon the Chalca called on their new allies for assistance. The allies, joined by a growing number of neighboring villages, continually forced their enemies to flee. When they did not arrive on the scene in time, Chalco successfully defended itself. The Mexica's power base in one of its most important granaries was starting to erode.[33]

Another attack on Chalco in early April prompted the allies to undertake a third major campaign, with Cortés personally heading the Spanish units. The campaign was directed against the region south of the lake, where, despite occasional successes, extensive control had yet to be achieved. It also intended to explore this area for further military operations. After they left Chimalhuacan behind them, about twenty thousand men from Tlaxcala, Chalco, Texcoco, and Huexocingo joined the already formidable army. According to Bernal Díaz, this was the largest allied contingent to date. Regardless, the fighting turned out to be more difficult than expected. The inhabitants of the towns they passed through attacked from hills and greeted their enemies with avalanches of stones. The cities supposedly finally surrendered in the end due to the lack of water. The army moved on through the cities of Oaxtepec, Yautepec, Jiutepec, and Tepotzlan, which were famous for their gardens. There were heavy battles in many locations with the townspeople and troops from Tenochtitlan. In mid-April, the army reached the mountain city of Cuernavaca, which was surrounded by ravines. They were able to take the city despite the inhabitants having destroyed the access bridges. Murder and rape were rampant, women and children were enslaved, and the cities were looted and burned to the ground. In particular, the hunt for

~~young~~ good women as spoils of war—Bernal Díaz spoke of the *"buenas indias"*— was conducted systematically and, along with the greed for gold, was one of the main driving forces of the conquistadors. Cortés's own claim that he was lenient and treated with mercy the inhabitants who submitted to him seems ludicrous.[34]

After several days of rest, the troops continued their arduous journey over the mountain range toward the island city of Xochimilco, which was connected to the mainland by three dams. There the inhabitants remained loyal to Tenochtitlan and prepared for the attack by building trenches and barricades. Because the Tlaxcala sappers filled in the breaches, the allies nevertheless managed to penetrate the city and conquer large parts of it. But then the Xochimilca, whose women and children had already fled across the lake, took on reinforcements from the Mexica, which gave rise to fierce skirmishes. Amidst the tumult, Cortés himself barely escaped after his horse fell. Under these circumstances, the Mexica warriors made a mistake that was typical of their way of fighting: they did not simply kill the captain general on the spot, but tried to capture him alive in order to sacrifice him later. Although they had already discarded this traditional way of fighting during the battles against their allies, they probably clung to it when fighting the commander of their enemies in part for religious reasons. In any case, the conquistador Cristóbal de Olea managed to save Cortés. Some of the captain general's men, who were careless in the frenzy of looting, were less fortunate, however. They were captured and taken to Cuauhtemoc, who had them sacrificed and their body parts sent to allied cities, both to demonstrate his resolve and to dispel any lingering doubts about the Europeans' mortality. The battle around Xochimilco lasted several days, and the Mexica fought both on land and water. In the end, the attackers had to retreat under the onslaught of constant Mexica attacks—but not before burning the city to the ground.[35]

Pursued by the Mexica troops and embroiled in combat, the Spaniards and their allies moved on to Coyoacán, whose inhabitants had fled to Tenochtitlan. After a short stay, during which they destroyed the village's temple and its idols, they marched to Tlacopan, where fierce fighting broke out again. From the great temple of the city, Cortés showed Alderete and the friar Melgarejo the lake and the capital, which they found highly impressive. They returned to Texcoco along the known route, passing through mostly deserted areas and having to defend themselves against the constant attacks of their enemies. Over the course of three weeks, the allies had circumnavigated the great lake. Cortés later claimed that he had conducted the campaign only for reconnaissance purposes, but he was unable to cover up the failure of the operation, which incurred numerous losses.[36]

The campaign had confirmed an important insight, namely that attacking the capital only by land was futile, as it allowed the Mexica to fully leverage their superiority on the water. In addition, the campaign helped to further reduce the prestige and deterrent potential of Tenochtitlan in the region. The mightier the allies appeared, the more cities joined their side. Nonetheless, since the invaders had not yet defeated their most formidable opponent, Tenochtitlan itself, many villages decided to bide their time by alternately reassuring both sides of their obedience. But these pledges were only valid as long as the respective military threat persisted. With this tactic, they followed proven survival strategies of the altepeme, which dated to before the arrival of the Europeans.

Siege and Demise of Tenochtitlan

With the completion of the brigantines in April, the Spaniards had a weapon that could greatly increase their chances of success in another campaign. A special channel was dug out to transfer the ships onto the lake. For this task, the allies mainly used indigenous workers and slaves. Reportedly, eight thousand men worked around the clock in alternating shifts for fifty days. At the end of the month, the ships sailed the lake for the first time. According to Cervantes de Salazar, the launch of the ships was not entirely free of hazards. For this reason, the Spaniards held a supplication service in which they begged God to protect the brigantines. As the pious Cervantes de Salazar wrote: "without [this service] it would not have been so easy to wage war against those who had their houses in the water and so many canoes with which to attack and defend themselves. Cortés, who, like any good caudillo, was ahead of the others in all moral matters, shed so many tears that day and prayed with such devotion that he aroused great piety even among his comrades-in-arms."[37] Doubtless, this was an exaggeration, but the religious dimension was nevertheless an important form of mobilization.

Meanwhile the military preparations were in full swing. The neighboring towns of Texcoco were obliged to supply a few thousand copper or hardwood arrowheads each for the crossbows. According to Bernal Díaz, they were "better than (those of) the Spanish."[38] In addition, the supreme command requested reinforcements from Tlaxcala, Cholula, and Huexotzinco. Twenty thousand men were ordered to bolster the army. Finally, a military review was performed on the day of Pentecost in 1521. According to the sources, the total number of Spanish conquistadors who were standing by to attack Tenochtitlan ranged from six hundred-fifty to nine hundred men. The vast majority were infantrymen; the cavalry probably comprised eighty-six horsemen, plus more than a hundred crossbowmen and arquebusiers. The troops had three large cannons, fifteen culverins, and enough powder, brought by ship from Spain. Cortés again issued a strict order of the day to ensure the discipline of his men in the forthcoming hostilities. In particular, the captain general urged his soldiers to refrain from attacks against the allies, under all circumstances. This was especially important with regard to conflicts over the distribution of booty.[39] He also reminded them that they were Spanish and thus "not worth any less than Romans and Greeks" and that they were fighting for God's cause.[40]

Then the Spanish supreme command divided up its own men. For each brigantine there were twelve oarsmen, six infantrymen, six crossbowmen, a helmsman, and a captain. Since there were not enough oarsmen, the officers assigned soldiers from the port cities to this task. The land forces were divided into three battalions of roughly equal strength. The first was under the command of Alvarado and consisted of thirty horsemen, one hundred and fifty foot soldiers, eighteen crossbowmen, and several thousand indigenous warriors. Alvarado's brother Jorge, Gutierrez de Badajoz, and Andrés de Monjaras were to act as unit leaders. The unit carried two cannons and was to take up quarters in Tlacopan. The second battalion was under the command of Olid and his lieutenants Andrés de Tapia, Francisco Verdugo, and Francisco de Lugo. Their destination was Coyoacán. The third unit was commanded by Sandoval and his sub-commanders Luis Marín and Pedro de Ircio. The indigenous warriors of this force came from Cholula, Huexotzinco, and Chalco. This unit was to march to Itztapalapa, destroy the city, and then move to Tenochtitlan, under the protection of the brigantines, to join with Olid's battalion. The boats were under the command of Cortés, who would embark with his three hundred men sometime after the departure of the land forces. The strategy behind this division of troops was obvious: The commanders had learned from experience in the first three campaigns and concluded that it was necessary to besiege Tenochtitlan and cut it off from its surroundings in order to strike at the provisioning of the city. At the same time, it seems that Cortés also pursued a plan of keeping an escape route open for the Mexica to avoid the total destruction of the city and high losses on both sides.[41]

Cervantes de Salazar concluded his report on the mustering of the troops with the following impassioned words: "It was only with these men, and not with more, that the very brave and happy Cortés besieged the strongest, richest, largest, most populated and most illustrious city in this New World, which has elements within it to be among the first in the Old World as well."[42] What he did not mention was the fact that the Spaniards only made up a fraction—probably around 1 percent—of the troops. A huge army gathered in Texcoco and entered the city in waves of enthusiasm. According to Bernal Díaz, there were cheers to the monarch and a chorus of calls of "Castilla, Castilla, Tlascala, Tlascala."[43] Although the exact number of indigenous allies is unknown, there were most certainly tens of thousands of them. In accordance with Mesoamerican custom, they were recruited from units that were raised among the capultin and led by local nobles and battle-hardened warriors. These troops provided the real strength of the army. The men were not just Tlaxcalans, but came from numerous cities, although not all of them contributed equally to the mobilization. Cholula thus continued to adopt a wait-and-see approach. The leaders of these indigenous contingents had the critical task of coordinating the fighters and ensuring communication in the coming battles.[44]

In May 1521, the decisive campaign began. The mass of the Tlaxcala warriors was deployed in front of the rest of the army to disperse the march. Chichimecatecle discovered that Xicotencatl the Younger, who was to take over a commanding role, was missing. He had garnered the reputation of refusing to cooperate with the Spanish from the very beginning. It is said that he went to Tlaxcala to seize power there and to fight against the strangers. When he did not return despite repeated demands, the chronicles note that he was captured by a ten-man special commando and hauled off to Texcoco. There, he was given a short trial and publicly executed by hanging. If this is how events actually unfolded—which is questionable—Chichimecatecle was thus able to dispose of a rival and Cortés of a potential troublemaker.[45]

In the meantime, Cuauhtemoc was not idle. His spies had kept him informed about the preparations of his enemies. Together with the supreme council, he had the city fortified and sharpened stakes to be rammed into the lake to hinder the brigantines. In addition, iron objects and weapons captured from the conquerors were used to make long lances, for example, which were to be used against the horsemen. The fact that spring was not actually a time of war for the Mexica no longer mattered, as the traditional rules had long since been suspended due to the presence of the Spanish. The Mexica in Tenochtitlan therefore offered sacrifices to the gods and prayed no less fervently, in their own way, than the Christians did. The gods of the Mexica, however, stopped supplying answers through the oracles. Friar Durán, who drew on numerous indigenous sources and eyewitnesses, wrote: "They thought [their gods] were silent or dead, or else they believed that the newly arrived gods had robbed them of all their powers and virtues, and that they now had no more power, and they wept bitterly over this."[46] But the Mexica had no intention of giving up. They were prepared to fight to the death. For this reason, Cuauhtemoc rejected all the messages of peace that Cortés allegedly sent him, right up to the end. According to Durán, the young tlatoani made a speech to his people:

> Fearless Mexica, as you can see, all our vassals have risen up against us. We now have not only the Tlaxcalans, Cholula, and Huexozinca as enemies, but also the Texcoca, Chalca, Xochimilca, and the Tepaneca. Everyone has turned away from us and abandoned us. They have gone over to the Spaniards and are now marching against us. Therefore, I ask you to remember the brave heart and courage of the Mexica-Chichimeca, our ancestors, who, despite their small numbers, dared to

come to this country with its many millions of people. They conquered this whole new world with their powerful arm . . .[47]

According to Durán, the Mexica responded to Cuauhtemoc's invocation of the glorious past with great enthusiasm. However, the ruler had not bothered to provide the city with enough food to withstand a long siege. Surely the tlatoani and his advisors had not forgotten the supply problem; the difficulty lay in the fact that the producers of the food, such as the Chalca, were simply no longer available. Other neighbors took advantage of the plight of the Mexica to enrich themselves by exchanging corn for jewels and gold. The city's dependence on the surrounding areas had become a significant liability. Ultimately, Tenochtitlan lived on the tributes, which were mainly brought to the city across the lake. Even the drinking water came from the outside, since the brackish lake water was undrinkable. The supply was ensured by an aqueduct, which was built at the end of the fifteenth century, under the tlatoani Ahuizotl, and carried water from the hills of Chapultepec into the city.[48]

In the second week of May, the battalions, whose Spanish contingents were commanded by Alvarado and Olid, marched together from Texcoco. Along the way, there were disagreements between the two Spanish captains, which were further inflamed by the allocation of the quarters. A personal animosity developed between them, which Cortés was able to mediate only temporarily through the dispatch of pastor Melgarejo de Urrea and captain Luis Marín. Subsequently, the soldiers traveled along already-familiar paths through deserted villages until they reached Tlacopan. The first skirmishes between the Tlaxcalans and the Mexica took place there, along the causeway, the night they arrived. The Mexica tried to provoke their enemies by shouting out to them and luring them onto the dam.[49]

The next day, after a mass, the army marched toward its first major objective, the destruction of the water pipeline on Chapultepec. After heavy combat, the men fulfilled their mission. From this point onward, the inhabitants of Tenochtitlan were dependent on the few freshwater wells in the city itself. The battles on subsequent days concentrated on the dam. Once again, the Mexica followed their strategy of smashing large craters into the street. While the allies tried to fill the cavities with their sappers, they had limited success, as they were exposed to fierce land and water attacks. According to Bernal Díaz, the allies suffered a defeat and lost many lives. Soon the battalion to which Olid belonged continued on to Coyoacán, where it encountered the same difficulties. Olid and Alvarado parted amicably, but remained enemies. Their subsequent avoidance of contact hampered the coordination of the troops. They cooperated only when absolutely necessary, such as to fortify the road for the cavalry or locate provisions in the hinterland.[50]

Meanwhile, the third battalion of Sandoval's Spaniards had also begun its march. At the end of May, they moved from Texcoco through already "pacified" territory to Iztapalapa. Here numerous houses were destroyed and the first battles with the Mexica, who attacked via the lake, ensued. The allies spotted smoke signals rising from an island in the lake that were apparently answered from other Mexica bases. It was precisely this messaging station on the small rocky island of Tepepolco that Cortés wanted to conquer with his brigantines and the canoe fleet from Texcoco under the command of Ixtlilxochitl. One hundred and fifty Spaniards invaded the island, leaving no Mexica men alive, only women and children. Then, the Spaniards were confronted by a naval force from Tenochtitlan, which had been alerted by the smoke signals. The first great naval battle thus commenced. Cortés was fortunate that a favorable wind had set in; this enabled the brigantines to make use of their speed advantage. He described the scene in his report: "Although they fled where they could, we attacked them head-on, smashing countless canoes and killing or drowning many enemies; it was a splendid sight. . . . And so it pleased our Lord to give us a greater and more glorious victory than we had prayed for and desired."[51] In fact, the brigantines deeply impressed the Mexica. As López de Gómara writes, the Spanish were able to gain control of the lake.[52]

Ixtlilxochitl and Cortés seized the opportunity to pass through the dyke of Nezahualcoyotl, which was destroyed in the first battle of Itztapalapa. Thereupon they led an attack on the well-fortified Fort of Xoloc at the junction of the causeways of Coyoacán and Itztapalapa. The battalion in Coyoacán correctly assessed the situation and simultaneously advanced on land. The warriors benefited greatly from the protection of the brigantines on the eastern side of the dam. The Tlaxcalans fought their way to the frontline in the bloody battle, while Cortés brought ashore three large cannons from the ships and fired on the defenders. The military effect of the artillery was limited, however. A fire that burned the remaining gunpowder prevented further salvos. The captain general was so furious about this mishap that, according to Cervantes de Salazar, "Cortés had to greatly restrain himself so as to not punish the artilleryman."[53] Just how little the traditional rules of warfare still applied to the Mexica is evident from a counterattack they launched after midnight, that is, in the dark. The allies were able to hold their ground, however, not least due to the use of their light artillery, the so-called falconets.[54]

Cuauhtemoc, who took command of the troops himself, divided his warriors into four divisions, three of which were to face the enemies on the causeways. He had planned the fourth as a mobile task force with the goal of preventing the brigantines from making landfall. The ruler himself appeared before his men in a war canoe at the various battle sites to cheer them on. The Mexica undeniably fought with tremendous vigor; they had also adapted their tactics to the new circumstances. To prevent the attackers from advancing, they repeatedly dug new holes in the causeways at night; these became deadly traps for their enemies during daytime fighting. In addition, extra-long lances were employed against the horses. Contrary to their traditions, they avoided open terrain and sought refuge behind rubble and barricades. Hand-to-hand combat on the embankments was certainly advantageous for the Mexica. However, the Spaniards were able to continually discharge their firearms at the defenders, inflicting heavy casualties. At least at the beginning of the battle, Tenochtitlan did not stand alone. In this phase, cities such as Xochimilco, Mixcoac, Colhuacán, Mexicaltzingo, and Itztapalapa continued to support the Mexica and helped to supply the city. This made it possible to hinder the enemy's advance, though not stop it entirely.[55]

At the start of the siege, the Mexica could still launch their own diversionary attacks. Accordingly, they sent a fleet of canoes, their most effective weapon, to Itztapalapa to penetrate the dam there and thus cut off Sandoval's battalion from the rest of the troops. Once again, the brigantines succeeded in thwarting this maneuver. However, after having taken control of the Fort of Xoloc, Itztapalapa had less strategic importance from the point of view of the attackers. Since Tenochtitlan was fed with supplies via the northern causeway to Tepeyac, the allies decided to seal off this passage, originally kept open to provide an escape route for the besieged. For this purpose, the battalion was ordered from Itztapalapa to Tepeyac, where it managed to fight quickly and successfully. A few brigantines were supposed to be positioned there for support. As Cervantes de Salazar observed: "In this way, the great and powerful city of Mexico was completely enclosed so that none of the enemy could get out or in unnoticed."[56]

On the causeways, the bitter and costly battles continued day after day, with no decisive progress made by either side. During the day, the attackers fought their way forward with heavy losses, conquered a number of barricades, filled in trenches, and repaired bridges. The indigenous sappers in particular excelled in this work, which was extremely dangerous due to the constant onslaught. At night, when the enemy retreated to their fortified camps, the Mexica destroyed everything. Even the deployment of night guards at specially erected barricades did not change this significantly.[57] Bernal Díaz described the bloody fighting:

> While we fought, the barrage of hurled spears and arrows was so great that we sustained injuries, no matter how robust our armor was. . . . The Mexica kept deploying new divisions, attacking the brigantines from the roof terraces with a hail of bullets. It was more than hail. I don't know how to describe it. No one will be able to understand it except those who were there, like us. . . . When the night separated us from our enemies, we dressed our wounds with oil. and a soldier named Juan Catalán incanted the wounds and our Lord Jesus Christ truly gave us

strength . . . and they healed quickly. And so we wounded had to fight with our rag-wrapped wounds from morning till night. If the wounded had all remained in their quarters, the companies would not even have had twenty men to go into battle.[58]

During the fighting, it soon became clear that the brigantines gave the attackers a decisive advantage. They always gained the most ground on the causeways when the ships fended off the canoes of the Mexica in a flanking maneuver. Cortés therefore divided the fleet between the various units. Alvarado was supported by four ships, and six stayed with Cortés, who also established his headquarters in Coyoacán. The remaining two were already with Sandoval. The smallest boat was taken out of service because it could not hold its own against the canoes. The crew was divided among the other ships and replaced the many seriously wounded. Also, the brigantines were of vital importance for logistical purposes, carrying troops, materiel, and provisions. In addition, it was possible to post advanced guards on them, which helped to better protect the warriors' sleep at night. However, they were also needed during the night to disrupt the provisioning of Tenochtitlan, which was carried out by supply boats from the cities allied with the capital. This was not entirely successful, though, and so Tenochtitlan's water supply became smaller with each passing day.[59]

Recognizing the danger, the leaders of the Mexica army tried to eliminate the ships commanded by the Spaniards. One night, they lured one of the two patrolling brigantines into a trap. When they tried to repeat this ruse later, the Spanish turned the tables on them, destroying numerous canoes. The Mexica commanders certainly noticed other weaknesses of their enemies. In Tlacopan, for instance, the allies had stationed only a small garrison to protect the entourage of Tlaxcala women who prepared corn cakes and other food for the fighting forces. It is not known whether the few Spanish women who accompanied the conquistadors on their campaigns, such as Isabel Rodriguez, Beatriz de Palacios, María de Estrada, and Beatriz Bermúdez de Velasco, helped them in their work. In any case, Cuauhtemoc tried to cut off this important supply line from the enemy with the support of his allies. The effort ultimately failed because captured officers exposed the plan, probably under torture.[60]

With high losses and only meager terrain gains in the fierce fighting, the attackers decided to change their strategy. Instead of retreating at night to their quarters behind the lines, they occupied the more spacious areas on the causeways, which were secured in a makeshift fashion and guarded around the clock. The canals were supposed to be filled up with rubble from the destroyed houses in order to create further passageways for advancing. The first targets of this round of attacks were those buildings whose roof terraces the Mexica used to lob their projectiles. The new style of combat also meant that the battles continued at night, making the war seem interminable. Bernal Díaz, who provided the most detailed description of these battles in his report of over a thousand pages, doubted whether the fighting could even be depicted:

> I understand all too well that readers get tired of hearing about the daily skirmishes, but I cannot restrict myself any further, because we were fighting a war, day and night, that dragged on for ninety-three days . . . I am not even recounting here all the details of what we went through each day, because it seems to me that would be too long-winded, and then, like Amadís [de Gaula] and the other chivalry novels, we would never reach the conclusion.[61]

Nonetheless, the battles introduced a new element to the attackers' strategy. Around June 9, the army commanders decided to bring the war to the city. Flanked by brigantines on the water, they aimed to attack from the west, north, and south simultaneously in a combined assault. The southern battalion was headed by Cortés, who declared Axayacatl Palace, where the Spaniards had resided until La Noche Triste, to be a rallying point for the troops. After a series of bloody clashes, the attackers reached the city gate, the Gate of the Eagle, where the bridge had been demolished.[62] The brigantines were used as pontoons to facilitate the crossing and, thanks to the artillery fire, the Spaniards and their allies successfully entered the city. The Spaniards' enemies, who had not set up any barriers, obviously had not anticipated this turn of events. Thus, the further the Spanish advanced, the easier their task became. The invaders were even able to penetrate the district of the Great Temple. Their forces were overstretched, however, and they met with the bitter resistance of the combined forces of the Mexica. Since the north and west battalions were still far from the city center, the attackers managed to save themselves only by leaving behind a valuable piece of artillery that the Mexica subsequently sunk in the lake. All the same, the Spaniards had sufficient time to destroy numerous buildings in order to facilitate their next incursion.[63]

In the weeks that followed, there were further raids on the city center, resulting in the destruction of the Palace of Axayacatl, among other things. The war increasingly turned into a campaign of annihilation that devastated Tenochtitlan. However, the attackers' goal of forcing the Mexica to surrender proved elusive. The defenders were still able to tear down bridges, destroy the causeways, and drive back their opponents, at least sporadically. And so the fighting raged back and forth. The warriors ambushed Alvarado's battalion on the causeway of Tlacopan, inflicting heavy casualties because the brigantines could not get close enough due to the stake barriers. Still, the Mexica were not able to regain the offensive. For the defenders, it was particularly distressing that allied cities such as Iztapalapa, Mixcoac, and Xochimilco sided at least half-heartedly with their enemies Thanks to the mediation of Ixtlilxochitl.[64] By the end of June, the captain general came to an important realization:

> When I saw that the inhabitants of the city were so resistant and so determined to die or defend themselves, I concluded two things: first, that we would get little or nothing of the treasures they had taken from us; second, that we would be forced to completely destroy the city.[65]

Allegedly, the latter observation weighed especially "heavily on the soul" of Cortés, for he had originally announced that he would hand over the magnificent city, intact, to his monarch.[66] It is debatable how heavy this burden actually may have been. In any event, the now-impatient captain general was not dissuaded from preparing the deathblow for Tenochtitlan toward the end of June. According to Bernal Díaz, he convened a war council that included Alvarado and Sandoval, and Cortés presented his captains with a plan to advance to the marketplace of Tlatelolco, unite the battalions there, and set up camp. According to Bernal, Alvarado's regiment, to which he belonged, voiced serious reservations about the plan, because of the danger of being encircled. This view was even expressed in writing: "so that we would not end up like we did when we fled Mexico." The concern was that they would once again be blamed for a plan they had not approved.[67] In Cortés's letter-report, however, the situation looked rather different. According to him, he hesitated to venture deeper into the city, hoping for the surrender of the enemy and fearing the risks. And yet: "When the Spaniards, who had now been fighting continuously for twenty days, noticed the delay, they pressed me to . . . take the marketplace. . . . When I resisted, your majesty's treasurer [Alderete] told me that the whole camp was in support of it and that I therefore had no choice."[68] The question of who exactly bore responsibility for the decision would prove important later on. For the time being, however, the decision was made to attack the next day from three sides, all the way to Tlatelolco. Again, the old and new indigenous allies, who had thousands of warriors and all the canoes at their disposal, would bear the greatest burden.

The target of the attack, Tlatelolco, had gained new significance with the siege. So far, the Tlatelolca had been largely spared from the fighting, having defended themselves more successfully against the invaders than the Tenochca in the south of the city area, who had to fend off the main brunt of the attacks. Tlatelolco thus now found itself in a position to make demands on its neighbors, to whom they had been tributary since their defeat in the fratricidal war of 1473 and to accuse them of weakness, even cowardice. Apparently, there was at least one unsuccessful attempt by the Spanish to draw the Tlatelolca to their side. Going forward, the district demanded a leadership role in the triple alliance from the Tenochca. It seems that under the pressure of the invaders, Cuauhtemoc assented and, in June, he moved his headquarters to the palace of Yacalulco, near the great marketplace. The most important divine statues were also transferred to Tlatelolco. By and large, the army and population of Tenochtitlan also retreated there.[69]

It was on this day that, from the Spanish perspective, "the wheel of fortune turned in the wrong direction . . ."[70] The advance, which, according to the Annals of Tlatelolco, was under the command of Ixtlilxochitl, at first seemed successful. Although the three troop units were engaged in heavy fighting, the invaders apparently advanced according to plan. They overcame barricades and pursued the enemy, which was forced to retreat further and further. What they failed to realize, however, was that the warriors were leading them into an ambush. During a counterattack, the Mexica succeeded in driving one of the enemy units into a trench that had not been filled in. Due to this tactical mistake, Cortés put himself and his unit in mortal danger. Only at the cost of his own life was Cristóbal de Olea able to save the captain general from certain death a second time. According to Cortés's own report, Antonio de Quiñones, the captain of the bodyguard, had to literally drag him off the battlefield to get him to safety. In the face of the terrible fate of so many of his men, he allegedly would have preferred to "die fighting."[71]

The attack turned into a panicked escape. For their part, the Mexica succeeded in capturing numerous enemies alive. They immediately cut off the heads of some of them and threw the bloody skulls at the feet of Alvarado and Sandoval's units, who were still unaware of the disastrous turn of events. As the enormous drum of the Great Temple sounded, the attackers rightly suspected that the first prisoners had been sacrificed. The drum was accompanied by the call of the horns, which spurred on the fighting frenzy of the Mexica. In the meantime, all the invading battalions were retreating to their camps, under heavy attacks that lasted well into the night and left many dead and wounded. As Bernal Díaz remarked, it was due to the heavy artillery that the attacks of the pursuers at last slowly subsided.[72] But the night still held a terrible spectacle in store for the Spaniards and their allies, which Bernal described in extraordinarily vivid detail:

> After we had finally found refuge near our camps, . . . the drums of the Huitzilopochtli and other timpani, shell trumpets and horns, could be heard making a terrifyingly plaintive sound. We saw how they violently herded our comrades . . . under blows and thrusts up to the high temple for sacrifice. We saw how they put feathers on the heads of many of them on the platform, where they had the chapels with their cursed idols and forced them to dance with something like fans in front of

Huitzilopochtli. Then they laid them on their backs on sacrificial stones and cut open their chests with great flint knives to pluck out their throbbing hearts and offer them to their idols. They pushed their bodies down the temple steps with their feet.[73]

The cruel spectacle produced its intended effect—the sight shocked the survivors to their core. Díaz del Castillo, who found little to blame for Cortés in his chronicle, described a captain general who seemed weak and overwhelmed by the situation. Paralyzed by his mistake while the fighting raged on, he tried to shift the blame to Alderete, who allegedly disobeyed his orders in battle and thus triggered the panic. The other captains were stunned by Cortés's self-pitying behavior and were shaken by the heavy losses, which included numerous brigantines. Nevertheless, the Mexica once again failed to decisively pursue their badly beaten enemies, who could rest and regroup in their additionally fortified camps despite ongoing defensive skirmishes.[74]

From the Mexicas' point of view, this day was undoubtedly one of the greatest triumphs in the history of the struggle for their capital, which had been steeped in disappointments. The victory was also symbolically charged by the capturing of the Spanish banner. The Florentine Codex describes the scene from the Mexica point of view:

The brave warriors who had lain crouched then all together threw themselves upon [the Spaniards]. They quickly forced them to run along among the houses. And when the Spaniards saw this, they were just like drunk men. Thereupon captives were taken. Many Tlaxcallans, Acolhuans, Chalcans, Xochimilcans, etc., were taken. Indeed in abundance they were made captive, indeed in abundance there were slain. Indeed they forced the Spaniards and all the [allied] people into the water. . . . And thereupon they brought the captives there to Yacacolco. Each was forced to go. They went rounding up their captives. One went weeping; one went singing; one went crying out while striking the mouth with the palm of the hand. And when they made them reach Yacacolco, thereupon they were put in rows. They were put in rows. One by one the multitude went to the small pyramid, where they were slain as sacrifices. The Spaniards went first; they went first. But only at the last, following, were all the dwellers of the allied cities. And when they had all been slain as sacrifices, then they strung each of the Spaniards' heads on the [skull rack] staves. Also they strung up the horses' heads. They placed them below. And the Spaniards heads were above. As they were strung up, they were facing the sun. . . . And of Spaniards overtaken there were fifty-three. And there were four horses."[75]

The victory not only gave the Mexica a tremendous boost, but the high priests also predicted a favorable outcome of the war in only eight days. Cuauhtemoc quickly seized the opportunity to send messengers to Chalco, Xochimilco, and other provinces. They presented the skulls and bones of horses and conquistadors, proclaimed the prophecy of their high priests, and, with the threat of severe punishment, called upon the provincial rulers to rejoin Tenochtitlan's side. The Europeans' vulnerability to defeat had once again been demonstrated. The Mexica mocked their enemies. They also continued to wage psychological warfare by sacrificing their prisoners in the days that followed. In fact, most cities in the immediate vicinity of the lake broke away from the allies and took a wait-and-see attitude. Only a few allies, such as Ixtlilxochitl and Chichimecatecle, remained loyal to the Spaniards, but their troop contingents had shrunk considerably due to casualties and desertions.[76]

In addition, there were disturbances in the outlying areas. Messengers from allied Cuernavaca reported that the neighboring town of Malinalco, allied with Tenochtitlan, attacked them. Despite the urgency of his own predicament, Cortés promptly dispatched Captain Andrés de Tapia with a small force to "pacify" the region. This was important not only because the (albeit weakened) control over the hinterland remained a lifeline for the Spanish. It was crucial, too, for the Otomí, who had turned to the Europeans because of threats from Matalcingo. The captain general again assigned a unit under Sandoval to protect the allies and to punish the "rebels," as Cortés called them. Both expeditions proved successful, which instilled fresh courage in their allies. A contributing factor to a change of heart was the fact that Chichimecatecle, who had been disappointed by the inaction of his Spanish allies, made a new advance into Tenochtitlan with four hundred men and successfully fought his way to the city.[77]

The most important driver of the new tactic, however, lay in the catastrophic supply situation in the Mexica capital, which deteriorated daily. True, the invaders also repeatedly suffered from hunger, as Bernal Díaz reported in detail, but they were still able to access the hinterland for supplies. Despite the loss of a number of brigantines, the attackers, together with the canoes of the indigenous allies, managed to restore the siege ring, having learned to avoid the stake barriers. According to Brother Durán, "more people died of hunger than from the iron" of the Spaniards.[78] The Annals of Tlatelolco reported that the inhabitants even ate the wood of the tzompantlis.[79] Sahagún's eyewitnesses described the dire circumstances in the most vivid terms:

> There was famine. Many died of hunger. No more did they drink good water, pure water. Only nitrous water did they drink. Many people died of it. And many people thus contracted a bloody flux; because of it they died. And all was eaten—the lizard, the barn swallow, and maize straw,

and saltgrass. And they gnawed *colorín* wood, and they gnawed the glue orchid and the frilled flower, and tanned hides and buckskin . . . Never had there been such suffering. It terrified one, when they were shut in, that indeed in large numbers they died of hunger. And quite tranquilly [the foe] pressed us back as if with a wall, quite tranquilly they herded us.[80]

In view of their plight, it is hardly surprising that the Mexica were no longer able to strike a decisive blow against their enemies. Thus, even after a fortnight, the prophecy of their priests still had not been fulfilled. This was opportune for the Spanish, as the allies from Texcoco, Cholula, and Tlaxcala, who had taken the prophecies and the supposed strength of the Mexica seriously, returned with fresh troops. Cortés greeted them cordially, though he also admonished them for their desertion. He further promised them abundant spoils if they supported him in the looming decisive battle. Finally, he asked the allies to spare the conquered city districts, still hoping to take possession of at least parts of the city without destruction. The fact that the military prospects were viewed more positively was also due to the reinforcements that came from Vera Cruz, where a ship had arrived with gunpowder, weapons, and new recruits.[81]

The final attack against the Mexica capital would go on for several weeks. The invaders resumed their attacks in mid-July and, although they met with stubborn resistance from the defenders, it weakened gradually. What remained for the Mexica was the courage that comes from desperation and the determination to fight to the bitter end. Cortés could not fathom this, writing in his report: "When I saw that the city's inhabitants were more rebellious and determined to die than any generation before them, I didn't know what to do . . . without destroying their city, because it was the most beautiful place in the entire world."[82] Nevertheless, the captain general decided to intensify his warfare in order to break the Mexica's will and finally prevail: "[So I decided] that as we advanced through the streets of the city we would demolish all the buildings on both sides, so that we would not make a step forward without having devastated everything and turned the water into solid ground."[83] Cortés entrusted this task of annihilation to the indigenous sappers, who were well versed in razing cities.[84]

The new strategy was prepared meticulously. After a few days of ceasefire, the allies attacked again with even greater ferocity, thoroughly executing the work of destruction. During the struggle, Ixtlilxochitl managed to capture his brother Coanacoch, who led the loyal Texcocas in the army of the Mexica. At this moment, the troops from Texcoco changed sides.[85] The attackers were able to advance during the day with relatively little difficulty to the temple district of Tenochtitlan, where Cortés would regularly climb the highest temple to demonstrate his power to the Mexica. The conquerors systematically filled in the trenches and also gained full access to the Tlacopan causeway, enabling them to move freely in the center of Tenochtitlan. The emaciated and decimated Mexica no longer had the strength to reopen the trenches at night, as they had previously. Toward the end of July, Alvarado's battalion gained access to the marketplace of Tlaltelolco for the first time. They were unable to hold it at first, since the Mexica had stationed the majority of their warriors there. On the next day, Alvarado's troops were able to join up with Cortés' men. The captain general climbed the main temple of Tlatelolco, where he found the heads of his sacrificed comrades. However much the sight may have shocked him, he relished the fact that almost ninety percent of the city was in the hands of the attackers and that their advance could not be stopped. Sheer necessity resulted in a tendency to disband, at least among the civilian population. Nevertheless, the prospect of falling into the hands of the enemy was hardly better than starving or dying of thirst. Indeed, as Cortés himself reported: "Our allies treated the prisoners with such cruelty that they did not leave a single one alive, even though we rebuked and punished them."[86]

Faced with these new developments, the Mexica started to weigh the option of opening negotiations. For this, the Spaniards were more likely to be their interlocutors, as their indigenous enemies had the greatest interest in the complete destruction of the city. The initial efforts, however, oscillated between propaganda, ambushes, and desperate attempts to buy time. According to Spanish sources, Cortés consistently responded to the Mexica's offers to negotiate, even after he had been deceived several times. In turn, he probably also made several offers to negotiate. For example, he reportedly sent three high-ranking prisoners with an offer of peace to Cuauhtemoc, upon which the royal council consulted. This is confirmed by the Annals of Tlatelolco. The tlatoani is said to have been personally inclined to stop the fighting, because the enemy controlled almost the entire surrounding area, and the supply situation was catastrophic. His advisors, however, spoke out against this idea. So far, they argued, all the concessions made to the enemy, chiefly by Moctezuma, had only ever brought disadvantages to the Mexica. The priests, who undoubtedly had the most to lose in a surrender, underscored this rationale, predicting the favor of the gods and imminent victory. As a result, Cuauhtemoc is said to have in the end opposed further negotiations.[87]

The last assault on Tlatelolco took place in August. Despite the defenders' frantic resistance, the invaders were soon able to move freely around the huge marketplace and, above all, to use their cavalry in a more targeted manner. A short time later, they even set up their headquarters there. Cuauhtemoc was forced to retreat to the eastern part of the district, which was surrounded by water. Once again, the Mexica seem to have made an offer to negotiate, but this turned out to be a deception. In a two-day cease-fire unilaterally declared by Cortés, the last contingent of fighters used the opportunity to build more barricades and trenches. The Spanish allies, whose number ran into the thousands and who were impossible to rein in, did not stick to the moratorium, anyway. Yet the appalling example of the massacres, allegedly committed only by the indigenous warriors, made surrender less attractive. As Cortés wrote, the atrocities cost the lives of tens of thousands of half-starved elderly people, women, and children who were desperately trying to flee. The Tlaxcalans were getting ever closer to their war aim: the complete destruction of Tenochtitlan.[88]

But the sense of desperation was also great among the Mexica warriors, so they took the last possible recourse. Cuauhtemoc entrusted to the exceptional warrior Tlapaltecatl Opuchtzin the weapons and armor of his father Ahuizotl; this was a unique ensemble, designed both to protect its wearer and terrify its observer. It was called and its wearer became "Quetzalteculotl." He was also given the bow and arrow of the god Huitzilopochtli and assigned four captains who were to accompany him in battle. The tlatoani then said: "May our foes behold it; may they marvel at it."[89] In fact, the Florentine Codex tells us that the enemies froze at the sight of the Quetzalteculotl and fled. The very next night, however, they saw a fire that approached "like a whirlwind. It went continually spinning about; it went revolving. It was as if the blazing coal broke into many pieces" and then struck in the middle of the lagoon.[90] Since the Spanish sources do not mention this natural wonder, this heavenly omen was presumably only later included in the narrative by Sahagún's eyewitnesses in order to explain the demise of the great empire.

A final major attack took place on August 13, 1521, during which the heavy artillery was also employed. Sandoval was ordered to strike with the brigantines from the seaside and to prevent the warriors, especially the Mexica nobles, from escaping. This attack crushed the last stand. According to Alva Ixtlilxochitl, "on that day they inflicted on the unfortunate Mexica one of the greatest atrocities this world has ever seen. The men were completely broken by the wailing of the women and children."[91] According to indigenous sources, Cuauhtemoc went to his enemies in a canoe to surrender, as his people wept and said: "There goes our ruler. He goes to surrender to the Spanish gods."[92] In contrast, the Spanish sources claim that the tlatoani tried to flee across the lake with the highest nobles aboard several canoes, but was captured by captain García de Holguín in the fastest brigantine. His commander, Sandoval, claimed the royal prisoner himself to hand him over to Cortés. There was even a dispute about this between the Spaniards, which the captain general had to settle. In the end, both were allowed to present Cuauhtemoc. Cortés supposedly received him graciously, but, according to Bernal Díaz, the tlatoani said "Master Malinche, I have done what I was obliged to do to defend my city and my subjects. Now I stand before you as

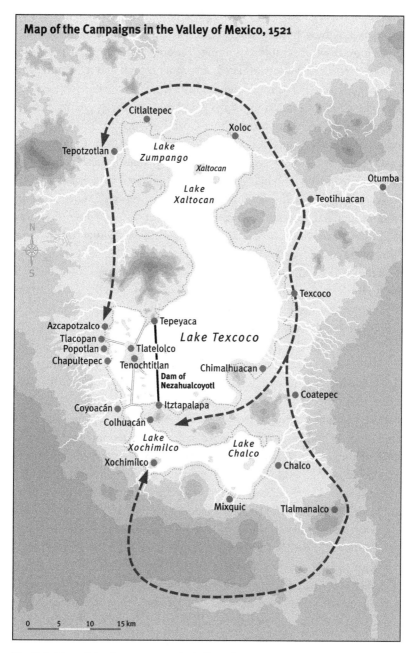

Map of the Campaigns in the Valley of Mexico, 1521

Citlaltepec

Xoloc

Tepotzotlan

Lake Zumpango

Xaltocan

Lake Xaltocan

Otumba

Teotihuacan

Texcoco

Azcapotzalco

Tepeyaca

Lake Texcoco

Tlacopan

Popotlan

Tlatelolco

Chapultepec

Tenochtitlan

Dam of Nezahualcoyotl

Chimalhuacan

Coatepec

Coyoacán

Itztapalapa

Colhuacán

Lake Xochimilco

Lake Chalco

Xochimilco

Chalco

Mixquic

Tlalmanalco

0   5   10   15 km

Fig. 7.4 Map of the Campaigns in the Valley of Mexico, 1521

a prisoner and I beg you: Take the dagger you carry on your belt and kill me."[93] But Cortés did not want to do this, since he still needed his royal prisoner.[94]

After months of acrimonious fighting, Tenochtitlan had fallen. Although, as Bernal reports, a terrible storm raged, it seemed to him and his comrades as if great peace had finally returned after the hellish roar of constant battle. The city was a scene of utter devastation. Corpses and body parts clogged the paths, and the stench of decay was so terrible that Cortés became ill. The few remaining Mexica rose out of the ruins and trudged towards the mainland. They became easy prey not only for the indigenous allies, but also for the Spanish conquistadors, who proceeded to loot and pillage and take the refugees' last possessions. Those Mexica were in fact lucky to get away with their lives at all. Even though the captain general had allegedly promised safe escort, the slaughter continued at will. Those who remained in reasonably good health were enslaved and branded. Women were raped. As the Florentine Codex reports, many women smeared dirt on their faces and dressed in rags in an attempt to escape this fate. Though looting, killing, raping, and pillaging was commonplace on both Mesoamerican and European battlefields at the time, the extent of the atrocities, which continued over several days, unsettled even a veteran such as Bernal Díaz.[95]

On the day after the surrender, the victors called another official meeting with Cuauhtemoc and his highest advisors Coanacoch, the ruler of Texcoco, and Tetlepanquetzal, the ruler of Tlacopan, who had also been captured. All three wore splendid robes that were soiled as a sign of their capitulation. Cortés did not waste any time getting to the point. Through Malinche, who was still performing indispensable translation work, he asked where the gold was that he had left behind on La Noche Triste after fleeing from Tenochtitlan. The princes then ordered all the gold they still had at their disposal to be brought to him. As Sahagún relates, Cortés then exclaimed: "Is this all the gold? That which was guarded in Mexico?"[96] The princes responded evasively. The prime minister (Cihuacoatl) even suggested that only the Tlatelolca had fought from canoes in the Battle of the Toltec Canal. Hence, they must have the gold as well. But Cuauhtemoc made clear that all the gold was seized at that time and that what they had managed to collect was all that they had. Other princes pointed out that it was possible that refugees from the common people had taken some of the gold and that the women hid it under their clothing. Yet, in their greed for the precious metal, the Spaniards stressed that they were by no means satisfied with these answers.[97]

Very quickly the captain general sent the allies home with their share of the loot. Countless Mexica were forced to spend the rest of their lives as slaves in the cities of the victors or were sacrificed there. To celebrate the victory, Cortés ordered a banquet for the Spanish officers and select soldiers. Wine and pork were sent from Vera Cruz, where another ship with supplies had arrived from

Santo Domingo. Due to a lack of available seats, there was dissatisfaction from the start. The conquistadors boasted of their new wealth, which they wanted to use to buy golden saddles or golden arrowheads. Soon most of them were drunk, playing cards, and dancing. Díaz del Castillo, who described the scene extensively, emphasized that there were many faux pas. Making a rather ridiculous impression were the few Spanish ladies who belonged to the retinue and their armored gallants. Friar Olmedo was very angry about the celebration's orgiastic excesses. But Cortés said he could not forbid the exuberance of his men on their day of triumph. The next day, however, the priest ordered a mass with a procession and a sermon, which everyone had to attend to atone for their sins.[98]

One thing that was not considered at the time to be a sin requiring repentance was responsibility for the deaths of tens of thousands of people as a result of the Fall of Tenochtitlan. The Spanish had lost about half of their soldiers since their arrival in Mesoamerica; these numbered about one thousand men. This

Fig. 7.5 Surrender of the Mexica (Lienzo de Tlaxcala). The image shows the enthroned Cortés with decorative quetzal feathers on his hat. Noble Mexica stand before him. The title in Nahuatl says: "This is how the Mexica were defeated." Smithsonian Libraries and Archives. Internet Archive.

was a great loss, but it paled in comparison to the thousands upon thousands of indigenous warriors and civilians who lost their lives on the battlefields while fighting alongside and against the Europeans. Of course, the Mexica suffered the most, losing almost their entire leadership, but also countless women and children. Nevertheless, they were by no means annihilated. Not even their city had been entirely destroyed, although the ruins in August 1521 may have suggested otherwise.[99]

Endless Conquest

With the Fall of Tenochtitlan, the most important, but by no means the only center of power in Mesoamerica before the arrival of the Spaniards, was lost. The battles of the previous years had shown that it was precisely the diversity of states and the rivalries among them that made such a powerful state, such as that of Mexica, vulnerable to defeat. But what followed the conquest? The indigenous city-states allied with the Spaniards had achieved their goal. At first glance, they seemed to be the actual victors, not the Spaniards, who had taken possession of a destroyed city but not gained hoped-for riches from it. A new political order was in the cards, one in which the Europeans could play an important role, but did not have to. The reason they did so was due to the continued fluidity of the Mesoamerican political landscape and the logic of Spanish colonization in the New World, which was designed to exploit the country's resources and labor force. For Cortés, therefore, the war was far from over with the Fall of Tenochtitlan. His goal was to consolidate power, supplant the Mexica rulers, and even to surpass them by creating a unified body politic with a single religion. Challenges loomed both in the New World and in Europe, where the crown still had not decided how things would proceed across the ocean. The conquistadors who had fought and suffered great privations were probably not sympathetic to the lofty plans of their captain general. They were interested in gold, and, for their taste, the triumph had yielded far too little of it. The interplay of these motives ensured that the Conquest would endure for decades to come and may well have seemed endless to many of those involved.

The Insatiable Greed for Gold

Cortés set up his camp in the palace of the former ruler of Coyoacán and tackled what he called the "pacification" of the country.[1] Undoubtedly, he regarded himself as the new legitimate ruler, subject only to his monarch in distant Europe.

The captured tlatoani Cuauhtemoc, who remained in office pro forma, was given the task of instructing his subordinates to retrieve and bury the dead from the ruins. Besides this, there was clean-up work to do, and above all the water supply to Chapultepec needed to be restored. In order to protect the brigantines, a harbor was built to the east of the destroyed city. For supplies, the Spaniards relied on the Mexica tribute system. Many rulers, such as Tetlepanquetzal, the tlatoani of Tlacopan, who had been captured together with Cuauhtemoc, remained in office or were replaced by servile deputies. Villages in the Valley of Mexico that had been hesitant during the battle submitted to the new rulers. From then on, they owed obedience to the Spaniards, who, when they had the slightest suspicion of resistance, used terror tactics in an attempt to nip in the bud any future uprisings. Even weeks after the surrender, numerous local rulers and other officials—especially priests—were arbitrarily murdered.

One reason for the persecutions was the problematic supply situation, which hindered the required tribute payments. This was due less, however, to a resistant attitude on the part of the producers than to the destruction caused by the prolonged war.[2] Another reason for the atrocities was the Spaniards' concern with recovering lost treasure. Specifically, the search for the gold lost on La Noche Triste was given the highest priority. The Spanish busily continued to gather everything they could find, which, as Bernal Díaz reported, was "very little."[3] Disappointment prevailed among the conquistadors, and a rumor arose that Cuauhtemoc had all the riches dumped in the lake a few days before the fall of his city. Others suspected that the captain general had set aside a large sum for himself, a slander that would stick to Cortés for some time and result in legal problems. Allegedly, under pressure from his men and especially the royal treasurer Alderete, the captain general, who recognized the danger of these suspicions, agreed to interrogate his prisoners under torture.[4]

In fact, the martyred Mexica, who had the soles of their feet burned, among having been subjected to other kinds of torture, confessed that some treasures had been submerged in the lake and gave clues as to where they were hidden. In the end, only small amounts of gold were found. Even the best Spanish divers found hardly anything. Cortés also tried to blackmail one of his closest allies, Ixtlilxochitl; the latter offered a ransom for the freedom of his brother Coanacoch, but this did not satisfy the captain general. Consequently, Ixtlilxochitl had all the gold of his hometown Texcoco collected, whereupon Cortés showed mercy and released Coanacoch. In any case, the greed for gold still was not satiated. As the Codex Durán reports: "The Marqués [Cortés] had many more Indians mauled by dogs, hung or burned alive so that they would reveal the secret to him," but without success. "The conquistadors shed more tears over this than for the crimes they had committed."[5]

Fig. 8.1 Códice del Aperreamiento. The single-sheet codex from the sixteenth century (ca. 1540) with numerous annotations and glyphs in Nahuatl shows the cruel punishment of a Mexica nobleman in Coyoacán. On the upper left is Cortés with Malinche; on the lower left, the friar Andrés de Tapia, who instructs two indigenous people. At the right margin, there are five more bound nobles who were forced to watch the torture. The Spaniards frequently used this form of terror to instil fear in the defeated and force confessions out of them. Bibliothèque Nationale de France, Ms. 374.

The allocation of the loot thus caused widespread resentment. Cortés had the precious metal melted down and took the fifth part for the crown and another twenty percent for himself. The remaining sixty percent was to be split up. The captains were awarded particularly high shares. What was left over was so meager compared to the large number of conquistadors that, according to Bernal, the soldiers did not even want to accept the payment in the first place. It was simply out of proportion to the costs and dangers they had borne in the preceding years. The discontentment, which was particularly pronounced among the longtime opponents of the captain general and the men of Narváez, was also directed against Alderete. The treasurer, however, emphasized that the small amount of loot to be distributed could be explained by the high share belonging to Cortés and the fact that he had other jewelry reserved for the royal court. The captain general, conversely, claimed that he had summoned the entire army and asked for their consent, whereupon everyone "agreed with great enthusiasm."[6]

Bernal Díaz reports that the enthusiasm was modest, to say the least. He mentions the debts that weighed on the conquistadors: the army surgeons and pharmacists wanted their bills paid and the goods that merchants brought from Vera Cruz were overpriced. In addition, there were forgers on the scene, whom Cortés had hanged as a deterrent. Finally, even the ordinary soldiers had to give back the little gold they had received in order to pay for their slaves. To forestall a rebellion by his men and to keep the hope of acquiring prosperity alive, Cortés sent expeditions into the surrounding countryside. Another reason for the ventures: the Spaniards had discovered Mexica administrative documents that made reference to gold-rich provinces in areas not yet explored by the Europeans.[7]

Beginning in 1521, the troops launched various campaigns from the destroyed Tenochtitlan, which was rebuilt as Mexico City, to the neighboring regions to the north, west, and especially south. In doing so, the conquistadors followed the old trade routes and thus profited from indigenous knowledge. What they usually failed to mention in their reports, however, was the fact that thousands of indigenous allies once again took part in the campaigns as warriors, porters, and retinue. Among these were not only the familiar allies from Tlaxcala and its environs, but also the subjugated Mexica. They provided the vast majority of the fighters, suffered the highest losses, and followed traditional pre-Hispanic ideas of warfare without the Europeans even realizing it. Cortés granted some privileges to the indigenous rulers who accompanied the Spaniards on the war campaigns; they were given the rank of captain and allowed to ride horses. They were also entitled to wear European clothing, and Cortés granted the title of "Don" to especially high-ranking nobles.[8]

After the gold deposits near the capital were quickly exhausted, silver deposits were discovered as early as 1522 in the southwest, in the so-called silver province between Temazcaltepec and Taxco. There was also tin there, which was important as a raw material for the production of cannons.[9] In addition, Cortés instructed Sandoval, together with several hundred Spaniards and several thousand Texcoca under the command of several brothers of Ixtlilxochitl, to march to

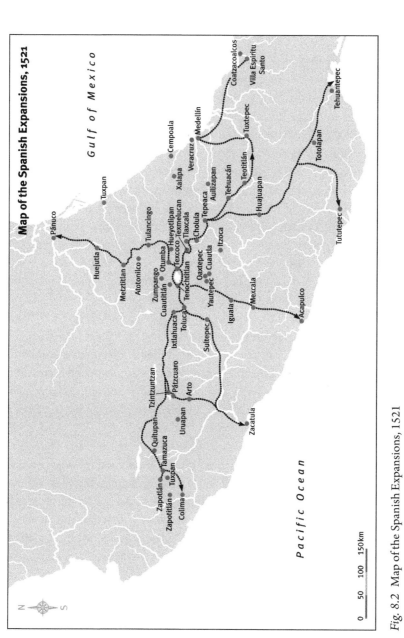

Fig. 8.2 Map of the Spanish Expansions, 1521

Tuxtepec, where they founded a city they called Medellín in Cortés's honor. The purpose of the expedition was, among other things, to punish "rebellious" provinces that had opposed the Spanish during the last campaign. From Medellín, Sandoval moved on to Coatzalcoalcos, where he wanted to look for a suitable alternative to the port of Vera Cruz. Although the indigenous people living there had been friendly toward the Spaniards when they explored the region under Diego de Ordás in 1520, they actively resisted the foundation of a city. Sandoval and his allies crushed the struggle violently. Luis Marín and Bernal Díaz, among others, settled for some time in the new city of Espíritu Santo, located near the mouth of the Coatzalcoalco, and were awarded rich encomiendas. From there, the conquistadors also subjugated neighboring provinces such as Centla, Tabasco, Chinantla, and Zapotec areas in the present-day state of Oaxaca.[10]

Pedro de Alvarado was assigned to the southwest. He headed to the Tututepec region, which was also located in Oaxaca. There he looted a lot of gold, which he was not willing to share with his crew. His men therefore planned a mutiny. The plan was exposed, however, and Alvarado had two soldiers hanged. On the spot where they died, he founded the city of Segura de la Frontera, whose inhabitants came from the settlement of the same name near Tepeaca. Years later, a legal dispute arose between the two men over the loot that the captain sent to Cortés.[11] Captain Francisco de Orozco was also sent southward to Oaxaca, where the Spaniards, based on the tribute lists believed there to be rich gold deposits. Although he formally conquered the Valley of Oaxaca, Orozco did not succeed in completely quashing the resistance of the Zapotecs and Mixes living there. Rodrigo Rangel was ordered to reinforce the garrison at Vera Cruz, while Juan Rodriguez de Villafuerte and Juan Álvarez were commanded to march to Zacatula on the Pacific coast.[12]

There was a special reason for Cristobal de Olid's order to march to Michoacán. The news of Tenochtitlan's fall had spread quickly throughout Mesoamerica. As a result, not only did many of the Mexicas' allies surrender, but their enemies also paid their respects to the victors. Among them was, not least, the cazonci Zinzicha of the Tarascans of Michoacán, who sent a legation to the Spaniards. He had already welcomed three envoys of the Spaniards under Antonio Caicedo in the fall of 1521 and a little later four more under Francisco Montaño. Cortés warmly welcomed the cazonci's delegation, which brought lavish gifts, and he ordered the customary exercises of his riders and firing of artillery. The Tarascan envoys were visibly impressed and informed their ruler of what they had witnessed. When Olid arrived in Michoacán with his army in the summer of 1522, the cazonci initially remained hidden out of fear. Olid plundered the palace in Tzintzuntzan and amassed a considerable treasure of gold, which he sent to Cortés, along with the nobleman Cuinierangari. Cuinierangari was later christened Pedro and wrote down the history (relación) of Michoacán. After

Olid had found the cazonci, he pressed him for more gold. In the end, the dignitary agreed to relocate with the treasure to Tenochtitlan, where he was treated hospitably. He subsequently proved to be a loyal subject of the Spaniards, to whom he had to relinquish his tributes and perform a variety of services.[13]

After the purportedly successful "pacification" of the Tarascans, Olid turned west, where Álvarez and Villafuerte had failed to establish a settlement. In the province of Colima, on the Pacific coast, he led various campaigns to subjugate the smaller city-states there, which had belonged neither to the empire of the Mexica nor to that of the Tarascans. It was not until 1523 that this undertaking was completed, when with Sandoval he founded the Spanish city of Villa de la Concepción de Zacatula, which was used as a port and wharf. Settlers with shipbuilding skills came from Vera Cruz, and, with the help of the Tarascans, brought equipment such as anchors and sails. The main goal was to build brigantines and caravels, for which the region's abundance of wood provided ample material. Cortés, who had already sent small expeditions westward and had taken possession of this stretch of the Pacific Ocean, had great plans for what was then called the "Mar del Sur." He wanted to launch voyages of discovery across the sea and along the coast in order to finally discover the passage between the oceans that Columbus had sought and to open a new sea route to Asia. In his third report to the monarch in May 1522 he wrote: "those who have knowledge and experience of seafaring in the Indies are very sure that with the discovery of the South Sea in this region, many islands rich in gold, pearls, precious stones and spices will open up and many secrets and remarkable things will be discovered."[14]

At the end of 1522, Cortés went to Pánuco in the Huasteca Alta mountains in the far north of the present state of Veracruz. His adversary Garay from Jamaica, who had been acting on royal orders since 1521 and had garnered the title of adelantado of Pánuco, had sent his captain Diego de Camargo there. The captain general, who also claimed this region for himself, wanted to beat him to it. Cortés was also told that the province was in a state of uprising. This was dubious, however, as the province had never paid tributes to the Mexica. With all his captains deployed at that time, Cortés gathered the remaining troops and set out on their march, reinforcing the small band of Spaniards with thousands of Mexica warriors. The heavy fighting against the Huaxtecs resulted in considerable losses, especially among the Mexica.

During the fighting, Cortés's troops stumbled upon the severed heads of some of Camargo's men. The survivors had made their way to Vera Cruz. The combat lasted several weeks before the troops were able to break the indigenous resistance. At the end of December 1522, Cortés founded the Villa de Santesteban del Puerto, today's city of Pánuco. It included a garrison of 130 citizens (vecinos) endowed with encomiendas, including several horsemen and crossbowmen, with Pedro Vallejo as captain. Here, as in the other regions, the conquerors' strategy was to hang rebellious caciques and put compliant ones in their place. Cortés incurred high costs from the expedition, and he later unsuccessfully sought to gain reimbursement from the crown. Malinche, who best understood the details of the indigenous constellations of interests, remained his most important advisor. When in doubt, she was the one who gave advice as to which old elites should be dethroned and which new and submissive ones should be installed.[15]

Despite all the progress that had been made, the conquests in Mesoamerica in the 1520s were by no means over. In some regions, the Spaniards and their allies, who continued to bear the brunt of the fighting, also encountered stubborn opposition from the indigenous inhabitants. This was the case, for example, with the Yucatán, whose conquest under Francisco de Montejo and later his son of the same name, dragged on for decades after 1527. Only after several unsuccessful campaigns and the suppression of an uprising in Valladolid in 1547 did it formally conclude, at least in the eyes of Spanish chroniclers. In reality, numerous Maya groups managed to hold on to their autonomy for centuries. The campaigns to the north, in particular, revealed that these were vast territories that the conquistadors only partially explored—if at all—and took possession of for the crown. Neither the president of the first audiencia, Nuño de Guzmán, who led a particularly brutal campaign of conquest in Michoacan in 1530 and 1531, nor Viceroy Antonio de Mendoza ultimately achieved the desired "pacification." Again and again, revolts were instigated, and in the far north Spanish rule remained so piecemeal until the end of the colonial period that it was more a theoretical claim than an actual fact.[16]

Consolidation of Rule

Despite his legitimate concern about the possibility of an uprising by the conquistadors, the greatest threat to Cortés's claim to power came not from his surroundings in New Spain, but from the motherland. His situation had not improved following the dispatch of his messengers in 1520. Revolutionary changes in Europe demanded the court's undivided attention. In May 1520, Charles V was forced to leave Spain. He was yet to be crowned emperor but had already to worry about Martin Luther's influence dividing the Church. While Charles himself was considered an alien in Spain, his vice-regent Adrian of Utrecht, later Pope Hadrian VI, was respected even less. The most important cities of Castile, led by the *comuneros* (councilmen), rebelled against the government, which was perceived as a foreign regime. They demanded limitations on the power of the crown and the restoration of the old rights of the Estates Assembly.[17]

Although the uprising temporarily crippled the power and influence of Cortés's great adversary in Spain, Bishop Fonseca, who was responsible for policy in the Indies, as well as that of the proponents of Governor Velázquez, it was unreasonable to expect that the monarch and his advisers would make any crucial decisions under these circumstances. Cortés's father Martín subsequently retreated to Medellín to bide his time. After the defeat of the cities at the Battle of Villalar in April 1521, Fonseca regained his power and once again took charge of the policy concerning the Indies. Fonseca had Cortés most important representative—Hernández Portocarrero—jailed because he had allegedly seduced a noblewoman years earlier. Portocarrero would soon die in prison. Meanwhile, in the fall, Ordás and Mendoza arrived in Seville with the second letter-report and new gifts. They reported for the first time on the splendor of Tenochtitlan. The money they had brought, intended to be used to bribe the court and to be given to Cortés's father, was successfully smuggled past the Casa de la Contratación, the commercial administration for the Indies. Only the crown's share and other funds belonging to Sandoval were left in Seville, where they were confiscated. The two envoys secretly went to Medellín to avoid being caught by Fonseca's agents, who had given orders to arrest all intermediaries of Cortés. From there, the procurators travelled on to Vitoria to the regent Adrian of Utrecht, to whom they delivered Cortés's letters. Adrian was persuaded and even allowed the two of them to bring charges against Bishop Fonseca before the crown council. However, this did not lead anywhere for the time being, and, when Adrian was elected pope in January 1522, he had more important matters to attend to than Cortés's concerns.[18]

A few months earlier, Bishop Fonseca had succeeded in convincing Adrian that his confidant Cristóbal de Tapia, who held the office of inspector of the crown (*veedor*) in Santo Domingo, should assume the power to govern in the new countries. The instructions, which were issued on April 11, 1521, arrived in Santo Domingo in late summer. The audiencia there had no interest in disrupting Cortés's endeavors, but Tapia overcame any reservations of the institution and traveled to Vera Cruz. The instructions declared that Velázquez had financed and commissioned all voyages of discovery and conquest, but that his subordinate, Cortés, had defied his authority by having himself elected captain general. Narváez was also severely rebuked for his conduct toward Judge Ayllón. Tapia was given the order to arrest the accused "for their disobedience," to transport them to Spain, and to confiscate all their property. All the monarch's subjects were obliged to show obedience to and support Tapia, the new vice-regent.[19]

The new mayor of Vera Cruz, Gonzalo de Alvarado, one of Pedro's brothers, received the mandates that had been issued in the name of the crown, but he reserved the right for himself and the members of the city council to examine the documents. Tapia, after all, was completely unknown and, Alvarado argued, it would first be necessary to determine how he had obtained the documents. Moreover, Tapia was advised to travel inland to meet with Cortés. At first, there was an exchange of letters in which Cortés offered to meet with Tapia in Texcoco. There was one problem, however: Tapia had also written to the royal treasurer Alderete, who had formed an alliance with Olid. Both were displeased with Cortés's leadership and the distribution of the spoils. They therefore advocated the unconditional recognition of the new governor. In fact, they even planned to conspire against Cortés, along with some of Velázquez's former associates.[20]

When Cortés heard about this, he cancelled the trip to Texcoco. In a letter to Tapia, he justified his decision by stating that an uprising might break out if he left the Valley of Mexico. Instead, he preferred to send his confidant, friar Pedro de Melgarejo, to meet Tapia. Eventually, after some back and forth, the representatives of the town councils of Tenochtitlan, Segura de la Frontera, and Vera Cruz were tasked with verifying Tapia's documents. They asked the captain general to remain in Coyoacán to maintain peace there. The councilmen in question were naturally close confidants of Cortés and among his leading officers. They included Vázquez de Tapia, Jorge de Alvarado, Francisco Álvarez Chico, and Simón de Cuenca, who represented the council of Vera Cruz; Cristóbal del Corral, representing Segura de la Frontera; Andrés de Monjaras for Medellín; Pedro de Alvarado, whom Cortés had appointed as mayor of Tenochtitlan; and Sandoval and several others, who represented the captain general himself.[21]

The meeting took place on Christmas Day 1521 in Cempoala. Upon examining the documents, Cortés's men found them to be genuine and treated Tapia's people deferentially. Nevertheless, they refused to follow the instructions until they had lodged an objection. After all, the documents clearly showed the influence of Fonseca, who was interested only in promoting Diego Velázquez. The councilmen moreover argued that Tapia was unsuitable for the office of governor, as he was unfamiliar with the local conditions and would undoubtedly provoke a rebellion among the indigenous population. Tapia's legalistic responses were not recognized. Ultimately, the inspector gave in, whereupon Cortés rewarded him with some slaves and horses. In exchange, Tapia was to immediately leave for Santo Domingo. When he showed reluctance after receiving a letter from Alderete, Sandoval and Vázquez de Tapia applied gentle force and placed Tapia on board the next ship bound for Santo Domingo.[22]

Having happily survived this threat to his power, Cortés punished all of those whom he even suspected of wanting to submit to Tapia's demands. Olid, among others, fell out of favor, although he still received military orders, such as to join the march to Michoacán. No sooner did Cortés implement these measures to consolidate his power than a ship from Cuba arrived in Vera Cruz under the command of Juan Bono de Quejo, one of Narváez's followers who had been allowed to return. As Bernal Díaz reports, Bono de Quejo believed that Tapia had replaced Cortés as governor. He was equipped with letters of appointment and even with carte blanche from Bishop Fonseca, who had promised great benefactions to all of Tapia's supporters. But Bono de Quejo arrived too late and no longer posed a danger to Cortés, who received him cordially.[23]

In the meantime, Alonso de Ávila had succeeded in championing Cortés's cause before the audiencia in Santo Domingo. The bribes he paid at the behest of the captain general doubtless helped. At the time, Ávila had departed with Portocarrero and Montejo and made a stopover in Hispaniola. While inspector Tapia fell from grace on his return, the audiencia authorized Cortés to conquer all of New Spain, to brand slaves, and to distribute indigenous labor by means of encomienda. These far-reaching allowances were to remain in force until the crown reached a final decision. Cortés had thus accomplished an important secondary goal, because, for the time being, Velázquez no longer posed a danger. The captain general thanked Ávila by appointing him mayor of the new city of Mexico in April 1522 and granting him a generous encomienda. Ávila was not, however, one of Cortés's closer confidants; in fact, he always preferred to keep him "as far away from himself as possible."[24]

What was still missing was the monarch's affirmation. In May 1522, Cortés completed his third extensive letter-report, designed for publication, in which he described the conquest of Tenochtitlan in considerable detail. He added a personal letter to Charles V, in which he expressed his regret about the crown's silence:

> . . . for more than three years I have always reported to Your Majesty and to your Indian Council about the important events in your service, and so far I have received no reply. The reason for this is, I believe, that my letters and reports did not arrive because of the great distance or negligence of the persons in charge of my affairs . . .[25]

Cortés supplemented the papers intended for the monarch with a power of attorney for his father and funds for the latter's use. The conquistadors also wrote a letter in which they accused Velázquez, Fonseca, Tapia, and Garay of having jeopardized the successful conclusion of the war. They also asked that missionaries be sent and, above all, that Cortés's services be recognized. On top of this, there was a treasure trove that measured up to that of the first mission. Among the shipped items were gold, precious stones, pearls, handicrafts (especially feather mosaics), strange rarities such as giant bones, and three live jaguars. A further part of the cargo were some native people and the treasure of the cazonci from Michoacán. The monarch, who was heavily indebted to the Fugger family business in Augsburg that had paid the enormous expenses for his election, was not the only one who received gifts. Other beneficiaries included the crown council, including Cortés's rivals, especially Bishop Fonseca, as well as high-ranking nobles. In addition, the captain general remembered important churches and monasteries in his home country. The recipients were chosen wisely, since they were politically influential personalities and institutions.[26]

Cortés instructed Ávila and his bodyguard Quiñones to transport the valuable cargo on two caravels. Traveling on a third ship, which carried copies of the letters, the messages for Martín Cortés, and smaller pieces of jewelry, was the secretary to the captain general, Juan de Ribera. The three caravels set sail on May 22, 1522. Alderete, who had since become a bitter adversary of the captain general, was also on board, but he died of food poisoning after a few days. There was an incident at sea with one of the jaguars, which broke out of its cage and killed and injured some sailors. What's more, when the ships reached the Azores for a stopover, Quiñones fell victim to a stabbing. Finally, on the last leg of the voyage, the flotilla was attacked by the French pirate Jean de Fleury, who was sailing on behalf of Admiral Jean Ango from Dieppe. Fleury captured the two treasure-bearing ships and took them to Dieppe, where the gold was probably melted down and the rest of the jewels vanished. Ávila fell into French captivity. Only the ship with Ribera managed to safely get to Spain, where it arrived in November 1522.[27]

A lot had changed in Spain. Charles V, back in the country since July 1522, moved the court to his capital, Valladolid. By that time, the conquest of Tenochtitlan had been known about for around three months. Charles V finally got to read the first letters from Cortés. In order to negotiate Cortés's dispute with Velázquez, he convened a commission of which Bishop Fonseca was no longer a member. This was at least partly attributable to the influence of Pope Hadrian. Fonseca's protégés also lost their posts. The special commission was headed by the Italian grand chancellor Mercurino Gattinara. The members examined the documents in their possession and interrogated eyewitnesses, with advocates and opponents of Cortés alike having their say. In the end, the success of the conquest was decisive, but Cortés was also helped by the fact that Velázquez had disregarded instructions from the audiencia of Santo Domingo. The commission thus decided in Cortés's favor and granted him rule in New Spain, while the governor had to undergo a formal investigation.[28]

The authorizations and instructions signed by the emperor in Valladolid on October 15, 1522, were comprehensive, as they formed the basis for the government of New Spain. In the letter of appointment, Cortés was given political, military, and judicial power over the new country, which the emperor officially called New Spain. He also received the titles of governor, captain general, and chief justice and was granted the authority to fill all offices in New Spain and to dismiss officials. Furthermore, Charles V expressed his fullest confidence in

Cortés and promised to forbid any action by Velázquez against him. Beyond this, it was also important that the "Indians" be treated well and instructed in matters of faith.[29]

While these provisions were entirely consistent with Cortés's desires, the second letter contained some items that might result in conflicts. Thus, the emperor announced the dispatch of his officials Alonso de Estrada as treasurer (*tesorero*), Gonzalo de Salazar as administrator (*factor*), Rodrigo de Albornoz as accountant (*contador*), and Pedro Almíndez Chirinos as inspector (veedor). These officials were required to abide by Cortés's authority, who in turn was expected to treat them well and with respect. In another decree, Charles V specified the salaries of his commissioners. Cortés was awarded a much lower salary than the royal officials. Finally, specific instructions followed in June 1523 concerning the treatment of the indigenous population in the newly conquered territories; they prohibited the right to demand tribute (repartimiento, encomienda) from the indigenous population.[30]

Shortly after the documents were signed, the ship with Ribera and the latest reports arrived in Spain, and the news of Cortés's exploits began to spread throughout Europe. Pietro Martire vividly described what had transpired in New Spain. Although most of the treasure was lost, the Italian humanist was impressed by the artifacts that Ribera showed him and by the simulated struggle and human sacrifice that the Mexica who had been transported to Spain had to perform in their original dress. He was particularly fascinated by their game played with rubber balls.[31] From a European perspective, the story of the conquest of the exotic Mexica Empire's capital resembled a knightly romance, whose hero was unquestionably Hernán Cortés. For the moment, his fame seemed assured.

The exhibition of Moctezuma's so-called hospitality gifts, which Charles V had displayed in Spain and the Spanish Netherlands, caused quite a stir. Albrecht Dürer, who observed the objects in Brussels in 1520, wrote with astonishment in his diary:

> I, too, have seen the things that were brought to the king from the new golden land; a very golden sun, a whole fathom wide, likewise a very silvery moon, of the same size, likewise two chambers full of armor, likewise of all sorts of weapons, armor, ordnances, marvelous weaponry, strange clothing, bedding, and all sorts of marvelous things for multiple use, which are so much more beautiful to behold than some fantastical things. These things have all been exquisite, that one estimates them to be worth a hundred thousand guilders. And all my life I have never seen anything that has so pleased my heart as these things. Because I saw in

them wonderful artistic things, and was amazed at the subtle genius of people in foreign lands. I do not know how to express the things that I saw there.[32]

Not all the onlookers were as artistically minded as the painter or Pietro Martire. The gold objects were soon melted down, while the other items made their way to princely libraries, treasure chambers, and curiosity cabinets as exotica.[33]

In addition to the objects briefly made available to a restricted public, it was above all Cortés's letter-reports that contributed to the spread of his fame. Although the conquistador had written his letters as accounts for the monarch and in an effort to justify his deeds, there were many descriptive passages in them that were addressed to a broader audience. He emphasized the beauty and power of Tenochtitlan as well as the discipline and reason in the social structures of Mexica, even though in his eyes they were barbarians because they had no knowledge of God. The comparison with his own European society was inevitable, and Pietro Martire, one of the earliest readers of Cortés's letters, concluded that, in the end, it was purely a matter of taste. For example, the Mexicas' facial jewelry with ear plugs and lower lip piercings may have seemed strange to European observers, and yet: "In this example we see how foolishly people succumb to their own prejudices and how much we indulge in all kinds of misconceptions."[34]

The German-born publisher Jacob Cromberger in Seville issued the second and third letter-reports in 1522 and 1523, while the fourth appeared in Toledo in 1525. The publications, printed with lurid headlines, were quickly translated into numerous European languages. In February 1524, for example, a Latin edition was published in Nuremberg, to which was added the first pictorial representation of Tenochtitlan in Europe. By the time the publication of the letter-reports was banned in 1527 for legal reasons at the instigation of Pánfilo de Narváez, the fame of Cortés and his version of the conquest was already ubiquitous. Although the ban on publication was lifted the same year, there was no new edition in Spain for around two hundred years. The first Mexican edition would not appear until 1770.[35]

The Height of Power

In mid-1522, Cortés could not yet know about the personally promising developments in Europe; it would take more than a year for the royal mandates to reach Mexico. But this did not stop him from acting like a viceroy. Although he usually dressed relatively plainly in "black silk," he nevertheless surrounded himself with a large retinue of chamberlains, servants, and officials. When he traveled, four indigenous nobles rode with him, and he was preceded by officers carrying ornamental maces. As they had done when the tlatoani approached, the Indians threw themselves to the ground when the captain general passed by. On account of his vast power, some contemporary witnesses expressed doubts about his loyalty to the monarch, while others felt there was no reason to question this.[36] When the royal decrees finally arrived in the fall of 1523, and his two most dogged opponents, Bishop Fonseca and Governor Velázquez, died the following year, he undoubtedly felt himself to be at the height of his power.

Cortés had baptized the country New Spain to subordinate it directly to the crown. The boundaries of the new country were not precisely defined in his certificate of appointment as governor. It was in fact impossible to do so because of the lack of geographic knowledge of the region. An integral part of the colonial program was the expansion and founding of new cities. The use of the word "new" in the naming of places or territories would also become established as a model in many European languages, reflecting the colonial attachment to the old homeland. After they consolidated their rule, the Spaniards and their allies were interested in enlarging this "new" Spain, as well as the riches that were suspected to exist, especially in the south.

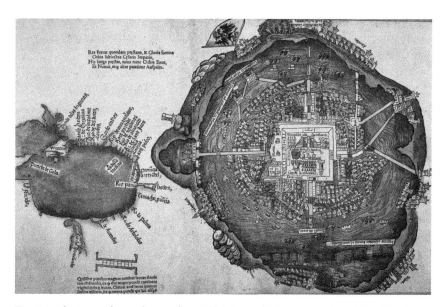

Fig. 8.3 The Nuremberg edition of Cortés's letters of February 1524 contained the first pictorial representation of Tenochtitlan in Europe and was reprinted countless times. The anonymous author claimed that the map was based on an indigenous template, but it is strongly oriented toward European conventions. The map shows both signs of human civilization through the orderly cityscape and barbarism through the human sacrifices in the city center. Map of Tenochtitlan 1524 (Hernán Cortés, Praeclara Ferdinandi Cortesii De nova maris Oceani Hyspania Narratio . . ., Nuremberg 1524). Wikimedia Commons.

Cortés still faced potential rivals even after Velázquez's death. Among others, there was Pedro Arias de Avila, known as Pedrarias, who had been governor of Darién in present-day Panama since 1514 and, above all, there was the ambitious Garay.[37] After his various failures, Garay again assembled an armada of a dozen ships and more than eight hundred soldiers in 1523, and this time he personally commanded the company. At the end of July, he landed north of Pánuco on the Río Palmas and founded the city of Garayana. From there, Garay and his men fought their way through the arduous land route to Santesteban del Puerto. Despite the cordial welcome that Cortés's vice-regent Vallejo extended to Garay's deputy, Gonzalo de Ocampo, who had been sent ahead, disputes subsequently developed between the Spaniards. It was at this very time, on September 13, 1523, that two of Cortés's cousins, Rodrigo de Paz and Francisco de las Casas, delivered the royal mandates and a decree prohibiting Garay from settling in Pánuco.[38]

Cortés promptly sent a legation under the command of Alvarado and Sandoval to Garay and invited him to Tenochtitlan. There, Cortés received him in a courteous and hospitable manner, "as a true brother." During his stay at the end of December 1523, Garay died suddenly under the mysterious circumstances of indigestion. According to Cortés, his "brother" had "taken the news so much to heart that the Huaxtecs had exploited the discord among the Spaniards to stage an uprising that he fell ill with grief, so much so that he died within three days."[39] For Cortés, this removed another major rival, though the warfare conducted against the Huaxtecs in the province of Pánuco proved unusually brutal. There were heavy losses on both sides, but the Spaniards and their allies were able to prevail in the end. For their part in the uprising, the Huaxtec leaders were burned alive.[40]

The presence of indigenous conquistadors remained highly important, both in the Pánuco campaign and in other undertakings. The fact that they were willing to fight alongside the Spaniards even after the Fall of Tenochtitlan shows that they were not concerned just with casting off the yoke of the Mexica and cheerfully accepted Christianity, as they later often claimed in their chronicles. Rather, they were also focused on the conquest of land and slaves. For instance, the allied Tlaxcalans viewed Christianity, whose proliferation Cortés and his men always touted, as a religion of conquest, like so many pre-Hispanic beliefs which had contained expansive elements, too. Many decades later, they documented their participation in the wars and triumphs visually in the great depictions of the Lienzos of Tlaxcala, Quauhquechollan, and Analco. Even the contingents of Mexica troops, who took part in many war campaigns, were by no means merely hostages being carried along to prevent an uprising in the capital. They pursued their own goals in order to make room for themselves in the new constellation of power.[41]

The collaboration succeeded once more when Cortés entrusted his confidant Alvarado with the conquest of Guatemala and the exploration of a sea route between the Gulf of Mexico and the "South Sea." At the same time, Cortés, who had just been promoted to governor, wanted to extend his sphere of influence as far south as possible and to gain access to the riches of the region, which he had first heard about in 1521. In 1522, he had sent two Spanish scouts and indigenous escorts to the Maya. Allegedly, envoys of the K'iche and the Kaqchikel then came to Tenochtitlan and swore allegiance to the crown. Shortly thereafter, Spanish allies in Soconusco complained about Mayan attacks. This is said to have been the decisive factor in Cortés's decision to dispatch Alvarado on December 13, 1523.[42]

Alvarado, who had already pushed deep into Oaxaca in 1522 and then "pacified" the region around Tututepec on the Pacific coast, gathered indigenous allies in the neighboring regions and in Oaxaca. With them he travelled across the Isthmus of Tehuantepec, along the Pacific coast toward Guatemala. This campaign can also be regarded as a continuation of the pre-Hispanic expansion under Moctezuma into cocoa-rich Soconusco, for the tlatoani had probably already planned to attack the region. Pedro de Alvarado thus had allies from many cities under his command, who, with their own commanders, went into battle in December. It was the traditional season of warfare, before the wet harvesting period. While the epidemics had reduced the total number of indigenous allies, thousands of Nahua, Zapotecs, and Mixtecs still participated in this campaign as porters, soldiers, officers, and colonizers with their own specific aims.[43]

The Spaniards' diseases arrived in Guatemala before they did, which meant that the dying had begun. Alvarado and his troops won several battles in February 1524, destroying the K'iche capital of Q'umarkaj. By the end of 1523, they had already found new partisans in the Kaqchikel, who were enemies of the K'iche. To get rid of the invaders as quickly as possible, the Kaqchikel formally agreed to acknowledge the sovereignty of the Spanish monarch and to pay tribute. However, because of the excessive tribute demands, war broke out as early as August 1524 and lasted for six years. Moreover, the allies had to fight and subjugate the numerous independent Mayan cities one by one. Not until around 1530 did the troops achieve a temporary "pacification" of the highlands. Many Mesoamerican allies were intentionally settled in the conquered Maya territories in order to establish a measure of control through ethnic differentiation. In large parts of present-day Guatemala, however, the Conquest was far from over.[44]

As Cortés had learned of the supposed prodigious wealth of these countries, the neighboring region of Hibueras (also known as Higueras), today's Honduras, bordering on Guatemala, was also a target of the expansion to the south. Supposedly, the indigenous people there hung "gold pieces mixed with

Fig. 8.4 This detail from the Lienzo de Quauhquechollan shows the fraternization of the ruler of this territory near Cholula with the leader of the Spanish. Together with Alvarado, warriors and porters marched to Guatemala. Unrestored Lienzo de Quauhquechollan. Universidad Francisco Marroquín. Wikimedia Commons.

copper" on their nets instead of the usual lead weights.[45] Cortés also hoped to find the passage there that Columbus had been looking for. In parallel to Alvarado's cross-country expedition, Cristóbal de Olid was tasked with sailing six ships along the Gulf of Mexico to Hibueras, where the two units were to join forces. Yet another reason to conduct this campaign was that Gil González de Ávila, the conqueror of Costa Rica and Nicaragua and a favorite of Bishop Fonseca, had broken away from Pedrarias and also reached Honduras in 1524. On his way south, Olid made a stopover in Cuba, where he was supposed to buy horses. There, his old patron Velázquez asked him to renounce Cortés and carry out the conquest of Honduras with him; in doing so, Velázquez defied the royal instructions. Having agreed, when Olid reached the coast of Hibueras, he founded the port city of Triunfo de la Cruz.[46]

As soon as Cortés learned of the intrigue, he became enraged. As he informed the monarch, he even wanted to go to Cuba himself to arrest Velázquez and send him back to Spain. In June 1524, he sent a fleet of five ships, under the command of his cousin Francisco de las Casas, to Honduras to arrest Olid. However, after a shipwreck off the coast, Las Casas as well as Gil González fell into Olid's hands. Olid soon let his guard down, though, and a short time later, in the village of Naco, the two managed to ambush Olid and severely injure him. After the attack, Las Casas and González had Olid tried and executed. The two Spaniards were already on their way back to Mexico when the impatient Cortés himself set out in mid-October. Shortly before this, he had completed his fourth letter-report.[47]

Next to the conquest of Tenochtitlan, the expedition to Hibueras proved to be one of the most bitter, prolonged, and fruitless undertakings. To prevent an uprising, the governor took with him Cuauhtemoc and Tetlepanquetzal, as well as the members of the Mexican high nobility who had survived the Conquest. In Chalco, a contingent of about three thousand indigenous warriors from the high valley and Michoacán, under the command of Ixtlilxochitl, joined the Spaniards, led by Cortés, who left with a large entourage and his best men, including Sandoval, Bernal Díaz, and several clergymen. As Bernal reported, Cortés also brought with him shawm, flageolet, and trombone players; falconers; and even a large herd of pigs. Of course, Malinche was also present. During this march, she was married to Captain Juan Jaramillo, apparently because Cortés had grown tired of his concubine. The conspicuously grand conquest march was designed to make the governor's fame radiate into the deep south of New Spain and beyond.[48]

Indeed, the army was lavishly received and celebrated on its way through the already conquered provinces. Nonetheless, the elation of their leader would soon evaporate, as the march proved anything but easy. Against the advice of the indigenous people, who pointed out the lack of land routes, the governor wanted to advance to Honduras via Tabasco and Campeche across the tropical lowlands of the Petén. Often in the pouring rain, the troops had to cross countless smaller and larger rivers, jungles, swamps, and mountain ranges. The local indigenous communities had fled and left no food behind, so the army soon suffered from hunger. The deprivations were so severe that dead and desperate people were left behind. The soldiers were even angered by the musicians playing. "Having corn to eat was more valuable than music," Bernal wrote.[49]

When, south of the Laguna de Términos, the haggard troops returned to more hospitable areas, an incident occurred that had grave consequences. Allegedly, after being baptized, an indigenous man named Mexicalcingo told Cortés that Cuauhtemoc and the other nobles had been discussing an attack against the Spanish and intended to incite the local Maya. Cortés probably had the accused Cuauhtemoc, Tetlepanquetzal, and Cohuanacotzin tortured, causing them to confess. In response, he had sentenced them to death and had them hanged in the village of Acalan at the end of February 1525. According to Alva Ixtlilxochitl, the accusations were all false, which made the execution murder. Those who were responsible for the turmoil in the capital had supposedly spread lies to draw attention away from their own misdeeds. We can no longer know whether this was the case. However, even Bernal Díaz, who believed that the Mexica princes had indeed betrayed the Spaniards, felt that the harsh sentence was excessive and unjustified.[50]

The expedition then continued for many weeks through the Chontal and Itza Maya territory. Many more hardships and casualties were incurred before the men finally reached their destination in Honduras. There, they recognized that the entire undertaking had been in vain. The few inhabitants of the Spanish city founded by Gil Gonzalez were destitute and they were all sick, so they had nothing to offer the starving troops. In his report, Cortés deliberately omitted these facts. He instead mentioned that he continued to explore the region's hinterland and founded the port cities of Trujillo and Natividad de Nuestra Señora at the end of 1525. On his return by sea in April 1526, Cortés learned during a stopover in Cuba that he was presumed dead in Mexico. He arrived in Vera Cruz on May 24, 1526, and on June 19, after more than a year and a half, he returned to Mexico to a hero's welcome.[51]

The Limits of Success

The march to Hibueras not only cost an unknown number of lives but also a great deal of money. Later, Cortés would unsuccessfully ask for restitution from the crown. Even more infuriating for him was the turmoil in the capital caused by his absence.

The four royal administrators had arrived before Cortés's departure in 1524. He appointed Estrada and Albornoz as vice-regents, while Salazar and Chirinos were assigned to travel to the Mayan lands with him. Alonso de Zuazo also remained in Mexico as mayor and chief justice; this decision was made in response to the officials having tried to dissuade Cortés from the expedition because they feared problems with the indigenous population in Central Mexico. Cortés was ill-disposed toward the administrators because they received a salary around 35 percent higher than his, even though, in his opinion, he had to bear "two hundred times more costs" than "all four together." In the end, he clearly prevailed.[52] In his reply to the monarch, he had self-assuredly declared that he would not tolerate interference in the affairs of government by officials from the motherland who had no experience on the ground. This, he suggested, would only have negative consequences, as seen for instance in Hispaniola's decline.[53]

Cortés had already received reports on the march south, before Espíritu Santo, that there was a dispute in the capital between Estrada and Albornoz, which allegedly triggered unrest among the Mexica. He therefore sent Salazar and Chirinos back to settle the matter. Together with Judge Zuazo, they were to take over the government if the quarrels could not be resolved. The pacification did not last for long, however. At the beginning of 1525, there was an uprising on the part of the indigenous people, which Zuazo brutally suppressed. Further discord followed among the leadership, whereupon Salazar and Chirinos seized power, deposed Zuazo, and shipped him to Cuba. After the rumor of Cortés's death emerged, the two officials confiscated the expedition members' assets, persecuted the governor's supporters, and had his court minister, Rodrigo de Paz, tortured and executed in order to obtain the supposedly hidden treasures. When news from Cortés arrived in the capital at the end of January 1526, the now reconciled Estrada and Albornoz reinstated themselves at the head of the government and had their colleagues imprisoned. It was not until Cortés's return in June 1526 that the situation quieted down.[54]

Nevertheless, word of Cortés's error of judgment and the resulting problems had spread to Spain, as had word of his style of governance, which the royal officials considered presumptuous. Albornoz composed a letter to the crown in a specially designed secret code. In his view, Cortés was behaving like a viceroy, and he also suspected that the governor was hiding large amounts of gold. The communications nourished the doubts about Cortés that had already existed in the motherland since the dispute with Velázquez. For this reason, the crown sent Luis Ponce de León, an examining magistrate, to New Spain to carry out a review of the administration (a residencia) against Cortés. It was a routine procedure of the Spanish administration, not to be confused with criminal proceedings. Cortés received the judge respectfully, kissed the royal orders, and then held them over his head, as was customary. But like many crew members of his ship, Ponce de León died of an epidemic illness shortly after his arrival in July 1526. Thereafter, his companion Marcos de Aguilar was appointed vice-governor ad interim.[55]

The residencia was thus initially put on hold. In September, Aguilar called on Cortés to temporarily give up the governorship, which was suspended during the trial anyway, as well as his offices as captain general and administrator of indigenous affairs. Cortés went along with this to demonstrate his obedience to the monarch and his deputy. As he admitted to his father, he subsequently felt as if he were in "limbo."[56] Soon, on March 1, 1527, Aguilar also died, and the city council elected Sandoval and Estrada as new regents. A few months later, Estrada was appointed sole regent by royal decree and remained so until December 1528, when the first audiencia arrived in Mexico and took over the affairs of government. Its members consisted of Nuño de Guzmán—the governor of the province of Pánuco, who had only been in New Spain since 1526—and the *oidores* (interrogation judges) Juan Ortiz de Matienzo, Diego Delgadillo, Alonso de Parada, and Francisco de Maldonado. While Estrada was still in office, he had a falling out with Cortés. As a consequence, the interim governor temporarily expelled the conquistador, including from the capital. Cortés's power was on the wane.[57]

Against this backdrop, Cortés's activities in exploring the "South Sea" and a new sea route to the Spice Islands can be understood as a way to counteract his threatened loss of significance. Cortés had emphasized the importance of this ocean for Spain already in his letter to the crown in May 1522, a few months before the remnants of Ferdinand Magellanes's (Fernão de Magalhães) fleet under the command of Juan Sebastián Elcano were to return from their first circumnavigation of the globe. Like many of his contemporaries, he was inspired by ancient myths and the search for the land of gold, especially the land of the Amazons. He saw it as an opportunity to make himself indispensable to the crown into the future. He directed his father to present the idea at court in order to obtain the royal commission. In the meantime, Cortés had ships built in Zacatula on the Pacific coast, which he intended to use to realize his objective. To the monarch, he wrote in his fifth letter-report:

> I consider these ships more important than I can say, for I am sure that with them I will make your Imperial Highness the ruler of more kingdoms and dominions than can be imagined in our nation so far. [...] Your Majesty will have so many advantages from this that you will, I believe, have nothing more to do to become ruler of the whole world.[58]

Cortés did not receive the order until 1526, after the crown had sent García Jofre de Loaísa and Sebastián Caboto on their exploratory journey. The royal decree ordered, among other things, the search for the ships of Loaísa and Caboto. Cortés had a fleet equipped at his own expense, which he placed under the command of his cousin, Álvaro de Saavedra. He gave him detailed instructions and a letter for Caboto and Loaísa. The documents also contained a letter to the "King of Cebú," which Cortés had translated into Latin, in the hope that perhaps a Jew would be found who understood this universal language. Otherwise, Saavedra was supposed to search for an Arab or Indian from Calicut. Cortés had learned during his own hueste that such an undertaking required the help of translators. The flotilla set sail at the end of October 1527, but it met with little success. Soon after its departure, two ships were lost and only the captain's ship with Saavedra on board managed to reach Asia. After the commander (in October 1529) and large parts of the crew had died, the few survivors returned to Spain via Portugal in 1534. Once again, an undertaking that Cortés had pursued with great hopes and considerable financial expenditure turned out to be a failure.[59]

Thus, his return to Spain could not have come at a better time. As early as the beginning of 1528, Cortés had received instructions from the president of the Indian Council, Francisco García de Loaísa, to return to Spain to present himself to the crown, which was confirmed a few months later by a royal decree.

As López de Gómara reports, this trip was entirely in accordance with Cortés's wishes. He wanted to marry, have legitimate children, and report in person to the monarch about the situation in New Spain. Even before he left, the sad news reached him: his father and tireless advocate, Martín Cortés, had died. On the crossing, he was accompanied by his loyal captains Sandoval and Tapia, various close relatives of Moctezuma, including his son Pedro Tlacahuepan, a son of Maxixcatzin from Tlaxcala, and other indigenous high nobles. Also onboard were Malinche and her six-year-old son Martín, Cortés's illegitimate child. The governor also took on board numerous indigenous acrobats, servants, and slaves, along with animal species that were unknown in Europe. The flotilla arrived in Spain at the end of May.[60]

Even before Cortés left the port of Palos for the royal court in Toledo via the monastery La Rábida, where Columbus had previously taken up residence, he had to cope with another loss. Sandoval fell ill on arrival and died a few days later. The fact that Cortés was received honorably at court was by no means a matter of course. Still, despite the recent problems in New Spain and the intrigues of his many adversaries, the Duke of Bejar and the Count of Aguilar had championed his cause. The monarch thus ordered the cities through which Cortés and his rather outlandish looking retinue passed to throw festive receptions. The exotic procession astonished his contemporaries, including the German-born painter Christoph Weiditz, who painted portraits of Cortés (Fig. 2.1). Moreover, during his travels, at the Guadalupe Monastery in Extremadura Cortés met the wife of the most important imperial advisor, Francisco de los Cobos, and her sister, whom he showered with gifts and who subsequently strongly advocated for him.[61]

The personal reception by Charles V was a particularly gratifying experience and undoubtedly a highlight of the conquistador's life. After his speech, the monarch granted him high honors and promised him a fitting reward, whose terms were to be more closely negotiated in subsequent months. When Cortés fell seriously ill a short time later and was fighting for his life, the monarch granted him the rare honor of a personal visit to his sickbed. Though numerous other privileges aroused envy in others, according to Díaz del Castillo, his intercessors defended him with the words: "His Majesty had ordered that it should be demonstrated to him that Cortés and his men had won so many countries that all Christianity was indebted to them."[62]

Cortés seized this auspicious moment to send a legation with lavish gifts to Rome. Pope Clement VII thanked him by legitimizing three of his illegitimate children, including his son Martín. The conquistador also married a second time. His first wife, Catalina Suárez, had followed her husband from Cuba to New Spain in mid-1522, where Cortés received her honorably and had her come to the capital with a large escort. Bernal Díaz reported that his feelings of joy were nevertheless tempered by the fact that, besides Malinche, he had had affairs with other women. Catalina died a few months later, after a banquet at which tensions between the couple had become apparent. The sudden death of his wife led to suspicions that would plague Cortés for a long time. Seven years later, Cortés still remained a very good marital prospect in the homeland. His father, though, had previously arranged a marriage with Juana de Zúñiga, daughter of the Count of Aguilar and niece of the Duke of Béjar. This marriage was in keeping with his social standing, which opened the door for Cortés to the influential circles of the Spanish high nobility. With his new wife, the conquistador would go on to have six more children, including his son and heir in 1532. He, too, bore the name Martín, underlining the particularly close relationship Cortés had had with his father.[63]

At the end of July 1529, Cortés was allowed to submit a memorandum to the monarch with his ideas for the future government of New Spain, in which he focused on the protection of the indigenous peoples and the expansion of tax revenues. He emphasized the need to let the indigenous population go on living according to their own way of life. Of course, religion remained an exception, and Cortés called for priests of exemplary character to see to their conversion. Furthermore, he noted, the Spanish landowners must be bound to their land in order to secure and increase the crown's income in the long term. He himself wanted to set a good example. In the same month, the crown granted Cortés over twenty-two villages with 23,000 subjects, although it remained unclear whether the number actually referred to the heads of household or to the inhabitants as a whole. In connection with this, the monarch also conferred on Cortés the title of Marqués of the Valley of Oaxaca, membership in the Order of Santiago, and the title of Captain General of New Spain and the South Sea. Mexican historian José Luis Martínez has carefully analyzed the significance of the royal favors. He concludes that, while Cortés received the highest possible honors for his merits, he was not conferred power. Specifically, the title of governor was not restored to him.[64]

The court intended to decide on the question of power without Cortés and in the interests of the crown. The request that he return home already followed this rationale, as the government wanted to make use of his absence to reorganize governmental power. The crown had advised Cortés of this in April 1528 and, as was customary in the Caribbean, had already appointed an audiencia as the ruling body. The fact that Nuño de Guzmán, one of Cortés's fiercest opponents, was president of the committee did not bode well for Cortés. Under Guzmán, the audiencia certainly did not make itself popular in New Spain. Its measures brought about discontent and discord. For example, Cortés's possessions were confiscated and his devotees persecuted. The exorbitant increase in tribute demands from the subjects also contributed to the unease.[65]

Guzmán moreover was the driving force behind the rapid restoration of the residencia in 1529. In the process, the residencia raised fifty-three issues concerning Cortés's actions since his departure to Cuba. The very selection of witnesses made it clear that the aim was a conviction. The interrogation led to an indictment that included no fewer than 101 charges: from the destruction of the ships in 1519, the Cholula massacre and La Noche Triste, to self-enrichment and gambling. In total, the accusations focused on embezzlement of royal funds, mistreatment of indigenous people, nepotism, obstruction of justice, disregard of royal decrees, inept administration at the expense of the community, and sin against the laws of God. Beyond this, in February 1529, the audiencia commenced a trial against Cortés on behalf of his mother-in-law on the suspicion that he had murdered his first wife, Catalina. The trial, however, was never concluded. The mother-in-law and her heirs further demanded part of his property, as it had been acquired during his marriage to Catalina. Some of the court proceedings dragged on until 1599 and ended with a settlement. The residencia itself never reached a final verdict. In the Council of the Indies, where the indictment was received together with the marqués's extensive defense, the proceedings were left pending in order to keep up the pressure on Cortés and prevent his renewed rise to caudillo.[66]

Cortés learned of the machinations of the first audiencia while he was preparing to return to New Spain. In accordance with his rank, he brought with him four hundred people, including his new wife and his mother, but also many craftsmen and missionaries. The ships arrived in Vera Cruz in mid-1530. However, the crown had forbidden him to travel to the capital until the arrival of the newly appointed audiencia. The latter was to replace the incompetent body under Guzmán, who was then conducting a bloody conquest in New Galicia, northwest of the capital. However, Cortés arrived too early and his followers, among them many indigenous princes, gave him a triumphant welcome. This gave rise to numerous disputes with the first audiencia, which was still in power. The marqués had to stay in Texcoco, where his mother died without having had a chance to admire the capital. The situation improved only when the new audiencia under Bishop Sebastián Ramírez de Fuenleal arrived. Despite hostilities and legal disputes, and though he was still denied participation in government, Cortés was able to maintain large portions of his property. As far as the administration of his vast estates was concerned, however, the marqués had behaved no better than the other encomenderos and shamelessly exploited his subordinates. Thus, the newly appointed viceroy, Antonio de Mendoza, who had taken office in 1535 with the royal mandate to further limit Cortés's powers, had to intervene to secure tribute and work relief for the indigenous inhabitants of Cuernavaca. Nevertheless, the two leaders initially got along well, as the viceroy treated the conquistador very tactfully.[67]

The crown commissioned Cortés to undertake further exploration of the "South Sea," partly to keep Cortés busy, but also out of genuine interest in such activities. The marqués had stressed in his letter-reports that only the discovery and mastery of the sea route through the Pacific would make Charles V "the monarch of the world."[68] After his return to New Spain, these endeavors became Cortés's primary focus, alongside his efforts in trade and mining. These four voyages, which were financed from his own resources and in one case even personally led by him, were not entirely successful, however. A faster sea route to the Spice Islands was not discovered. Neither did the support for another conquistador from Extremadura, Francisco Pizarro, and the initiation of trade transactions with Peru bear the desired fruit. The competition with viceroy Mendoza that broke out in 1539 for the discovery of the legendary seven golden cities of Cíbola in the unknown north of New Spain further darkened Cortés's future. At any rate, his vessels explored California, named after the chivalric novel character Califia, along with the gulf, which bears the name of the marqués: Mar de Cortés, the Sea of Cortés. But the mythical island inhabited by black women and full of gold, pearls, and precious stones was not found here, either.[69]

The years from 1530 to 1540 were the last years that the marqués spent in New Spain. Besides his expeditions and undertakings, he was mainly preoccupied with legal issues—complaints that his numerous opponents brought against him and those that he himself raised to the court in many letters, albeit without being heard. In 1539, when he felt that he was being deprived of his privileges by the viceroyal initiative in the "South Sea," and even his shipyard installations in Tehuantepec were confiscated, Cortés decided to return to Spain. The circumstances, however, were far less glorious than twelve years earlier. The monarch no longer wanted to hear from the relentless petitioner, who in his opinion had been more than richly rewarded, and he rebuked him accordingly. Nor did it help that the marqués took part in the imperial campaign against Algiers in October 1541, which ended disastrously. His subsequent petitions to Charles V were in vain; his power had eroded, and his wealth melted away through the countless court cases. His fame, too, was fading rapidly.[70]

In order at least to ease his conscience, in his testament of October 1547, Cortés instructed his heirs to return to the indigenous owners all property that he might have acquired unlawfully. The old conquistador should have known that Martín, his legitimate son and successor as Marqués del Valle, had no interest in returning this property and did not even make any inquiries in this regard. Cortés died on December 2, 1547, at the age of 62 in Castilleja de la Cuesta, a small town near Seville. According to his instructions, his body was to be transferred to New Spain and buried in a family crypt in his town of Coyoacán. The tomb was to become the basis for a new Franciscan convent, but that was never built due to the lack of funds from his descendants. In the end, Cortés's dying wishes were only partially fulfilled after a variety of detours. His mortal remains arrived in the New World in 1566 and, after several reburials, were finally laid to rest in the Church of Jesus Nazareno in the heart of the new capital of Mexico.[71]

The Legacy of the Conquest

Long before Cortés's death, the Conquest had become a self-sustaining institution. It transformed into a process of colonization in which the marqués played only a minor, though significant, role. The creation of a new realm, in which Spanish and indigenous worlds mixed under diverse conditions, had begun with the arrival of the Europeans in 1519 and intensified after the Fall of Tenochtitlan in 1521. At the same time, the conquests were far from a fait accompli. The form of the new rule was by no means fixed from the start, but rather evolved out of the interaction of different elements, motives, and interests. Over time, the type of rule, economy, culture, and everyday life of the people underwent fundamental changes.

The New Capital

The basis for these developments was the reconstruction of the war-ravaged capital of the Mexica Empire, which began just a few months after the city was captured at the end of 1521. Cortés himself wanted to have the city rebuilt at its original site "because of its magnificence and wonderful location." There was some resistance to the idea, however.[1] Critics complained about the problematic drinking water supply and the danger of flooding, and so pleaded for a location on the mainland, for example in Texcoco or Coyoacán. But Cortés rejected these arguments and commissioned the master builder Alonso García Bravo to supervise the work. He also reinstated Tlacotzin, the prime minister (*chiuacoatl*), and other high nobles to their administrative posts and ordered the return of the surviving inhabitants to Tenochtitlan, where they were to cultivate Spanish agricultural products. Security was a major concern for Cortés, which is why he had a fort built and neighborhoods with canals separating indigenous and European residents. Nevertheless, close contact between the two populations would lay the foundation for city life.[2]

Due to the extensive devastation, the reconstruction proved to be an enormous challenge. Still, the city of the Mexica had not been razed, as the Spanish chroniclers later claimed for propaganda reasons. The indigenous slaves first had to bury the dead, clean the city, and then rebuild the aqueduct. Contemporary sources reported on the great human toll suffered by the indigenous workers during the reconstruction. In fact, Motolinía called this work the proverbial "seventh plague" of the Mexica, for, as he remarked, it cost more lives than the construction of the temple in Jerusalem. From the summer of 1522, hundreds of thousands of locals were forced to undertake this work. Many came from Chalco, the city of master builders. As a sign of Christian triumph, a cathedral was built next to the site of the great temple, which like the other places of worship served as a quarry. On the site of Moctezuma's palace, Cortés had his own city palace built. Within a few years, numerous church buildings, monasteries, markets, hospitals, and administrative buildings were erected. During the construction work, many Spaniards stayed in Coyoacán. Cortés, for instance, lived there with Malinche until the arrival of his wife Catalina.[3]

The construction work closely followed pre-Hispanic patterns and retained the indigenous functional characteristics of the area. Nonetheless, European construction techniques and equipment were introduced and quickly adopted by the indigenous people. The indigenous population were not only forced laborers, but also played a significant role in the design of the new city. There was spatial continuity, for example, in use of dams and neighborhood design in the reconstruction: again, an indigenous city subdivided into the traditional four districts and with its typical markets was created around the center, which remained reserved for the Spanish. The construction was supervised by the only surviving son of Moctezuma, given the Christian name Don Pedro, and by other princes. Commodities helped to establish continuity between Tenochtitlan and Mexico, a name that became naturalized for the new city over time and included Tlatelolco, renamed Santiago Tlatelolco. Christian and secular celebrations took place in urban spaces in which the different groups mingled. On August 13, for instance, while the Spanish commemorated the surrender of Cuauhtemoc with the feast of San Hipólito, the natives celebrated their salvation from the devil. Mexico thus became a place where indigenous and European elements mixed. The maintenance of the indigenous identity and local customs was in the Spaniards' interest, not least because it allowed for a more effective collection of tributes.[4]

At first, the cost of living in the city of Mexico was exorbitant. As Bernal Díaz reports, imported items, in particular, such as medicine and weapons, required enormous sums of money. Cortés had two tax officials specifically assigned to facilitate loans and moratoriums. Attempts were also made to introduce a separate

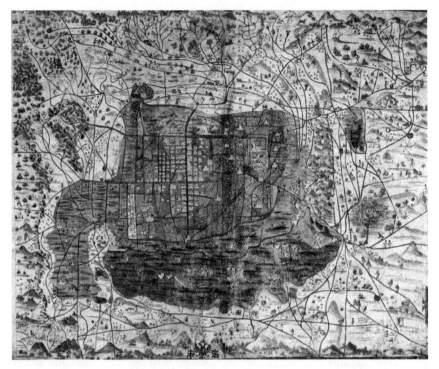

Fig. 9.1 Map of México-Tenochtitlan around 1550. This is one of the earliest extant maps of México-Tenochtitlan (Uppsala University Library), probably created around 1550 in the surroundings of the Colegio de Santa Cruz de Tlatelolco. It shows the fusion of Mesoamerican and European elements not only in the new urban landscape, but also cartographically. The previous road network was thus maintained, but new buildings and Catholic churches were built to replace the temples. Library of Congress https://www.loc.gov/item/2021668313/.

copper currency, although this did not bring any relief. Many conquistadors were soon forced to return to battle, as they had no other means of earning a living. When it became clear to everyone that there was not nearly as much gold for distribution as had been expected and hoped for, the often heavily indebted veterans sought an encomienda to secure their livelihood.[5] The arrangement over the control of the indigenous labor force would become a central problem of the emerging colonial society.

Systems of Rule

Cortés realized early on that the mistakes that had led to the catastrophic depopulation of the Caribbean islands should not be repeated. In his letters to the monarch, he repeatedly expressed the need for a policy that would ensure that the settlers remained in the country permanently rather than simply sapping it of its resources with the aim of returning to Europe as quickly as possible. At the same time, the type of settler mattered as well. The Spanish concept of the "purity of blood" (*limpieza de sangre*) also applied in New Spain. Jews, Moors, New Christians—with the exception of the indigenous peoples—and heretics were not allowed entry. Nevertheless, this could not always be effectively enforced. At the same time, Cortés informed the crown of the need to treat the natives well, so that there would be enough workers to increase the wealth of the crown. Each of these goals was in fact contrary to the interests of the conquistadors. Soon, the marqués lacked the authority to implement his ideas, especially as he did not live up to his own principles in the treatment of the indigenous subjects.[6]

The decrease in population among the native inhabitants could not be thwarted through policy. On the other hand, the extinction that some Spanish observers expected in the sixteenth century did not come to pass. Instead, a multiethnic society emerged; this was utterly unique at the time. Even before the Spaniards arrived, Mesoamerican societies and cultures were characterized by great ethnic and linguistic diversity. However, the addition of Europeans and Africans brought new elements. As a consequence, the colonial category of the "Indio" emerged, which subsumed the various indigenous ethnic groups. It was a new nomenclature for everyone involved and constantly renegotiated. The social dichotomy between Spaniards and indigenous peoples was evolving gradually, as was the equation of "Indio" with poverty and backwardness. In the beginning, there were numerous alliances that did not reflect this duality; after the Fall of Tenochtitlan, Mexico was politically a blend of overlapping and competing regimes.[7]

Accordingly, the indigenous allies and their elites initially negotiated on an equal footing with the Spaniards. In the 1520s in particular, when the situation in Mexico was still unstable, Cortés placed great emphasis on fear and deterrence. There were still many millions of indigenous people living in the region, and their long-term subjugation could not be taken for granted. The Spaniards were weak in numbers and needed allies to assert their claim to power. After his victory over the Mexica, Cortés exercised a form of charismatic power. From 1520 onward, he secured his position by appointing new tlatoque whenever possible, such as after military successes or the death of incumbents. The rulers who depended on him were baptized and then served as mediators between the Spaniards and the subjugated.[8]

The former tributary city-states that were allied with the Spaniards must have felt great satisfaction in the victory. For them, the defeat of the Mexica Empire was an act of liberation. It also was in keeping with their historical frame of reference, which was marked by constant wars and the rise and fall of powerful empires. At first, the situation appeared to improve considerably. The tribute payments to the Mexica were no longer necessary, and the constant threat of war evaporated. Right after the end of the fighting, the indigenous allies still greatly outnumbered the Europeans. But because Cortés successfully continued to play them against each other, no alliances were formed against the Spaniards. Even the Tlaxcalans remained strong only in their own region. In general, the improvement in the regional situation was short-lived. This was because the Spaniards pursued long-term plans for domination, which they systematically based on the European model of territorial rule with control over all ethnic groups, the introduction of a centralized power structure, and high tribute demands. The indigenous people could not have foreseen this, being unfamiliar with this form of statehood. The actual subjugation of Mesoamerica began gradually in the years following the Fall of Tenochtitlan. For their part, the former allies realized the extent of their loss of power only once the process of colonization could no longer be stopped.[9]

Regardless of whether they had been allies of the Spanish, the nobles eventually recognized the supremacy of the Spanish crown. They consequently sought to maintain their prominent position in their own communities by keeping the Spanish sphere apart from the indigenous sphere. In relation to their own subjects, they were able to act as mediators and interpreters. They derived power from their greater knowledge. The nobility of the allies enjoyed numerous privileges from the Spaniards, such as permission to carry swords and own horses, to possess a coat of arms, keep their own land, be exempt from tribute, and bear the honorary titles of "Don" or "Hidalgo." In colloquial language, the term "cacique," chief, which originated in the Caribbean, became generally accepted, while "tlatoani" lost favor. Even official Spanish titles such as "alcalde," mayor, and "regidor," city councilor, were given to the indigenous nobles. Signs of distinction were accorded great importance. A marriage with a local noble daughter initially proved advantageous for the Spanish conquistadors and resulted in gained prestige. In theory, the monarch recognized the rights of the indigenous nobles, who were supposed to pass on Christianity to their subjects and maintain order. Only over time did the structural disadvantages of the indigenous officials compared to the Spanish landowners become evident in the struggle for the dwindling resources of tributes and labor. These officials were increasingly marginalized and either lost access to their subordinates or were absorbed into the Creole elite.[10]

By the time the Spaniards established themselves as the ruling class, the power structure of the Mexica Empire had already long since disintegrated and the trend toward fragmentation was underway. The colonial rulers had to deal directly with the individual altepeme, which attached great importance to diversity. They allowed the altepeme to govern themselves, even if only up to the level of the city administration. The highest authorities of the subjugated empires disappeared entirely, and the natives had to adopt European forms of administration such as city councils (cabildos) and courts, while retaining the district boundaries of the so-called Repúblicas de Indios. Simple macehualtin, commoners, could now sue the *gobernador*, which indicated his loss of authority. Elected local officials increasingly ousted the former nobility and the indigenous governors from the ruling families. The local administration thus also passed increasingly into the hands of Spanish officials. The *corregidores*, as crown officials, replaced the old tlatoque in growing numbers, contributing to their disempowerment.[11]

Special standing was extended to the descendants of Moctezuma, who allegedly had submitted voluntarily to the Spanish crown and whose lineage could thus make legitimate claims to participation in the rule. The daughters of the tlatoani received numerous privileges, such as membership in prestigious orders of knights, or an annuity, and married into the Spanish nobility. Tecuichpo, who later took the Christian name Doña Isabel de Montezuma, was first the wife of Cuitlahuac; after the conquest, she became concubine of Cortés, with whom she had a daughter. Later, the governor married her to conquistador Alonso de Grado; after de Grado's death, he married her to Pedro Gallego, and, after the Gallego's demise, he finally married her to Juan Cano. Cano intensively represented his wife's economic interests, although he was unsuccessful in petitioning for the restitution of her entire inheritance in 1536. The question of inheritance certainly preoccupied the numerous other descendants of Moctezuma, who is said to have fathered around one hundred and fifty children.[12]

Don Pedro Tlacahuepan, the only legitimate son of Moctezuma recognized by the crown, even travelled with an entourage to Spain in 1540. Another son, Don Martín Cortés Nezahualteculuchi, married in Spain. While no claims to power were recognized, the Spanish authorities strove to respect traditional notions of legitimacy in the election of the indigenous governors of Tenochtitlan. This came after a transitional phase in the 1520s and 1530s, when Cortés installed illegitimate and wholly subservient puppets. Viceroy Mendoza thus had Moctezuma's direct relative, Diego de Alvarado Huanitzin, who enjoyed the recognition of the Mexica, appointed in 1538. The ruling dynasty would remain in power until 1565, even though its actual authority was tightly constrained. The Spaniards may very well have feared attempts at rebellion, but the risk was low at the time, as the indigenous leaders were already reliant on the Spanish governors for their status.[13]

The creeping erosion of indigenous authority provoked conflicts between the former rulers and the new Spanish encomenderos, mostly over labor. Not only did the indigenous people insist on their privileges, but around the middle of the century they were also willing and able to fight for them through legal channels. The plaintiffs and petitioners repeatedly invoked Moctezuma's submission and loyalty to the crown, their own age-old and therefore legitimate governmental tradition, and the aid provided during the war of conquest, which underpinned the legitimacy of their concerns. As early as 1532, Moctezuma's son Martín petitioned the king regarding the decline of the legitimate power of the leaders of Mexico. He requested financial support and the confirmation of his rights.[14]

The Spaniards' most loyal ally, Tlaxcala, played a key role in the emerging colonial society, if only a formal one. Cortés specified that because of its great merits the city should remain exempt from having to provide indigenous labor to Spanish encomenderos. The Tlaxcalans nevertheless had to pay tribute to the Spanish crown and were forced to build a fortress and a monastery for the Spaniards. As early as 1527, a Tlaxcala delegation visited Spain and, in 1534, the town received the honorary title of "the Loyal City" for its municipality as well as a Spanish coat of arms. The Lienzo de Tlaxcala illustrated the glorious history of the alliance with Cortés from the Tlaxcala perspective. Later, the Tlaxcalans unilaterally claimed exemption from the tribute, citing the alleged assurances of the marqués. In 1585, they won their demand through a skillful manipulation of historical facts. Yet this victory did not protect Tlaxcala against relative decline. The city-state, like the rest of Mesoamerica, was struck by epidemics and compelled to build the Spanish neighboring city of Puebla, whose settlers soon bought up Tlaxcala land holdings. Despite its prominent position and relative autonomy, there were telling signs of Tlaxcala's gradual impoverishment.[15]

A royal decree confirmed the privileges of the indigenous elites on February 26, 1557. It would be incorporated into the legal code for America (the Recopilación de Leyes) in 1560. Subsequently, numerous petitions were made to the crown. The petitioners usually cited four arguments: first, their noble origin; second, their role in the Conquest; third, their conversion to Christianity and its spread; and fourth, their contribution to good governance as caciques and governors. Increasingly, the petitions also included complaints about excessive tributes and compulsory labor, the widespread decline of the population, and the expansion of Spanish possessions at the expense of the indigenous population. Moreover, the European wars consumed more and more money, which increased the tax pressure on the American possessions. It was in this context that the local elites lost influence over the course of the sixteenth century, and their appeals to the crown were increasingly ignored.[16]

These trends were a source of great disappointment, especially among the former allies. Even the Tlaxcalans complained about how poorly they were treated by the colonizers. The latter ousted them everywhere from leadership positions and mistreated them. Other groups suffered a similar fate, including the Tarascans, whose leaders had freely acquiesced to the Spaniards' assurances. The threat of indigenous uprisings continued until the middle of the century, as the Mixton War in New Galicia abundantly demonstrated. This uprising, led by

Tenamatzle, even prompted the reactivation of Pedro de Alvarado in 1541, who then fell victim to a riding accident during the campaign. In the end, Viceroy Mendoza himself had to deploy indigenous troops to crush the rebellion. Further wars against the Mixtecs, Zapotecs, and Mixes would follow.[17]

The perpetuation of rivalries between ethnic groups, such as Tenochca and Tlatelolca, proved helpful for the Spanish, even though they had been allies in the war for the capital. As a direct consequence, the number of revolts in colonial Mexico remained comparatively low. When unrest did occur, it was usually local in scope and had local motives. As a rule, the crown was accepted as a distant but fair ruler who enjoyed the trust of the people; grievances were blamed on the supposedly inept local administrators. Additionally, armed conflicts were usually suppressed, ringleaders were punished with a deterrent effect, and some reforms were implemented to mitigate public discontent.[18]

There was no dispute about the emperor's rule in faraway Europe; it was even tied to the idea of a global empire, which, although not new, took on a novel dimension in its current form. In his second letter-report, Cortés had already addressed Charles V as the "new emperor of this country," a title "worth no less than that of Germany."[19] He repeatedly tried to make the notion appealing to the monarch in the subsequent reports. Cortés was well familiar with the idea, dating back to the Middle Ages, that Spain, whose civilization and religion were superior to those of other peoples, was called by God to rule the world. As he saw it, this imperial mission justified the subjugation of the Mexica Empire as well as the repression of supposedly diabolical beliefs of the indigenous peoples. The name Nueva España, New Spain, that Cortés introduced was also intended to signal that a pioneering expansion of the European parts of the empire had taken place.[20]

The government's motto "Plus ultra," adopted by the monarch already in 1516, seemed to point to the creation of a global empire beyond the pillars of Hercules. It gave rise to the assumption that the court would take an interest in a Spanish global empire. Chroniclers were also mindful of this. They included courtier Fernández de Oviedo and López de Gómara, who later wrote in his dedication to Charles V: "You have chosen the motto 'Plus ultra' and, with this, made it clear that you aspire to rule over the New World."[21] This observation was based on the idea of the worldwide spread of Spanish civilization and Christianity, made possible by the conquest of the Mexica Empire and the recognition of the vastness of the new territories. The monarch understood himself in the tradition of an imperator Romanorum and concentrated his policies on achieving supremacy in Europe. His grand chancellor Gattinara had already propagated the idea of a universal monarchy—of an "empire in which the sun never sets."[22] This was taken up by chroniclers and historians such as Cervantes de Salazar, Bernal Díaz, and Alonso de Zuazo when they compared the deeds of the Spanish with those of the ancient Romans and concluded that the former had even surpassed the latter.[23]

The Encomienda and Indigenous Work

Such considerations were irrelevant for the vast majority of the common freemen in the calpulli. Their lives nevertheless changed profoundly, even though the ruptures were not as radical everywhere as in Tenochtitlan itself. By and large, they had to abandon their traditional way of life, and they received new masters who exploited their labor. The introduction of the encomienda by the Spaniards in the early phase of the colonial period would have crucial repercussions. This form of labor regime had its roots in medieval Spain and was frequently used during the Reconquest on the Iberian Peninsula. At the beginning of the sixteenth century, the institution was brought to the Caribbean under Governor Nicolás de Ovando. In this system, a victorious conqueror was "entrusted" (*encomendar*) with the work services and tributes of a certain number of subjects. Landholding and jurisdiction were not originally part of this system, although many encomenderos later claimed these rights as a matter of course. In return, the encomenderos were responsible for the military protection, education, and Christianization of the indigenous people in their care. However, the system was prone to abuse, as had already become apparent in the Caribbean. Conquistadors and colonists who wanted to become rich quickly treated the indigenous population like slaves and willingly accepted their exponential deaths.[24]

After the conquest of Tenochtitlan, Cortés swiftly issued the first encomiendas. When allocating them, he linked them to indigenous forms of labor. The fact that the encomenderos were culturally foreign collectors of tributes and labor was nothing new in the Mesoamerican context. The obligation to provide public services for the calpulli continued and was extended to certain areas such as mining. In organizing this work, the indigenous nobility initially played a central role as mediators. This was clearly demonstrated in 1555, when the first great flood disaster of the colonial era required a substantial amount of labor. Viceroy Luis de Velasco, who had replaced his predecessor Mendoza in 1550, decided to have the work coordinated on the model of the indigenous community services. The design of the encomienda districts and their administration was also based on pre-Hispanic structures. Former city-states, which were too large to be individual encomiendas, were partitioned. The capitals of the altepeme retained their status as judicial and administrative centers and were renamed *cabeceras*.[25]

The encomiendas, however, were hardly uncontroversial. As early as 1511, a fierce debate had developed in Spain about the proper treatment of the indigenous population in the Indies. The abuse was criticized, especially by clergy of the mendicant orders, with Dominican Bartolomé de las Casas a particularly prominent voice. As a result, the crown enacted legal provisions in 1512 to protect the entrusted inhabitants. These did little to change the situation, however. When Cortés's reports in the early 1520s highlighted the magnitude of the conquest of an empire that was far more civilized from the Spanish point of view, the crown took up the policy of protection in order to prevent excesses like those that had occurred on the Caribbean islands. He also wanted to prevent the development of hereditary feudal rule. For example, Charles V's instructions to Cortés dated June 26, 1523, explicitly prohibited the granting of encomiendas. The indigenous peoples were instead to be like the free subjects of the crown in the Iberian Peninsula and live with the Spanish in peace.[26]

Cortés, nonetheless, did not follow the royal instructions; he even kept them secret from his men. In his written reply to Charles V in October 1524, he justified his position as follows:

> ... in these countries the Spaniards have no other advantages and no other way to survive or earn a living than with the help they receive from the indigenous people. Without them they couldn't survive here and would have to leave the country. . . . If word of this got around, no [Spaniards] would come anymore, which would cause quite a lot damage, for example to the service to our Lord God, because the Christianization of the local people would stop. Royal income would also be reduced and this great dominion would be lost, as would the territories that will be available with it in the future, and that will be more than the world has suspected hitherto.[27]

His main argument, therefore, was that the survival of the Spaniards in the newly conquered territories and the maintenance of military control depended on the allocation of indigenous labor. Moreover, in his view, there was not enough material booty available for the soldiers, who consequently had to make do with the local population. Last but not least, as Cortés wrote, this was the only way to generate the surplus for the crown. Regarding the accusation that the encomienda was a hidden form of slavery, the captain general replied that, on the contrary, it was the only way he was able to liberate the Indians from captivity, for: "as they used to serve their previous masters, they were not only prisoners, but incredibly subjugated, for they (their masters) not only took everything they had . . . but also snatched from them their sons, daughters and relatives and even they themselves, in order to sacrifice them to their gods."[28]

Cortés also explained that he was familiar with the fate of the "Indios" on the Caribbean islands because he had lived there for more than twenty years. He wanted to prevent the abuses in his dominion that had led to depopulation there. One way was to forbid the encomenderos from using their entrusted workers to search for gold. In addition, the natives were not to be taken from their villages, and only a part of what was produced should be mandated as tribute to the Spanish masters. For other services, the Spaniards should only use those indigenous people who had already been slaves or who were captured in war because of their resistance to the Spanish conquest. According to the ideas of the time, natives could be rightfully enslaved under these circumstances. Cortés also argued that the introduction of direct taxation demanded by the crown was doomed to failure. For this reason, the encomienda seemed the best possible solution.[29]

As the crown did not insist on the ban, and even went so far as to grant encomiendas, the institution stayed in place until the eighteenth century. By 1560, there were already about 480 encomiendas in New Spain, and in the first half of the sixteenth century an encomendero class arose that aspired to hereditary nobility status. As a matter of fact, this concession was seen as a substitute for the disappointing amount of booty to be had. The encomiendas were allotted according to the same set distribution: twenty percent went to Cortés and the crown, respectively, and the rest went to the troops. This formula and the division of the districts again triggered disputes and feelings of resentment among the conquistadors. Ultimately, only about 40 percent of the surviving Spaniards were able to enjoy an encomienda. Most stayed in the Valley of Mexico, although not all of them did. Bernal Díaz, for example, moved to present-day Guatemala. Cortés himself wanted to secure vast territories such as Texcoco, Chalco, Otumba, and Coyoacán, but had to surrender most of them when he set off on his campaign to Honduras. When in 1529 he was awarded the Valley of Oaxaca, with 23,000 vassals, he became the richest man in the Indies and probably in the entire Spanish world. But all that remained of his former possessions in the center of power were Coyoacán and Tacubaya. The strategically important encomiendas of Otumba, Chalco, and Texcoco had been transformed into crown provinces.[30]

Cortés formally issued instructions on good governance to the Spanish settlers in March 1524. Therein, he stipulated that the encomenderos were obliged to remain in the country for at least eight years and to bring their wives to New Spain. He hoped to prevent the landowners, who like those in the Caribbean islands were also only interested in a speedy return to Europe, from ruthlessly exploiting their subordinates. Cortés ordered that the encomenderos "should exercise special care not only not to ruin and disperse their Indians, but to preserve and multiply them." If they treated those entrusted to them in this way, the captain general promised to make their encomiendas hereditary.[31]

Fig. 9.2 Mistreatment of the indigenous people by the Spanish authorities. The so-called Codex Osuna was created during the visitation of Jerónimo de Valderrama (1563–1565) in New Spain. It recorded in Spanish and Nahuatl the crimes of certain Spanish officials against the indigenous population. This page also contains glyphs depicting the crimes of the royal judge Dr. Vasco de Puga, in which even his wife participated. In 1566, Puga was relieved of his office and had to answer to the Council of the Indies in Spain. Biblioteca Digital Hispánica, España Biblioteca Nacional de España.

Ultimately, nothing actually changed regarding the exploitation of the indigenous labor force. Cortés himself set a bad example; his subjects from Cuernavaca even complained to the royal audiencia in January 1533. They not only had to regularly deliver tributes in kind and provide for the household of their master and his subordinates, but they also had to be available for all kinds of other services and were mistreated by the Spanish servants.[32] Under the encomienda system, the boundaries of slavery were in fact quite fluid. The landowners inflicted cruel corporal punishment at will, and they also hired out or sold the indigenous farm workers entrusted to them. In the process, they would often illegally appropriate the communal land of the natives. To justify any infringements, the encomenderos referred to the precariousness of their circumstances in a hostile environment. The encomiendas were also a source of soldiers and porters for the ongoing war campaigns until the end of the 1520s.[33]

As for the crown, its attitude toward the encomiendas and thus toward the indigenous subjects remained ambivalent. On the one hand, it made attempts to curtail the power of the encomenderos in the 1530s and 1540s by regulating connected services. The intention was to prevent the worst excesses of exploitation and to generally reduce the encomenderos' influence, not least in order to boost the royal income. Under secret instructions, the members of the second audiencia of 1530 were ordered to abolish the encomienda and to replace it with a centralized system of tribute collection by the corregidores, who were also to oversee religious instruction and administer justice locally. From the start, these officials were also paid with tribute revenues and entitled to indigenous labor, however. They often used their office solely for their own benefit. Although a residencia took place at the end of their terms of office, they rarely had to fear harsh punishment, even in the event of mistreatment. In many places, moreover, the encomenderos were simply appointed as corregidores, which opened the door to abuse of the new office. As a result, the regulations could not be enforced locally and later were even undermined by royal orders and special dispensations.[34]

When the crown introduced the "New Laws" (Leyes Nuevas) in 1542 and 1543, it attempted yet again to combat arbitrariness and abuse with respect to the indigenous population and to limit the power of the encomenderos. The enslavement of the indigenous people—forbidden for some time—was to permanently end. In addition, the inheritability of the encomienda was banned. However, following the encomenderos' objections, the prohibition was later weakened so that at least a one-time inheritance remained possible. New encomiendas were only to be awarded by the viceroy. The tribute ceilings that had been in place since the 1530s were enforced more stringently. The crown also determined that, while the landowners could continue to receive tributes, they were no longer allowed to demand labor. Beginning in the middle of the century, visitations by royal officials were initiated to ensure that the provisions were being implemented on the ground. Moreover, the natives were given rights of appeal, which led to numerous court cases, as documented in the Codex Osuna. Despite all this, forms of forced labor and even indigenous slavery continued for many years.[35]

The royal dictates aroused much criticism and resistance among the New Spanish encomenderos. After the establishment of the viceroyalty, the audiencia, and the corregidores, they had steadily lost influence in a permanent clash with the royal authorities. This trend only worsened around the middle of the century. The crown's reaction to an alleged conspiracy among the encomenderos in the 1560s revealed just how much their position had eroded. The presumed ringleaders were severely punished, sometimes with death, and their possessions fell to the crown. Cortés's sons, including his legitimate heir Martín, who had come to New Spain after their father's death, were suspected of complicity, if not incitement. In the end, they had to answer for their actions in Spain. They were also not allowed to return to New Spain. The crown confiscated Cortés's lavish possessions of the Marquesado del Valle de Oaxaca and did not release them again until 1593, even though the marqués Martín Cortés had already been vindicated in 1574.[36]

The Christian Mission and Its Limitations

For the proponents of the encomienda, a key argument was its importance in the Christianization of the indigenous population and the eradication of their religious ideas. From the conquerors' point of view, the indigenous religions were nothing more than the work of the devil. The mission was at the very heart of the colonization process. The sources place special emphasis on this dimension: if the victory of the Spaniards was presented as being divinely ordained, it was also the starting point for the Christianization mandate. The Spanish conquistadors invoked this to legitimize the conquest of a highly civilized empire. From the beginning, however, Christianization also served political purposes and substantiated foreign rule. On the other hand, it was implemented systematically only after several years, once there was no longer any danger of a major uprising by various indigenous groups. The targeted destruction of temples, books, and other cultlike objects began in the mid-1520s. From this point forward, military subjection and spiritual submission would go hand in hand.

As early as the 1519 march into the interior, Cortés had ordered the destruction of indigenous religious artifacts whenever the Spanish triumphed militarily. After the Fall of Tenochtitlan, the measures were at first pursued only systematically in the former heartland of the Mexica Empire. In particular, the decision to destroy the main temple did not fail to have an impact on the Mexica's will to resist. The Spanish punished any public practice of the traditional faith, and the indigenous priests were severely persecuted and killed. They assumed that the memory of the religious practices and rites would be lost along with the priests. From the point of view of the Mesoamerican people, the destruction of the temples after a military defeat or religious submission to the victors was hardly unprecedented. On the other hand, what was unique and shocking was the fact that they were expected to completely abandon their own religion and adopt a wholly different faith. The Spaniards' view, conversely, was informed by the experiences of the Reconquest, the expulsion of Jews and Moors from the Iberian Peninsula, and the Reformation in Central Europe.[37] They could therefore see no alternative.

Once the Mexica capitulated, Cortés prohibited the practice of human sacrifice, although he lacked the power to enforce this ban everywhere. Moreover, in his instructions on good governance in March 1524, he entrusted to the encomenderos the responsibility to bar idolatry and, above all, human sacrifice, among their indigenous serfs and to build churches in their villages. The sons of the indigenous nobles were to be educated in the Christian faith in monasteries or parishes. Large encomiendas with more than two thousand servants had to provide for their own priest or friar; smaller encomenderos were supposed to jointly organize to do so.[38] At the beginning of the 1520s, however, there were insufficient funds to implement these measures. The Franciscan Toribio de Benavente, also known as "Motolinía," wrote about the initial phase of the mission in 1541:

> In all the idolatrous temples of Mexico, which had not yet been destroyed or burned, the people served and worshipped the demons not only in the countryside, but also in the city. The Spaniards were busy building their houses and living quarters, and were therefore content that the human sacrifices did not take place in public right before their eyes. Secretly, however, they continued to take place throughout Mexico.[39]

Even during the campaigns, Cortés had occasionally given sermonlike speeches not only to his men, but also to the subjugated population. Also, the religious services that the priests and hueste members Díaz, Olmedo, and Pedro de Villagrán held in public were always addressed to the locals. Malinche was assigned to translate, but she had only limited success. Consequently, Cortés soon requested that the crown send clergy. In order for their work to bear fruit, the priests needed to set a good example. It was thus especially important to Cortés that the future missionaries demonstrate impeccable conduct. Cortés believed that members of the mendicant orders, especially the Franciscans, were the most suitable candidates.[40] He argued that sending secular clergymen could even be counterproductive:

For if we were to receive bishops and prelates, they would adhere to their customs . . . and dispose of the church goods; that is, they would indulge in pomp and other vices and hand out estates to their children and relatives. This would result in yet another great difficulty, because the local natives had their clergymen in their day, who knew all the rites and ceremonies and lived in such an upright and chaste manner that they were punished with death in case of any aberration. Now, if they saw our church affairs and our services in the hands of those canons and other dignitaries and learned that they were servants of God, and they saw all the vices and profanities that they were currently practicing in these kingdoms, it would be very damaging to us, for they would no longer believe any of the sermons that were preached to them."[41]

Cortés neglected to mention in his letter that well-connected noble prelates in Spain might also have posed a threat to his claims to power. In fact, in 1521, Pope Leo X had issued a bull allowing two Franciscans to go to New Spain. His successor, Hadrian VI, modified the decree the following year and spoke of the order Friars Minor as being "strictly observant." For various reasons, it would take more than two years before the arrival of the first friars. In 1523, three Flemish Franciscans went to the New World of their own accord. One of them, Pieter van Gent, or Pedro de Gante, would go on to have a remarkably long and productive period of activity. In line with their millenarian orientation, they hoped for the restoration of a pure early Christianity in the New Spanish setting. They regarded the indigenous people as innocent children with whom they hoped to establish a church without sin. This tendency became even stronger when in May of the following year an official delegation of twelve Franciscans— the so-called Twelve Apostles, including Motolinía—arrived from Spain. Cortés dramatically staged their arrival in the presence of indigenous nobles. He first drew closer to them; then, kneeling down, he kissed their hands.[42]

The marqués offered the Franciscans a plot of land in the central square of the capital. They instead preferred to settle in the Moyotlan district in the southwest, where they would maintain their convent of San José de los Naturales, which included a school and an indigenous chapel. They also spread out in their new Franciscan province to Tlaxcala, Texcoco, and Huexotzinco. Over time, the Spanish authorities gave them far-reaching powers. They deliberately chose locations far from the city centers in order to be able to pursue their utopian ideals far away from the Europeans and the secular clergy, who, in their view, were already corrupt. At least a portion of the Franciscans pursued the goal of creating a new church that would turn away from the sinful Old World. The first bishop of Michoacán, Vasco de Quiroga, for example, wanted to create model parishes in the 1530s based on the example of Thomas More's work "Utopia," published in 1516. In this way, he thought he could revive early Christianity.[43]

In their missionary activity, the Friars Minor had a twofold strategy. On the one hand, they relentlessly demolished what they considered to be pagan cult objects, including the books of the Mexica and Maya. The indigenous calendars, which were so important for ritual purposes, were abolished and replaced by the Christian calendar. Thousands of the local inhabitants under-went mass baptisms beneath the open sky in the antechambers of the unfinished churches. The true purpose of these actions was undoubtedly rarely revealed to those being baptized. On the other hand, the Minorites began to reach out to the local population. In everyday missionary practice, they founded religious brotherhoods for the indigenous people and consciously drew on indigenous religious traditions. They employed songs, theatrical elements, flowers, and even integrated some Mesoamerican deities by equating them with Christian saints. One example of this was the use of a specially developed pictorial language in the catechisms, based on the indigenous glyphs. By appearing as poor mendi-cant friars, the Franciscans expected to be able to appeal to the mass population, especially the common freemen. In the year of their arrival, they even engaged in a religious dispute with the Mexica priests to convert them to Christianity. It became apparent, however, that the Mexica were not at all disposed to simply abandon their beliefs, which the Christian missionaries reacted to with different strategies.[44]

One of the priorities of the Franciscans was the teaching of Christianity to children by founding schools. Immediately after their arrival, they established the first educational facilities in Tenochtitlan and Texcoco in 1523, and by 1532 there were already about five thousand children in their various convents. Pedro de Gante created the largest of these schools in the capital. One of the initial milestones was the founding of the first secondary school, Santa Cruz de Tlaltelolco; its goal was to educate young indigenous nobles as the new elite for New Spain. There was no interest in preparing them for service as priests. Rather, graduates trained in the Spanish language and Christian faith were to transmit European values to their communities and serve as role models. They also were responsible for bringing home the Latin script, which led to the transformation of the Nahuatl into a written language. A profound cultural change was thus set into motion. In pre-Hispanic times, writing was a privilege of the elites used to establish historical property rights. In the colonial period, the indigenous people used this medium extensively in countless court cases. Nevertheless, the educa-tional efforts of the Europeans could replace the lost education system of the Mexica only to a limited extent.[45]

In the first years after the conquest, the mendicant orders determined church life in New Spain. After the Franciscans, the Dominicans arrived in 1526 and then the Augustinians in 1533. The secular clergy also gradually expanded over time. The encomienda usually corresponded to a parish district, with ecclesiastical instruction taking place in the cabeceras, where the first churches were built. Christian names were added to precede the indigenous place names. Dioceses were founded in the capital and later in Tlaxcala, Antequera, Michoacán, Chiapas, and Guadalajara. In 1546, the diocese in Mexico was promoted to an archdiocese. Pursuant to the royal patronage law, the crown determined the establishment of the church administrative structures, the appointment of high dignitaries, and the church tithes.[46]

In principle, the missionaries were initially the only Europeans allowed to live directly in the settlements of the indigenous population. The crown deliberately separated the different spheres to shield its new subjects. While the members of the mendicant orders originally acted as protectors of the indigenous people and denounced the exploitation by the encomenderos, over time they themselves increasingly became economic exploiters of indigenous labor. Moreover, the clergy as a whole rose to the status of large landowners by taking over of the property of the Mexica priests, and later through inheritance. More and more, their behavior toward those who were entrusted to them resembled that of their worldly overlords. Consequently, there was a gradual decline in the number of church visits and devoutness, in general. This gradual alienation was partly due to the clergy's use of physical violence in dealing with those natives who did not meet expectations or who refused to abandon "pagan customs" quickly enough. In responding to the criticism, the Franciscans pointed to the need for punishment as an educational measure. The "Indios," in their view, were nothing more than stubborn children who were, after all, accustomed to corporal punishment.[47]

The first bishop of New Spain, Franciscan Juan de Zumárraga, took a hard line against all real or suspected forms of religious nonconformity. Zumárraga came to the New World in 1528, together with the members of the first audiencia, and was endowed with the title of "protector of the Indians." After he was given the office of general inquisitor in 1535, the bishop intensified his efforts in the fight against the material remnants of the Mesoamerican religions. For example, that year he had numerous valuable codices collected and burned at the Texcoco market. Temples were also destroyed, and inquisition processes were carried out at his instigation. The latter were mainly directed against conquistadors and settlers, who were persecuted for blasphemy and other transgressions, but also against indigenous people who had been converted and had violated the rules of faith. The most prominent culprit was the tlatoani Don Carlos Ometochtzin of Texcoco, who died at the stake in late November 1539. Yet Zumárraga's radicalism went too far for the crown. There were fears of an uprising, yes, but the inquisition proved counterproductive; the number of converts among the increasingly wary population was declining rapidly. The crown consequently prohibited the abuses and later the inquisition trials against indigenous people altogether.[48]

The inquisition proceedings were another important catalyst for the collection of information on the subjugated communities. In his instructions to Cortés in June 1523, the Charles V had already expressed his optimism regarding the conversion of the indigenous population, since they appeared to be dealing with a highly evolved empire. The crown was hopeful that once human sacrifice and ritual cannibalism were eradicated, the population would quickly turn to the "true" faith. In the first decade of the colony, the main focus was on gaining geographic and economic information for planning further conquests and managing division of the encomiendas. However, as it became apparent that the missionary work was more difficult than originally anticipated, information gathering concentrated on ethnographic details. An event that spurred this was the trial against the priest Martín Ocelotl, who had secretly continued to practice the old faith in Texcoco. He was both respected and feared there because of his magical powers. It was the fear of an indigenous conspiracy that prompted the Franciscans in particular to conduct systematic ethnographic efforts in order to better understand the indigenous religion—and to better persecute it.[49]

For this purpose, learning the native languages was critical. The crown was very keen to have the missionaries learn Nahuatl and teach Spanish to the locals. Indeed, the Franciscans quickly mastered Nahuatl, the lingua franca in multilingual Mesoamerica, and later learned many other regional languages. Andrés de Olmos compiled a first grammar of Nahuatl in 1547. Later, missionaries in remote regions where unknown languages were spoken were even expected to teach Nahuatl, since the indigenous population learned it more easily than Spanish.[50]

The base of knowledge concerning the many different societies with which the missionaries in Mesoamerica came into contact was constantly expanded during the sixteenth century. Early on, the crown commissioned as full an appraisal as possible of the lives of its new subjects. First, a no-longer-extant economic geography of New Spain, the Descripción de la Nueva España, was drawn up and completed by 1532. Afterward, the Council of the Indies continuously requested further documentation and thereby initiated the first ethnographic studies. First and foremost, the involved Franciscans were interested in the social and cultural aspects of the different ethnic groups before and during the Conquest. In their information gathering, they interviewed caciques and religious experts. This resulted in numerous reports and chronicles, the most famous of which is that of Bernardino de Sahagún. Nevertheless, as the purported rebellion of Martín Cortés aroused fears on the part of the crown, King Philip II had the ethnographic books to do with Old Mexico confiscated in 1577 and subsequently kept them under lock and key.[51]

At first glance, the result of Christianization toward the end of the sixteenth century was extraordinary. A network of churches and monasteries had spread in

New Spain on the ruins of the indigenous temples. Hundreds of thousands had been baptized by the missionaries, and pre-Hispanic beliefs were as nonexistent in public as human sacrifice and cannibalism. A closer look reveals a different picture, however. The old beliefs certainly lived on in private, for the daily life of the Mexica was steeped in religious significance. This was reflected in, among other things, nutrition, clothing, language, and even hairstyles. Although Mexica and their neighbors were quick to accept the large church buildings, ceremonies, processions, and images of saints, they usually did not acquire a deeper understanding of Christianity. The voluntary acceptance of baptism was often only a strategy to continue living undisturbed, while retaining as much as possible the rituals that were considered essential for survival. The indigenous population of the colonial period remained polytheistic and integrated the Christian God and his saints into their own pantheon.[52]

From the Spanish point of view, the legitimacy of the Conquest was based on the successful Christianization of a previously pagan, even devil-possessed world. However, for the local clergy entrusted with this task, the reality on the ground was sobering. Often the missionaries complained in their writings that idolatry and superstition lived on. Particularly in the 1520s, the Mesoamerican cults, including human sacrifices, still survived in many places. They were practiced in secret, especially during Cortés's absence. Given their own expectations, the missionaries had only very limited success in the period that followed. This strengthened their conviction that the indigenous people were like feeble and immature children who needed to be dominated and chastised. In New Spain, however, new hybrid forms of Catholicism emerged; they built on adaptations on both sides. Until the end of the colonial era and beyond, the situation was mostly unchanged.[53]

Everyday Life in the Colonial Society

Daily colonial life was overshadowed by the mass deaths of the indigenous population, which lasted throughout the sixteenth and the first half of the seventeenth century. Historian Ross Hassig estimates that the population decreased from about twenty-five million in 1519 to about one million in 1599, a loss of more than 95%. After the plague of 1520 and 1521, which was instrumental in the allies' victory, various waves of epidemics shook Mesoamerica. Diseases such as smallpox, typhus, measles, mumps, diphtheria, and influenza swept away countless people and brought a sense of despair to those left behind. Household structures also changed as a result, with greater emphasis placed on the immediate family. The indigenous population's lack of immunity to the European pathogens, which were transmitted not only by humans but also by animals, as well as the general weakening and demoralization that heightened susceptibility to disease, contributed to a vicious cycle of famine and epidemics.[54]

The struggle for the daily *tlaxcalli* (corn tortilla) was the focus of the daily life for the vast majority of the survivors. This is what characterized their lives before the Spaniards arrived and it would continue to be the case after the Fall of Tenochtitlan. Corn cultivation stayed firmly rooted in tradition and, under the favorable climatic conditions in the Valley of Mexico, initially continued to yield good harvests. The indigenous markets also persisted or were revived. At first, the new settlers from Spain had to rely on what the land could provide in terms of food. However, after the end of the war they quickly strove to change this. Apart from the demand for bread and wine for liturgical reasons, they regarded the preservation of southern European eating habits, such as the consumption of wheat products, wine, and olive oil, as essential for preserving their bodily integrity. By the same token, it was thought that indigenous food would transform and weaken the Spaniards' bodies. In colonial society, nutrition became a central feature of social distinction, alongside one's physical attributes, clothing, language, profession, and surname.[55]

Consequently, new agricultural techniques and crops were introduced from Europe. The plough pulled by draught animals was soon widely used, and the cultivation of wheat, rye, rice, wine, citrus and other fruits, sugar cane, olives, onions, garlic, lentils, and much more was intended to provide a proper diet. Some of these products, such as sugar, required large tracts of land and transformed the landscape. With the import of new tools and household items made of iron, ceramics, and glass, the preparation of food also changed. Furthermore, European farm animals were imported in large numbers. Donkeys, goats, sheep, cattle, horses, dogs, mules, and also rats made the long journey across the Atlantic. While the indigenous population quickly adopted farm animals such as chickens and pigs, horses were reserved for the Spaniards for military and social reasons. Livestock husbandry, both large and small-scale, became ubiquitous.[56]

These changes had far-reaching ecological and social consequences. European cattle species spread and multiplied very quickly in Mesoamerica. One reason for this was the depopulation of large areas of land due to the demographic collapse of the indigenous people. The sprawling Spanish encomenderos contributed to the expansion of this economic form, which was completely new to the region. European crops such as wheat and sugar cane, which occupied the most fertile land, required a considerably higher level of labor and irrigation than the native corn. As a rule, however, these crops were produced for the Spanish diet, or else exported.[57]

One unexpected consequence was soil erosion. This led to considerable productivity declines in certain regions of Mesoamerica and was partly due to deforestation during the reconstruction of the country. Because of the leaching of the soil, the water levels of the lakes rose during the summer rains, which caused flooding in cities, especially in the capital. When the Spaniards then had the lakes drained, a salt desert was the result. As a consequence, canoe traffic collapsed, and more expensive land transport became necessary. Although the new livestock made it possible to transport agricultural products over long distances, much of it flowed into the capital, causing problems in the provinces. In addition, horses, cattle, sheep, and goats, all of which remained mostly under Spanish ownership, needed the land that the indigenous farmers could no longer use for cultivation. The encomenderos' cattle moreover regularly trampled the fields of the indigenous communities, which led to frequent litigation.[58]

All in all, the question of land ownership became a major problem for the everyday lives of large sectors of the population. With the emergence of the great estates, the *latifundias* and *haciendas*, at the expense of indigenous communal property, more and more land went to the descendants of the conquistadors and Spanish immigrants; Cortés's vast property was just one such tract. Added to this was the fact that the Spanish notoriously overestimated the indigenous population in requiring tribute payment, even though it was constantly decreasing due to the demographic catastrophe, making it increasingly difficult for the indigenous communities to pay. Even the judge at the audiencia in Mexico (1556–1566), Alonso de Zorita, described the tribute demands of the Spaniards in some areas as so "exorbitantly high" that they defied all reason.[59] The tribute collectors ruthlessly and violently enforced these demands. Impoverishment resulted for large portions of the population, and many peasants had to sell their homes. By the end of the century, the destitution of the ever-dwindling indigenous population had become so serious that the colonial masters had to arrange for their resettlement to ensure that tributes could be earned and collected in a controlled manner.[60]

It is hardly surprising that different forms of resistance spread in the face of these developments. At the onset of colonial rule, there were repeated local uprisings against encomenderos and their tribute collectors. This was especially true in remote provinces such as Oaxaca and Chiapas. Economic hardship led to people being uprooted, which was reflected in a rise in vagrancy. Orphans were especially affected, but so were many mestizos who had emerged from the not-always-voluntary associations of Spanish men and indigenous women. Alcohol abuse was also rampant. Spaniards considered this stigma to be more or less endemic and "racially typical" for the native population.[61]

Deviant behavior, however, remained the exception. The indigenous peoples' ability to adapt was typical of the Mesoamerican colonial period. Lacking alternatives, they became accustomed to Spanish rule—the one hand, for fear of punishment, and on the other, as in the case of the allies, in the expectation of receiving benefits. Over time, colonial rule came to appear as a normal, even natural order, especially since there was undoubtedly room to maneuver in the local context of the altepetl. Sources show that the locals quickly learned to distinguish between the various groups of Spaniards—the priests, the officials, the soldiers, and so on. They were able to incorporate them into their own world and, under the new circumstances, sought advantages wherever they could. In everyday life, for instance, there was unreserved acceptance of the wheel, pulley, nails, candles, and steel. In other matters, the natives were more reserved. Even though the Spanish monetary economy grew over time, barter and even the cocoa currency long persisted. The Spaniards themselves used the latter to procure various indigenous products such as pharmaceuticals, tobacco, and rubber. The clothing of the Mexica people, which had earned the admiration of the conquistadors, also underwent only gradual changes. Initially, the nobles alone were allowed the privilege of dressing like Spaniards. Later, even the common population would come to embrace long shirts more quickly than pants.[62]

Despite all the processes of adaptation and hybridization, indigenous identities remained largely local. People defined themselves by belonging to a community, to their altepetl with its own origin myth, to their own dynasty, and to a central market. Their leaders used various strategies to acquire certain privileges, from conducting campaigns to initiating legal proceedings to protecting communal land. The documents that emerged in indigenous languages were crucial, since they engendered ideas of a common identity and history and legitimized those in power. Indigenous identities, moreover, changed over time and were influenced by immigrants from Europe and Africa as well as by progressive mestizization. A homogeneous indigenous identity did not emerge during the colonial period or afterward.[63]

From the perspective of the various ethnic groups, the Conquest unquestionably brought profound changes to political structures. At the same time, it did not represent an abrupt end to the old way of life of the vast majority of the population. Particularly in the first half of the sixteenth century, there are many discernible continuities at all levels. The conquerors, after all, neither wanted to nor could they immediately implement all of the changes they sought. The transformation took place slowly. As had been the case under the Mexica, the Spanish conquerors' rule prevailed over the conquered, but the latter's altepemes remained largely intact. Over time, though, tensions were heightened greatly by the demographic collapse and the misguided policies of the Spaniards. Around 1570, an extended economic depression took hold in New Spain. The once integrated economic area of Mesoamerica had disintegrated and there was a retreat to local markets. In the end, the new colonial masters harmed themselves because they failed to anticipate the grave consequences of their actions.

Conclusion

Today, we know that Cortés's personal account in his riveting letter-reports as well as the favored version of events of many sympathetic chroniclers (and even some contemporary history schoolbooks) is false. To be precise, it was not the small group of indomitable Spaniards, under their heroic leader Cortés, who defeated the barbaric empire of the Mexica more or less single-handedly. The fact remains, however, that the empire of the Mexica and its magnificent capital Tenochtitlan perished in 1521. On its ruins, a new type of colonial empire was born, and it would survive for several centuries and become a model for European colonial rule throughout the world. How can this be explained?

Even contemporary observers, starting with Cortés, have focused on psychological factors. The bad omens and the fear of the return of the gods would have paralyzed the Mexica and, above all, their ruler. The Spanish, by contrast, believed that they confronted the enfeebled indigenous population with their superior civilization and rational viewpoint, and were aided by the one true God. To be sure, Moctezuma and his subjects were deeply religious and uncertain about the ways of the Spanish. For this reason, they created tests to prove that the strangers were not gods who had returned. This realization, in any case, did not exclude the possibility that the Spanish could, if only temporarily, become teotl, that is, become animated by a god. Moctezuma's actions, and especially his decision to let the invaders into the capital, must be seen in this context. This does not necessarily imply a paralysis of the Mexica, for they had a different relationship to their gods than the Europeans did to their Christian god. During the war, any reverence for the Spaniards dissipated. And by the end, the Mexica regarded their enemies as nothing more than barbarians. To convince the inhabitants of the remote provinces of this, Cuauhtemoc displayed the severed heads of Spaniards and their horses. The Spanish, too, held supernatural beliefs—for instance, a belief in miracles and a fear of ghosts. When they

considered their successes, the victorious conquistadores glorified this very tendency by claiming that St. Jacob astride his white horse had allegedly stood by
them in battle.

Scholars have often blamed the Mexicas' fighting style for their inability to
prevail against their enemies, despite their clear numerical superiority. Their
ritualized warfare, which involved capturing rather than killing the enemy and
led to high casualties, was contrasted with the "total" warfare of the Spanish,
which did not spare even civilians. Moreover, the Europeans more often used war
ruses and killed with their firearms from a distance, ways of fighting for which
Mexicans had nothing but contempt. Even the idea of conducting a siege, with
the aim of weakening the enemy before battle, was foreign to them. Nevertheless,
when one carefully reads the sources, it is difficult to dispute the more recent research that assumes that the Spaniards greatly exaggerated the number of their
enemies in order to put their own heroic actions into a better light.

The victory of the Spaniards and their allies was not due to their civilizational
and religious superiority or to their exceptional strategy, as the chroniclers liked
to claim. Both warring sides could only partially interpret the actions of their
enemies accurately, and their own actions suffered as a result. Still, the factions
learned during the fighting and adjusted their tactics accordingly. Thus, the
Mexica, over time, adapted their way of fighting to the demands of the situation
and, for practical reasons, became less and less concerned with traditional ideas
of warfare. What both had in common was the necessity, indeed the compul-
sion, to wage the war to a decisive conclusion. Cortés, after all, could not return
to Cuba, and for the Mexica, unlike the small altepeme, subjugation was out of
the question.

In the course of the conflicts, the Mexica tried to seize and employ their
enemies' iron weapons. The superiority of Spanish swords, lances, cannons,
crossbows, and arquebuses was especially evident in close combat. Obsidian
swords, bows, slingshots, and javelins were simply no match. The notable extent
to which the Florentine Codex, for example, deals with European armor and
weapons is an evidence for the importance the Mexica attached to this dimension of the conflict. The Spaniards' horses were another aspect of their upper
hand; though the locals' initial shock at seeing the animals did not last long, the
cavalry gave the Europeans a decisive advantage in the open field battle, albeit
less so in the house-to-house skirmishes of the final few weeks. The significance
that the Mexica attributed to the horses is reflected in their own actions: they
sacrificed captured animals as they did humans, and their heads also wound up
on tzompantli.

But the superiority of weapons alone would not have been enough to win
the victory against the powerful Tenochtitlan, especially since the vast majority
of the attackers fought with the same weapons as the Mexica. The indigenous

allies not only formed a clear numerical majority, but their fighting strength also proved pivotal, due to its effectiveness. If they were mentioned at all in the Spanish reports, it was merely as auxiliary troops. They filled in the trenches or carried the equipment; they also froze to death and died of thirst during the exhausting marches, while the Spaniards and their horses enjoyed protection against the elements and plenty of water. Truth be told, they were also warriors who fought on the front line and paid dearly, and sustained the far higher death toll.

If we read Bernal Díaz carefully, we find that he repeatedly hints at the actual role of the indigenous allies—notwithstanding the fact that the conquistador preferred to gloss over this so as not to diminish his own performance. The relatively small number of Spanish casualties compared to that of their allies might indicate that the most dangerous part of the battle was left to the indigenous troops.[1] Of course, the Spanish chroniclers took a very different view. In their eyes, it was always their brave compatriots who led the way and overcame the fiercest battles. The indigenous allies, conversely, primarily attacked the enemy when the latter was already weakened. They allegedly murdered, raped, and looted without restraint and could hardly be brought under control. Thus, Díaz reported about one of the battles at Chalco in March 1521:

> . . . When our soldiers had broken the resistance and fled [the enemy], they no longer inflicted any harm on any Indian, because it seemed overly cruel. All they did was to look for a good Indian female and plunder. They also often quarreled with their allies because they were so merciless, and wrested some Indians from them so that they would not kill them.[2]

The dubious nature of such descriptions becomes most apparent when indigenous sources such as the Lienzos of Tlaxcala or Quauquechollan are consulted, along with texts such as the Codex Ramírez or the famous letter from Xochimilco. In this testimony, the authorities of the city confidently wrote to King Philip II: "We provided the Marqués with two thousand canoes with equipment and twelve thousand warriors, who saved them and with whom they conquered Mexico. Even the Tlaxcalans, who came from a distant land and were tired, were saved. Following God, then, Xochimilco had the greatest merit in victory."[3] The Spanish are thus portrayed as being equal allies or as respected opponents, but by no means as superhuman. If we are to believe them, indigenous princes were the first to plunge into battle and lead the allied armies to victory over the fearsome Mexica. As a rule, the documents were created long after the events. They served as proof of services rendered and merits earned by one's own ethnic group vis-à-vis the king, from whom privileges could be expected in return. This also applied to the Spanish sources, which were equally designed to justify and exaggerate individual achievements.

In addition, indigenous accounts reveal that the Spanish troops and their leader by no means always determined the course of the campaigns. Often, they were only an auxiliary force, if a particularly powerful one, in the pursuit of the war goals of the Tlaxcalans, for example. The Cholula massacre is the best example of this. Not only could the flight after La Noche Triste and the Battle of Otumba hardly be classified as proof of Spanish heroism, but they also revealed the weakness of the Europeans and their dependence in a foreign environment. Even the frenzied looting and killing in the defeated city of Tenochtitlan underscores how little influence Cortés had on his allies. After the fall of the capital, colonial rule consolidated slowly. Support from indigenous allies therefore remained crucial for maintaining status.

There were manifold reasons why the allies followed the Spaniards. Some marched along with the Spaniards by force, others went into battle voluntarily and returned home again after the victorious battles, and still others continued to fight together with the Spaniards even after 1521. Young warriors wanted to win fame and honor for themselves and their altepetl. In addition to the pursuit of prestige, successful campaigns with the Spaniards brought material advantages. New settlement areas, tributes, and male and female slaves beckoned as rewards. The Spanish marriage policy also contributed to forging alliances, as for example when Cortés accepted the daughters of the indigenous rulers as gifts and married them to his officers.

It is necessary, therefore, to abandon the idea that the conquest of Tenochtitlan was solely a struggle between Europeans and indigenous peoples. Stereotypes of barbarian man-eaters, on the one hand, and genocidal conquistadors, on the other, are obsolete. They say more about the ideological context of the time in which they were written and continue to be propagated than they do about the interpretation of the past. Various indigenous groups fought together with the Spaniards against the Mexica and their allies, although the alliances changed rapidly under the pressure of the hostilities. For Cortés and his men, these alliances were essential for their survival, as Cortés needed to understand how to exploit the rivalries between and within the city-states. For this, Malinche's translation services were invaluable.

A decisive factor was thus the structural instability of the Mesoamerican world of city-states, in which the parties simply bided their time until a neighbor showed weakness and then subjugated them or freed themselves from an oppressive tribute. For some indigenous groups, the Spanish might have appeared, if only at first, as liberators from the yoke of the Mexica, as they later liked to present themselves. City-states that did not cooperate directly with the attackers also took advantage of the weakening of the Mexica Empire to stop paying their tributes, which in turn aggravated Tenochtitlan's crisis. Within the altepeme, a succession arrangement that produced a large number of discontented sons of the tlatoani contributed to rivalries and open conflict, which further benefited the Spanish. The war over Tenochtitlan also had the characteristics of a bitterly fought fratricidal war. In this volatile environment, Cortés was able to become a kingmaker by learning how to use conflict for his own ends, often with the help of the forces of contingency.

The conquest of Tenochtitlan was thus the culmination of a Mesoamerican war, which must be understood as part of a long history of military conflicts between the Mexica and their countless enemies. It constituted a successful uprising of indigenous ethnic groups against their tribute rulers. In this Cortés and his hueste ultimately played a secondary role. The fact that the Mexica lost a war was nothing new. What was actually new was that the Spaniards suspended the rules of Mesoamerican warfare, that Cortés managed to become the leader of the campaign to take over the rule of Tenochtitlan, and, on this basis, that he later conquered the entire Mexica Empire. The indigenous allies played a central role again in these later campaigns. But the decisive factor was that none of these allied altepeme—whether Tlaxcala or Texcoco or the many others—pursued a plan of their own to achieve overall domination.

Certainly, the epidemics brought from Europe, which killed thousands in a few weeks and had a serious impact not just on the Mexica people, played a key role in the indigenous city-states' acceptance of the foreigners' domination over time. Simultaneously, the Spaniards had a substantial, even life-saving advantage because of their immunity. That both sides sought explanations for this demographic catastrophe in the work of supernatural powers was in keeping with the ideas of the time. Europeans and indigenous peoples proved to be very similar in this regard. The "great leprosy" (*hueyzahuatl*), as the Nahua called the epidemic, struck the Mexica and their enemies en masse and severely weakened the resistance of the indigenous population of Mesoamerica at the critical moment of the establishment of colonial rule.[4]

The actors involved in the Conquest had diverse values and world views, which were radically changed by the momentous events. Their interpretations were an effort to classify and categorize the new and the foreign in order to put it into a form understandable to themselves and the social and ethnic group to which they belonged. There were, moreover, many misunderstandings and ambiguities in communication, which were complicated by the need to translate not only words but also the concepts behind them. The text reports and pictorial representations, lienzos, maps, chronicles, annals, and archives that have come down to us bear witness to this. At the same time, they are the expression of a process of worldmaking that spanned the Atlantic and created new orders in which Mesoamerican and European elements merged.

NOTES

Introduction

1. "López Obrador asegura en su carta al rey que los abusos de la conquista 'aún generan encendidas polémicas'," *El País*, May 4, 2017, https://elpais.com/internacional/2019/03/27/mexico/1553651641_263448.html.
2. "Mexica" was the proper name of the population of Tenochtitlan and Tlaltelolco. The term "Aztec" was introduced in the 18th century in allusion the mythical Aztlan. In the following, I will use the proper nomenclature. See: Hanns J. Prem, *Die Azteken: Geschichte, Kultur, Religion* (München: C. H. Beck, 1999), 9–10.
3. David A. Lupher, *Romans in a New World: Classical Models in Sixteenth-Century Spanish America* (Ann Arbor: University of Michigan Press, 2003), 8.
4. The estimates vary considerably. I follow: Serge Gruzinski, *La ciudad de Mexico: Una historia* (México: Fondo de Cultura Económica, 2004), 263.
5. John H. Elliott, *Die Neue in der Alten Welt: Folgen Einer Eroberung, 1492–1650* (Berlin: Wagenbach, 1992), 44.
6. In Western languages the spellings of this ruler's name differ widely. Montezuma, Moctezoma and many other versions are in circulation. My own spelling follows: Prem, *Die Azteken*, 18. The meaning of the name: *Teuc* means "Lord," and *Mo . . . zoma* means "he rages," as explained by: Berthold Riese, *Das Reich der Azteken: Geschichte und Kultur* (München: C.H. Beck, 2011), 251.
7. Stefan Rinke, *Kolumbus und der Tag von Guanahani: 1492, Ein Wendepunkt der Geschichte* (Stuttgart: Theiss, 2013), 73–75.
8. David A. Boruchoff, "Indians, Cannibals, and Barbarians: Hernan Cortes and Early Modern Cultural Relativism," *Ethnohistory* 62, no. 1 (January 1, 2015): 26–28, https://doi.org/10.1215/00141801-2821657.
9. Stephanie G. Wood, *Transcending Conquest: Nahua Views of Spanish Colonial Mexico* (Norman: University of Oklahoma Press, 2003), 23. Gordon Whittaker, "The Principles of Nahuatl Writing," *Göttinger Beiträge zur Sprachwissenschaft* 16 (2009): 47–81. Camilla Townsend, *Annals of Native America: How the Nahuas of Colonial Mexico Kept Their History Alive* (Oxford: Oxford University Press, 2016), 1–17.
10. Kenneth Pomeranz, *The Great Divergence: China, Europe, and the Making of the Modern World Economy* (Princeton: Princeton University Press, 2009), 12–15.
11. Bernd Hausberger, *Die Verknüpfung der Welt: Geschichte der frühen Globalisierung vom 16. bis zum 18. Jahrhundert*, Expansion, Interaktion, Akkulturation, Band 27 (Wien: Mandelbaum Verlag, 2015), 37–56.
12. Carlo Klauth, *Geschichtskonstruktion bei der Eroberung Mexikos: am Beispiel der Chronisten Bernal Díaz del Castillo, Bartolomé de las Casas und Gonzales Fernández de Oviedo* (Hildesheim: Olms, 2012), 64–65.

13. Roland Bernhard, *Geschichtsmythen über Hispanoamerika: Entdeckung, Eroberung und Kolonisierung in deutschen und österreichischen Schulbüchern des 21. Jahrhunderts* (Göttingen: V & R unipress, 2013), 130.

14. Arif Dirlik, "Performing the World: Reality and Representation in the Making of World Histor(Ies)," *Journal of World History* 16, no. 4 (2005): 391–401, https://doi.org/10.1353/jwh.2006.0016.

15. Barbara Caine, *Biography and History* (Basingstoke: Palgrave Macmillan, 2010), 23–27.

16. Caine, 27.

17. A standard work for the concept of "worldmaking" is: Nelson Goodman, *Ways of Worldmaking* (Indianapolis: Hackett, 1978).

18. Baltasar Dorantes de Carranza as quoted in: Iván Vélez Cipriano, *El mito de Cortés: De héroe universal a icono de la leyenda negra* (Madrid: Ediciones Encuentro, 2016), 94–95. On Cortés's veneration, see also Vélez Cipriano, 112–127; Ingrid Simson, *Amerika in der spanischen Literatur des Siglo de Oro: Bericht, Inszenierung, Kritik* (Frankfurt am Main: Vervuert, 2003), 185–186; Michael J. Schreffler, *The Art of Allegiance: Visual Culture and Imperial Power in Baroque New Spain* (University Park: Pennsylvania State University Press, 2007).

19. William Prescott, *History of the Conquest of Mexico* (New York: Modern Library, [1841] 2001).

20. José Vasconcelos, *Hernán Cortés, creador de la nacionalidad* (México: Xochitl, 1941), 14.

21. José Luis Martínez, *Hernán Cortés*, Breviarios del Fondo de Cultura Económica (México: Fondo de Cultura Económica, 1992), 10.

22. Vélez Cipriano, *El mito de Cortés*, 14–15.

23. Vélez Cipriano, 145–157; Matthew Bennett Restall, "Spanish Creation of the Conquest of Mexico," in *Invasion and Transformation: Interdisciplinary Perspectives on the Conquest of Mexico*, eds. Rebecca Parker Brienen and Margaret Ann Jackson (Boulder: University Press of Colorado, 2008), 99; Monika Wehrheim, "De enemigos a antecesores: Cortés, Clavijero y Pesado y la construcción de los aztecas," *Romanische Forschungen* 3, no. 116 (2004): 346–360.

24. Regarding earlier literature, see: Rafael Heliodoro Valle, *Bibliografía de Hernán Cortés*, Publicaciones de La Sociedad de Estudios Cortesianos (México: Editorial Jus, 1953). The most important works of contemporary research include: Martínez, *Hernán Cortés*; Demetrio Ramos Pérez, *Hernán Cortés: mentalidad y propósitos* (Madrid: Ediciones Rialp, 1992); John H. Elliott et al., *Hernán Cortés y México* (Sevilla: Diputación Sevilla, 2000); Christian Duverger, *Cortés* (Paris: Fayard, 2001); Juan Miralles Ostos, *Hernán Cortés: inventor de México* (Barcelona: Tusquets Editores, 2001); Bartolomé Bennassar, *Cortez der Konquistador: die Eroberung des Aztekenreiches* (Düsseldorf: Artemis und Winkler, 2002). See also the discussion in: Karl Kohut, "Literatura y cultura coloniales: Cuestiones teóricas y Nueva España," *Iberoamericana* 4, no. 14 (2004): 189–210. Many more works have been published since then, among them: José Antonio Vaca de Osma, *Hernán Cortés* (Madrid: Espasa Calpe, 2000); Francisco Martínez Hoyos, *Breve historia de Hernan Cortés* (Madrid: Nowtilus, 2014). A good and recent literature review is found in: Esteban Mira Caballos, *Hernán Cortés: el fin de una leyenda* (Trujillo: Palacio de Barrantes Cervantes, 2010). On the monument controversy, see: Vélez Cipriano, *El mito de Cortés*, 196–197. In an article for *El País* of October 12, 1985, Octavio Paz succinctly summarizes the ambivalence in the evaluation of Cortés, which now can also be found in Mexico, see: Octavio Paz, "Hernán Cortés: exorcismo y liberación," in *México en la obra de Octavio Paz; 1: el peregrino en su patria* (México: Fondo de Cultura Económica, 1988), 100–112.

25. Susan D. Gillespie, "Blaming Moteuczoma," in *Invasion and Transformation: Interdisciplinary Perspectives on the Conquest of Mexico*, eds. Rebecca Parker Brienen and Margaret Ann Jackson (Boulder: University Press of Colorado, 2008), 26–30.

26. Inga Clendinnen, "'Fierce and Unnatural Cruelty': Cortés and the Conquest of Mexico," *Representations*, no. 33 (Winter 1991): 69; James Lockhart, *The Nahuas after the Conquest: A Social and Cultural History of the Indians of Central Mexico, Sixteenth through Eighteenth Centuries* (Stanford: Stanford University Press, 1992).

27. Camilla Townsend, "Burying the White Gods: New Perspectives on the Conquest of Mexico," *The American Historical Review* 108, no. 3 (2003): 679.

28. Bernard Grunberg, *Histoire de la conquête du Mexique* (Paris: L'Harmattan, 1995), 207–217.

29. A good summary of the arguments can be found in; Ross Hassig, *Mexico and the Spanish Conquest*, 2nd ed. (Norman: University of Oklahoma Press, 2006), 4.

30. Tzvetan Todorov, *Die Eroberung Amerikas: Das Problem des Anderen*, trans. Wilfried Böhringer (Frankfurt am Main: Suhrkamp, 1985).

31. Wolfgang Gabbert, *Kultureller Determinismus und die Eroberung Mexikos: Zur Kritik eines dichotomischen Geschichtsverständnisses* (Freiburg: Alber, 1995), 276–280; Jeanne Gillespie, *Saints and Warriors: Tlaxcalan Perspectives on the Conquest of Tenochtitlan* (New Orleans: University Press South, 2004), 27.

32. Hassig, *Mexico and the Spanish Conquest*, 3.

33. For this view see, e.g.: Hugh Thomas, *Die Eroberung Mexikos: Cortés und Montezuma* (Frankfurt am Main: Fischer-Taschenbuch-Verl, 1993); Clendinnen, "'Fierce and Unnatural Cruelty': Cortés and the Conquest of Mexico," 65. A discussion of the criticism is found in Gillespie, "Blaming Moteuczoma," 25.

34. Laura Matthew and Michel Oudijk, "Conclusion," in *Indian Conquistadors: Indigenous Allies in the Conquest of Mesoamerica*, eds. Laura Matthew and Michel Oudijk (Norman: University of Oklahoma Press, 2007), 319–321.

35. For example: Inga Clendinnen, *Ambivalent Conquests: Maya and Spaniard in Yucatan, 1517–1570* (Cambridge: Cambridge University Press, 1987); Matthew Restall, *Maya Conquistador* (Boston: Beacon Press, 1998).

36. Michel Oudijk and Matthew Restall, "Mesoamerican Conquistadors in the Sixteenth Century," in *Indian Conquistadors: Indigenous Allies in the Conquest of Mesoamerica*, eds. Laura Matthew and Michel Oudijk (Norman: University of Oklahoma Press, 2007), 30; Danna Levin Rojo and Federico Navarrete Linares, eds., *Indios, mestizos y españoles: Interculturalidad e historiografía en la Nueva España* (Azcapotzalco: Universidad Autónoma Metropolitana, 2007).

37. Restall, *Maya Conquistador*, 43; Matthew Restall, "The New Conquest History," *History Compass* 10, no. 2 (2012): 151–160.

38. For the sources, see the overviews in: Georges Baudot, *Utopía e Historia en México: Los primeros cronistas de la civilización mexicana (1520–1569)* (Madrid: Espasa-Calpe, 1983); Francisco Esteve Barba, *Historiografía indiana*, 2a ed. (Madrid: Gredos, 1992).

39. José Luis Martínez, *Documentos cortesianos (DC) 1: 1518–1528*, vol. I (México: Universidad Nacional Autónoma de México, 1990), 9–10.

40. Hernán Cortés, *Cartas de relación*, ed. Manuel Alcalá, XXI (México: Editorial Porrúa, 2005); Ricardo Padrón, *The Spacious Word: Cartography, Literature, and Empire in Early Modern Spain* (Chicago: University of Chicago Press, 2004), 116–136; Elizabeth Wright, "New World News, Ancient Echoes: A Cortés Letter and a Vernacular Livy for a New King and His Wary Subjects (1520–23)," *Renaissance Quarterly* 61, no. 3 (2008): 712.

41. Beatriz Aracil Varón, "Hernán Cortés y sus cronistas: la última conquista del héroe," *Atenea*, no. 499 (2009): 61–76; Viviana Díaz Balsera, "The Hero as Rhetor: Hernán Cortés's Second and Third Letters to Charles V," in *Invasion and Transformation: Interdisciplinary Perspectives on the Conquest of Mexico*, eds. Rebecca Parker Brienen and Margaret Ann Jackson (Boulder: University Press of Colorado, 2008), 57–74; Glen Carman, *Rhetorical Conquests: Cortés, Gómara, and Renaissance Imperialism* (West Lafayette: Purdue University Press, 2006), 55–71; Felix Hinz, *"Hispanisierung" in Neu-Spanien 1519–1568: Transformation kollektiver Identitäten von Mexica, Tlaxkalteken und Spaniern*, vol. 3 (Hamburg: Dr. Kovač, 2005), 648–654.

42. Bernal Díaz del Castillo, *Historia verdadera de la conquista de la Nueva España*, eds. Juan Gil and Carmen Sáenz de Santa María (Madrid: Fundación José Antonio de Castro, 2012).

43. Michel Graulich, "'La mera verdad resiste a mi rudeza:' forgeries et mensonges dans l'Historia verdadera de la conquista de la Nueva España de Bernal Diaz del Castillo," *Journal de la société des américanistes* 82, no. 1 (1996): 63–95. See also: Angelina Hartnagel, *Bernal Díaz Del Castillo, Doña Marina und die hohe Kunst der Historiographie: Eine Umfeldanalyse der Historia verdadera de la Conquista de la Nueva España* (Frankfurt am Main: Peter Lang, 2013); Juan Miralles Ostos, *Y Bernal Mintió: El lado oscuro de su Historia verdadera de la conquista de la Nueva España*, Taurus Historia (México: Taurus, 2008). Adorno argues that Bernal wrote not only in opposition to López de Gómara, but also to Bartolomé de las Casas, see: Rolena Adorno, "Discourses on Colonialism: Bernal Díaz, Las Casas, and the Twentieth-Century

Reader," *Modern Language Notes* 103, no. 2 (1988): 239–258. Duverger even assumes that Cortés himself is the author of the *Historia verdadera*, which he would have had to write under a pseudonym because he was banned from writing, and that Bernal Díaz did not exist because there were no indications of his existence before 1544, see: Christian Duverger, *Crónica de la eternidad: ¿Quién escribió La historia verdadera de la conquista de la Nueva España?* (México: Taurus, 2012); Christian Duverger, *Cortés et son double: Enquête sur une mystification* (Paris: Seuil, 2013). María del Carmen Martínez Martínez has shown, however, that Bernal Díaz co-signed the "Primera carta de relación" of the Cabildo of Veracruz from the middle of 1519, which disproves Duverger's thesis, in: María del Carmen Martínez Martínez, *Veracruz 1519: Los Hombres de Cortés* (León: Universidad de León, 2013), 11. Schwaller and Nader have confirmed this in: John Frederick Schwaller and Helen Nader, *The First Letter from New Spain: The Lost Petition of Cortés and His Company, June 20, 1519* (Austin: University of Texas Press, 2014), 40. On the debate surrounding Duverger in Mexico and Spain, see: María Beatriz Aracil Varón, *"Yo, Don Hernando Cortés": reflexiones En torno a la escritura cortesiana* (Madrid: Iberoamericana, 2016), 45–48.

44. Guillermo Turner, *Los soldados de la conquista: Herencias culturales* (México: Ediciones el Tucán de Virginia, 2013), 19–78.

45. Díaz del Castillo, *Historia verdadera de la conquista de la Nueva España*, 931.

46. Francisco de Aguilar, "Relación breve de la conquista de la Nueva España [1892]," in *La Conquista de Tenochtitlan*, ed. Germán Vázquez (Madrid: Historia 16, 1988), 155–206.

47. Andrés de Tapia, "Relación de algunas cosas de las que acaecieron al muy iluestre Señor Don Hernando Cortés [1866]," in *La Conquista de Tenochtitlan*, ed. Germán Vázquez (Madrid: Historia 16, 1988), 59–123.

48. Bernardino Vásquez de Tapia, "Relación de Méritos y Servicios [1939]," in *La Conquista de Tenochtitlan*, ed. Germán Vázquez (Madrid: Historia 16, 1988), 125–154.

49. Conquistador Anónimo, "Relación de algunas cosas de la Nueva España, y de la gran ciudad de Temestitán México; Escrita por un compañero de Hernán Cortés," in *CDM*, ed. Joaquín García Icazbalceta, 1, n.d., http://www.cervantesvirtual.com/obra-visor/coleccion-de-doc umentos-para-la-historia-de-mexico-version-actualizada--0/html/21bcd5af-6c6c-4b27- a9a5-5edf8315e835_20.html#I_12_. See also: Esteve Barba, *Historiografía indiana*, 169– 175; Baudot, *Utopía e historia en México*, 37–40.

50. Klauth, *Geschichtskonstruktion bei der Eroberung Mexikos*, 60–63.

51. Gillespie, "Blaming Moteuczoma," 26; Hassig, *Mexico and the Spanish Conquest*, 4–5.

52. Baudot, *Utopía e historia en México*, 78–79.

53. Peter Martyr von [Pietro Martire d'] Anghiera, *Acht Dekaden über die Neue Welt*, ed. Hans Klingelhöfer, 2nd ed. (Darmstadt: Wiss. Buchges., 1973).

54. Gonzalo Fernández de Oviedo, *Historia general y natural de las Indias, Islas y Tierra-Firme del Mar Océano* (Madrid: Imprenta de la Real Academia de la Historia, 1851 [1532]).

55. Kathleen Ann Myers, *Fernández de Oviedo's Chronicle of America: A New History for a New World*, (Austin: University of Texas Press, 2007), 1; Esteve Barba, *Historiografía indiana*, 64–82; Mariano Cuesta Domingo, "Los cronistas oficiales de Indias: De López de Velasco a Céspedes del Castillo," *Revista Complutense de Historia de América*, no. 33 (2007): 119.

56. Francisco López de Gómara, *La conquista de México*, ed. José Luis de Rojas Gutiérrez de Gandarilla (Madrid: Dastin, 1987); Carman, *Rhetorical Conquests*, 9 and 72–112; Hinz, *"Hispanisierung" in Neu-Spanien 1519–1568*, 3:742–748; Nora Edith Jiménez, *Francisco López de Gómara: Escribir historias en tiempos de Carlos V* (México: Colegio de Michoacán, 2001); Cristián Andrés Roa-de-la Carrera, *Histories of infamy: Francisco López de Gómara and the ethics of Spanish imperialism*, trans. Scott Sessions (Boulder: University Press of Colorado, 2012), 1–2. On Díaz del Castillo's reckoning with López de Gómara, see Díaz del Castillo, *Historia verdadera de la conquista de la Nueva España*, 43–46.

57. The Latin original with Spanish translation in: Juan Ginés de Sepúlveda, *Del Nuevo Mundo*, ed. Luis Rivero García, Obras completas 11 (Pozoblanco: Excmo. Ayuntamiento, 2005); Esteve Barba, *Historiografía indiana*, 103–105.

58. Bartolomé de las Casas, *Historia de Las Indias*, vol. 3, 5 vols., Obras Completas 3 (Madrid: Alianza Editorial, 1994); Esteve Barba, *Historiografía Indiana*, 88–98.

59. Toribio de [Motolinía] Benavente, *Memoriales: O libro de las cosas de la Nueva España y de los naturales de ella*, ed. Edmundo O'Gorman, 2. ed (México: Universidad Nacional Autónoma de México, Instituto de Investigaciones Históricas, 1971); Baudot, *Utopía e historia en México*, 247–387; Hinz, *"Hispanisierung" in Neu-Spanien 1519–1568*, 3:725.

60. Gerónimo de Mendieta, *Historia eclesiástica indiana*, ed. Joaquín García Icazbalceta and Antonio Rubial García, 2nd ed., vol. 1 (México: Consejo Nacional para la Cultura y las Artes, 1997); Esteve Barba, *Historiografía indiana*, 198–204.

61. Alonso de Zorita, *Edición crítica de la relación de la Nueva España y de la breve y sumaria relación escritas por Alonso de Zorita*, ed. Wiebke Ahrndt, trans. Luis Felipe Segura (Bonn: Sauerwein, 2001).

62. Francisco Cervantes y Salazar, *Cronica de la Nueva España*, ed. Manuel Magallón, 2nd ed. (Madrid: Ed. Atlas, 1971). See also: Esteve Barba, *Historiografía indiana*, 178–191.

63. José Rabasa, *Inventing America: Spanish Historiography and the Formation of Eurocentrism*, (Norman: University of Oklahoma Press, 1993), 3.

64. "Visión de los vencidos" was the original title of the source edition by Miguel León Portilla. In the following, I quote from the German translation, first published in 1962:Renate Heuer, *Rückkehr Der Götter: Die Aufzeichnungen Der Azteken Über Den Untergang Ihres Reiches* (Köln: Middelhauve, 1962). See also: James Lockhart, ed., *We People Here: Nahuatl Accounts of the Conquest of Mexico* (Berkeley: University of California Press, 1993); Robin Blackburn and Heraclio Bonilla, eds., *Los conquistados: 1492 y la población indígena de las Américas* (Santafé de Bogotá: Tercer Mundo Editores, 1992).

65. John Bierhorst, ed., *Cantares Mexicanos: Songs of the Aztecs* (Stanford: Stanford University Press, 1985).

66. Heinrich Berlin and Robert H. Barlow, eds., *Anales de Tlatelolco: Unos anales históricos de la nación mexicana y Códice de Tlatelolco* (México: Antigua Libr. Robredo, de José Porrua e Hijos, 1948).

67. Lockhart and Townsend claim that there are no indigenous sources from the 1520s and 30s. Lockhart, *We People Here*, 3; Townsend, "Burying the White Gods," 665.

68. Gabriel Miguel Pastrana Flores, *Historias de la conquista: Aspectos de la historiografía de tradición náhuatl* (México: Universidad Nacional Autónoma de México, 2004).

69. Federico Navarrete Linares, "La Malinche, la Virgen y la montaña: El juego de la identidad en los Códices Tlaxcaltecas," *História (São Paulo)* 26, no. 2 (2007): 289; Gillespie, *Saints and Warriors*, 34–170.

70. Wood, *Transcending Conquest*, 8–9.

71. Diego Muñoz Camargo, *Historia de Tlaxcala*, ed. Alfredo Chavero (México: Oficina Tip. de la Secretaría de Fomento, 1892 [1531]).

72. Fernando Alvarado Tezozomoc, *Crónica Mexicana*, ed. Gonzalo Díaz Migoyo (Madrid: Historia 16, 1997).

73. Bradley Benton, "The Outsider: Alva Ixtlilxochitl's Tenuous Ties to the City of Tetzcoco," *Colonial Latin American Review*, no. 23 (2014): 37–52.

74. Fernando de Alva Ixtlilxóchitl, "Décima tercia relación, de la venida de los españoles y principio de la ley evangélica," in *Historia general de las cosas de Nueva España*, ed. Bernardino de Sahagún, vol. 4 (México, 1938), 237–336; Fernando de Alva Ixtlilxóchitl, *Obras históricas: Incluyen el texto completo de las llamadas Relaciones e historia de la nación Chichimeca en una nueva versión establecida con el cotejo de los manuscritos más antiguos que se conocen*, eds. Edmundo O'Gorman and Miguel León Portilla, 2nd ed., vol. 3, Biblioteca Nezahualcóyotl (Toluca: Instituto Mexiquense de Cultura, 1997).

75. Domingo Francisco de San Antón Muñón Chimalpahin Quauhtlehuanitzin, *Relaciones originales de Chalco Amaquemacan*, ed. Silvia Rendón (México: Fondo de Cultura Económica, 1965).

76. Verónica Rodríguez and Monica Styles, "Domingo Francisco de San Antón Muñón Chimalpahin Cuatlehuanitzin (1579–1660)," in *Narradores indígenas y mestizos de la época xolonial (aiglos XVI–XVII): Zonas andina y Mesoamericana*, eds. Rocío Cortés and Margarita Zamora (Lima: Centro de Estudios Literarios "Antonio Cornejo Polar," 2016), 111–117; Susan Schroeder, "Writing the Nahuatl Canon: Ethnicity, Identity, and Posterity According to Chimalpahin," in *To Be Indio in Colonial Spanish America*, ed. Mónica Díaz

(Albuquerque: University of New Mexico Press, 2017), 226–229; David Tavárez, "Reclaiming the Conquest," in *Chimalpahin's Conquest*, ed. Susan Schroeder (Stanford: Stanford University Press, 2010), 18. The tradition was continued with Juan Buenaventura Zapata y Mendoza (ca. 1620–1688), who rejected Spanish sources and instead relied on Nahuatl texts for his work: Juan Buenaventura Zapata y Mendoza, "Historia xronológica de la noble ciudad de Tlaxcala," in *Narradores indígenas y mestizos de la época colonial (siglos XVI–XVII): Zonas andina y mesoamericana*, eds. Rocío Cortés and Margarita Zamora (Lima: Centro de Estudios Literarios "Antonio Cornejo Polar," 2016), 139–151; Camilla Townsend, "Don Juan Buenaventura Zapata y Mendoza," in *Narradores indígenas y mestizos de la época colonial (siglos XVI–XVII): Zonas andina y mesoamericana*, eds. Rocío Cortés and Margarita Zamora (Lima: Centro de Estudios Literarios "Antonio Cornejo Polar," 2016), 136–138.

77. Hassig, *Mexico and the Spanish Conquest*, 4.
78. Bernardino de Sahagún, *Historia general de las cosas de Nueva España*, eds. Alfredo López Austin and Josefina García Quintana, 2nd ed. (Madrid: Alianza, 1988). In the following, I will be using the English translation by Arthur J. O. Anderson and Charles E. Dibble: Bernardino de Sahagún, *Florentine Codex: General History of the Things of New Spain, Book 12–The Conquest of Mexico*. Translated by Arthur J. O. Anderson and Charles E. Dibble. 2nd ed. Vol. 13. 13 vols. Santa Fe: The School of American Research and the University of Utah, 1975. On Sahagún in-depth: Miguel León Portilla, *Bernardino de Sahagún* (Madrid: Historia 16, 1987); Victoria Ríos Castaño, *Translation as Conquest: Sahagún and Universal History of the Things of New Spain* (Madrid: Iberoamericana, 2014); José Rubén Romero Galván and Pilar Máynez, eds., *El universo de Sahagún: pasado y presente* (México: Universidad Nacional Autónoma de México, 2007).
79. David Anthony Brading, *The First America: The Spanish Monarchy, Creole Patriots, and the Liberal State, 1492–1867* (Cambridge: Cambridge University Press, 1991), 120; David M. Solodkow, *Etnógrafos coloniales: Alteridad y escritura en la conquista de América (siglo XVI)* (Madrid: Iberoamericana, 2014), 313–325.
80. Jongsoo Lee, "The Europeanization of Prehispanic Tradition: Bernardino de Sahagún's Transformation of Aztec Priests (Tlamacazque) into Classical Wise Men (Tlamatinime)," *Colonial Latin American Review*, no. 26 (2017): 291–312.
81. Juan de Tovar, *Códice Ramírez: manuscrito del siglo XVI intitulado: Relación del origen de los Indios que habitan esta Nueva España, según sus historias* (México: Ed. Innovación, 1979).
82. Baudot, *Utopía e historia en México*, 483–485.
83. Elizabeth Hill Boone and Walter D. Mignolo, eds., *Writing without Words: Alternative Literacies in Mesoamerica and the Andes* (Durham: Duke University Press, 1994), https://doi.org/10.1215/9780822379263; Daniela Bleichmar, "The Imperial Visual Archive: Images, Evidence, and Knowledge in the Early Modern Hispanic World," *Colonial Latin American Review* 24, no. 2 (2015): 236–266.
84. Federico Navarrete Linares, "Beheadings and Massacres: Andean and Mesoamerican Representations of the Spanish Conquest," *Anthropology and Aesthetics*, no. 53/54 (Spring-Autumn 2008): 78.
85. Navarrete Linares, "La Malinche, La virgen y La montaña: El juego de la identidad en los Códices Tlaxcaltecas," 292; Florine Asselbergs, "The Conquest in Images: Stories of Tlaxcalteca and Quauhquecholteca Conquistadors," in *Indian Conquistadors: Indigenous Allies in the Conquest of Mesoamerica*, eds. Laura Matthew and Michel Oudijk (Norman: University of Oklahoma Press, 2007), 66; Gillespie, *Saints and Warriors*, 82–86; Byron Ellsworth Hamann, "Object, Image, Cleverness: The Lienzo de Tlaxcala," *Art History* 36, no. 3 (2013): 523–525.

Chapter 1

1. John Huxtable Elliott, *Imperial Spain 1469–1716*, 2nd ed. (London: Penguin, 2002), 15–163; Miguel Ángel Ladero Quesada, *La España de los reyes Católicos*, 4th ed. (Madrid: Alianza Editorial, 2014).
2. Lucio Marineo Sículo, *Hernán Cortés: su primera y olvidada biografía. La obra de Lucio Marineo Sículo*, 1530, ed. Miguel León Portilla (México: Editorial Ambos Mundos, 1985), 75; Thomas, *Die Eroberung Mexikos*, 174–183.

3. Quoted after Martínez, *Hernán Cortés*, 107–108.

4. López de Gómara, *La conquista de México*, 35. The biographical details are very contradictory; even the year of birth is disputed. See, for example: Mira Caballos, *Hernán Cortés*, 75–118; Miralles Ostos, *Hernán Cortés*, 45–64; Martínez, *Hernán Cortés*, 107–114.

5. Ida Altman, *Emigrants and Society: Extremadura and America in the Sixteenth Century* (Berkeley: University of California Press, 1989), 21.

6. López de Gómara, *La conquista de México*, 35; Cervantes y Salazar, *Cronica de la Nueva España*, Chapter XV.

7. Mira Caballos, *Hernán Cortés*, 95–118.

8. Antonio de Nebrija, *Gramática de la lengua castellana*, ed. Antonio Quilis (Madrid: Editora Nacional, 1981), 97.

9. Oscar Barrau, "Framing the Literary: Jacob Cromberger of Seville and the Incipient Spanish American Narrative," *Colonial Latin American Review*, no. 17 (2008): 7–12; Eduardo Daniel Crespo Cuesta, *Continuidades medievales en la conquista de América* (Pamplona: Eunsa, 2010), 53–54.

10. Hinz, "Hispanisierung" in Neu-Spanien 1519–1568, 1:118–119.

11. López de Gómara, *La conquista de México*, 1:36; Casas, *Historia de las Indias*, 1869. According to Suárez de Peralta, a Mexican-born nephew of Cortés, the future conquistador from Medellín went to the court in Valladolid, where he was apprenticed to a scribe: Juan Suárez de Peralta, *Tratado del descubrimiento de las Indias: Noticias históricas de la Nueva España*, ed. Teresa Silva Tena (México: Consejo Nacional para la Cultura y las Artes, 1990), 81. For the different points of view of research: Mira Caballos, *Hernán Cortés*, 122–129; Jaime Marroquín Arredondo, *Diálogos con Quetzalcóatl: Humanismo, etnografía y ciencia (1492–1577)* (Madrid: Iberoamericana, 2014), 82; Martínez Martínez, *Veracruz 1519*, 14–15; Martínez, *Hernán Cortés*, 107–114.

12. Antonio de Solís, *Historia de la conquista de México, población y progresos de la América septentrional, conocida por el nombre de Nueva España*, ed. Edmundo O'Gorman, 3. ed. (México: Porrúa, 1978[1634]), 41.

13. López de Gómara, *La conquista de México*, 1:36.

14. Suárez de Peralta, *Tratado del descubrimiento de las Indias*, 81; Francisco López de Gómara, *Historia general de las Indias y vida de Hernán Cortés*, ed. Jorge Gurría Lacroix (Caracas: Biblioteca Ayacucho, 1991), 324.

15. López de Gómara, *La conquista de México*, 1:37.

16. Rinke, *Kolumbus und der Tag von Guanahani*, 109.

17. William F. Keegan, *The People Who Discovered Columbus: The Prehistory of the Bahamas* (Gainesville: University Press of Florida, 1992), 1–19; Irving Rouse, *The Tainos: Rise and Decline of the People Who Greeted Columbus* (New Haven: Yale University Press, 1992), 105–137.

18. José R. Oliver, *Caciques and Cemí Idols: The Web Spun by Taíno Rulers between Hispaniola and Puerto Rico* (Tuscaloosa: University of Alabama Press, 2009), 157–189; Antonio M. Stevens Arroyo, *Cave of the Jagua: The Mythological World of the Taínos*, 2nd ed. (Scranton: University of Scranton Press, 2006), 37–70.

19. David Abulafia, *The Discovery of Mankind: Atlantic Encounters in the Age of Columbus* (New Haven: Yale University Press, 2008), 199–207.

20. Luis N. Rivera-Pagán, "Freedom and Servitude: Indigenous Slavery and the Spanish Conquest of the Caribbean," in *General History of the Caribbean: Volume I: Autochthonous Societies*, ed. Jalil Sued-Badillo (New York: Palgrave Macmillan US, 2003), 316–362.

21. María Dolores Maestre, *Frey Don Nicolás de Ovando, primer gobernador real de las Indias y tierra firme de la mar océana La Española, 1501, 1509 y 1511* (Sevilla: Padilla Libros, 2011), 120–135.

22. Anghiera, *Acht Dekaden über die Neue Welt*, 1:300.

23. Carlos Esteban Deive, *La Española y la esclavitud del indio* (Santo Domingo: Ed. Fundación García Arévalo, 1995); Noble David Cook, "Sickness, Starvation, and Death in Early Hispaniola," *The Journal of Interdisciplinary History* 32, no. 3 (2002): 349–386.

24. Cervantes y Salazar, *Cronica de la Nueva España*, 177.

25. Maestre, *Frey Don Nicolás de Ovando*, 143–160.

26. Cervantes y Salazar, *Crónica de la Nueva España*, 177–178; Luis Barjau, *Voluntad e infortunio en la conquista de México* (México: Instituto Nacional de Antropología e Historia, 2015), 260.

27. Stefan Rinke, *Lateinamerika* (Darmstadt: Theiss, 2015), 53.

28. López de Gómara, *La conquista de México*, 1:38; Cervantes y Salazar, *Crónica de la Nueva España*, 178–179.

29. Cervantes y Salazar, *Crónica de la Nueva España*, 178.

30. For Diego Colón, see: Luis Arranz Márquez, *Don Diego Colón, almirante, virrey y gobernador de las Indias* (Madrid: Consejo Superior de Investigaciones Científicas, 1982).

31. Las Casas, *Historia de las Indias*, 1841–1842; López de Gómara, *Historia general de las Indias y vida de Hernán Cortés*, 327–328. The idea that Velázquez actually had to persuade Cortés to come along, as López de Gomara claims, strains credulity.

32. Barjau, *Voluntad e infortunio en la conquista de México*, 268.

33. Bartolomé de las Casas, *Kurzgefasster Bericht von der Verwüstung der westindischen Länder*, ed. Hans Magnus Enzensberger (Frankfurt am Main: Insel-Verl, 2003 [1790]), 29.

34. Las Casas, 25–27.

35. Las Casas, *Historia de las Indias*, 1865.

36. López de Gómara, *La conquista de México*, 39.

37. López de Gómara, *Historia General de las Indias y vida de Hernán Cortés*, 332–334; Las Casas, *Historia de las Indias*, 1868–1869. Cervantes de Salazar supports Las Casas's versión. Cervantes y Salazar, *Crónica de la Nueva España*, 179–180.

38. Hans-Joachim König, *Die Entdeckung und Eroberung Amerikas, 1492–1550* (Freiburg: Ploetz, 1992), 56–66.

39. Thomas, *Die Eroberung Mexikos*, 92.

40. Fernando Colón, *Historia del almirante Don Cristóbal Colón en la cual se da particular y verdadera relación de su vida y de sus hechos, y del descubrimiento de las Indias Occidentales, llamadas Nuevo-Mundo* (Madrid: Minuesa, 1892 [1561]), 2:148.

41. Colón, 2:149–150; Anghiera, *Acht Dekaden über die Neue Welt*, 1: 248–249.

42. Thomas, *Die Eroberung Mexikos*, 93.

43. Cervantes y Salazar, *Crónica de la Nueva España*, 189.

44. Cervantes y Salazar, 190–194.

45. Díaz del Castillo, *Historia verdadera de la conquista de la Nueva España*, 4.

46. Díaz del Castillo, 4–5; Anghiera, *Acht Dekaden über die Neue Welt*, 1:341.

47. Diego de Landa, *Bericht aus Yucatán*, ed. Carlos Rincón, 2nd ed. (Leipzig: Reclam, 1993), 12; Cervantes y Salazar, *Crónica de la Nueva España*, 151–152.

48. "Probanza sobre las causas que se dieron a la suplicación de las provisiones del veedor Cristóbal de Tapia (Coyoacán, April 20, 1522)," *Boletín del archivo general de la nación*, 1938, 231. This document contains the testimony of Alaminos.

49. Robert J. Sharer, *The Ancient Maya*, 5th ed. (Stanford: Stanford University Press, 1994), 20–24.

50. Anthony P. Andrews, "The Political Geography of the Sixteenth Century Yucatan Maya: Comments and Revisions," *Journal of Anthropological Research* 40, no. 4 (1984): 589–590.

51. Nikolai Grube and Simon Martin, "The Dynastic History of the Maya," in *Maya: Divine Kings of the Rain Forest*, eds. Nikolai Grube, Eva Eggebrecht, and Matthias Seidel (Postdam: H. F. Ullmann, 2012), 169–171.

52. John F. Chuchiak IV, "La Conquista de Yucatán," in *Historia general de Yucatán*, ed. Sergio Quezada, Fernando Robles C., and Anthony P. Andrews, vol. 2, *Yucatán en el orden colonial, 1517–1811* (Mérida: Universidad Autónoma de Yucatán, 2014), 29–58; Sharer, *The Ancient Maya*, 417–421.

53. Sharer, *The Ancient Maya*, 559–581.

54. Landa, *Bericht aus Yucatán*, 30; Clendinnen, *Ambivalent Conquests*, 3–4; Antje Gunsenheimer, "Geschichtstradierung in den yukatekischen Chilam Balam-Büchern: Eine Analyse der Herkunft und Entwicklung ausgewählter historischer Berichte" (Bonn, Universität Bonn, 2002), 9; and passim.

55. Anghiera, *Acht Dekaden über die Neue Welt*, 1:342.

56. Díaz del Castillo, *Historia verdadera de la conquista de la Nueva España*, 5–6.

57. Clendinnen, *Ambivalent Conquests*, 7–8.

58. Díaz del Castillo, *Historia verdadera de la conquista de la Nueva España*, 6–7; Anghiera, *Acht Dekaden über die Neue Welt*, 342–343.
59. Prudence M. Rice, "Time, History, and Worldview," in *Maya Worldviews at Conquest*, eds. Leslie G. Cecil and Timothy W. Pugh (Boulder: University Press of Colorado, 2009), 17–38; Gabrielle Vail, "Cosmology and Creation in Late Postclassic Maya, Literature and Art," in *Maya Worldviews at Conquest*, 83–110; Sharer, *The Ancient Maya*, 513–555.
60. Sharer, *The Ancient Maya*, 449–452 and 462–464.
61. Díaz del Castillo, *Historia verdadera de la conquista de la Nueva España*, 8–11; Anghiera, *Acht Dekaden über die Neue Welt*, 1:344–345.
62. Sharer, *The Ancient Maya*, 476–491; Berthold Riese, *Die Maya: Geschichte, Kultur, Religion*, 5th ed. (München: Beck, 2002), 116.
63. Díaz del Castillo, *Historia verdadera de la conquista de la Nueva España*, 11–14.
64. Díaz del Castillo, 14–18.
65. Bernardino de Santa Clara to Francisco de los Cobos (Santiago de Cuba, October 20, 1517), in: Luis Torres de Mendoza, Francisco de Cárdenas, and Joaquín Francisco Pacheco, eds., *Colección de documentos inéditos relativos al descubrimiento, conquista y colonización de las posesiones españolas en América y Oceanía* (CDIA) (Madrid: Imprenta de M.B. de Quirós, 1864), 11:556–559.
66. Díaz del Castillo, *Historia verdadera de la conquista de la Nueva España*, 18–20.
67. Díaz del Castillo, 22–26; Antonio Gutiérrez Escudero, *Pedro de Alvarado: el conquistador del país de los Quetzales* (Madrid: Anaya, 1988), 19.
68. Juan Díaz, "Itinerario de la Armada del Rey Católico a la isla de Yucatán [1520]," in *La conquista de Tenochtitlan*, ed. Germán Vázquez (Madrid: Historia 16, 1988), 33.
69. Díaz, 41.
70. Díaz del Castillo, *Historia verdadera de la conquista de la Nueva España*, 25–26.
71. Díaz, "Itinerario de la Armada" 41.
72. Anghiera, *Acht Dekaden über die Neue Welt*, 1:347; Fernández de Oviedo, *Historia general y natural de las Indias*, 509.
73. Díaz, "Itinerario de la Armada," 42.
74. Fernández de Oviedo, *Historia general y natural de las Indias*, 510.
75. Díaz, "Itinerario de la Armada," 44–45; Díaz del Castillo, *Historia verdadera de la conquista de la Nueva España*, 27.
76. Díaz, "Itinerario de la Armada," 47.
77. Thomas, *Die Eroberung Mexikos*, 160.
78. Díaz, "Itinerario de la Armada," 48.
79. Díaz del Castillo, *Historia verdadera de la conquista de la Nueva España*, 31.
80. Díaz del Castillo, 32.
81. Díaz, "Itinerario de la Armada," 49–50; Anghiera, *Acht Dekaden über die Neue Welt*, 1:350.
82. Walter Krickeberg, *Las antiguas culturas mexicanas* (México: Fondo de Cultura Económica, 1977), 323–344.
83. Díaz, "Itinerario de la Armada," 51–52. Díaz del Castillo later claimed that Grijalva had definitely wanted to settle. The background is his attempt to discredit the chronicle of López de Gómara. Díaz del Castillo, *Historia verdadera de la conquista de la Nueva España*, 33–34 and 37. For the annoyance of the disappointed men, see also: Anghiera, *Acht Dekaden über üie Neue Welt*, 1:351; Cervantes y Salazar, *Crónica de la Nueva España*, 165–166.
84. Fernández de Oviedo, *Historia general y natural de las Indias*, 522.
85. Díaz, "Itinerario de la Armada," 56–57; Díaz del Castillo, *Historia verdadera de la conquista de la Nueva España*, 38–41.
86. Díaz del Castillo, *Historia verdadera de la conquista de la Nueva España*, 53–54.
87. Las Casas, *Historia de las Indias*, 2249.
88. Díaz, "Itinerario de la Armada," 57.

Chapter 2

1. Cervantes y Salazar, *Crónica de la Nueva España*, 179.

2. Hernán Cortés, "Interrogatorio presentado por el dicho Don Hernándo Cortés (Temistlan 1529)," in CDIA, vol. 27 (Madrid: Imprenta de M.B. de Quirós, 1864), 346; Las Casas, Historia de las Indias, 2249; Díaz del Castillo, Historia verdadera de la conquista de la Nueva España, 47–48.

3. Causa seguida por María de Marcaido en contra de Cortés y sus descendientes por gananciales, Declaraciones del Marqués (Mexico, January 14, 1531), in: Martínez, ed., Documentos cortesianos 1518–1548, 2:100–101.

4. Las Casas, Historia de las Indias, 2250–2251; Díaz del Castillo, Historia verdadera de la conquista de la Nueva España, 42; Antonio de Herrera y Tordesillas, Historia general de los hechos de los castellanos en las islas y tierrafirme del mar océano (Madrid: Tipografía de Archivos, 1934 [1601–1615]), 4:263–267.

5. Instrucciones de Diego Velázquez a Hernán Cortés (October 23, 1518), in: Martínez, Documentos cortesianos 1518–1548, 1:45–57. See also: Martínez, Hernán Cortés, 141–144.

6. Juan Ochoa de Lejalde, Probanza a nombre de Hernán Cortés (Segura de la Frontera, October 4, 1520), in: Martínez, ed., Documentos cortesianos 1518–1548, 1:148–155. Especially López de Gomara's version, according to which Velázquez and Cortés shared the costs, was very controversial: López de Gómara, La conquista de México, 46–47. See the discussion in: Martínez, Hernán Cortés, 128–129.

7. Las Casas, Historia de las Indias, 2253.

8. "Amici, sequamur crucem, et si nos fidem habemus vere, in hoc signo vincemus," as in: Tapia, "Relación de Algunas Cosas", 67; Cervantes de Salazar, Crónica de la Nueva España, 182–183; López de Gómara, La conquista de México, 45–46.

9. Cervantes de Salazar, Crónica de la Nueva España, 183–184.

10. Las Casas, Historia de las Indias, 2255–2257; Díaz del Castillo, Historia verdadera de la conquista de la Nueva España, 5051; Suárez de Peralta, Tratado del descubrimiento de las Indias, 86–87; Guillermo Goñi, Las conquistas de México y Yucatán (México: Instituto Nacional de Antropología e Historia, 2008), 64–66.

11. Las Casas, Historia de las Indias, 2258. See also the court records of 1529: Interrogatorio presentado por el dicho Don Hernando Cortés (Temistlán, 1529), in: Torres de Mendoza, Cárdenas, and Pacheco, CDIA, 27:310–316.

12. Díaz del Castillo, Historia verdadera de la conquista de la Nueva España, 52–53; López de Gómara, La conquista de México, 49.

13. Díaz del Castillo, Historia verdadera de la conquista de la Nueva España, 54–56; Juan de Torquemada, Monarquía indiana: De los veinte y un libros rituales y monarquía indiana, con el origen y guerras de los Indios occidentales, de sus poblazones, descubrimiento, conquista, conversión y otras cosas maravillosas de la mesma tierra, ed. Miguel León Portilla (México: Universidad Nacional Autónoma de México, 1975), 2:35–39; Herrera y Tordesillas, Historia general, 4:267–272; Las Casas, Historia de las Indias, 2257–2258.

14. Díaz del Castillo, Historia verdadera de la conquista de la Nueva España, 57–58.

15. Torres de Mendoza, Cárdenas, and Pacheco, CDIA, 22:38–46; Marta Milagros del Vas Mingo, Las capitulaciones de Indias en el siglo XVI (Madrid: Cultura Hispánica, 1986), 169–172.

16. The sources contradict each other with regard to the departure dates. Bernal Díaz, like most authors, mentions February 10, while López de Gómara mentions February 18. Díaz del Castillo, Historia verdadera de la conquista de La Nueva España, 61; López de Gómara, La conquista de México, 52.

17. López de Gómara, La conquista de México, 50–51. The number of soldiers varies between four hundred and six hundred, depending on the source. See: Bernard Grunberg, "The Origins of the Conquistadores of Mexico City," The Hispanic American Historical Review 74, no. 2 (1994): 263.

18. Grunberg, "The Origins of the Conquistadores of Mexico City," 259–273. See also the comprehensive biographical dictionaries: Bernard Grunberg, Dictionnaire des conquistadores de Mexico (Paris: Harmattan, 2001); Hugh Thomas, Who's Who of the Conquistadors (London: Cassell, 2000).

19. Ynformación de Diego Dordáz (Santo Domingo, September 26, 1521), in: Torres de Mendoza, Cárdenas, and Pacheco, *CDIA*, 40:74–131; Martínez Martínez, *Veracruz 1519*, 18.

20. Schwaller and Nader, *The First Letter from New Spain*, 2; Goñi, *Las conquistas de México y Yucatán*, 18–19; María del Carmen León Cazáres, "Entre el breviario y la espada: los Mercedarios como capellanes en las huestes conquistadoras," in *El mundo de los Conquistadores*, ed. Martín Ríos Saloma (México: Universidad Nacional Autónoma de México, 2015), 600. For the best study on the issue of booty, see Vitus Huber, *Beute und Conquista: Die politische Ökonomie der Eroberung Neuspaniens* (Frankfurt: Campus, 2018)

21. Bernard Grunberg, "Hernán Cortés y la guerra de los conquistadores," in *El Mundo de los conquistadores*, ed. Martín Ríos Saloma (México: Universidad Nacional Autónoma de México, 2015), 557–558.

22. Louis Cardaillac, "Lo morisco peninsular y su proyección en la conquista de América," in *El Mundo de los conquistadores*, ed. Martín Ríos Saloma (México: Universidad Nacional Autónoma de México, 2015), S. 438–440.

23. Hernán Taboada, *La sombra del Islam en la conquista de América* (México: Fondo de Cultura Económica, 2004), 212.

24. Taboada, 192.

25. König, *Die Entdeckung und Eroberung Amerikas, 1492–1550*, 96–98; Eberhard Straub, *Das Bellum Iustum des Hernán Cortés in Mexico* (Köln: Böhlau, 1976).

26. Grunberg, "Hernán Cortés y la guerra de los conquistadores," 567; Navarrete Linares, "Beheadings and Massacres: Andean and Mesoamerican Representations of the Spanish Conquest," 59–60; Crespo Cuesta, *Continuidades medievales en la conquista de América*, 113.

27. An example for that in: "Ordenanzas militares mandadas pregonar por H. Cortés (December 22, 1520)", in: Martínez, *DC*, 1:165.

28. Grunberg, "Hernán Cortés y la guerra de los conquistadores," 557–562.

29. Jacques Lafaye, *Los conquistadores: figuras y escrituras*, 2nd ed. (México: Fondo de Cultura Económica, 1999), 13–19; Hinz, "Hispanisierung" in *Neu-Spanien 1519–1568*, 1:99–101.

30. Díaz del Castillo, *Historia verdadera de la conquista de la Nueva España*, 61–62; Anghiera, *Acht Dekaden über die Neue Welt*, 1:358–359.

31. Anghiera, *Acht Dekaden über die Neue Welt*, 1:358.

32. Anghiera, 365.

33. Díaz del Castillo, *Historia verdadera de la conquista de la Nueva España*, 62–63; Torquemada, *Monarquía indiana*, 2:40–46. Cortés described the situation as his having to win back the confidence of the islanders, who had been frightened by his predecessors Hernández de Córdoba and Grijalva. Cortés, *Cartas de relación*, 13.

34. Chuchiak IV, "La conquista de Yucatán," 29–33; Clendinnen, *Ambivalent Conquests*, 16–17. Stenzel supposes that the Maya probably regarded the Spaniards as a people who were looking for new land under the leadership of their prince; see: Werner Stenzel, *Das kortesische Mexiko: Die Eroberung Mexikos und der darauf folgende Kulturwandel* (Frankfurt am Main: P. Lang, 2006), 14.

35. Díaz del Castillo, *Historia verdadera de la conquista de la Nueva España*, 64–66; Cortés, *Cartas de relación*, 14.

36. Landa, *Bericht aus Yucatán [Report from Yucatán]*, 11; Tapia, "Relación de algunas cosas," 70–71; López de Gómara, *La conquista de México*, 55–60; Díaz del Castillo, *Historia verdadera de la conquista de la Nueva España*, 69–71; Cervantes de Salazar, *Crónica de la Nueva España*, 186–194; Aguilar, "Relación breve de la conquista de la Nueva España [1892]," 164; Cortés, *Cartas de relación*, 14–16; Vásquez de Tapia, "Relación de méritos y servicios [1939]," 134; Alva Ixtlilxóchitl, *Obras históricas*, 3:2:195–196. The sources give different information about the fate of the two shipwrecked men. This is discussed in detail by: Thomas Bargatzky, "Aguilar und Guerrero: Zwei versprengte Spanier in Yukatan im Zeitalter der Conquista," *Zeitschrift Für Ethnologie* 106, no. 1/2 (1981): 161–175. As well as: Hinz, "Hispanisierung" in *Neu-Spanien 1519–1568*, 1:127–131.

37. López de Gómara, *La conquista de México*, 60–61; Díaz del Castillo, *Historia verdadera de la conquista de la Nueva España*, 67.

38. Cervantes de Salazar, *Crónica de la Nueva España*, 196.
39. Vásquez de Tapia, "Relación de méritos y servicios [1939]," 135–136. Marqués del Valle was the title of nobility that Cortés received after the conquest of Tenochtitlan. See also: López de Gómara, *La conquista de México*, 66–68; Cortés, *Cartas de relación*, 17–19.
40. According to Cortés's own account he even waited a few days before he went over to the attack; Cortés, *Cartas de relación*, 18.
41. Vásquez de Tapia, "Relación de méritos y servicios," 135; Díaz del Castillo, *Historia verdadera de la conquista de la Nueva España*, 74–77.
42. Cortés, *Cartas de relación*, 20. For the exaggerations, see: Straub, *Das Bellum Iustum*, 51.
43. Cortés, *Cartas de relación*, 19–20.
44. Díaz del Castillo, *Historia verdadera de la conquista de la Nueva España*, 82; Herrera y Tordesillas, *Historia general*, 4:346–347; Anghiera, *Acht Dekaden über die Neue Welt*, 1:363–364.
45. Díaz del Castillo, *Historia verdadera de la conquista de la Nueva España*, 83–84; Tapia, "Relación de Algunas Cosas," 76–77; Torquemada, *Monarquía indiana*, 2:50–54; López de Gómara, *La conquista de México*, 72–75.
46. Vásquez de Tapia, "Relación de méritos y servicios," 136; Cervantes de Salazar, *Crónica de la Nueva España*, 197. Andrés de Tapia also reported about the apparition: Tapia, "Relación de algunas cosas," 75–76; Sepúlveda, *Del Nuevo Mundo*, 89–91. On the other hand see: Díaz del Castillo, *Historia verdadera de la conquista de la Nueva España*, 84. For a comparison with the ancient heroes see; Anghiera, *Acht Dekaden über die Neue Welt*, 2:5.
47. Díaz del Castillo, *Historia verdadera de la conquista de la Nueva España*; Torquemada, *Monarquía indiana*, 2:54–56; Sepúlveda, *Del Nuevo Mundo*, 92–93.
48. Vásquez de Tapia, "Relación de méritos y servicios," 136; Anghiera, *Acht Dekaden über die Neue Welt*, 1:365; Herrera y Tordesillas, *Historia general*, 4:351–352; Cervantes de Salazar, *Crónica de la Nueva España*, 201–203.
49. Díaz del Castillo, *Historia verdadera de la conquista de la Nueva España*, 89. See also: López de Gómara, *La conquista de México*, 76.
50. López de Gómara, *La conquista de México*, 78–79; Tapia, "Relación de algunas cosas," 76; Landa, *Bericht aus Yucatán [Report from Yucatán]*, 16.
51. Margo Glantz, "La Malinche: la lengua en la mano," in *La Malinche, sus padres y sus hijos*, ed. Margo Glantz (México: Taurus, 2001), 93.
52. Díaz del Castillo, *Historia verdadera de la conquista de la Nueva España*, 92–94; Cervantes de Salazar, *Crónica de la Nueva España*, 203–204; Sepúlveda, *Del Nuevo Mundo*, 94; Benton, "The Outsider: Alva Ixtlilxochitl's Tenuous Ties to the City of Tetzcoco," 2:198; Camilla Townsend, *Malintzin's Choices: An Indian Woman in the Conquest of Mexico* (Albuquerque: University of New Mexico Press, 2006), 37.
53. Townsend, *Malintzin's Choices*, 11–29.
54. Roberto A. Valdeón, *Translation and the Spanish Empire in the Americas* (Amsterdam: John Benjamins Publishing Company, 2014), 49–52.
55. Hinz, "Hispanisierung" in Neu-Spanien 1519–1568, 1:180.
56. Townsend, *Malintzin's Choices*, 56–59; Navarrete Linares, "La Malinche, la virgen y la montaña: el juego de la identidad en los Códices tlaxcaltecas," 292–293; Georges Baudot, "Malintzin, imagen y discurso de mujer en el primer México virreinal," in *La Malinche, sus padres y sus hijos*, ed. Margo Glantz (México: Taurus, 2001), 71.
57. One example is: Cristóbal del Castillo, *Historia de la venida de los mexicanos y otros pueblos: e historia de la conquista*, ed. Federico Navarrete Linares (México: Asociación de Amigos del Templo Mayor, 2001), 133. See also: Gordon Brotherston, "La Malintzin de los códices," in *La Malinche, sus padres y sus hijos*, ed. Margo Glantz (México: Taurus, 2001), 22–24.
58. Goñi, *Las conquistas de México y Yucatán*, 66–70; Navarrete Linares, "La Malinche, la virgen y la montaña: el juego de la identidad en los Códices tlaxcaltecas," 293; Hinz, "Hispanisierung" in Neu-Spanien 1519–1568, 1:180.
59. Townsend, *Malintzin's Choices*, 56.
60. Susan Dale Gillespie, *The Aztec Kings: The Construction of Rulership in Mexica History* (Tucson: University of Arizona Press, 1989), 59; Luis Barjau, *La conquista de la Malinche* (México: CONACULTA, 2009); Brotherston, "La Malintzin de los códices," 19–37.
61. Cortés, *Cartas de relación*, 20; Cervantes de Salazar, *Crónica de la Nueva España*, 204–205.

Chapter 3

1. William T. Sanders, Jeffrey R. Parsons, and Robert S. Santley, *The Basin of Mexico: Ecological Processes in the Evolution of a Civilization* (New York: Academic Press, 1979), 33–87; María Castañeda de la Paz, *Conflictos y alianzas en tiempos de cambio: Azcapotzalco, Tlacopan, Tenochtitlan y Tlatelolco (siglos XII–XVI)* (México: Universidad Nacional Autónoma de México, 2013), 27–70; Christopher A. Pool, "The Formation of Complex Societies in Mesoamerica," in *The Oxford Handbook of Mesoamerican Archaeology*, eds. Deborah L. Nichols and Christopher A. Pool (Oxford: Oxford University Press, 2012), 169–187; Teresa Rojas Rabiela, "Las cuencas lacustres del Altiplano Central," *Arqueología mexicana* 12, no. 68 (2004): 20–27.

2. Frances Berdan, *Aztec Archaeology and Ethnohistory* (New York: Cambridge University Press, 2014), 35; René Millon, "Teotihuacan: City, State and Civilization," in *Supplement to the Handbook of Middle American Indians*, ed. Jeremy Sabloff, vol. 1, Archaeology (Austin: University of Texas Press, 1981), 198–243; Linda Manzanilla, "Teotihuacan," in *The Aztec Empire*, ed. Felipe Solis (New York: Guggenheim Museum, 2004), 114–123.

3. Castañeda de la Paz, *Conflictos y alianzas en tiempos de cambio*, 27–70; Richard Diehl, "Tula and the Tolteca," in *The Aztec Empire*, ed. Felipe Solis (New York: Guggenheim Museum, 2004), 124–129.

4. Federico Navarrete Linares, *Los orígenes de los pueblos indígenas del Valle de México: Los Altépetl y sus historias* (México: Universidad Nacional Autónoma de México, 2011), 103–113; Riese, *Das Reich der Azteken*, 78–82; Ulrich Köhler, *Vasallen des linkshändigen Kriegers im Kolibrigewand: Über Weltbild, Religion und Staat der Azteken*, Ethnologische Studien (Berlin: Lit, 2009), 7–8. For the origin of the Mexica, see also: Sahagún, *Historia general de las cosas de Nueva España*, 2:973–978.

5. Riese, *Das Reich der Azteken*, 83–84; Berdan, *Aztec Archaeology and Ethnohistory*, 37–39.

6. Riese, *Das Reich der Azteken*, 92–94; Carlos Santamarina Novillo, "El sistema de dominación azteca: El imperio Tepaneca" (PhD Dissertation, Madrid, Universidad Complutense de Madrid, 2005), 348–360; Enrique Florescano, *Los orígenes del poder en Mesoamérica* (México: Fondo de Cultura Económica, 2009), 407–409. For the latest criticism of 1325 as the date of foundation, see: Patrick Johansson, "La fundación de México-Tenochtitlan: Consideraciones 'cronológicas,'" *Arqueología Mexicana* 23, no. 135 (2015): 70–77.

7. Castañeda de la Paz, *Conflictos y alianzas en tiempos de cambio*, 141–156; Riese, *Das Reich der Azteken*, 97–100; Santamarina Novillo, "El sistema de dominación azteca," 75–76 and 360–362.

8. Riese, *Das Reich der Azteken*, 149–151; Santamarina Novillo, "El sistema de dominación azteca," 553–599; Isabel Bueno Bravo, *La guerra en el imperio Azteca: Expansión, ideología y arte* (Madrid: Editorial Complutense, 2007), 22–48.

9. Edward E. Calnek, "The Internal Structure of Tenochtitlan," in *The Valley of Mexico* (Albuquerque: University of New Mexico Press, 1976), 287–302. In estimating the population I follow: José Luis de Rojas, *Tenochtitlan: Capital of the Aztec Empire* (Gainesville: University Press of Florida, 2012), 50–53.

10. Charles Gibson, *The Aztecs under Spanish Rule: A History of the Indians of the Valley of Mexico; 1519–1810*, 2nd ed. (Stanford: Stanford University Pr, 1991), 5; Pablo Escalante Gonzalbo, "La ciudad, la gente y las costumbres," in *Historia de la vida cotidiana en México*, vol. 1 (Mexico: El Colegio de México, 2004), 199.

11. Grunberg, *Histoire de la conquête du Mexique*, 90.

12. Michael Ernest Smith, *Aztec City-State Capitals* (Gainesville: University Press of Florida, 2008), 27–70.

13. Cortés, *Cartas de relación*, 79.

14. Rojas, *Tenochtitlan*, 56; Alfredo López Austin and Leonardo López Luján, *Monte sagrado, Templo Mayor: El cerro y la pirámide en la tradición religiosa mesoamericana* (México: Universidad Nacional Autónoma de México, 2009), 265–468.

15. Cervantes de Salazar, *Crónica de la Nueva España*, 349; Gruzinski, *La ciudad de Mexico*, 266–79; López de Gómara, *La conquista de México*, 172–173; Susan Toby Evans, "Aztec Palaces and Gardens: Intertwined Evolution," in *The Oxford Handbook of the Aztecs*, eds. Deborah L. Nichols and Enrique Rodríguez Alegría (New York: Oxford University Press, 2017), 229–245.

16. Alejandro Alcántara Gallegos, "Los barrios de Tenochtitlan: Topografía, organización interna y tipología de sus predios," in *Mesoamérica y los ámbitos indígenas de la Nueva España*, ed. Pablo Escalante Gonzalbo, Historia de la vida cotidiana en México (México: El Colegio de México, 2004), 167–198; Smith, *Aztec City-State Capitals*, 94–135.

17. Navarrete Linares, *Los orígenes de los pueblos indígenas del valle de México*, 24–28; Berdan, *Aztec Archaeology and Ethnohistory*, 135–140.

18. Navarrete Linares, *Los orígenes de los pueblos indígenas del valle de México*, 24–28; Berdan, *Aztec Archaeology and Ethnohistory*, 135–140.

19. Christopher T. Morehart, "Aztec Agricultural Strategies: Intensification, Landesque Capital, and the Sociopolitics of Production," in *The Oxford Handbook of the Aztecs*, ed. Deborah L. Nichols and Enrique Rodríguez Alegría (New York: Oxford University Press, 2017), 263.

20. Berdan, *Aztec Archaeology and Ethnohistory*, 74–81; Teresa Rojas Rabiela, *Las siembras de ayer: La agricultura indígena del siglo 16* (México, D.F.: SEP—Secr. de Educación Pública, 1988), 54–74.

21. Smith, *Aztec City-State Capitals*, 190–195; Luz María Mohar Betancourt, *El tributo mexica en el siglo XVI: Análisis de dos fuentes pictográficas* (México: Centro de Investigaciones y Estudios Superiores en Antropología Social, 1987), 21–35.

22. Berdan, *Aztec Archaeology and Ethnohistory*, 70.

23. Philip P. Arnold, "Eating Landscape: Human Sacrifice and Sustenance in Aztec Mexico," in *Aztec Ceremonial Landscapes*, ed. David Carrasco (Niwot: University Press of Colorado, 1991), 219–232; Johanna Broda, "The Sacred Landscape of Aztec Calendar Festivals: Myth, Nature and Society," in *Aztec Ceremonial Landscapes* (Niwot: University Press of Colorado, 1991), 74–120.

24. Kenn Hirth, *The Aztec Economic World: Merchants and Markets in Ancient Mesoamerica* (New York: Cambridge University Press, 2016), 59–89.

25. Hirth, 102–236. According to the unknown conquistador, the market of Tlatelolco was three times the size of that of Salamanca, and around twenty-five thousand people traded there daily: Conquistador Anónimo, "Relación de algunas cosas de la Nueva España," Chapter 20.

26. Berdan, *Aztec Archaeology and Ethnohistory*, 98–104.

27. Berdan, 104–108.

28. Geoffrey McCafferty and Sharisse McCafferty, "Pregnant in the Dancing Place: Myths and Methods of Textile Production and Use," in *The Oxford Handbook of the Aztecs*, eds. Deborah L. Nichols and Enrique Rodríguez Alegría (New York: Oxford University Press, 2017), 375–384.

29. Michael E. Smith and Frederic Hicks, "Inequality and Social Class in Aztec Society," in *The Oxford Handbook of the Aztecs*, eds. Deborah L. Nichols and Enrique Rodríguez Alegría (New York: Oxford University Press, 2017), 423.

30. Berdan, *Aztec Archaeology and Ethnohistory*, 177–180.

31. Goñi, *Las Conquistas de México y Yucatán*, 27. See also: Jacques Soustelle, *So Lebten Die Azteken Am Vorabend Der Spanischen Eroberung* (Stuttgart: Dt. Verl.-Anst., 1956).

32. Lockhart, *The Nahuas after the Conquest*, 96–102; Smith and Hicks, "Inequality and Social Class in Aztec Society," 425–427.

33. Berdan, *Aztec Archaeology and Ethnohistory*, 180–184.

34. Berdan, 189–191; Smith and Hicks, "Inequality and Social Class in Aztec Society," 430; Riese, *Das Reich der Azteken*, 231.

35. Inga Clendinnen, *Aztecs: An Interpretation* (Cambridge: Cambridge University Press, 1993), 216–300; María Rodríguez-Shadow, *La mujer azteca*, 2nd ed. (Toluca: Universidad Autónoma del Estado de México, 1991), passim.

36. Pablo Escalante Gonzalbo, "Los otomies," in *Historia general del Estado de México*, eds. María Teresa Jarquín Ortega and Manuel Miño Grijalva, vol. 2 (Zinacantepec: Colegio Mexiquense, 1998), 161–185.

37. Berdan, *Aztec Archaeology and Ethnohistory*, 191–197.

38. Riese, *Das Reich der Azteken*, 234–237; Pablo Escalante Gonzalbo, "La cortesía, los efectos y la sexualidad," in *Historia general del Estado de México*, eds. María Teresa Jarquín Ortega and Manuel Miño Grijalva (Zinacantepec: Colegio Mexiquense, 1998), 270–278.

39. Escalante Gonzalbo, "La ciudad, la gente y las costumbres," 205–222.
40. Berdan, *Aztec Archaeology and Ethnohistory*, 214.
41. Berdan, 215 and 225–229; Gruzinski, *La ciudad de Mexico*, 266; Alfredo López Austin, *Cuerpo humano e ideología: las concepciones de los antiguos nahuas* (México: Universidad Nacional Autónoma de México, 1984), 1:58–70.
42. Anthony F. Aveni, "The Measure, Meaning, and Transformation of Aztec Time and Calendars," in *The Oxford Handbook of the Aztecs*, eds. Deborah L. Nichols and Enrique Rodríguez Alegría (New York: Oxford University Press, 2017), 110–111.
43. Hermann Trimborn, "Zum Weltbild und Geschichtsbewußtsein in den Hochkulturen des alten Amerika," in *Archäologie und Geschichtsbewußtsein*, ed. Hermann Müller-Karpe (München: Beck, 1982), 109; Tzvi Medin, *Mito y pragmatismo e imperialismo: La conciencia social en la conquista del imperio azteca* (Frankfurt am Main: Vervuert, 2009), 95–96; Emily Umberger, "Schrift und Kalender," in *Die Azteken und ihre Vorläufer: Glanz und Untergang des alten Mexiko*, ed. Arne Eggebrecht (Mainz am Rhein: P. von Zabern, 1986), 126–131.
44. Riese, *Das Reich der Azteken*, 35–40; Clendinnen, *Aztecs*, 236–265; Gruzinski, *La ciudad de Mexico*, 268.
45. Köhler, *Vasallen*, 7–8.
46. Guilhem Olivier, "Humans and Gods in the Mexica Universe," in *The Oxford Handbook of the Aztecs*, eds. Deborah L. Nichols and Enrique Rodríguez Alegría (New York: Oxford University Press, 2017), 575–576.
47. Berdan, *Aztec Archaeology and Ethnohistory*, 230–234; John Bierhorst, *The Mythology of Mexico and Central America*, 2nd ed. (Oxford: Oxford University Press, 2002), 144–146.
48. López Austin and López Luján, *Monte sagrado, templo mayor*, 178.
49. Bierhorst, *The Mythology of Mexico and Central America*, 16; Gruzinski, *La ciudad de Mexico*, 266.
50. Diego Durán, "Historia de las Indias de Nueva-España y Islas de Tierra Firme" (Manuscript, Biblioteca Digital Hispánica, 1579), 1:355. Camilla Townsend, *Fifth Sun: A New History of the Aztecs*. New York: Oxford University Press, 2019.
51. Yolotl González Torres, "El sacrificio humano: Poder y sumisión," in *El sacrificio humano en la tradicion religiosa mesoamericana*, ed. Leonardo López Luján (México: Instituto Nacional de Antropologia e Historia, 2009), 397–406; Juan Alberto Román Berrelleza and Leonardo López Luján, "El papel de los infantes en las prácticas sacrificiales mexicas," in *El sacrificio humano en la tradición religiosa mesoamericana*, 345–366. See also: Michel Graulich, *Le sacrifice humain chez les Aztèques* (Paris: Fayard, 2005), passim.
52. Gillespie, *The Aztec Kings*, xxiii–xxv.
53. Anghiera, *Acht Dekaden über die Neue Welt*, 1:370–371.
54. Trimborn, "Zum Weltbild und Geschichtsbewußtsein in den Hochkulturen des alten Amerika," 109; Berdan, *Aztec Archaeology and Ethnohistory*, 36.
55. Bueno Bravo, *La guerra en el imperio azteca*, 3–8; Norbert Díaz de Arce, "Bezeichnungen für den Krieg bei den Azteken: die Metapher Teoatl Tlachinolli," *Indiana* 16 (2000): 7–8.
56. Bueno Bravo, *La guerra en el imperio azteca*, 192–197; Berdan, *Aztec Archaeology and Ethnohistory*, 152–156.
57. Ross Hassig, *Aztec Warfare: Imperial Expansion and Political Control* (Norman: University of Oklahoma Press, 1988), 48–62; Riese, *Das Reich der Azteken*, 141–143; Berdan, *Aztec Archaeology and Ethnohistory*, 156–162.
58. Hassig, *Aztec Warfare*, 95–100. For weapons, see: Marco Antonio Cervera Obregón, *El armamento entre los mexicas* (Madrid: Consejo Superior de Investigaciones Científicas, 2007), 117–148.
59. Hassig, *Aztec Warfare*, 17–26; Marco Antonio Cervera Obregón, *Guerreros aztecas* (Madrid: Nowtilus, 2011), 149–168.
60. Riese, *Das Reich der Azteken*, 139–141; Bueno Bravo, *La guerra en el imperio azteca*, 158–174.
61. Berdan, *Aztec Archaeology and Ethnohistory*, 159.
62. Inga Clendinnen, *The Cost of Courage in Aztec Society: Essays on Mesoamerican Society and Culture* (New York: Cambridge University Press, 2010), 8–25; Cervera Obregón, *Guerreros aztecas*, 61–82; Hassig, *Aztec Warfare*, 100.

63. Hassig, *Aztec Warfare*, 23; Berdan, *Aztec Archaeology and Ethnohistory*, 148.
64. Hassig, *Aztec Warfare*, 17–26; Gabbert, *Kultureller Determinismus und die Eroberung Mexikos*, 282–84; Pedro Carrasco Pizana, *The Tenochca Empire of Ancient Mexico: The Triple Alliance of Tenochtitlan, Tetzcoco, and Tlacopan*, v. 234 (Norman: University of Oklahoma Press, 1999).
65. Gibson, *The Aztecs under Spanish Rule*, 22; Carrasco Pizana, *The Tenochca Empire of Ancient Mexico*, 29–40.
66. Castañeda de la Paz, *Conflictos y Alianzas En Tiempos de Cambio*, 123–174; Wolfgang Gabbert, "Warum Montezuma weinte: Anmerkungen zur Frühphase der europäischen Expansion in den Atlantischen Raum," in *Atlantik: Sozial- und Kulturgeschichte in der Neuzeit*, eds. Ulrike Schmieder and Hans-Heinrich Nolte (Wien: Promedia, 2010), 38–39. In their research, Gibson and Gillespie argue that the overemphasis on the triple alliance in the sources produced under Spanish rule was due to the desire to subsequently enhance the role of Texcoco and Tlacopan; see: Gibson, *The Aztecs under Spanish Rule*; Gillespie, *The Aztec Kings*. Lee, on the other hand, argues that the importance of Texcoco and Tlacopan should not be underestimated; Jongsoo Lee, "The Aztec Triple Alliance: A Colonial Transformation of the Prehispanic Political and Tributary System," in *Texcoco: Prehispanic and Colonial Perspectives*, eds. Jongsoo Lee and Galen Brokaw (Boulder: University Press of Colorado, 2014), 63–92.
67. Berdan, *Aztec Archaeology and Ethnohistory*, 142–144.
68. Riese, *Das Reich der Azteken*, 154.
69. Riese, 251–252; Domingo Francisco de San Antón Muñón Chimalpahin Quauhtlehuanitzin, *Codex Chimalpahin: Society and Politics in Mexico Tenochtitlan, Tlatelolco, Texcoco, Culhuacan, and Other Nahua Altepetl in Central Mexico*, eds. Arthur J.O. Anderson and Susan Schroeder, vol. 1 (Norman: University of Oklahoma Press, 1997), 157–165.
70. Berdan, *Aztec Archaeology and Ethnohistory*, 151–152.
71. Santiago Ávila Sandoval, "La vida cotidiana del último tlatoani mexica," in *Historia de la vida cotidiana en México*, ed. Pablo Escalante Gonzalbo, vol. 1, Mesoamérica y los ámbitos indígenas de la Nueva España (Mexico: El Colegio de México, 2004), 279–284.
72. Berdan, *Aztec Archaeology and Ethnohistory*, 152–155; Ávila Sandoval, "La vida cotidiana del último tlatoani mexica," 285–292; Smith, *Aztec City-State Capitals*, 46.
73. Riese, *Das Reich der Azteken*, 253.
74. Alva Ixtlilxóchitl, *Obras históricas*, 2:177–179; Bueno Bravo, *La guerra en el imperio azteca*, 122–124.
75. Bueno Bravo, *La Guerra En El Imperio Azteca*, 124–125.

Chapter 4

1. López de Gómara, *La conquista de México*, 81–82. On Malinche's translating: Townsend, *Malintzin's Choices*, 41.
2. Cervantes de Salazar, *Crónica de la Nueva España*, 205; López de Gómara, *La conquista de México*, 83.
3. López de Gómara, *La conquista de México*, 83.
4. The source is the entry of the *cabildo* of Veracruz to the monarch of July 10, 1519, which is discussed in more detail below. Cortés, *Cartas de relación*, 21.
5. López de Gómara, *La conquista de México*, 84. Also in: Díaz del Castillo, *Historia verdadera de la conquista de la Nueva España*, 96; Cervantes de Salazar, *Crónica de la Nueva España*, 213. Tendile is more reserved.
6. López de Gómara, *La conquista de México*, 85. In Diego Durán the illustrators already appear during Grijalva's visit. Durán, "Historia de las Indias," 2:10–13.
7. From Libro de los Guardianes y Gobernadores de Quauhtinchan, sheet 11, quoted from: Riese, *Das Reich der Azteken*, 265.
8. López de Gómara, *La conquista de México*, 85; Sahagún, *Florentine Codex*, 13:5.
9. Durán, "Historia de las Indias," 2:1–2; Díaz del Castillo, *Historia verdadera de la conquista de la Nueva España*, 98–101.
10. Berlin and Barlow, *Anales de Tlatelolco*, 62. Quoted from the translation of Riese, *Das Reich der Azteken*, 266. See also: Juan de Tovar, *Origen de los mexicanos* (Barcelona: Linkgua, 2011),

93, according to which the messengers addressed Cortés with the following words: "Put on, O Lord, the clothes you wore earlier, when you were our god and king among us."

11. See the report of the eyewitness Juan Alvarez, Información promovida de Diego Velázquez contra Hernán Cortés (Santiago de Cuba, June 28–July 6, 1521), in: Martínez, DC, 1:205. See also: Aguilar, "Relación breve de la conquista de la Nueva España [1892]," 165; Herrera y Tordesillas, Historia general, 4:385–386; Torquemada, Monarquía Indiana, 2:71–74. From a Nahua perspective: Berlin and Barlow, Anales de Tlatelolco, 62.

12. López de Gómara, La conquista de México, 87; Cervantes de Salazar, Crónica de la Nueva España, 214–215. See also: Antonio Aimi, La "verdadera" visión de los vencidos: la conquista de México en las fuentes aztecas (Alicante: Publicaciones de la Universidad de Alicante, 2009), 172.

13. Sahagún, Florentine Codex, 13: 1–3; Muñoz Camargo, Historia de Tlaxcala, 173. Motolinía had already reported on the prophecies before: Benavente, Memoriales, 1:213–215. The historicity of the story of the bad omens has long been questioned by research. Undoubtedly, it was a subsequent interpretation—Riese, speaks of a "post-factum rationalization" by the Mexica in order to make the traumatic experiences explainable afterward; Riese, Das Reich der Azteken, 25. See also Diana Magaloni Kerpel, "Albores de la Conquista: la historia pintada del Códice Florentino," in The Aztec Empire, ed. Felipe Solís (New York: Guggenheim Museum, 2004), 114–123.

14. Sahagún, Florentine Codex, 13: 11. According to Diego Durán, Moteuczoma had already learned ten years before the arrival of the Spaniards of a comet at night, which was considered a bad omen. Since his own soothsayers had not seen the heavenly body, he asked Nezahualpilli, the prince of Texcoco, for advice. The latter predicted a terrible catastrophic event with many dead, whereupon Moteuczoma despaired; Durán, "Historia de las Indias," 1:490–491.

15. Díaz del Castillo, Historia verdadera de la conquista de la Nueva España, 98.

16. Durán, "Historia de las Indias," 2:4; Alvarado Tezozomoc, Crónica mexicana, 452–453.

17. Sahagún, Florentine Codex, 13:12–13.

18. Información promovida de Diego Velázquez contra Hernán Cortés (Santiago de Cuba, June 28–July 6, 1521), in: Martínez, DC, 1:205. On Malinche: Muñoz Camargo, Historia de Tlaxcala, 168.

19. Domingo Francisco de San Antón Muñón Chimalpahin Cuauhtlehuanitzin, Chimalpahin's Conquest: A Nahua Historian's Rewriting of Francisco López de Gómara's La Conquista de México, eds. Susan Schroeder et al. (Stanford: Stanford University Press, 2010), 178. Fair skin (albinism) was known to the Mexica and was considered a blemish. Light-skinned people were sacrificed during a solar eclipse, for example. Stenzel, Das kortesische Mexiko, 12.

20. Sahagún, Florentine Codex, 13: 19–20. Alvarado Tezozomoc, Crónica mexicana, 459–463. See also: Riese, Das Reich der Azteken, 262–263.

21. Wood, Transcending Conquest, 72; Aimi, La verdadera visión de los vencidos, 158; Gillespie, "Blaming Moteuczoma," 34–38; Pastrana Flores, Historias de la conquista, 15–25.

22. See, e.g., Mira Caballos, Hernán Cortés, 25; Medin, Mito y pragmatismo e imperialismo, 176; Todorov, Die Eroberung Amerikas, 80–151.

23. Especially emphatically in Townsend, "Burying the White Gods," 659. See also: Ross Hassig, Time, History, and Belief in Aztec and Colonial Mexico (Austin: University of Texas Press, 2001), 58–59; Lockhart, The Nahuas after the Conquest, 20; Clendinnen, "'Fierce and Unnatural Cruelty': Cortés and the Conquest of Mexico"; Wood, Transcending Conquest, 72; Carman, Rhetorical Conquests, 30.

24. Werner Stenzel, "Quetzalcoatl von Tula: Die Mythogenese einer postkortesischen Legende," Zeitschrift Für Lateinamerika 18 (1980): 7–91; Diana Magaloni, "Painting a New Era: Conquest, Prophecy, and the World to Come," in Invasion and Transformation: Interdisciplinary Perspectives on the Conquest of Mexico, eds. Rebecca Parker Brienen and Margaret Ann Jackson (Boulder: University Press of Colorado, 2008), 149.

25. Wood, Transcending Conquest, 137–142.

26. According to Barjau there is even an indigenous source from 1519, from which he concludes that the authenticity of the Quetzalcoatl narrative cannot be disputed. However, the authenticity of this source is doubted in the research. Luis Barjau, Hernán Cortés y Quetzalcóatl, Segunda edición (México: Ediciones El Tucán de Virginia, 2011), 186–188.

27. Köhler, *Vasallen*, 234–238.
28. Valdeón, *Translation and the Spanish Empire in the Americas*, 114–117. Townsend has argued that the address "*teotl*" is not proof of the god myth because it has been mistranslated. Townsend, "Burying the White Gods," 672.
29. Molly H. Bassett, *The Fate of Earthly Things: Aztec Gods and God-Bodies* (Austin: University of Texas Press, 2015), 26–44.
30. Anghiera, *Acht Dekaden über die Neue Welt*, 1:368.
31. Félix Báez-Jorge and Sergio Vásquez Zárate, *Cempoala* (México: Fondo de Cultura Económica, 2011), 70–86; Krickeberg, *Las antiguas culturas mexicanas*, 323–325. For the archaeological findings, see above all: Jürgen K. Brüggemann, *Zempoala: El estudio de una ciudad prehispánica* (México: Instituto Nacional de Antropología e Historia, 1991).
32. José Luis Melgarejo Vivanco, *Los Totonaca y su cultura* (Xalapa: Universidad Verracruzana, 1985), 112–134; Joaquín Roberto González Martínez, "Veracruz, perfiles regionales, económicos y poblacionales," in *Historia general de Veracruz*, eds. Martín Aguilar Sánchez and Juan Ortiz Escamilla (Veracruz: Universidad Veracruzana, 2011), 30–38.
33. Báez-Jorge and Vásquez Zárate, *Cempoala*, 104–119.
34. Agustín García Márquez, *Los aztecas en el centro de Veracruz* (México: Universidad Nacional Autónoma, 2005), 125–182.
35. López de Gómara, *La conquista de México*, 88–89; Tapia, "Relación de Algunas Cosa," 78–79.
36. Cervantes de Salazar, *Crónica de la Nueva España*, 210–211; López de Gómara, *La conquista de México*, 90; Díaz del Castillo, *Historia verdadera de la conquista de la Nueva España*, 101 and 112; Martínez Martínez, *Veracruz 1519*, 79.
37. Díaz del Castillo, *Historia verdadera de la conquista de la Nueva España*, 106.
38. Díaz del Castillo, 107–109.
39. Cortés, *Cartas de Relación*, 22.
40. Las Casas, *Historia de Las Indias*, 2294. Statement by Martín Vázquez, Presentaciones e xuramentos de los testigos que presentó la parte del Marqués del Valle para prueba de sus descargos, in: Torres de Mendoza, Cárdenas, and Pacheco, *CDIA*, 28:134; Cervantes de Salazar, *Crónica de la Nueva España*, 219–220; López de Gómara, *La conquista de México*, 92.
41. Sepúlveda, *Del Nuevo Mundo*, 98; Martínez Martínez, *Veracruz 1519*, 69. For a detailed review of the literature on this subject see: Martínez Martínez, 80–83. Margo Glantz, "Ciudad y escritura: La Ciudad de México en las cartas de relación," *Hispamérica* 19, no. 56–57 (1990): 167.
42. Carta del ejército de Cortés al emperador (October 1520), in: Martínez, *DC*, 1:156–163; Cervantes de Salazar, *Crónica de la Nueva España*, 219–221. See also: Hinz, *"Hispanisierung" in Neu-Spanien 1519–1568*, 3:1:101.
43. Sepúlveda, *Del Nuevo Mundo*, 99.
44. Statement by Luis Marín, Presentaciones e xuramentos de los testigos que presentó la parte del Marqués del Valle para prueba de sus descargos, in: Torres de Mendoza, Cárdenas, and Pacheco, *CDIA*, 28:55. Díaz del Castillo, *Historia verdadera de la conquista de la Nueva España*, 109–113. The agreements between Cortés and the city government were put into writing shortly thereafter: Escriptura convenida entre Hernando Cortés y el regimiento de la Villa-Rica en la Vera-Cruz, sobre defensa de sus habitantes y derechos que había de recaudar (Cempoala, August 5, 1519), in: Torres de Mendoza, Cárdenas, and Pacheco, *CDIA*, 26:5–16; Anghiera, *Acht Dekaden über die Neue Welt*, 1:367–368. See also: Martínez Martínez, *Veracruz 1519*, 89.
45. Hassig, *Mexico and the Spanish Conquest*, 66–70.
46. Díaz del Castillo, *Historia verdadera de la conquista de la Nueva España*, 114–115; Cervantes de Salazar, *Crónica de la Nueva España*, 223–224; López de Gómara, *La conquista de México*, 95–98.
47. Díaz del Castillo, *Historia verdadera de la conquista de la Nueva España*, 116; Cervantes de Salazar, *Crónica de la Nueva España*, 224; López de Gómara, *La conquista de México*, 98–101; Sepúlveda, *Del Nuevo Mundo*, 101; Anghiera, *Acht Dekaden über die Neue Welt*, 1:372–373.
48. Aguilar, "Relación breve de la conquista de la Nueva España," 165; Cervantes de Salazar, *Crónica de la Nueva España*, 226; Cortés, *Cartas de relación*, 38; Alva Ixtlilxóchitl, *Obras Históricas*, 2:203–204.

49. Anghiera, *Acht Dekaden über die Neue Welt*, 2:4–5; Sepúlveda, *Del Nuevo Mundo*, 102; López de Gómara, *La conquista de México*, 102; Herrera y Tordesillas, *Historia general*, 4:403–405.

50. Díaz del Castillo, *Historia verdadera de la conquista de la Nueva España*, 117–118; López de Gómara, *La conquista de México*, 102–103.

51. Tapia, "Relación de algunas cosas," 81; Díaz del Castillo, *Historia verdadera de la conquista de la Nueva España*, 118–122; López de Gómara, *La conquista de México*, 102–103; Cervantes de Salazar, *Crónica de la Nueva España*, 226–228.

52. Díaz del Castillo, *Historia verdadera de la conquista de la Nueva España*, 122–123; López de Gómara, *La conquista de México*, 107–108; Sepúlveda, *Del Nuevo Mundo*, 105.

53. López de Gómara, *La conquista de México*, 104–105; Cervantes de Salazar, *Crónica de la Nueva España*, 231–232.

54. Sepúlveda, *Del Nuevo Mundo*, 106–107; López de Gómara, *La conquista de México*, 108–109; Díaz del Castillo, *Historia verdadera de la conquista de la Nueva España*, 125–126; Cervantes de Salazar, *Crónica de la Nueva España*, 232–233.

55. Díaz del Castillo, *Historia verdadera de la conquista de la Nueva España*, 128–133; Herrera y Tordesillas, *Historia general*, 5:17–28.

56. Hassig, *Mexico and the Spanish Conquest*, 70–77.

57. Díaz del Castillo, *Historia verdadera de la conquista de la Nueva España*, 136–137. Statement by Martín Vázquez, Presentaciones e xuramentos de los testigos que presentó la parte del Marqués del Valle para prueba de sus descargos, in: Torres de Mendoza, Cárdenas, and Pacheco, *CDIA*, 28:122.

58. Capitulación que se tomó con Diego Velázquez para la conquista de ciertas islas (November 13, 1519), in: Torres de Mendoza, Cárdenas, and Pacheco, *CDIA*, 22:38–46.

59. Hassig, *Mexico and the Spanish Conquest*, 66–70.

60. Díaz del Castillo, *Historia verdadera de la conquista de la Nueva España*, 137; López de Gómara, *La conquista de México*, 110. See also: Goñi, *Las conquistas de México y Yucatán*, 71–74; Bernard Grunberg, "Las relaciones entre Cortés y sus hombres y el problema de la unidad en la conquista de México (Febrero 1519–Agosto 1521)," *Revista de Indias* 43, no. 171 (1983): 304.

61. Instrucciones de Hernán Cortés a los procuradores Francisco de Montejo y Alonso Hernández Portocarrero enviados a España (Veracruz, July 1519), in: Martínez, *DC*, 1:77–85. Escritura convenida entre el ayuntamiento de la Vera Cruz y Hernán Cortés (Cempoala, August 5, 1519), in: Martínez, 86–91. See also: Martínez Martínez, *Veracruz 1519*. Almost at the same time the study by Schwaller and Nader (*The First Letter from New Spain*) appeared, which arrives at deviating findings.

62. The text of the document is printed in facsimile and transcription by: Schwaller and Nader, *The First Letter from New Spain*, 64–101.

63. Cortés, *Cartas de relación*, 3–34; quote from page 25. In Madariaga as well Cortés is the planner who pulled the strings in the background to reach his goal: Salvador de Madariaga, *Hernán Cortés: der Eroberer Mexikos* (Zürich: Manesse, 1997), 148–149. Some scholars also consider the "Carta-Relación" of July 10, 1519, to be the first of the letter-reports of Cortés from Mexico—including Manuel Alcalá, the editor of the edition of Cartas used here. Others, however, above all Martínez, are of the opinion that there must have been another report by the hand of Cortés—the first Carta de Relación—which, however, has disappeared; see: Martínez Martínez, *Veracruz 1519*, 27–28; Marroquín Arredondo, *Diálogos con Quetzalcóatl*, 83–85. For Schwaller and Nader, the petition of June 20 is the first letter which was believed to have been lost: Schwaller and Nader, *The First Letter from New Spain*, 1.

64. Henry Raup Wagner, *The Discovery of New Spain in 1518 by Juan de Grijalva* (Berkeley: The Cortes Society, 1942), 120–121. A description of the gifts can be found in: Anghiera, *Acht Dekaden über die Neue Welt*, 1:374–376; López de Gómara, *La conquista de México*, 111–113; Cortés, *Cartas de relación*, 31–34.

65. Díaz del Castillo, *Historia verdadera de la conquista de la Nueva España*, 141–142. The other chronicles do not report on the deceitfulness of Montejo. However, this is also well documented in the archive sources: Información recibida ante el gobernador y adelantado Diego Velázquez, sobre una expedición sospechosa emprendida desde la Habana por Alonso Fernandez Portocarrero y Francisco Montejo, con pretesto de que iban a nuevos

descubrimientos (October 7, 1519), in: Torres de Mendoza, Cárdenas, and Pacheco, *CDIA*, 12:151–203. On Cortés's messages to his family: Thomas, *Die Eroberung Mexikos*, 308.

66. Diego Velázquez to Juan Rodríguez de Fonseca (Santiago de Cuba, October 12, 1519), in: Martínez, *DC*, 1:91–93. Información recibida en La Coruña sobre la armada que Diego Velásquez dispuso para el descubrimiento de Nueva España (April 29–30, 1520), in: Francisco del Paso y Troncoso, ed., *Epistolario de Nueva España 1505–1818*, vol. 1, 1505–1529 (Mexico: Porrúa, 1939), 44–50. Benito Martín to His Majesty (Seville, October/November 1519), in: Martínez, *DC*, 1:95–97. Memorial presentado al Real Consejo por Don Martín Cortés de Monroy, padre de Hernán Cortés, en nombre de su hijo (March 1520), in: Martínez, 102–104. Declaraciones de Francisco de Montejo y Alonso Hernández Portocarrero sobre la armada que hizo el descubrimiento de la Nueva España, in: Martínez, 109–113; Díaz del Castillo, *Historia verdadera de la conquista de la Nueva España*, 144–147; Anghiera, *Acht Dekaden über die Neue Welt*, 1:376–377.

67. Díaz del Castillo, *Historia verdadera de la conquista de la Nueva España*, 147–148; López de Gómara, *La conquista de México*, 115–116; Residencia, *Documentos para la historia de México: Archivo mexicano*, Sumario de la residencia tomada a D. Fernando Cortes, vol. 1 (Mexico: Tipografía de Vicente García Torres, 1852), 120; Anghiera, *Acht Dekaden über die Neue Welt*, 2:6–7. See also: Miralles Ostos, *Hernán Cortés*, 119; Cervantes de Salazar, *Crónica de la Nueva España*, 236–238; Tapia, "Relación de algunas cosas," 81. In later court cases, these incidents were repeatedly referred to. See for example: Declaraciones de testigos en la pesquisa secreta contra Hernando Cortés (1529), in: Torres de Mendoza, Cárdenas, and Pacheco, *CDIA*, 26:423 and passim.

68. Cortés, *Cartas de relación*, 4. Díaz del Castillo presents it as though the men had ordered Cortés to destroy the ships, and as though this had been done in front of the men: Díaz del Castillo, *Historia verdadera de la conquista de la Nueva España*, 149. According to López de Gómara, the action took place in secret. Cortés himself justified his actions in the second letter-report: López de Gómara, *La conquista de México*, 116–117; Cortés, *Cartas de relación*, 39. See also: Sepúlveda, *Del Nuevo Mundo*, 109–110.

Chapter 5

1. On the number of one hundred thousand men: López de Gómara, *La conquista de México*, 106.
2. Díaz del Castillo, *Historia verdadera de la conquista de la Nueva España*, 151.
3. Díaz del Castillo, 151.
4. López de Gómara, *La conquista de México*, 118–119; Díaz del Castillo, *Historia verdadera de la conquista de la Nueva España*, 152–154; Anghiera, *Acht Dekaden über die Neue Welt*, 2:7–8; Cortés, *Cartas de relación*, 39–41.
5. Díaz del Castillo, *Historia verdadera de la conquista de la Nueva España*, 155; Herrera y Tordesillas, *Historia general*, 5:37–41; Cervantes de Salazar, *Crónica de la Nueva España*, 211–212; Cortés, *Cartas de relación*, 41–42. On the still debated route of Cortés, see also: Fernando Benítez, *La ruta de Hernán Cortés*, 2nd ed. (Mexico: Fondo de Cultura Económica, 1992); Goñi, *Las conquistas de México y Yucatán*, 77–80.
6. Grunberg speaks of ten percent in the first six months; Grunberg, *Histoire de la conquête du Mexique*, 64–65.
7. López de Gómara, *La conquista de México*, 121; Cortés, *Cartas de relación*, 42–43.
8. López de Gómara, *La conquista de México*, 122; Tapia, "Relación de algunas cosas," 86; Cervantes de Salazar, *Crónica de la Nueva España*, 243–245.
9. Sepúlveda, *Del Nuevo Mundo*, 112; Díaz del Castillo, *Historia verdadera de la conquista de la Nueva España*, 158–159.
10. Sepúlveda, *Del Nuevo Mundo*, 113; Cortés, *Cartas de relación*, 43–44; López de Gómara, *La conquista de México*, 123.
11. Muñoz Camargo, *Historia de Tlaxcala*, 31–39; Cándido Portillo Cirio, *Camaxtli: Dios tutelar de los tlaxcaltecas* (Tlaxcala: CAZATMEX, 2009).
12. Lane F. Fargher, Richard E. Blanton, and Heredia Espinoza, "The Independent Republic of Tlaxcallan," in *The Oxford Handbook of the Aztecs*, eds. Deborah L. Nichols and Enrique

Rodríguez-Alegría (New York: Oxford University Press, 2017), 535. See also: Charles Gibson, *Tlaxcala in the Sixteenth Century* (New Haven: Yale UniversityPress, 1952).

13. Ricardo Rendón Garcini, *Breve historia de Tlaxcala* (Mexico: Fondo de Cultura Económica, 1996), 15–27; Angel García Cook, *Tlaxcala a la llegada de los españoles según las evidencias arqueológicas* (Mexico: Instituto Nacional de Antropología e Historia, 2014); Antonio Peñafiel, *Ciudades coloniales y capitales de la república mexicana: La ciudad virreinal de Tlaxcala* (Mexico: Cosmos, 1978), 31–46; Lucina M. Toulet Abasolo, *Tlaxcala en la conquista de México: El mito de la traición* (Tlaxcala: Tlaxcallan, 1996), 13–20.

14. Riese, *Das Reich der Azteken*, 140–141; Hassig, *Aztec Warfare*, 10–11.

15. Rendón Garcini, *Breve historia de Tlaxcala*, 29.

16. Hassig, *Aztec Warfare*, 23.

17. Fargher, Blanton, and Espinoza, "The Independent Republic of Tlaxcallan," 535–539.

18. Fargher, Blanton, and Espinoza, 539–541; Toulet Abasolo, *Tlaxcala en la conquista de México*, 26–31.

19. Especially the Lienzo of Tlaxcala analyses this in: Gillespie, *Saints and Warriors*, 46–81; Cervantes de Salazar, *Crónica de La Nueva España*, 245–250. See also: Andrea Martínez Baracs, *Un Gobierno de Indios: Tlaxcala, 1519–1750* (Mexico: Fondo de Cultura Economica, 2008), 80–86.

20. Muñoz Camargo, *Historia de Tlaxcala*, 187–188; Durán, "Historia de las Indias," 2:28–32; Domingo Francisco de San Antón Muñón Chimalpahin Quauhtlehuanitzin, *Séptima relación de las différentes histoires originales*, ed. Josefina García Quintana (Mexico: Universidad Nacional Autónoma de México, 2003), 197.

21. Díaz del Castillo, *Historia verdadera de la conquista de la Nueva España*, 162.

22. Díaz del Castillo, 163. See also: Aguilar, "Relación breve de la conquista de la Nueva España [1892]," 169; Tapia, "Relación de algunas cosas," 87; Cortés, *Cartas de relación*, 45.

23. Díaz del Castillo, *Historia verdadera de la conquista de la Nueva España*, 164.

24. Anghiera, *Acht Dekaden über die Neue Welt*, 2:10–14; Cortés, *Cartas de relación*, 46–47. An exception is the court testimony of a confidant of Cortés, Francisco de Solis, regarding the importance of the Totonac allies: "If it weren't for them, we wouldn't have won." Thomas, *Die Eroberung Mexikos*, 349–350.

25. Navarrete Linares, "La Malinche," 294.

26. Alva Ixtlilxóchitl, *Obras históricas*, 2:209–210; López de Gómara, *La conquista de México*, 128–133; Sepúlveda, *Del Nuevo Mundo*, 114–123; Cortés, *Cartas de relación*, 43–48. On the problem of the siege, see: Hassig, *Mexico and the Spanish Conquest*, 85.

27. Díaz del Castillo, *Historia verdadera de la conquista de la Nueva España*, 167–177; Anghiera, *Acht Dekaden über die Neue Welt*, 2:17–18; Cervantes de Salazar, *Crónica de la Nueva España*, 253–271; López de Gómara, *La conquista de México*, 135–140; Tapia, "Relación de algunas cosas," 90. The extent of the exaggerations on the part of the Spaniards is shown by the fact that Cortés estimated the size of the enemy army at 149,000 men; Cortés, *Cartas de relación*, 47. On the danger of a mutiny, see especially: Hassig, *Mexico and the Spanish Conquest*, 90.

28. Hassig, *Mexico and the Spanish Conquest*, 91. Rendón assumes that the Tlaxcalans considered the Spanish invincible; Rendón Garcini, *Breve historia de Tlaxcala*, 31. See also: Martínez Baracs, *Un gobierno de indios*, 37–40.

29. Díaz del Castillo, *Historia verdadera de la conquista de la Nueva España*, 171–177.

30. Díaz del Castillo, 187–197; Cortés, *Cartas de relación*, 49–50; Alvarado Tezozomoc, *Crónica mexicana*, 465; López de Gómara, *La conquista de México*, 140–142; Tapia, "Relación de algunas cosas," 91; Vásquez de Tapia, "Relación de méritos y servicios," 139–140; Sepúlveda, *Del Nuevo Mundo*, 123–124; Anghiera, *Acht Dekaden über die Neue Welt*, 2:18.

31. Díaz del Castillo, *Historia verdadera de la conquista de la Nueva España*, 190–191; Cortés, *Cartas de relación*, 51; Sepúlveda, *Del Nuevo Mundo*, 125; Cervantes de Salazar, *Crónica de la Nueva España*, 271–272.

32. Díaz del Castillo, *Historia verdadera de la conquista de la Nueva España*, 197–199; Cortés, *Cartas de relación*, 50; López de Gómara, *La conquista de México*, 143–145; Sepúlveda, *Del Nuevo Mundo*, 124; Anghiera, *Acht Dekaden über die Neue Welt*, 2:18–19; Muñoz Camargo, *Historia de Tlaxcala*, 192–193; Taboada, *La sombra del islam en la conquista de América*, 192.

33. Díaz del Castillo, *Historia verdadera de la conquista de la Nueva España*, 200–204; López de Gómara, *La conquista de México*, 146.

34. Hassig, *Mexico and the Spanish Conquest*, 93.

35. Muñoz Camargo, *Historia de Tlaxcala*, 187–190. On the Lienzo: Gillespie, *Saints and Warriors*, 46–81; Hinz, *"Hispanisierung" in Neu-Spanien 1519–1568*, 1:192.

36. Townsend, *Malintzin's Choices*, 63.

37. Gillespie, *Saints and Warriors*, 24 and 120–126; Navarrete Linares, "La Malinche," 302–303. On marriage policy in general, see: Robinson A. Herrera, "Concubines and Wives: Reinterpreting Native-Spanish Intimate Unions in Sixteenth-Century Guatemala," in *Indian Conquistadors: Indigenous Allies in the Conquest of Mesoamerica*, eds. Laura Matthew and Michel Oudijk (Norman: University of Oklahoma Press, 2007), 130.

38. Hassig, *Aztec Warfare*, 21; Oudijk and Restall, "Mesoamerican Conquistadors in the Sixteenth Century," 44–47.

39. Díaz del Castillo, *Historia verdadera de la conquista de la Nueva España*, 175; Susan Schroeder, "Introduction," in *The Conquest All Over Again: Nahuas and Zapotecs Thinking, Writing, and Painting Spanish Colonialism*, ed. Susan Schroeder (Brighton: Sussex Academic Press, 2010), 14; Oudijk and Restall, "Mesoamerican Conquistadors in the Sixteenth Century," 38–42.

40. Díaz del Castillo, *Historia verdadera de la conquista de la Nueva España*, 212; López de Gómara, *La conquista de México*, 148.

41. Vásquez de Tapia, "Relación de méritos y servicios," 140–142.

42. López de Gómara, *La conquista de México*, 149; Cortés, *Cartas de relación*, 53. See also: Martínez Baracs, *Un gobierno de indios*, 50–54.

43. Tapia, "Relación de algunas cosas," 95–96; Díaz del Castillo, *Historia verdadera de la conquista de la Nueva España*, 215–217. According to Rojas, the Cholultecas were free: Gabriel de Rojas, "Relación de Cholula," ed. Fernando Gómez de Orozco, *Revista mexicana de estudios históricos*, no. 1 (October 1927): 160–163. On its role as a spiritual center, see: Benavente, *Memoriales*, 1:83–86. See also: Patricia Plunket and Gabriela Uruñela, "Cholula in Aztec Times," in *The Oxford Handbook of the Aztecs*, eds. Deborah L. Nichols and Enrique Rodríguez-Alegría (New York: Oxford University Press, 2017), 523–524. On the question of relations with Tenochtitlan: Plunket and Uruñela, 530.

44. Tapia, "Relación de algunas cosas," 97–99; Aguilar, "Relación breve de la conquista de la Nueva España," 175; Díaz del Castillo, *Historia verdadera de la conquista de la Nueva España*, 218–230; López de Gómara, *La conquista de México*, 150–152; Cervantes de Salazar, *Crónica de la Nueva España*, 287–290; Muñoz Camargo, *Historia de Tlaxcala*, 208–209; Sepúlveda, *Del Nuevo Mundo*, 127–129.

45. Cortés, *Cartas de relación*, 54–55; Cervantes de Salazar, *Crónica de la Nueva España*, 291–292; Torquemada, *Monarquía Indiana*, 2:137–140; Alva Ixtlilxóchitl, *Obras históricas*, 3:2:216. On the districts, see: Plunket and Uruñela, "Cholula in Aztec Times," 530. The massacre of Cholula was also mentioned in Las Casas as an example of Spanish cruelty: Las Casas, *Kurzgefasster Bericht*, 41–43.

46. Hassig, *Mexico and the Spanish Conquest*, 94–97. See also: Clendinnen, " 'Fierce and Unnatural Cruelty': Cortés and the Conquest of Mexico," 70–74. For the opposite opinion, see for example: Grunberg, *Histoire de la conquête du Mexique*, 80–82. See also: Navarrete Linares, "Beheadings and Massacres: Andean and Mesoamerican Representations of the Spanish Conquest," 64. In the Relación de Cholula of Rojas, written in 1581 and partly based on eyewitness accounts, it is stated that the "Naturales" still denied a conspiracy, "which cannot be believed," as Rojas remarked; Rojas, "Relación de Cholula," 158.

47. Sahagún, *Florentine Codex*, 13: 29.

48. Cortés, *Cartas de relación*, 56–57; López de Gómara, *La conquista de México*, 157; Anghiera, *Acht Dekaden über die Neue Welt*, 2:24–25; Sepúlveda, *Del Nuevo Mundo*, 129–130. With slight variations: Díaz del Castillo, *Historia verdadera de la conquista de la Nueva España*, 231–234.

49. Aguilar, "Relación breve de la conquista de la Nueva España," 176.

50. Ynformación de Diego Dordáz (Santo Domingo, September 26, 1521), in: Torres de Mendoza, Cárdenas, and Pacheco, *CDIA*, 40:80–82; Díaz del Castillo, *Historia verdadera de la conquista de la Nueva España*, 235; Cortés, *Cartas de relación*, 57–58; López de Gómara, *La*

conquista de México, 158; Sepúlveda, *Del Nuevo Mundo*, 131; Anghiera, *Acht Dekaden über die Neue Welt*, 2:25–26.

51. Díaz del Castillo, *Historia verdadera de la conquista de la Nueva España*, 236; Tapia, "Relación de algunas cosas," 100.
52. Sahagún, *Florentine Codex*, 13: 31.
53. Sahagún, 13: 31–32.
54. Sahagún, 13: 34.
55. Sahagún, 13: 34.
56. Cortés, *Cartas de relación*, 60.
57. Cortés, 61; Díaz del Castillo, *Historia verdadera de la conquista de la Nueva España*, 239–244; Cervantes de Salazar, *Crónica de la Nueva España*, 298–299; *Aus der Welt der Azteken*, 261; Durán, "Historia de Las Indias," 2:34; López de Gómara, *La conquista de México*, 160–162; Sepúlveda, *Del Nuevo Mundo*, 132–133; Tapia, "Relación de algunas cosas," 100.

Chapter 6

1. Sahagún, *Florentine Codex*, 13:39–41.
2. Díaz del Castillo, *Historia verdadera de la conquista de la Nueva España*, 244–245; Aguilar, "Relación breve de la conquista de la Nueva España," 178. For the description of the dam: Anghiera, *Acht Dekaden über die Neue Welt*, 2:29–31; Chimalpahin Quauhtlehuanitzin, *Codex Chimalpahin*, 1:157–159.
3. Díaz del Castillo, *Historia verdadera de la conquista de la Nueva España*, 245–247; Cortés, *Cartas de relación*; Tapia, "Relación de algunas cosas," 102; López de Gómara, *La conquista de México*, 164–165; Sepúlveda, *Del Nuevo Mundo*, 134. On the reception by the princes: *Crónica Mexicayotl: die Chronik des Mexikanertums des Alonso Franco, des Hernando de Alvarado Tezozomoc und des Domingo Francisco de San Antón Muñón Chimalpahin Quauhtlehuanitzin: aztekischer Text ins Deutsche übersetzt und erläutert* (Sankt Augustin: Academia, 2004), 297.
4. Díaz del Castillo, *Historia verdadera de la conquista de la Nueva España*, 247–248; Aguilar, "Relación breve de la conquista de la Nueva España," 180; Anghiera, *Acht Dekaden über die Neue Welt*, 2:33–34; Cervantes de Salazar, *Crónica de la Nueva España*, 302–303; Tovar, *Origen de los mexicanos*, 160; Durán, "Historia de las Indias," 2:34–36; Berlin and Barlow, *Anales de Tlatelolco*, 62; Alva Ixtlilxóchitl, *Obras Históricas*, 2:217–218.
5. Cortés, *Cartas de relación*, 64–65.
6. López de Gómara, *La conquista de México*, 165–166; Sepúlveda, *Del Nuevo Mundo*, 134–135; Cervantes de Salazar, *Crónica de la Nueva España*, 308; Díaz del Castillo, *Historia verdadera de La conquista de la Nueva España*, 248–249; Aguilar, "Relación breve de la conquista de la Nueva España," 179; Tapia, "Relación de algunas cosas," 104–105; Alva Ixtlilxóchitl, *Obras Históricas*, 2:218; Sahagún, *Florentine Codex*, 13:44; Durán, "Historia de las Indias," 2:36.
7. Townsend, "Burying the White Gods," 674. In detail with a discussion of the literature by: Francis J. Brooks, "Motecuzoma Xocoyotl, Hernán Cortés, and Bernal Díaz Del Castillo: The Construction of an Arrest," *The Hispanic American Historical Review* 75, no. 2 (1995): 149–183. For the narrative perspective, see especially: Carman, *Rhetorical Conquests*, 46–52 and 46–167.
8. Bassett, *The Fate of Earthly Things*, 42. Thomas defends the authenticity of the speech with arguments that unilaterally refer to Cortés: Thomas, *Die Eroberung Mexikos*, 390–393. See also: Martínez, *Hernán Cortés*, 244.
9. On the reporting to Moteuczoma: Alvarado Tezozomoc, *Crónica mexicana*, 466; Hassig, *Mexico and the Spanish Conquest*, 77; Hassig, *Aztec Warfare*, 242; Pastrana Flores, *Historias de la conquista*, 65–118; Townsend, "Burying the White Gods," 683; Aimi, *La verdadera visión de los vencidos*, 193–200. For a different interpretation see Matthew Restall, *When Montezuma Met Cortes: The True Story of the Meeting that Changed History* (New York: HarperCollins, 2018).
10. Hassig, *Mexico and the Spanish Conquest*, 100–102.
11. Díaz del Castillo, *Historia verdadera de la conquista de la Nueva España*, 251–252.
12. Díaz del Castillo, 261–267; Conquistador Anónimo, "Relación de algunas cosas de la Nueva España," Chapter XVIII–XXII; Cortés, *Cartas de relación*, 77–82. See also: López de Gómara, *La conquista de México*, 180–190.

13. Díaz del Castillo, *Historia verdadera de la Conquista de la Nueva España*, 267–271. See also: Anghiera, *Acht Dekaden über die Neue Welt*, 2:44–47; Sepúlveda, *Del Nuevo Mundo*, 135–137; López de Gómara, *La conquista de México*, 190–191.

14. Díaz del Castillo, *Historia verdadera de la conquista de la Nueva España*, 273–274, quote: 273; Aguilar, "Relación breve de la conquista de la Nueva España," 181–182; Alva Ixtlilxóchitl, *Obras Históricas*, 2: 218; López de Gómara, *La conquista de México*, 192–193; Durán, "Historia de las Indias," 2:37–38.

15. Cortés, *Cartas de relación*, 65; Díaz del Castillo, *Historia verdadera de la conquista de la Nueva España*, 274–278; Aguilar, "Relación breve de la conquista de la Nueva España," 182; Anghiera, *Acht Dekaden über die Neue Welt*, 2:36–37.

16. Cortés, *Cartas de relación*, 66–67; Tapia, "Relación de algunas cosas," 102–103; Aguilar, "Relación breve de la conquista de la Nueva España," 183; Díaz del Castillo, *Historia verdadera de la conquista de la Nueva España*, 278–281; Chimalpahin Quauhtlehuanitzin, *Séptima relación de las différentes histoires originales*, 199; López de Gómara, *La conquista de México*, 193–195; Tovar, *Origen de los mexicanos*, 162.

17. Cortés, *Cartas de relación*, 68; López de Gómara, *La conquista de México*, 200–201; Sepúlveda, *Del Nuevo Mundo*, 140–141; Vásquez de Tapia, "Relación de méritos y servicios," 109–110; Díaz del Castillo, *Historia verdadera de la conquista de la Nueva España*, 282–284; Anghiera, *Acht Dekaden über die Neue Welt*, 2:37–38; Cervantes de Salazar, *Crónica de la Nueva España*, 340–347; Fernández de Oviedo, *Historia general y natural de las Indias*, 287–290; Alva Ixtlilxóchitl, *Obras históricas*, 2:219.

18. Cortés, *Cartas de relación*, 66. Stenzel therefore presents the view that the capture had already been carried out in a surprise attack when entering the city. Cortés had deliberately misrepresented this in order to conceal the illegality of his actions: Stenzel, *Das kortesische Mexiko*, 38–40. On the models of his approach, see: Gabbert, "Warum Montezuma weinte," 38–39. See also: Aimi, *La verdadera visión de los vencidos*, 193. Townsend concludes from the contradictory source statements on the subject that the capture must have taken place much later: Townsend, *Malintzin's Choices*, 93–94.

19. Cortés, *Cartas de relación*, 68–69; Díaz del Castillo, *Historia verdadera de la conquista de la Nueva España*, 287–290; Alva Ixtlilxóchitl, *Obras históricas*, 2:220; Cervantes de Salazar, *Crónica de la Nueva España*, 347–353.

20. Díaz del Castillo, *Historia verdadera de la conquista de la Nueva España*, 284–287 and 291–295. On Grado and Sandoval: Declaraciones de testigos en la pesquisa secreta contra Hernando Cortés (1529), in: Torres de Mendoza, Cárdenas, and Pacheco, *CDIA*, 26:394–395.

21. Cortés, *Cartas de relación*, 69; Díaz del Castillo, *Historia verdadera de la conquista de la Nueva España*, 304–309; López de Gómara, *La conquista de México*, 203–205; Cervantes de Salazar, *Crónica de la Nueva España*, 367–371. On the Mixtecs: Ronald Spores, *The Mixtecs in Ancient and Colonial Times* (Norman: University of Oklahoma Press, 1984), 10–63.

22. Díaz del Castillo, *Historia verdadera de la conquista de la Nueva España*, 310–313; Cortés, *Cartas de relación*, 75–76; Anghiera, *Acht Dekaden über die Neue Welt*, 2:43–44.

23. Sahagún, *Florentine Codex*, 13:47–48. See also Durán, "Historia de las Indias," 2:38.

24. Díaz del Castillo, *Historia verdadera de la conquista de la Nueva España*, 313–318.

25. Cervantes de Salazar, *Crónica de la Nueva España*, 371–376; Alva Ixtlilxóchitl, *Obras históricas*, 2:222–224. On the throne dispute of Texcoco: Hinz, *"Hispanisierung" in Neu-Spanien 1519–1568*, 1:198; Eduardo de J. Douglas, *In the Palace of Nezahualcoyotl: Painting Manuscripts, Writing the Pre-Hispanic Past in Early Colonial Period Tetzcoco, Mexico* (Austin: University of Texas Press, 2010), 8–9.

26. Díaz del Castillo, *Historia verdadera de la conquista de la Nueva España*, 296–302; Cortés, *Cartas de relación*, 72–73; Tovar, *Origen de los mexicanos*, 164. See also: Clendinnen, " 'Fierce and Unnatural Cruelty,' " 74–75.

27. López de Gómara, *La conquista de México*, 207.

28. López de Gómara, 207–209; Díaz del Castillo, *Historia verdadera de la conquista de la Nueva España*, 302–304; Cortés, *Cartas de relación*, 74–75; Alva Ixtlilxóchitl, *Obras históricas*, 2:225–226; Sepúlveda, *Del Nuevo Mundo*, 143–144. See also Thomas, who quotes testimonies from later trials that confirm this version: Thomas, *Die Eroberung Mexikos*, 442–443. See also: Goñi, *Las conquistas de México y Yucatán*, 92–98.

29. Díaz del Castillo, *Historia verdadera de la conquista de la Nueva España*, 318–320; Tapia, "Relación de algunas cosas," 110–112; Cervantes de Salazar, *Crónica de la Nueva España*, 353–63; Anghiera, *Acht Dekaden über die Neue Welt*, 2:53–55.

30. Cervantes de Salazar, *Crónica de la Nueva España*, 357; Cortés, *Cartas de relación*, 80.

31. Díaz del Castillo, *Historia verdadera de la conquista de la Nueva España*, 320–323; Cervantes de Salazar, *Crónica de la Nueva España*, 381–385; López de Gómara, *La conquista de México*, 211–212.

32. Díaz del Castillo, *Historia verdadera de la conquista de la Nueva España*, 143.

33. Diego Velázquez to Juan Rodríguez de Fonseca (Santiago de Cuba, October 12, 1519), in: Martínez, *DC*, 1:91–93; Testimonio de una ynformación fecha en Sancto Domingo a ystancias del fiscal de aquelle Audiencia, sobre aber formado una armada Diego Velázquez (Isla Fernandina [Cuba], November 17, 1519), in: Torres de Mendoza, Cárdenas, and Pacheco, *CDIA*, 35:5–18.

34. Díaz del Castillo, *Historia verdadera de la conquista de la Nueva España*, 323–324. Cortés assumed only about eight hundred soldiers with Narváez: Cortés, *Cartas de relación*, 87. See also: López de Gómara, *La conquista de México*, 216–217; Sepúlveda, *Del Nuevo Mundo*, 144–145; Cervantes de Salazar, *Crónica de la Nueva España*, 386–388.

35. Lucás Vázquez de Ayllón to His Majesty (Santo Domingo, January 8, 1520), in: Torres de Mendoza, Cárdenas, and Pacheco, *CDIA*, 35:241–244; Ders. to His Majesty (San Juan de Ulóa, April 23, 1520), in: Martínez, *DC*, 1:105–108; Miguel de Pasamonte to His Majesty (Santo Domingo, January 15, 1520), in: Martínez, 1:244–247; Interrogatorio presentado por el dicho Don Hernán Cortés al exámen de los testigos que presentáre, para su descargo en la pesquisa secreta, in: Martínez, 27:348–350; Díaz del Castillo, *Historia verdadera de la conquista de la Nueva España*, 325–328.

36. Díaz del Castillo, *Historia verdadera de la conquista de la Nueva España*, 328–331; Ynformación fecha en la Ysla de Cuba a petycion del Adelantado Diego Velázquez (June 28, 1521), in: Torres de Mendoza, Cárdenas, and Pacheco, *CDIA*, 35:284–286; Residencia, *Documentos Para la historia de Mexico*, 2:389–390; Cervantes de Salazar, *Crónica de la Nueva España*, 390–391.

37. Cortés, *Cartas de relación*, 86; Tapia, "Relación de Algunas Cosas," 113; Cargos que resultan contra Hernando Cortés (Tenochtitlan, May 8, 1529), in: Torres de Mendoza, Cárdenas, and Pacheco, *CDIA*, 27:9–10; Presentaciones e xuramentos de los testigos que presentó la parte del Marqués del Valle para en prueba de sus descargos [statement of Luis Martínez] (1534), in: Torres de Mendoza, Cárdenas, and Pacheco, 28:36–37; Díaz del Castillo, *Historia verdadera de la conquista de la Nueva España*, 327–338; Sepúlveda, *Del Nuevo Mundo*, 327–328. On Olmedo's role, see also: León Cazáres, "Entre el breviario y la espada," 607.

38. Díaz del Castillo, *Historia verdadera de la conquista de la Nueva España*, 331. See also: Cervantes de Salazar, *Crónica de la Nueva España*, 391–3; Cortés, *Cartas de relación*, 86–87.

39. Tapia, "Relación de algunas cosas," 113–114; Díaz del Castillo, *Historia verdadera de la conquista de la Nueva España*, 332–333; Cortés, *Cartas de relación*, 86–87; López de Gómara, *La conquista de México*, 217–220; Alva Ixtlilxóchitl, *Obras históricas*, 2:226; Cervantes de Salazar, *Crónica de la Nueva España*, 394–396; Anghiera, *Acht Dekaden über die Neue Welt*, 2:61.

40. Díaz del Castillo, *Historia verdadera de la conquista de la Nueva España*, 328; Sepúlveda, *Del Nuevo Mundo*, 149; Cervantes de Salazar, *Crónica de la Nueva España*, 400–406.

41. Díaz del Castillo, *Historia verdadera de la conquista de la Nueva España*, 336–340; Sepúlveda, *Del Nuevo Mundo*, 149–150; Vásquez de Tapia, "Relación de méritos y servicios," 144; Aguilar, "Relación breve de la conquista de la Nueva España," 183; López de Gómara, *La conquista de México*, 220–222; Ynformación fecha en la ysla de Cuba a petycion del Adelantado Diego Velázquez (June 28, 1521), in: Torres de Mendoza, Cárdenas, and Pacheco, *CDIA*, 35:294 and 354; Cervantes de Salazar, *Crónica de la Nueva España*, 407–410.

42. Díaz del Castillo, *Historia verdadera de la conquista de la Nueva España*, 341–358; Cortés, *Cartas de relación*, 87–94; Sepúlveda, *Del Nuevo Mundo*, 150–151; Cervantes de Salazar, *Crónica de la Nueva España*, 410–411; López de Gómara, *La conquista de México*, 223–224; Residencia, *Documentos para la historia de Mexico*, 1:248–249; Durán, "Historia de las Indias," 2:39–40.

43. Tapia, "Relación de algunas cosas," 116–119; Díaz del Castillo, *Historia verdadera de la conquista de la Nueva España*, 358–365; Cortés, *Cartas de relación*, 94. On Cortés's bribes: Ynformación fecha en la ysla de Cuba a petycion del Adelantado Diego Velázquez (June 28, 1521), in: Torres de Mendoza, Cárdenas, and Pacheco, *CDIA*, 35:291, 340–343, 348.

44. Díaz del Castillo, *Historia verdadera de la conquista de la Nueva España*, 365–376; Aguilar, "Relación breve de la conquista de la Nueva España," 184–185; Cortés, *Cartas de relación*, 95; Residencia, *Documentos para la historia de Mexico*, 1:181–182; Residencia, 2:12, 436, 444; Ynformación fecha en la ysla de Cuba a petycion del Adelantado Diego Velázquez (June 28, 1521), in: Torres de Mendoza, Cárdenas, and Pacheco, *CDIA*, 35:264–266, 288–294, 346–353; López de Gómara, *La conquista de México*, 225–226; Sepúlveda, *Del Nuevo Mundo*, 151–152; Cervantes de Salazar, *Crónica de la Nueva España*, 2:18–24; Durán, "Historia de las Indias," 2:40; Anghiera, *Acht Dekaden über die Neue Welt*, 2:62–64.

45. Cortés, *Cartas de relación*, 96; Díaz del Castillo, *Historia verdadera de la conquista de la Nueva España*, 376–377.

46. *Proceso de residencia contra Pedro de Alvarado: Ilustrado con estampas sacadas de los antiguos códices mexicanos, y notas y noticias biográficas, críticas y arqueológicas* (Mexico: Valdés y Redondas, 1847).

47. Tovar, *Origen de los mexicanos*, 119–125; Izabela Wilkosz, "Power, Performance and Propaganda: Sociopolitical Aspects of the Aztec Feast of Toxcatl" (Doctoral Thesis, Berlin, Freie Universität Berlin, 2014). See also: Gutiérrez Escudero, *Pedro de Alvarado*, 39.

48. Alva Ixtlilxóchitl, *Obras históricas*, 2:228–229.

49. Testimony of Bernardino Vázquez de Tapia (Mexico, April 15, 1537), in: *Proceso de residencia contra Pedro de Alvarado*, 36–37; Statement of Alvarado (Mexico, June 4, 1537), in: *Proceso de residencia contra Pedro de Alvarado*, 66–68.

50. Sahagún, *Florentine Codex*, 13:51–54; Durán, "Historia de las Indias," 2:39–42. See also: López de Gómara, *La conquista de México*, 229.

51. Durán, "Historia de Las Indias," 2:42.

52. Testimony of Bernardino Vázquez de Tapia: Declaraciones de testigos en la pesquisa secreta contra Hernando Cortés (1529), in: Torres de Mendoza, Cárdenas, and Pacheco, *CDIA*, 26:397; López de Gómara, *La conquista de México*, 230–231.

53. Cortés, *Cartas de relación*, 97; Díaz del Castillo, *Historia verdadera de la conquista de la Nueva España*, 377; López de Gómara, *La conquista de México*, 231–232.

54. Díaz del Castillo, *Historia verdadera de la conquista de la Nueva España*, 378–380; López de Gómara, *La conquista de México*, 232; Aguilar, "Relación breve de la conquista de la Nueva España," 185–186; Vásquez de Tapia, "Relación de méritos y servicios," 141–142; Las Casas, *Kurzgefasster Bericht*, 44–46; Cervantes de Salazar, *Crónica de la Nueva España*, 2:33–38. See also: Pablo García Loaeza, "Telling Violence: The Toxcatl Massacre at the Templo Mayor in Sixteenth-Century Sources," *Journal of Iberian and Latin American Studies* 22, no. 2 (2016): 119.

55. Durán, "Historia de las Indias," 2:42–43; Sahagún, *Florentine Codex*, 13:51. On Codex Ramírez: Tovar, *Origen de los mexicanos*, 166. The Codex Aubin, the Anales de Tlatelolco and Alva Ixtlilxochitl, on the other hand, blame Alvarado; see: Walter Lehmann, Gerdt Kutscher, and Günter Vollmer, eds., *Geschichte der Azteken: Codex Aubin und verwandte Dokumente: aztekischer Text*, Bd. 13 (Berlin: Mann, 1981), 28–30; Berlin and Barlow, *Anales de Tlatelolco*, 62–63; Alva Ixtlilxóchitl, *Obras históricas*, 2:228–229. On the thesis of Cortés's order, see: Hassig, *Mexico and the Spanish Conquest*, 109.

56. Berlin and Barlow, *Anales de Tlatelolco*, 64; Sahagún, *Florentine Codex*, 13:61.

57. Cortés, *Cartas de relación*, 98; Díaz del Castillo, *Historia verdadera de la conquista de la Nueva España*, 380–388; López de Gómara, *La conquista de México*, 234; Aguilar, "Relación breve de la conquista de la Nueva España," 187; Cervantes de Salazar, *Crónica de la Nueva España*, 2:38–46.

58. Berlin and Barlow, *Anales de Tlatelolco*, 64.

59. Díaz del Castillo, *Historia verdadera de la conquista de la Nueva España*, 383; Alva Ixtlilxóchitl, *Obras históricas*, 2:229; Tovar, *Origen de los mexicanos*, 165–166; Sahagún, *Florentine Codex*,

13:60–61; Durán, "Historia de las Indias," 2:44–45; Anghiera, *Acht Dekaden über die Neue Welt*, 2:64–68.

60. Díaz del Castillo, *Historia verdadera de la conquista de la Nueva España*, 380–381; Cervantes de Salazar, *Crónica de la Nueva España*, 2:38.

61. According to Díaz del Castillo, Moteuczoma had lost the will to live and died in great despair: Díaz del Castillo, *Historia verdadera de la conquista de la Nueva España*, 38–39. The eyewitnesses Aguilar and Vázquez de Tapia stated that the tlatoani did not manage to give his speech at all but was hit by a misguided projectile and died the next morning (Aguilar) or after three days (Vázquez), respectively: Aguilar, "Relación Breve de la conquista de la Nueva España," 189 and 191; Vásquez de Tapia, "Relación de méritos y servicios," 145. According to Cortés, Cervantes de Salazar, and Peter Martire, the tlatoani himself came up with the idea to call the Mexica to peace from the roof, which hardly seems likely: Cortés, *Cartas de relación*, 99; Cervantes de Salazar, *Crónica de la Nueva España*, 2:47–48; Anghiera, *Acht Dekaden über die Neue Welt*, 2:68. See also: López de Gómara, *La conquista de México*, 235. Also Durán's indigenous interlocutors as well as Alva Ixtlilxochitl, Suárez de Peralta, and Muñoz Camargo assumed that Moteuczoma was killed by the projectiles of the Mexica: Durán, "Historia de las Indias," 2:45; Alva Ixtlilxóchitl, *Obras históricas*, 2:229; Suárez de Peralta, *Tratado del descubrimiento de las Indias*, 122; Muñoz Camargo, *Historia de Tlaxcala*, 217.

62. This thesis is supported by the eyewitness: Vásquez de Tapia, "Relación de méritos y servicios," 146. On the indigenous sources: Tovar, *Origen de los mexicanos*, 166; Sahagún, *Florentine Codex*, 13:65; Castillo, *Historia de la venida de los mexicanos y otros pueblos*, 139; Chimalpahin Quauhtlehuanitzin, *Séptima relación de las différentes histoires originales*, 201.

63. Alva Ixtlilxochitl writes that the Mexica did not feel grief, but simply continued to fight: Alva Ixtlilxóchitl, *Obras Históricas*, 2:230. Similarly, Tovar, *Origen de los mexicanos*, 166. In the Codex Aubin it is said that the carrier of the corpse was turned away several times and had problems finding a place to burn the body: Lehmann, Kutscher, and Vollmer, *Geschichte der Azteken*, 31–32.

64. *Crónica Mexicayotl*, 298; Chimalpahin Quauhtlehuanitzin, *Codex Chimalpahin*, 1:165; Díaz del Castillo, *Historia verdadera de la conquista de la Nueva España*, 389–391; López de Gómara, *La conquista de México*, 235–236; Cervantes de Salazar, *Crónica de la Nueva España*, 2:51–54; Anghiera, *Acht Dekaden über die Neue Welt*, 2:69–70.

65. Aguilar, "Relación breve de la conquista de la Nueva España," 191. Translation based on: Thomas, *Die Eroberung Mexikos*, 549; Cervantes de Salazar, *Crónica de la Nueva España*, 2:54.

66. Cortés, *Cartas de relación*, 102–103; Díaz del Castillo, *Historia verdadera de la conquista de la Nueva España*, 389–391; Cervantes de Salazar, *Crónica de la Nueva España*, 2:54–56; López de Gómara, *La conquista de México*, 236–240; Muñoz Camargo, *Historia de Tlaxcala*, 218; Vásquez de Tapia, "Relación de méritos y servicios," 146. On the division of the gold: Ynformación fecha en la ysla de Cuba a petycion del Adelantado Diego Velázquez (06.28.1521), in: Torres de Mendoza, Cárdenas, and Pacheco, *CDIA*, 35:297–298; *Proceso de Residencia Contra Pedro de Alvarado*, 94–95.

67. Díaz del Castillo, *Historia verdadera de la conquista de la Nueva España*, 394–398; Sahagún, *Florentine Codex*, 13:67–69; *Crónica Mexicayotl*, 301; Muñoz Camargo, *Historia de Tlaxcala*, 218; Suárez de Peralta, *Tratado del descubrimiento de las Indias*, 123; Durán, "Historia de las Indias," 2:47–48; Cervantes de Salazar, *Crónica de la Nueva España*, 2:56–58.

68. Cortés, *Cartas de relación*, 104; Aguilar, "Relación breve de la conquista de la Nueva España," 191–193; Vásquez de Tapia, "Relación de méritos y servicios," 146; Anghiera, *Acht Dekaden über die Neue Welt*, 2:73; López de Gómara, *La conquista de México*, 242–243; Sepúlveda, *Del Nuevo Mundo*, 159; Alva Ixtlilxóchitl, *Obras históricas*, 2:230–231; Berlin and Barlow, *Anales de Tlatelolco*, 64.

Chapter 7

1. Alva Ixtlilxóchitl, *Obras históricas*, 2:233; Sahagún, *Sahagún, Florentine Codex*, 13:71; Díaz del Castillo, *Historia verdadera de la conquista de la Nueva España*, 398–399; Tovar, *Origen de los mexicanos*, 167; Durán, "Historia de las Indias," 2:49; Vásquez de Tapia, "Relación de

méritos y servicios," 146–147; Aguilar, "Relación breve de la conquista de la Nueva España," 192–193; Cervantes de Salazar, *Crónica de la Nueva España*, 2:58–60.

2. Berlin and Barlow, *Anales de Tlatelolco*, 64; Sahagún, *Florentine Codex*, 13:79–80; Díaz del Castillo, *Historia verdadera de la conquista de la Nueva España*, 400; Cervantes de Salazar, *Crónica de la Nueva España*, 2:60–63; Anghiera, *Acht Dekaden über die Neue Welt*, 2:73–75; Cortés, *Cartas de relación*, 105–106.

3. Durán, "Historia de las Indias," 2:50–51; Muñoz Camargo, *Historia de Tlaxcala*, 225–226; Díaz del Castillo, *Historia verdadera de la conquista de la Nueva España*, 400–404; Cortés, *Cartas de relación*, 107; Cervantes de Salazar, *Crónica de la Nueva España*, 2:63–65; López de Gómara, *La conquista de México*, 243–246.

4. Cortés, *Cartas de relación*, 107–109; Muñoz Camargo, *Historia de Tlaxcala*, 228–229; Díaz del Castillo, *Historia verdadera de la conquista de la Nueva España*, 404–406; Berlin and Barlow, *Anales de Tlatelolco*, 64; López de Gómara, *La conquista de México*, 247–248; Anghiera, *Acht Dekaden über die Neue Welt*, 2:75–76; Cervantes de Salazar, *Crónica de la Nueva España*, 2:65–68; Alva Ixtlilxóchitl, *Obras históricas*, 2:233–234; Durán, "Historia de las Indias," 2:51–53. On the importance of the Tlaxcalans, see, for example, the statement of Alonso de Villanueva in a later court case: Presentaciones e xuramientos de los testigos que presentó la parte del Marqués del Valle para en prueba de sus descargos (April 21, 1534), in: Torres de Mendoza, Cárdenas, and Pacheco, *CDIA*, 27:503.

5. Alva Ixtlilxóchitl, *Obras históricas*, 2:236–238; Muñoz Camargo, *Historia de Tlaxcala*, 232–236; Cervantes de Salazar, *Crónica de la Nueva España*, 2:78–81. On the opposition of Xicoténcatl, see: Martínez Baracs, *Un gobierno de indios*, 56–59.

6. López de Gómara, *La conquista de México*, 249.

7. Díaz del Castillo, *Historia verdadera de la conquista de la Nueva España*, 406–409; Cervantes de Salazar, *Crónica de la Nueva España*, 2:69 and 76–78.

8. Cortés, *Cartas de relación*, 110; Díaz del Castillo, *Historia verdadera de la conquista de la Nueva España*, 414–417; Cervantes de Salazar, *Crónica de la Nueva España*, 2:81–88; Alva Ixtlilxóchitl, *Obras históricas*, 2:238; López de Gómara, *La conquista de México*, 251–253; Sepúlveda, *Del Nuevo Mundo*, 164–65; Anghiera, *Acht Dekaden über die Neue Welt*, 2:77.

9. Residencia, *Documentos para la historia de México*, 2:165; Díaz del Castillo, *Historia verdadera de la conquista de la Nueva España*, 418–420; Cortés, *Cartas de relación*, 111. Statement by Diego Dávila: Ynformación fecha en la Ysla de Cuba a petycion del Adelantado Diego Velázquez (June 28, 1521), in: Torres de Mendoza, Cárdenas, and Pacheco, *CDIA*, 35:354, 403, and 465.

10. Cortés, *Cartas de relación*, 118–119; Residencia, *Documentos para la historia de México*, 1:259; Díaz del Castillo, *Historia verdadera de la conquista de la Nueva España*, 434–440. Statement by Diego Dávila: Ynformación fecha en la Ysla de Cuba a petycion del Adelantado Diego Velázquez (June 28, 1521), in: Torres de Mendoza, Cárdenas, and Pacheco, *CDIA*, 35:373 and 475; Cervantes de Salazar, *Crónica de la Nueva España*, 2:99; Vásquez de Tapia, "Relación de Méritos y Servicios," 148–149.

11. José Tudela, ed., *Relación de las ceremonias y ritos y población y gobierno de los indios de la provincia de Michoacán* (Morelia: Balsal Ed., [1541] 1977), 237–240; On Cuitlahuac: Castañeda de la Paz, *Conflictos y alianzas en tiempos de cambio*, 177–178; Berlin and Barlow, *Anales de Tlatelolco*, 65.

12. Díaz del Castillo, *Historia verdadera de la conquista de la Nueva España*, 420–423 and 427–431. According to Díaz del Castillo, Olid led the troops into battle. Other chronicles report that Cortés himself commanded the campaigns. Cortés, *Cartas de relación*, 112–118; López de Gómara, *La conquista de México*, 253–257; Cervantes de Salazar, *Crónica de la Nueva España*, 2:93–95; Alva Ixtlilxóchitl, *Obras históricas*, 2:238; Anghiera, *Acht Dekaden über die Neue Welt*, 2:78–79; Sepúlveda, *Del Nuevo Mundo*, 165–167.

13. Díaz del Castillo, *Historia verdadera de la conquista de la Nueva España*, 431–434.

14. Buenaventura Zapata y Mendoza, "Historia cronológica de la noble ciudad de Tlaxcala," 142; Díaz del Castillo, *Historia verdadera de la conquista de la Nueva España*, 437–438; López de Gómara, *La conquista de México*, 258; Cervantes de Salazar, *Crónica de la Nueva España*, 2:100–104; Alva Ixtlilxóchitl, *Obras históricas*, 2:238–239; Cortés, *Cartas de relación*, 130–131.

15. Torquemada, *Monarquía Indiana*, 2:244–246; Cervantes de Salazar, *Crónica de la Nueva España*, 2:107–110. Ordenanzas militares mandadas pregonar por Hernando Cortés (Tlaxcala, December 22, 1520), in: Martínez, *DC*, 1:164–169; Cortés, *Cartas de relación*, 132; Sepúlveda, *Del Nuevo Mundo*, 167; Alva Ixtlilxóchitl, *Obras históricas*, 2:240.

16. Chimalpahin Quauhtlehuanitzin, *Codex Chimalpahin*, 1:165; *Crónica Mexicayotl*, 317; Lehmann, Kutscher, and Vollmer, *Geschichte der Azteken*, 33; Díaz del Castillo, *Historia verdadera de la conquista de la Nueva España*, 427; López de Gómara, *La conquista de México*, 226–227; Tovar, *Origen de los mexicanos*, 168; Cervantes de Salazar, *Crónica de La Nueva España*, 2:98–99; Berlin and Barlow, *Anales de Tlatelolco*, 64. On the course of the disease, see: Hassig, *Mexico and the Spanish Conquest*, 123–124. According to the Codex Aubin, Cuitlahuac died at the annual festival of the Huitzilipochtli, Panquetzalitzli, see: Lehmann, Kutscher, and Vollmer, *Geschichte der Azteken*, 32. Brooks claims that the smallpox epidemic did not have the dimensions described in the sources, but was part of the "Franciscan myth"; McCaa argues that in some provinces up to 50 percent of people died, while in others it was slightly less: Francis J. Brooks, "Revising the Conquest of Mexico: Smallpox, Sources, and Populations," *The Journal of Interdisciplinary History* 24, no. 1 (1993): 29; Robert McCaa, "Spanish and Nahuatl Views on Smallpox and Demographic Catastrophe in Mexico," *The Journal of Interdisciplinary History* 25, no. 3 (1995): 399.

17. Sahagún, *Florentine Codex*, 13:83.

18. Chimalpahin Quauhtlehuanitzin, *Codex Chimalpahin*, 1:167; *Crónica Mexicayotl*, 321; Tovar, *Origen de los mexicanos*, 169; Díaz del Castillo, *Historia verdadera de la conquista de la Nueva España*, 560–561; Durán, "Historia de las Indias," 2:53. On the strategic considerations, see: Hassig, *Mexico and the Spanish Conquest*, 121–133; Anghiera, *Acht Dekaden über die Neue Welt*, 2:80.

19. Cortés, *Cartas de relación*, 120; López de Gómara, *La conquista de México*, 260–263.

20. Cortés, *Cartas de relación*, 119; Díaz del Castillo, *Historia verdadera de la conquista de la Nueva España*, 437; Vásquez de Tapia, "Relación de méritos y servicios," 149; López de Gómara, *La conquista de México*, 258–259; Cervantes de Salazar, *Crónica de la Nueva España*, 2:58; Sepúlveda, *Del Nuevo Mundo*, 167; Muñoz Camargo, *Historia de Tlaxcala*, 237–239.

21. Cortés, *Cartas de relación*, 134–136; Díaz del Castillo, *Historia verdadera de la conquista de la Nueva España*, 441–442; López de Gómara, *La conquista de México*, 263–264. On the succession dispute, see: Hassig, *Mexico and the Spanish Conquest*, 135–138.

22. Alva Ixtlilxóchitl, *Obras históricas*, 2:241; Durán, "Historia de las Indias," 2:55. The role of this prince, a brother of Coanacoch, who also asserted claims to the throne and ruled parts of the national territory, in this context remains unclear. It is certain, however, that he joined Cortés and was patronized by him. See also: Torquemada, *Monarquía indiana*, 2:252–254.

23. Alva Ixtlilxóchitl, *Obras históricas*, 2:242. See also: Juan Bautista Pomar, *Relaciones de Texcoco y de la Nueva España: Pomar-Zurita*, ed. Joaquín García Icazbalceta (México: Salvador Chavez Hayhos, 1941), 2.

24. Díaz del Castillo, *Historia verdadera de la conquista de la Nueva España*, 443–447; Cortés, *Cartas de relación*, 137–138; Alva Ixtlilxóchitl, *Obras históricas*, 2:242–244; López de Gómara, *La conquista de México*, 265–266; Cervantes de Salazar, *Crónica de la Nueva España*, 2:125–127.

25. Díaz del Castillo, *Historia verdadera de la conquista de la Nueva España*, 448–449; Cortés, *Cartas de relación*, 139–140; López de Gómara, *La conquista de México*, 266–267; Sepúlveda, *Del Nuevo Mundo*, 169–170; Cervantes de Salazar, *Crónica de la Nueva España*, 120–121.

26. Díaz del Castillo, *Historia verdadera de la conquista de la Nueva España*, 450–451; Cortés, *Cartas de relación*, 141–144; López de Gómara, *La conquista de México*, 268; Cervantes de Salazar, *Crónica de la Nueva España*, 2:122; Alva Ixtlilxóchitl, *Obras históricas*, 2:242–243.

27. Díaz del Castillo, *Historia verdadera de la conquista de la Nueva España*, 457–461; Cortés, *Cartas de relación*, 146–148; López de Gómara, *La conquista de México*, 269–271; Durán, "Historia de Las Indias," 2:56; Alva Ixtlilxóchitl, *Obras históricas*, 2:243; Torquemada, *Monarquía indiana*, 2:256–258; Sepúlveda, *Del Nuevo Mundo*, 170–171; Cervantes de Salazar, *Crónica de La Nueva España*, 2:122–124.

28. Díaz del Castillo, *Historia verdadera de la conquista de la Nueva España*, 461–465; Cortés, *Cartas de relación*, 148; López de Gómara, *La conquista de México*, 272; Sepúlveda, *Del Nuevo Mundo*, 172; Cervantes de Salazar, *Crónica de la Nueva España*, 2:138–139.

29. Díaz del Castillo, *Historia verdadera de la conquista de la Nueva España*, 466–467. The fact that Cortés does not go into these struggles further suggests that they were not very successful for him: Cortés, *Cartas de relación*, 150. See also Cervantes, who writes of "skirmishes:" Cervantes de Salazar, *Crónica de la Nueva España*, 2:139–141. Sepúlveda, *Del Nuevo Mundo*, 172–173.

30. *Residencia, Documentos para la historia de México*, 1:64, 175, 243. On the judgment against Díaz: Probanza sobre la fuga que intentaba Panfilo Narváez (Villa Rica de la Veracruz, February 16, 1521), in: Torres de Mendoza, Cárdenas, and Pacheco, *CDIA*, 26:287–297; Cortés, *Cartas de relación*, 215; Cervantes de Salazar, *Crónica de la Nueva España*, 2:118–120. See also: Miralles Ostos, *Hernán Cortés*, 229; Díaz del Castillo, *Historia verdadera de la conquista de la Nueva España*, 504–506.

31. Díaz del Castillo, *Historia verdadera de la conquista de la Nueva España*, 479–481; Cervantes de Salazar, *Crónica de la Nueva España*, 2:135–136.

32. Díaz del Castillo, *Historia verdadera de la conquista de la Nueva España*, 434–436. Información promovida por Diego Velázquez contra Hernán Cortés (Santiago de Cuba, June 28–July 6, 1521), in: Martínez, *DC*, 1:192.

33. Cortés, *Cartas de relación*, 145; Díaz del Castillo, *Historia verdadera de la conquista de la Nueva España*, 471–478; Cervantes de Salazar, *Crónica de la Nueva España*, 2:144–147; López de Gómara, *La conquista de México*, 274–275; Alva Ixtlilxóchitl, *Obras históricas*, 2:247–248.

34. Cortés, *Cartas de relación*, 153–158; Díaz del Castillo, *Historia verdadera de la conquista de la Nueva España*, 481–491; Alva Ixtlilxóchitl, *Obras históricas*, 2:250–252; Sepúlveda, *Del Nuevo Mundo*, 174–176; Cervantes de Salazar, *Crónica de la Nueva España*, 2:147–153; López de Gómara, *La conquista de México*, 275–278; Torquemada, *Monarquía indiana*, 2:263–265. On the rapes, see also: Wood, *Transcending Conquest*, 68–69.

35. Cortés, *Cartas de relación*, 158–161; Díaz del Castillo, *Historia verdadera de la conquista de la Nueva España*, 491–500; López de Gómara, *La conquista de México*, 278–281; Alva Ixtlilxóchitl, *Obras históricas*, 2:252–254; Sepúlveda, *Del Nuevo Mundo*, 176–179; Cervantes de Salazar, *Crónica de la Nueva España*, 2:153–159; Torquemada, *Monarquía indiana*, 2:265–268; Berlin and Barlow, *Anales de Tlatelolco*, 64–65.

36. Cortés, *Cartas de relación*, 161–162; Díaz del Castillo, *Historia verdadera de la conquista de la Nueva España*, 500–504; Durán, "Historia de las Indias," 2:57–58.

37. Cervantes de Salazar, *Crónica de la Nueva España*, 2:136; Cortés, *Cartas de relación*, 163–164; Torquemada, *Monarquía indiana*, 2:259–260; López de Gómara, *La conquista de México*, 281–282; Durán, "Historia de las Indias," 2:56; Muñoz Camargo, *Historia de Tlaxcala*, 237.

38. Díaz del Castillo, *Historia verdadera de la conquista de la Nueva España*, 507.

39. Díaz del Castillo, 508–510; Sepúlveda, *Del Nuevo Mundo*, 180–181; Alva Ixtlilxóchitl, *Obras históricas*, 2:255.

40. Cervantes de Salazar, *Crónica de la Nueva España*, 2:167 and 162–164.

41. Cortés, *Cartas de relación*, 164–166; Aguilar, "Relación breve de la conquista de la Nueva España," 197; Díaz del Castillo, *Historia verdadera de la conquista de la Nueva España*, 510–514; Durán, "Historia de las Indias," 2:61; Sahagún, *Florentine Codex*, 13:81; López de Gómara, *La conquista de México*, 283–284. On Cortés's strategic considerations, see also: Grunberg, *Histoire de la conquête du Mexique*, 185.

42. Cervantes de Salazar, *Crónica de la Nueva España*, 2:162.

43. Díaz del Castillo, *Historia verdadera de la conquista de la Nueva España*, 512.

44. Alva Ixtlilxóchitl, *Obras históricas*, 2:256–257. For an assessment of the military situation, see also: Hassig, *Mexico and the Spanish Conquest*, 146–148.

45. Díaz del Castillo, *Historia verdadera de la conquista de la Nueva España*, 514–515; Cervantes de Salazar, *Crónica de la Nueva España*, 2:174. According to Muñoz Camargo, Xicotencatl left the army to visit his mistress in Tlaxcala. Muñoz Camargo, *Historia de Tlaxcala*, 84.

46. Durán, "Historia de las Indias," 2:54.

47. Durán, 56; Cervantes de Salazar, *Crónica de la Nueva España*, 2:171–173.

48. Durán, "Historia de las Indias," 2:56–57; Hassig, *Mexico and the Spanish Conquest*, 151–154.

49. Cortés, *Cartas de relación*, 165–166; Díaz del Castillo, *Historia verdadera de la conquista de la Nueva España*, 516–517; Cervantes de Salazar, *Crónica de la Nueva España*, 2:169–170; Torquemada, *Monarquía indiana*, 2:268–270.

50. Cortés, *Cartas de relación*, 166–167; Díaz del Castillo, *Historia verdadera de la conquista de la Nueva España*, 517–519; Cervantes de Salazar, *Crónica de la Nueva España*, 2:170–171; Anghiera, *Acht Dekaden über die Neue Welt*, 2:103; Sepúlveda, *Del Nuevo Mundo*, 182; Alva Ixtlilxóchitl, *Obras históricas*, 2:257–258.; López de Gómara, *La conquista de México*, 284–285.

51. Cortés, *Cartas de relación*, 168.

52. Díaz del Castillo, *Historia verdadera de la conquista de la Nueva España*, 519–521; Cervantes de Salazar, *Crónica de la Nueva España*, 2:175–176; López de Gómara, *La conquista de México*, 285–286.

53. Cervantes de Salazar, *Crónica de la Nueva España*, 2:177.

54. Cortés, *Cartas de relación*, 168–170; Sepúlveda, *Del Nuevo Mundo*, 183–184; Sahagún, *Florentine Codex*, 13:85–86.

55. Durán, "Historia de las Indias," 2:58–59.

56. Cervantes de Salazar, *Crónica de la Nueva España*, 2:179; Cortés, *Cartas de relación*, 170–171; Díaz del Castillo, *Historia verdadera de la conquista de la Nueva España*, 521–522; López de Gómara, *La conquista de México*, 288–289; Alva Ixtlilxóchitl, *Obras históricas*, 2:261.

57. Cortés, *Cartas de relación*, 171–172; Sepúlveda, *Del Nuevo Mundo*, 184–186.

58. Díaz del Castillo, *Historia verdadera de la conquista de la Nueva España*, 522–524.

59. Díaz del Castillo, 522–524.

60. Díaz del Castillo, 524–525; Cervantes de Salazar, *Crónica de la Nueva España*, 2:181–82.

61. Díaz del Castillo, *Historia verdadera de la conquista de la Nueva España*, 538. On the military significance of the roofs: Tovar, *Origen de los mexicanos*, 169.

62. Cervantes de Salazar, *Crónica de la Nueva España*, 2:180.

63. Cervantes de Salazar, 179–183; Cortés, *Cartas de relación*, 172–174; Sahagún, *Florentine Codex*, 13:87; López de Gómara, *La conquista de México*, 289–290; Alva Ixtlilxóchitl, *Obras Históricas*, 2:262–263; Sepúlveda, *Del Nuevo Mundo*, 186–188.

64. Tovar, *Origen de los mexicanos*, 170; Díaz del Castillo, *Historia verdadera de la conquista de la Nueva España*, 525–538; Cortés, *Cartas de relación*, 175–182; Sahagún, *Florentine Codex*, 13:99–101; López de Gómara, *La conquista de México*, 294–298; Sepúlveda, *Del Nuevo Mundo*, 187–191. On Alvarado's failures: *Proceso de residencia contra Pedro de Alvarado*, 70–71 and 87.

65. Cortés, *Cartas de relación*, 176.

66. Cortés, 176.

67. Díaz del Castillo, *Historia verdadera de la conquista de la Nueva España*, 539.

68. Cortés, *Cartas de relación*, 182. López de Gómara and Cervantes de Salazar follow Cortés: López de Gómara, *La conquista de México*, 299–300; Cervantes de Salazar, *Crónica de la Nueva España*, 2:193–194.

69. Berlin and Barlow, *Anales de Tlatelolco*, 66–70.

70. Díaz del Castillo, *Historia verdadera de la conquista de la Nueva España*, 540.

71. Díaz del Castillo, 540–542; Cortés, *Cartas de relación*, 183–185; Cervantes de Salazar, *Crónica de la Nueva España*, 2:194–198; Byron MacAfee and R. H. Barlow, "Anales de la conquista de Tlatelolco en 1473 y en 1521," in *Memorias de la Academia Mexicana de la Historia*, vol. 4, num. 3, Tlatelolco a través de los tiempos (México, D. F, 1945), 335–336.

72. Díaz del Castillo, *Historia verdadera de la conquista de la Nueva España*, 542–547; Cortés, *Cartas de relación*, 185–186; Cervantes de Salazar, *Crónica de la Nueva España*, 2:198–199; Sepúlveda, *Del Nuevo Mundo*, 191–195; López de Gómara, *La conquista de México*, 299–301; Solís, *Historia de la conquista de México, población y progresos de la América Septentrional, conocida por el nombre de Nueva España*, 2:339–343.

73. Díaz del Castillo, *Historia verdadera de la conquista de la Nueva España*, 548–549.

74. Díaz del Castillo, 547–548; Torquemada, *Monarquía indiana*, 2:286–289; Anghiera, *Acht Dekaden über die Neue Welt*, 2:104; Aguilar, "Relación breve de la conquista de la Nueva España [1892]," 198; Solís, *Historia de la conquista de México, población y progresos de la América Septentrional, conocida por el nombre de Nueva España*, 2:343–346.

75. Sahagún, *Florentine Codex*, 13:103–104. In the Anales de Tlatelolco, this victory is claimed for Tlatelolco. There it is also said that Cuauhtemoc himself performed the sacrifices: Berlin and Barlow, *Anales de Tlatelolco*, 70 and 71; Alva Ixtlilxóchitl, "Décima tercia relación, de la venida de los españoles y principio de la ley evangélica," 38–39. See also the representation in Durán, which, however, confuses the chronology: Durán, "Historia de las Indias," 2:59.
76. Díaz del Castillo, *Historia verdadera de la conquista de la Nueva España*, 549–555; Cervantes de Salazar, *Crónica de la Nueva España*, 2:199–200; Sepúlveda, *Del Nuevo Mundo*, 195–196.
77. Cortés, *Cartas de relación*, 187–191; Díaz del Castillo, *Historia verdadera de la conquista de la Nueva España*, 563–565; Cervantes de Salazar, *Crónica de la Nueva España*, 2:200–206; Alva Ixtlilxóchitl, "Décima tercia relación, de la venida de los españoles y principio de la ley evangélica," 40; Sepúlveda, *Del Nuevo Mundo*, 196–197; López de Gómara, *La conquista de México*, 302–303; Torquemada, *Monarquía indiana*, 2:290–292.
78. Durán, "Historia de Las Indias," 2:57.
79. Berlin and Barlow, *Anales de Tlatelolco*, 71.
80. Sahagún, *Florentine Codex*, 13:104–105. Díaz del Castillo also reported on the success of the siege: Díaz del Castillo, *Historia verdadera de la conquista de la Nueva España*, 557.
81. Díaz del Castillo, *Historia verdadera de la conquista de la Nueva España*, 557–559; Cortés, *Cartas de relación*, 191.
82. Cortés, *Cartas de relación*, 191.
83. Cortés, 192.
84. López de Gómara, *La conquista de México*, 303; Torquemada, *Monarquía indiana*, 2:295–297; Cervantes de Salazar, *Crónica de la Nueva España*, 2:210–214; Sepúlveda, *Del Nuevo Mundo*, 200; Sahagún, *Florentine Codex*, 13:107.
85. Alva Ixtlilxóchitl, "Décima tercia relación, de la venida de los españoles y principio de la ley evangélica," 42.
86. Cortés, *Cartas de relación*, 199; Cortés, 192–199; Díaz del Castillo, *Historia verdadera de la conquista de la Nueva España*, 566–567; Cervantes de Salazar, *Crónica de la Nueva España*, 2:218–227; López de Gómara, *La conquista de México*, 303–308; Solís, *Historia de la conquista de México, población y progresos de la América Septentrional, conocida por el nombre de Nueva España*, 2:346–350; Sahagún, *Florentine Codex*, 13:108.
87. Díaz del Castillo, *Historia verdadera de la conquista de la Nueva España*, 560–563; Berlin and Barlow, *Anales de Tlatelolco*, 71–73.
88. Cortés, *Cartas de relación*, 199–202; Díaz del Castillo, *Historia verdadera de la conquista de la Nueva España*, 568–571; Cervantes de Salazar, *Crónica de la Nueva España*, 2:227–235; Torquemada, *Monarquía indiana*, 2:303–307; Sepúlveda, *Del Nuevo Mundo*, 201–208. According to Sahagún, the Spaniards did not actually kill women. It is at least probable that the Europeans tended to spare them, as they were after slaves. In other cases, such as the Cholula massacre, they did not shy away from killing civilians, though this time they were motivated to incite terror, which no longer played a role in Tlatelolco: Sahagún, *Florentine Codex*, 13:116. Nonetheless, Alva Ixtlilxochitl reports that on at least one night the Spaniards ambushed starved and unarmed Mexicans desperately searching for food outside their position, killing most of them: Alva Ixtlilxóchitl, "Décima tercia relación, de la venida de los españoles y principio de la ley evangélica," 43.
89. Sahagún, *Florentine Codex*, 13:118.
90. Sahagún, 119.
91. Alva Ixtlilxóchitl, "Décima tercia relación, de la venida de los españoles y principio de la ley evangélica," 47.
92. Alva Ixtlilxóchitl, 859.
93. Díaz del Castillo, *Historia verdadera de la conquista de la Nueva España*, 573.
94. Díaz del Castillo, 571–574; Cortés, *Cartas de relación*, 202–5; Aguilar, "Relación breve de la conquista de la Nueva España," 199–200; Lehmann, Kutscher, and Vollmer, *Geschichte der Azteken*, 33; Berlin and Barlow, *Anales de Tlatelolco*, 74; Sahagún, *Florentine Codex*, 13:121; Durán, "Historia de las Indias," 2:62; Cervantes de Salazar, *Crónica de la Nueva España*, 2:227–236; Torquemada, *Monarquía indiana*, 2:303–307; Alva Ixtlilxóchitl, "Décima tercia relación, de la venida de los españoles y principio de la ley evangélica," 47–49; López de

Gómara, *La conquista de México*, 308–311; Sepúlveda, *Del Nuevo Mundo*, 209–210; Anghiera, *Acht Dekaden über die Neue Welt*, 2:104–105.

95. Díaz del Castillo, *Historia verdadera de la conquista de la Nueva España*, 574–577; Sahagún, *Florentine Codex*, 13:121; López de Gómara, *La conquista de México*, 311–312.

96. Sahagún, *Florentine Codex*, 13:125.

97. Sahagún, 123–126; Berlin and Barlow, *Anales de Tlatelolco*, 74–75; Alva Ixtlilxóchitl, "Décima tercia relación, de la venida de los españoles y principio de la ley evangélica," 49; López de Gómara, *La conquista de México*, 313; Torquemada, *Monarquía Indiana*, 2:310–314.

98. Díaz del Castillo, *Historia verdadera de la conquista de la Nueva España*, 578–579.

99. Estimates of the losses on both sides vary greatly. See: Hassig, *Mexico and the Spanish Conquest*, 156; Thomas, *Die Eroberung Mexikos*, 703–704.

Chapter 8

1. Cortés, *Cartas de relación*, 205.

2. Cortés, 205; Díaz del Castillo, *Historia verdadera de la conquista de la Nueva España*, 582–583; Cervantes de Salazar, *Crónica de la Nueva España*, 2:254.

3. Díaz del Castillo, *Historia verdadera de la conquista de la Nueva España*, 583.

4. Díaz del Castillo, 583–584; López de Gómara, *La conquista de México*, 314–315; Cervantes de Salazar, *Crónica de a Nueva España*, 2:244–245.

5. Durán, "Historia de las Indias," 2:64. See also: Alva Ixtlilxóchitl, "Décima tercia relación, de la venida de los españoles y principio de la ley evangélica," 50–51.

6. Cortés, *Cartas de relación*, 206; Residencia, *Documentos para la historia de México*, 1:259; Díaz del Castillo, *Historia verdadera de la conquista de la Nueva España*, 584–586; López de Gómara, *La conquista de México*, 315–316.

7. Díaz del Castillo, *Historia verdadera de la conquista de la Nueva España*, 588–589.

8. Alva Ixtlilxóchitl, "Décima tercia relación, de la venida de los españoles y principio de la ley evangélica," 50. On the importance of the indigenous conquistadors, see: Oudijk and Restall, "Mesoamerican Conquistadors in the Sixteenth Century," 49–50.

9. Cortés, *Cartas de relación*, 250–251; Jaime García Mendoza, *La provincia de la plata en el siglo XV:I Historia de los reales de minas de Temazcaltepec, Zultepec, Zacualpan y Taxco* (México, D.F.: Publicia, 2011), 38–48.

10. Díaz del Castillo, *Historia verdadera de la conquista de la Nueva España*, 608–614; López de Gómara, *La conquista de México*, 318–319.

11. Díaz del Castillo, *Historia verdadera de la conquista de la Nueva España*, 618–620. Testimonio jurado de Hernán Cortés en su pleito con Pedro de Alvarado (Toledo, March 10, 1529), in: Martínez, *DC*, 3:35–36.

12. Díaz del Castillo, *Historia verdadera de la conquista de la Nueva España*, 589–590; López de Gómara, *La conquista de México*, 318–321; Alva Ixtlilxóchitl, "Décima tercia relación, de la venida de los españoles y principio de la ley evangélica," 52.

13. Jerónimo de Alcalá, *La relación de Michoacán*, ed. Francisco Miranda (México: Secretaría de Educación Pública, 1988), 303–326; Cortés, *Cartas de relación*, 206; López de Gómara, *La conquista de México*, 316–318. On the legation of Montaño, see also Cervantes de Salazar, *Crónica de la Nueva España*, 2:255–261. The latter, however probably exaggerates the role of his friend, since he is mentioned only in passing in the relación. For the context: Joseph Benedict Warren, *The Conquest of Michoacán: The Spanish Domination of the Tarascan Kingdom in Western Mexico, 1521–1530* (Norman: University of Oklahoma Press, 1985), 42–72.

14. Cortés, *Cartas de relación*, 206. See also: Cortés, 214–215; López de Gómara, *La conquista de México*, 320–321; Luis Romero Solano, *Expedición cortesiana a las Molucas, 1527* (México: Editorial Jus, 1950), 14–16.

15. Cortés, *Cartas de relación*, 210; Díaz del Castillo, *Historia verdadera de la conquista de la Nueva España*, 590–600; López de Gómara, *La conquista de México*, 323–325. On Malinche's role in this period, see: Townsend, *Malintzin's Choices*, 127–129.

16. Robert Stoner Chamberlain, *Conquista y colonización de Yucatán, 1517–1550* (México, D.F.: Porrúa, 1982), 19–104; Chuchiak IV, "La conquista de Yucatán," 175–226, 131–132, 235–314; Goñi, *Las conquistas de México y Yucatán*, 50–53; Restall, *Maya Conquistador*,

passim; Ida Altman, "Conquest, Coercion, and Indigenous Allies: The Role of Indios Amigos in the Campaigns in New Galicia," in *Indian Conquistadors: Indigenous Allies in the Conquest of Mesoamerica* (Norman: University of Oklahoma Press, 2007), 145–174; José María Murià and Angélica Peregrina, eds., *Historia general de Jalisco*, vol. 1, desde los orígenes hasta mediados del siglo XVI (Zapopan: Porrúa, 2015), 289–318.

17. Aurelio Espinosa, *The Empire of the Cities: Emperor Charles V, the Comunero Revolt, and the Transformation of the Spanish System* (Boston: Brill, 2009), 46–81; José Antonio Maravall, *Las comunidades de castilla: Una primera revolución moderna*, 2nd ed. (Madrid: Alianza, 1979), 36–75.

18. Solís, *Historia de la conquista de México*, 2:291–294. On the Battle of Villalar: Rodolfo Puiggrós, *La España que conquistó el Nuevo Mundo*, 5th ed. (Bogotá: El Áncora Ed., 1989), 137–145.

19. Cristóbal de Tapia presenta sus provisiones reales para que Cortés le entregue la gobernación ... (Cempoala, December, 24–30, 1521): Martínez, *DC*, 1:210–213.

20. Cargos que resultan contra Hernando Cortés (Temistlan, May 8, 1529), in: Torres de Mendoza, Cárdenas, and Pacheco, *CDIA*, 27:17–19. Descargos dados por García de Llerena en nombre de Hernando Cortés a los cargos hechos a éste (Temistlan, October 12, 1529), in: Torres de Mendoza, Cárdenas, and Pacheco, *CDIA*, 27:227–228.

21. Cortés, *Cartas de relación*, 210–212.

22. Cristóbal de Tapia presenta sus provisiones reales para que Cortés le entregue la gobernación ... (Cempoala, December 24–30, 1521), in: Martínez, *DC*, 1:213–218; Díaz del Castillo, *Historia verdadera de la conquista de la Nueva España*, 590–592; Cortés, *Cartas de relación*, 212–213.

23. Díaz del Castillo, *Historia verdadera de la conquista de la Nueva España*, 616–617; Cortés, *Cartas de relación*, 225–227.

24. Díaz del Castillo, *Historia verdadera de la conquista de la Nueva España*, 601.

25. Hernán Cortés to Charles V. (Coyoacán, May 5, 1522), in: Torres de Mendoza, Cárdenas, and Pacheco, *CDIA*, 1:230.

26. On the power of attorney for Martín Cortés, see: Poder otorgado por Hernán Cortés en favor de su padre Martín Cortés ... (Coyoacán, May 8, 1522), in: Martínez, *DC*, 1:225–229. The letter of the conquistadors is summarized by Díaz del Castillo, *Historia verdadera de la conquista de la Nueva España*, 602–604. Relación del oro, plata, joyas y otras cosas que los procuradores de Nueva España llevan a Su Majestad (Coyoacán, March 19, 1522), in: Martínez, *DC*, 1:233–238. Memoria de los plumajes y joyas que enviaba Hernán Cortés a iglesias, monasterios y personas de España (Coyoacán, May 19, 1522), in: Martínez, 242–249. For an analysis of the recipient list, see: Thomas, *Die Eroberung Mexikos*, 750–754.

27. Díaz del Castillo, *Historia verdadera de la conquista de la Nueva España*, 604–608; Cortés, *Cartas de relación*, 255; Vásquez de Tapia, "Relación de méritos y servicios [1939]," 150; López de Gómara, *La conquista de México*, 315–316; Cervantes de Salazar, *Crónica de la Nueva España*, 2:246–247; Anghiera, *Acht Dekaden über die Neue Welt*, 2:106–107.

28. Díaz del Castillo, *Historia verdadera de la conquista de la Nueva España*, 676–689; López de Gómara, *La conquista de México*, 343–346. See also: Martínez, *Hernán Cortés*, 371–78; Thomas, *Die Eroberung Mexikos*, 758–761; Grunberg, *Histoire de la conquête du Mexique*, 57–58.

29. Real cédula de nombramiento de Hernán Cortés como gobernador y capitán general de la Nueva España (Valladolid, October 15, 1522), in: Martínez, *DC*, 1:251–253. Carlos V. and Hernán Cortés (Valladolid, October 15, 1522), in: Martínez, 1:254–256.

30. Real cédula en que se asignan a Hernán Cortés los sueldos y otras concesiones (Valladolid, October 15, 1522), in: Martínez, *DC*, 1:257–261. Instrucciones de Carlos V a Hernán Cortés sobre tratamiento de los indios ... (Valladolid, June 26, 1523), in: Martínez, 1:265–271.

31. Anghiera, *Acht Dekaden über die Neue Welt*, 2:120–138.

32. Albrecht Dürer, *Tagebuch der Reise in die Niederlande*, ed. Friedrich Leitschuh (Leipzig: Brockhaus, 1884), 83.

33. Anghiera, *Acht Dekaden über die Neue Welt*, 1:370–372; Ferdinand Anders, *Die Schätze des Montezuma: Utopie und Wirklichkeit* (Wien: Museum für Völkerkunde, 1996), 3–4.

34. Anghiera, *Acht Dekaden über die Neue Welt*, 1:368; Boruchoff, "Indians, Cannibals, and Barbarians," 26–27.

35. Aracil Varón, *Yo, Don Hernando Cortés*, 20; Carman, *Rhetorical Conquests*, 11 and 64. On the publisher, see: Barrau, "Framing the Literary," 16. On the Nuremberg edition, see: Barbara E. Mundy, "Mapping the Aztec Capital: The 1524 Nuremberg Map of Tenochtitlan, Its Sources and Meanings," *Imago Mundi* 50 (1998): 13; Padrón, *The Spacious Word*, 94.

36. Anghiera, *Acht Dekaden über die Neue Welt*, 2:281–282.

37. Real cedula de nombramiento de Hernán Cortés como gobernador y capitán general de la Nueva España (October 15, 1522), in: Martínez, *DC*, 1:251.

38. Real Provisión a Francisco de Garay (Valladolid, April 24, 1523), in: Torres de Mendoza, Cárdenas, and Pacheco, *CDIA*, 26:71–76. Provisión del Adelantado Francisco de Garay y consecuencias de la misma en la gobernación de Hernando Cortés (Chiachacata, October 4, 1523), in: Torres de Mendoza, Cárdenas, and Pacheco, 77–135.

39. Cortés, *Cartas de relación*, 241.

40. Cortés, 231–243; Díaz del Castillo, *Historia verdadera de la conquista de la Nueva España*, 621–638; López de Gómara, *La conquista de México*, 325–331; Anghiera, *Acht Dekaden über die Neue Welt*, 2:203–204.

41. Oudijk and Restall, "Mesoamerican Conquistadors in the Sixteenth Century," 54–56; Gillespie, *Saints and Warriors*, 107–110; Asselbergs, "The Conquest in Images: Stories of Tlaxcalteca and Quauhquecholteca Conquistadors," 82–84.

42. Cortés, *Cartas de relación*, 245; W. George Lovell, Christopher Hayden Lutz, and Wendy Kramer, *Strange Lands and Different Peoples: Spaniards and Indians in Colonial Guatemala* (Norman: University of Oklahoma Press, 2013), 3–17.

43. Díaz del Castillo, *Historia verdadera de la conquista de la Nueva España*, 641–643; Alva Ixtlilxóchitl, "Décima tercia relación, de la venida de los españoles y principio de la ley evangélica," 65–66; Laura Matthew, "Whose Conquest? Nahua, Zapoteca, and Mixtec Auxiliaries in the Conquest of Central America," in *Indian Conquistadors: Indigenous Allies in the Conquest of Mesoamerica*, eds. Laura Matthew and Michel Oudijk (Norman: University of Oklahoma Press, 2007), 104–105; Oudijk and Restall, "Mesoamerican Conquistadors in the Sixteenth Century," 29.

44. Díaz del Castillo, *Historia verdadera de la conquista de la Nueva España*, 643–648; López de Gómara, *La conquista de México*, 332–337; Lovell, Lutz, and Kramer, *Strange Lands and Different Peoples*, 3–17. On the epidemic, see: Ruud van Akkeren, *La visión indígena de la conquista* (Guatemala: Serviprensa, 2007), 41; Matthew, "Whose Conquest? Nahua, Zapoteca, and Mixtec Auxiliaries in the Conquest of Central America," 104–105. See also: Gutiérrez Escudero, *Pedro de Alvarado*, 56–67.

45. Díaz del Castillo, *Historia verdadera de la conquista de la Nueva España*, 648.

46. Díaz del Castillo, 649–652; Cortés, *Cartas de relación*, 245; López de Gómara, *La conquista de México*, 338–339. Relación de gastos que hizo Hernán Cortés en la armada que envió al cabo de Honduras al mando de Cristóbal de Olid (ca. 1524), in: Martínez, *DC*, 1:319–323.

47. Testimonio de una información (October 1524), in: Torres de Mendoza, Cárdenas, and Pacheco, *CDIA*, 12:268–277; Cortés, *Cartas de relación*, 256; Díaz del Castillo, *Historia verdadera de la conquista de la Nueva España*, 712–717; López de Gómara, *La conquista de México*, 350–354; Anghiera, *Acht Dekaden über die Neue Welt*, 2:320–328.

48. Alva Ixtlilxóchitl, "Décima tercia relación, de la venida de los españoles y principio de la ley evangélica," 72–73; Díaz del Castillo, *Historia verdadera de la conquista de la Nueva España*, 717–722. Regarding Malinche's wedding, Townsend comments that Cortés's mistress was provided with a good match: Townsend, *Malintzin's Choices*, 154.

49. Díaz del Castillo, *Historia verdadera de la conquista de la Nueva España*, 728. See also: Díaz del Castillo, 723–729; Cortés, *Cartas de relación*, 281–297; López de Gómara, *La conquista de México*, 360–369.

50. Berlin and Barlow, *Anales de Tlatelolco*, 9–10; Cortés, *Cartas de relación*, 297–298; Alva Ixtlilxóchitl, "Décima tercia relación, de la venida de los españoles y principio de la ley evangélica," 74–75; Díaz del Castillo, *Historia verdadera de la conquista de la Nueva España*, 734–738; López de Gómara, *La conquista de México*, 369–371. See also: Riese, *Das Reich der Azteken*, 293–295.

51. Cortés, *Cartas de relación*, 298–357; Díaz del Castillo, *Historia verdadera de la conquista de la Nueva España*, 738–792; López de Gómara, *La conquista de México*, 371–389; Alva Ixtlilxóchitl, "Décima tercia relación, de la venida de los españoles y principio de la ley evangélica," 76–104. See also: Castañeda de la Paz, *Conflictos y alianzas en tiempos de cambio*, 175–183; Oudijk and Restall, "Mesoamerican Conquistadors in the Sixteenth Century," 54.
52. Cortés, *Cartas de relación*, 271.
53. Cortés, 271–274 and 277. Relación de los gastos que hizo HC en el apresto de una armada que envió al Cabo de Honduras . . . (1529), in: Torres de Mendoza, Cárdenas, and Pacheco, *CDIA*, 12:386–403.
54. Cortés, *Cartas de relación*, 278–279. HC to Audiencia de Santo Domingo (La Habana, 13.5.1526), in: Martínez, *DC*, 1:362–367. Memoria de lo acaecido en la ciudad de México . . . (Temixtitán, 1526), in: Martínez, 1:423–431. Alva Ixtlilxóchitl, "Décima tercia relación, de la venida de los españoles y principio de la ley evangélica," 72–73. Cartas de Diego de Ocaña contra Hernán Cortés (Mexiko, August 31 and September 9, 1526), in: Alva Ixtlilxóchitl, 391–401. According to Díaz del Castillo, it was clear from the beginning that Salazar and Chirinos were only supposed to accompany them as far as Coatzacoalcos: Díaz del Castillo, *Historia verdadera de la conquista de la Nueva España*, 719–720. See also: Díaz del Castillo, 769–777.
55. Cortés, *Cartas de relación*, 362–366; Díaz del Castillo, *Historia verdadera de la conquista de la Nueva España*, 781–784 and 792–800. HC to Kaiser (Tenochtitlan, 3. September 1526), in: Torres de Mendoza, Cárdenas, and Pacheco, *CDIA*, 12:480–490. HC to García de Loaisa, Präsident des Indienrats (Cuernavaca, January 1, 1527), in: Martínez, *DC*, 1:432–434; Anghiera, *Acht Dekaden über die Neue Welt*, 2:321–332; López de Gómara, *La conquista de México*, 395–396.
56. HC to Martín Cortés (Tenuxtitan, September 26, 1526), in: Martínez, *DC*, 1:417.
57. Requerimiento y mandamiento que Marcos de Aguilar intimó a Hernán Cortés a fin de hacerle renunciar el cargo de Capitán General de la Nueva España y de la repartición de los indios. Respuesta y renuncia de Cortés (Tenustitan, September 5, 1526), in: Martínez, *DC*, 1:387–390; Cortés, *Cartas de relación*, 369–371; Díaz del Castillo, *Historia verdadera de la conquista de la Nueva España*, 810–819; López de Gómara, *La conquista de México*, 396–399.
58. Cortés, *Cartas de relación*, 248. See also: Torres de Mendoza, Cárdenas, and Pacheco, *CDIA*, 1:231; Alfredo Ruiz Islas, "Hernán Cortés y la isla California," *Iberoamericana* 7, no. 27 (2007): 41.
59. Charles V to HC (Granada, June 20, 1526), in: Martínez, *DC*, 1:373–376. On the instructions, see: HC to Saavedra Cerón (Temixtitan, May 27 and May 28, 1527), in: Martínez, 439–449, 452–453 and 459–460. HC to Sebastián Caboto (Temixtitan, May 28, 1527), in: Martínez, 454–458. On the course of the journey, see: Relación de todo lo que descubrió y anduvo el capitán Alvaro de Saavedra (o. D.), in: Torres de Mendoza, Cárdenas, and Pacheco, *CDIA*, 5:68–96. Relación de Vicente de Nápoles (1534), in: Torres de Mendoza, Cárdenas, and Pacheco, 142–175; Díaz del Castillo, *Historia verdadera de la conquista de la Nueva España*, 848–855; López de Gómara, *La conquista de México*, 399–401. On the costs that Cortés incurred, see: HC, Relación y cuenta (ca. 1528), in: Martínez, *DC*, 491–503.
60. Charles V to HC (Madrid, April 5, 1528), in: Martínez, *DC*, 3:11–313; López de Gómara, *La conquista de México*, 402–403; Díaz del Castillo, *Historia verdadera de la conquista de la Nueva España*, 819–821. Van Deusen recently examined the problems of the "free" Indians who came to Spain with Cortés and were suddenly considered slaves: Nancy E. Van Deusen, "Coming to Castile with Cortés: Indigenous 'Servitude' in the Sixteenth Century," *Ethnohistory* 62, no. 2 (April 1, 2015): 285–308.
61. Díaz del Castillo, *Historia verdadera de la conquista de la Nueva España*, 821–825.
62. Díaz del Castillo, 826. Charles V to HC (Zaragoza, April 1, 1529), in: Martínez, *DC*, 3:37. Charlies V, Cédulas (Barcelona, July 6, 1529), in: Martínez, 49–61; López de Gómara, *La conquista de México*, 403–404.
63. Clemens VII., Bulle für HC (Rom, April 16, 1529), in: Martínez, *DC*, 3:40–42; Díaz del Castillo, *Historia verdadera de la conquista de la Nueva España*, 828–830. On the marriage with Doña Juana: López de Gómara, *La conquista de México*, 404–405. On the death of Catalina Suárez: Díaz del Castillo, *Historia verdadera de la conquista de la Nueva España*, 614–615. For

the context, see: Vélez Cipriano, *El Mito de Cortés*, 269–275. One of the unfinished tasks of the judge Ponce de León was the investigation of the death of Catalina Suárez: Francisco Manzo-Robledo, *I, Hernán Cortés: The (Second) Trial of Residency* (New York: Peter Lang, 2013), 19; Mira Caballos, *Hernán Cortés*, 156–161.

64. HC, Memorial de peticiones a Carlos V (Madrid, July 25, 1528), in: Martínez, *DC*, 3:21–25; Martínez, *Hernán Cortés*, 510–512.

65. Charles V to HC (Madrid, April 5, 1528), in: Martínez, *DC*, 3:11–313; Díaz del Castillo, *Historia verdadera de la conquista de la Nueva España*, 830–839; López de Gómara, *La conquista de México*, 405–407. On the tributary demands, see: "Huexotzinco Codex, 1531," Library of Congress, Washington, accessed March 28, 2016, https://www.wdl.org/en/item/2657/view/1/1/. The Huexotzinca were able to prevail with their complaint.

66. Cargos que resultan contra Hernando Cortés (Temistlan, May 8, 1529), in: Martínez, *DC*, 2:102–131. The most comprehensive analysis of the Residencia is provided by: Manzo-Robledo, *I, Hernán Cortés*, passim.

67. Mayordomus Francisco de Terrazas an HC (Tenustitan, July 30, 1529), in: Martínez, *DC*, 3:63–75; Traslado de una real cédula prohibiendo a Hernando Cortés . . ., y a su mujer, entrar en México (March 22, 1530), in: Torres de Mendoza, Cárdenas, and Pacheco, *CDIA*, 12:403–405; Díaz del Castillo, *Historia verdadera de la conquista de la Nueva España*, 839–840. On the initial friendship between Cortés and the viceroy, see: Suárez de Peralta, *Tratado del descubrimiento de las Indias*, 138–140.

68. Cortés, *Cartas de relación*, 248.

69. Charlies V provision a HC (Madrid, 5.11.1529), in: Martínez, *DC*, 2:86–89; López de Gómara, *La conquista de México*, 409–415; Díaz del Castillo, *Historia verdadera de la conquista de la Nueva España*, 848–855 and 864–865. On the limitation of Cortés's powers: Charlies V, Cédula (Barcelona, April 17, 1535), in: Martínez, *DC*, 4:145. See also: Miguel Léon Portilla, *Hernán Cortés y La Mar Del Sur* (Madrid: Instituto de Cooperación Iberoamericana, 1985); Guadalupe Pinzon Ríos, "Descubriendo El Mar Del Sur. Los Puertos Novohispanos En Las Exploraciones Del Pacífico (1522–1565)," in *El Mundo de Los Conquistadores*, ed. Martín Ríos Saloma (México: Sílex-UNAM, 2015), 749–773.

70. Díaz del Castillo, *Historia verdadera de la conquista de la Nueva España*, 873–882. Cortés summarized the lawsuits against Mendoza in a memorandum in 1540: HC, Memorial (Madrid, June 25, 1540), in: Martínez, *DC*, 4:210–415. See also: María del Carmen Martínez Martínez, "Hernán Cortés en España (1540–1547): negocios, pleitos y familia," in *El Mundo de los conquistadores*, ed. Martín Ríos Saloma (México: Sílex-UNAM, 2015), 577–598.

71. HC, Testamento (Sevilla, October 11/12, 1547), in: Martínez, *DC*, 4:313–341; Martínez, *Hernán Cortés*, 778–796. On the odyssey concerning the mortal remains of Cortés, see: Jesús Ignacio Fernández Domingo, *Estudio del testamento de Don Hernando Cortés Marqués del Valle de Oaxaca* (Badajoz: Departamento de Publ. de la Diputación Provincial de Badajoz, 1999), 16–18; Vélez Cipriano, *El mito de Cortés*, 58–84.

Chapter 9

1. Cortés, *Cartas de relación*, 248.

2. Gibson, *The Aztecs under Spanish Rule*, 370; Gruzinski, *La Ciudad de Mexico*, 307.

3. Benavente, *Memoriales*, 1:27–28. Zorita adopted this metaphor: Zorita, *Edición crítica*, 267. See also: Glantz, "Ciudad y escritura: La Ciudad de México en las cartas de relación," 165–174. On the importance of Coyoacán: Rebecca Horn, *Postconquest Coyoacan: Nahua-Spanish Relations in Central Mexico, 1519–1650* (Stanford: Stanford University Press, 1997), 3–12. On the early hospitals: María Luisa Rodríguez-Sala, *Los cirujanos de hospitales de la Nueva España (siglos XVI y XVII): Miembros de un estamento profesional o de una comunidad científica?* (México, D. F: UNAM, 2005), 46–56.

4. Barbara E. Mundy, *The Death of Aztec Tenochtitlan, the Life of Mexico City* (Austin: University of Texas Press, 2015), 9; William F. Connell, *After Moctezuma: Indigenous Politics and Self-Government in Mexico City, 1524–1730* (Norman: University of Oklahoma Press, 2011), 5–7.

5. Díaz del Castillo, *Historia verdadera de la conquista de la Nueva España*, 418–419.

6. Cortés, *Cartas de relación*, 259–260. HC to Kaiser (Mexiko, o. D.), in: Torres de Mendoza, Cárdenas, and Pacheco, *CDIA*, 4:566–567. HC to Kaiser (Mexiko, October 15, 1524), in: Torres de Mendoza, Cárdenas, and Pacheco, 556–561.

7. Gabriela Ramos and Yanna Yannakakis, "Introduction," in *Indigenous Intellectuals: Knowledge, Power, and Colonial Culture in Mexico and the Andes* (Durham: Duke University Press, 2014), 7; Townsend, *Malintzin's Choices*, 170; Connell, *After Moctezuma*, 18.

8. HC, "Ordenanzas de buen gobierno dadas por Hernán Cortés para los vecinos y moradores de la Nueva España" (March 20, 1524), in: Torres de Mendoza, Cárdenas, and Pacheco, *CDIA*, 26:134–145.

9. Hassig, *Mexico and the Spanish Conquest*, 179–181.

10. Peter B. Villella, *Indigenous Elites and Creole Identity in Colonial Mexico, 1500–1800* (New York: Cambridge University Press, 2016), 29–72; Lockhart, *The Nahuas after the Conquest*, 110–112; Douglas, *In the Palace of Nezahualcoyotl*, 4–6.

11. Gibson, *The Aztecs under Spanish Rule*, 166–173; Lockhart, *The Nahuas after the Conquest*, 5; Woodrow Borah, "The Spanish and Indian Law: New Spain," in *The Inca and Aztec States, 1400–1800 Anthropology and History*, eds. George Allen Collier, Renato Rosaldo, and John D. Wirth (New York: Academic Press, 1982), 272.

12. Baudot, *Utopía e historia en México*, 73–74; Donald E. Chipman, *Moctezuma's Children: Aztec Royalty under Spanish Rule, 1520–1700* (Austin: University of Texas Press, 2005), 123–124.

13. Villella, *Indigenous Elites and Creole Identity in Colonial Mexico, 1500–1800*, 42–43; Hinz, "Hispanisierung" in Neu-Spanien 1519–1568, 2:463–464; Connell, *After Moctezuma*, 11–16.

14. Castañeda de la Paz, *Conflictos y alianzas en tiempos de cambio*, 215–226 and 335–337; Emma Pérez-Rocha and Rafael Tena, *La nobleza indígena del centro de México después de la conquista* (México, D.F.: Instituto Nacional de Antropología e Historia, 2000), 99–102; Villella, *Indigenous Elites and Creole Identity in Colonial Mexico, 1500–1800*, 30; Serge Gruzinski, *La colonisation de l'imaginaire: Sociétés indigènes et occidentalisation dans le Mexique Espagnol, XVIe–XVIIIe Siècle* (Paris: Gallimard, 1988), 139–188.

15. Cortés, *Cartas de relación*, 271; Martínez Baracs, *Un gobierno de indios*, 71–108; Gillespie, *Saints and Warriors*, 45; Hinz, "Hispanisierung" in Neu-Spanien 1519–1568, 488–520.

16. Pérez-Rocha and Tena, *La nobleza indígena del centro de México después de la conquista*, 16–17. For further examples, see the documents in: *Colección de Documentos Sobre Coyoacán*, 2 vols. (México, D.F.: Secretaría de Educación Pública, 1976).

17. Carlos Lázaro Avila, *Las fronteras de América y los "Flandes Indianos"* (Madrid: Consejo Superior de Investigaciones Científicas, 1997), 51–66; Matthew, "Whose Conquest?," 114; Friedrich Katz, "Rural Uprisings in Preconquest and Colonial Mexico," in *Riot, Rebellion, and Revolution: Rural Social Conflict in Mexico*, ed. Friedrich Katz (Princeton: Princeton University Press, 1988), 78.

18. Brian Philip Owensby, *Empire of Law and Indian Justice in Colonial Mexico* (Stanford: Stanford University Press, 2008), 1–2; Katz, "Rural Uprisings in Preconquest and Colonial Mexico," 79–80; John H. Coatsworth, "Patterns of Rural Rebellion in Latin America: Mexico in Comparative Perspective," in *Riot, Rebellion, and Revolution: Rural Social Conflict in Mexico*, ed. Friedrich Katz (Princeton: Princeton University Press, 1988), 49–54.

19. Cortés, *Cartas de relación*, 37. See also: Víctor Frankl, "Die Begriffe des Mexikanischen Kaisertums und der Weltmonarchie in den 'Cartas de Relación' des Hernán Cortés," *Saeculum* 13 (1962): 5–6.

20. Straub, *Das Bellum Iustum*, 5.

21. Quoted after: Hans-Joachim König, "Plus Ultra: Ein Weltreichs- und Eroberungsprogramm? Amerika und Europa in politischen Vorstellungen im Spanien Karls V," in *Von Kolumbus bis Castro: Aufsätze zur Geschichte Lateinamerikas* (Stuttgart: Heinz, 2006), 74. Fernández de Oviedo justified the imperial claim with the fact that the Mesoamerican territories had already belonged to Spain in early history and were nothing more than the mythical islands of the Hesperides, which had been suspected in the far west since ancient times and which in turn were named after the equally mythical ancient king of Spain, Hespero. See: Frankl, "Die Begriffe des mexikanischen Kaisertums," 15–16.

22. Alfred Kohler, *Karl V: 1500–1558, eine Biographie* (München: Beck, 1999), 97. The emperor also did not change his titulation, so that the "Indian islands and terrae firme" were always pronounced after the European empires: Kohler, 227–228.

23. Vélez Cipriano, *El mito de Cortés*, 308; Lupher, *Romans in a New World*, 11–12.

24. Gibson, *The Aztecs under Spanish Rule*, 58–59.

25. Gibson, 6–24 and 34–54; Lockhart, *The Nahuas after the Conquest*, 28.

26. Charles V to Cortés (Valladolid, June 26, 1523), in: Martínez, *DC*, 1:265–271.

27. Cortés to Charles V (Tenustitan, October 15, 1524), in: Martínez, *DC*, 1:287.

28. Martínez, 1:287–288.

29. Martínez, 1:288–295; Martínez, See also: Memorial de peticiones de H. Cortés a Carlos V (July 25, 1528), in: 3:23.

30. Schwaller and Nader, *The First Letter from New Spain*, 139–41; Gibson, *The Aztecs under Spanish Rule*, 58–61; Martínez, *Hernán Cortés*, 78–82.

31. Ordenanzas de buen gobierno dadas por Hernán Cortés para los vecinos y moradores de la Nueva España (March 20, 1524), in: Martínez, *DC*, 1:281.

32. Declaración de los tributos que los indios de Cuernavaca hacían al marqués del Valle (Mexiko, January 24, 1533), in: Martínez, 4:11–414.

33. Gibson, *The Aztecs under Spanish Rule*, 58–59.

34. Gibson, 58–59; Martínez, *Hernán Cortés*, 81–82; Hinz, *"Hispanisierung" in Neu-Spanien 1519–1568*, 2:420–421; Peggy K. Liss, *Orígenes de la nacionalidad mexicana 1521–1556: la formación de una nueva sociedad*, trans. Agustín Bárcena, 2nd ed. (México, D.F: Fondo de Cultura Económica, 1995), 83–92.

35. Gibson, *The Aztecs under Spanish Rule*, 61–63; Hinz, *"Hispanisierung" in Neu-Spanien 1519–1568*, 2:420–421.

36. Liss, *Orígenes de la nacionalidad mexicana*, 106–110.

37. Ordenanzas de buen gobierno dadas por Hernán Cortés para los vecinos y moradores de la Nueva España (March 20, 1524), in: Martínez, *DC*, 1:279–280; Hassig, *Mexico and the Spanish Conquest*, 183–185; Gruzinski, *La colonisation de l'imaginaire*, 226; Gillespie, *The Aztec Kings*, xxix.

38. Ordenanzas de buen gobierno dadas por Hernán Cortés para los vecinos y moradores de la Nueva España (March 20, 1524), in: Martínez, *DC*, 1:279–280.

39. Toribio [de Motolinía] Benavente, *Historia de los indios de la Nueva España: Escrita a mediados del siglo XVI; teniendo a la vista las ediciones de Lord Kingsborough y de García Icazbalceta*, ed. Daniel Sánchez García (Barcelona: Gili, 1914), 24.

40. HC to emperor (Mexiko, October 15, 1524), in: Torres de Mendoza, Cárdenas, and Pacheco, *CDIA*, 5:556–561; Torquemada, *Monarquía Indiana*, 5:17–20; Susanne Klaus, *Uprooted Christianity: The Preaching of the Christian Doctrine in Mexico based on Franciscan Sermons of the 16th Century written in Nahuatl* (Schwaben: Saurwein, 1999), 20–47.

41. Cortés, *Cartas de relación*, 257.

42. Mendieta, *Historia eclesiástica indiana*. 1:318–321. On the reception of the Twelve by Cortés, see: Mendieta, 1:352–356; Muñoz Camargo, *Historia de Tlaxcala*, 241–242; Hugh Thomas, *The Golden Age: The Spanish Empire of Charles V* (London: Allen Lane, 2010), 42.

43. Mendieta, *Historia eclesiástica indiana*. 1:359–533. On the construction of the convent, see: Mundy, *The Death of Aztec Tenochtitlan, the Life of Mexico City*, 116. On the powers of attorney under Philipp II, see: Torquemada, *Monarquía Indiana*, 5:384–386. On the mission in Tlaxcala: Martínez Baracs, *Un Gobierno de Indios*, 109–134. On the utopias, see: Baudot, *Utopía e historia en México*, 94–95.

44. Francisco Morales, "The Native Encounter with Christianity: Franciscans and Nahuas in Sixteenth-Century Mexico," *The Americas* 65, no. 2 (2008): 137–159. For the trans-formation of the god see: Richard Karl Nebel, *Altmexikanische Religion und christliche Heilsbotschaft: Mexiko zwischen Quetzalcóatl und Christus* (Immensee: Neue Zeitschrift für Missionswiss, 1983), vol. 2. On the dispute with the priests: Miguel León-Portilla, *Coloquios y doctrina cristiana: Con que los doce frailes de San Francisco, enviados por el Papa Adriano VI y por el Emperador Carlos V, convirtieron a los indios de la Nueva España* (México, D.F.: UNAM, 1986). On the tightening of the prohibitions from 1525: Gruzinski, *La Ciudad de Mexico*, 309–310; Hassig, *Time, History, and Belief in Aztec and Colonial Mexico*, 137–152.

45. José María Kobayashi, *La educación como conquista: Empresa franciscana en México* (México: El Colegio de México, 1974), 171–180; Morales, "The Native Encounter with Christianity," 146–149; Ramos and Yannakakis, "Introduction," 8–11; Ríos Castaño, *Translation as Conquest,* 66–82; Lockhart, *The Nahuas after the Conquest,* 330–331; Gruzinski, *La colonisation de l'imaginaire,* 70.

46. Martínez, *Hernán Cortés,* 93–94; Gibson, *The Aztecs under Spanish Rule,* 98–103.

47. Gibson, *The Aztecs under Spanish Rule,* 102–120.

48. Martínez, *Hernán Cortés,* 93; Josefina Edith Ruiz y Torres, *A puerta cerrada: Lectura e Inquisición en el siglo XVI novohispano* (México, D.F.: Ediciones Clandestino, 2014), 78–83; Patricia Lopes Don, *Bonfires of Culture: Franciscans, Indigenous Leaders, and the Inquisition in Early Mexico, 1524–1540* (Norman: University of Oklahoma Press, 2010), 3–5; Richard E. Greenleaf, *Zumárraga y la Inquisición mexicana 1536–1543* (México: Fondo de Cultura Económica, 1988), 121–125; Hassig, *Mexico and the Spanish Conquest,* 183–185. On the trial of Don Carlos, see: Martin Lienhard, *Disidentes, rebeldes, insurgentes: Resistencia indígena y negra en América Latina: Ensayos de historia testimonial* (Madrid: Iberoamericana, 2008), 29–50.

49. Charles V to Cortés (Valladolid, June 26, 1523), in: Martínez, *DC,* 1:265–271. See also: Baudot, *Utopía e historia en México,* 42–46; Don, *Bonfires of Culture,* 52–82. On the confrontation of the Spanish with ritual cannibalism, which they considered an infectious disease, see: Kelly L. Watson, *Insatiable Appetites: Imperial Encounters with Cannibals in the North Atlantic World* (New York: New York University Press, 2015), 92–94.

50. Baudot, *Utopía e historia en México,* 102–105.

51. Baudot, 47–56 and 495–496; Douglas, *In the Palace of Nezahualcoyotl,* 4–6.

52. Hinz, *"Hispanisierung" in Neu-Spanien 1519–1568,* 2:293–295; Gruzinski, *La colonisation de l'imaginaire,* 226; Don, *Bonfires of Culture,* 5–7.

53. Lockhart, *The Nahuas after the Conquest,* 205–206. Fundamental is: Louise M. Burkhart, *The Slippery Earth: Nahua-Christian Moral Dialogue in 16th-Century Mexico* (Tucson: University of Arizona Press, 1989). For the christianization of the Maya see also: William F. Hanks, *Converting Words: Maya in the Age of the Cross* (Berkeley: University of California Press, 2010).

54. Hassig, *Mexico and the Spanish Conquest,* 186; Noble David Cook, *Born to Die: Disease and New World Conquest, 1492–1650,* New Approaches to the Americas (Cambridge: Cambridge University Press, 1999), 60–133.

55. Gibson, *The Aztecs under Spanish Rule,* 308–309 and 53; Rebecca Earle, *The Body of the Conquistador: Food, Race, and the Colonial Experience in Spanish America, 1492–1700* (Cambridge: Cambridge University Press, 2012), 118–130.

56. Luis Alberto Vargas and Leticia E. Casillas, "El encuentro de dos cocinas: México en el siglo XVI," in *Conquista y comida: Consecuencias del encuentro de dos mundos,* ed. Janet Long (México, D.F.: UNAM, 1996), 155–168.

57. Elinor G. K. Melville, *A Plague of Sheep: Environmental Consequences of the Conquest of Mexico* (Cambridge: Cambridge University Press, 1994), 1–3. See also: Ramón María Serrera Contreras, *La América de los Habsburgo (1517–1700)* (Sevilla: Universidad de Sevilla, 2011), 109–119.

58. Melville, *A Plague of Sheep,* 12–13; Hassig, *Mexico and the Spanish Conquest,* 186–193; Peter Gerhard, *A Guide to the Historical Geography of New Spain,* 2nd ed. (Norman: University of Oklahoma Press, 1993), 3.

59. Zorita, *Edición Crítica,* 262.

60. Martínez, *Hernán Cortés,* 88; José Luis de Rojas, *A cada uno lo suyo: El tributo indígena en la Nueva España en el siglo XVI* (Zamora: Colegio de Michoacán, 1993), 77–86; Gibson, *The Aztecs under Spanish Rule,* 217–282.

61. Stenzel, *Das kortesische Mexiko,* 95–96; Gibson, *The Aztecs under Spanish Rule,* 150–152; Hinz, *"Hispanisierung" in Neu-Spanien 1519–1568,* 2:525–33; Vargas and Casillas, "El encuentro de dos Cocinas: México en el siglo XVI," 160–162. On passive resistance, see: Serrera Contreras, *La América de los Habsburgo (1517–1700),* 89–108; Frances Berdan, "Trauma and Transition in Sixteenth-Century Central Mexico," in *The Meeting of Two Worlds: Europe and America, 1492–1650,* ed. Warwick Bray (Oxford: Oxford University Press, 1993), 171.

62. Susan Kellogg, *Law and the Transformation of Aztec Culture, 1500–1700* (Norman: University of Oklahoma Press, 1995), XIX–XX; Schroeder, "Introduction," 2; Wood, *Transcending Conquest*, 141; Gibson, *The Aztecs under Spanish Rule*, 357–358; Pilar Gonzalbo Aizpuru, "Vestir al desnudo: Un acercamiento a la ética y la estética del vestido en el siglo XVI novohispano," in *Herencia española en la cultura material de las regiones de México: Casa, vestido, sustento* (Zamora: El Colegio de Michoacán, 1993), 333–335.

63. Rebecca Horn, "Indigenous Identities in Mesoamerica after the Spanish Conquest," in *Native Diasporas: Indigenous Identities and Settler Colonialism in the Americas,* eds. Gregory D. Smithers and Brooke N. Newman (Lincoln: University of Nebraska Press, 2014), 32.

Conclusion

1. Grunberg has shown that the losses of the Spanish were quite high overall. Thus 56.7 percent of the conquistadors he examined (1,189 out of 2,100) fell victim to the fighting, a further 4.8 percent (100) died of diseases, and only around 38.6 percent (810) died natural deaths. However, when one considers how many battles the troops had to fight from 1519 onward, and how high the number of those killed in action and those who died in the epidemics among the indigenous allies might have been, the losses need to be put into perspective: Bernard Grunberg, *L'univers des conquistadores: Les hommes et leur conquête dans le Mexique du XVIe siècle* (Paris: L'Harmattan, 1993), 106.

2. Díaz del Castillo, *Historia verdadera de la conquista de la Nueva España*, 476.

3. Carta de don Pedro de Santiago y de los principales de Xochimilco al rey Felipe II (Mexico, May, 20, 1563), in: Pérez-Rocha and Tena, *La nobleza indígena*, 281; Benavente, *Memoriales*, 1:21.

4. Benavente, *Memoriales*, 1:21.

BIBLIOGRAPHY

Primary Sources

Aguilar, Francisco de. "Relación breve de la conquista de la Nueva España [1892]." In *La conquista de Tenochtitlan*, edited by Germán Vázquez, 155–206. Madrid: Historia 16, 1988.

Alcalá, Jerónimo de. *La relación de Michoacán*. Edited by Francisco Miranda. México: Secretaría de Educación Pública, 1988.

Alva Ixtlilxóchitl, Fernando de. "Décima tercia relación, de la venida de los españoles y principio de la ley evangélica." In *Historia general de las cosas de Nueva España*, edited by Bernardino de Sahagún, 4:237–336. México, D.F., 1938.

Alva Ixtlilxóchitl, Fernando de. *Obras históricas: Incluyen el texto completo de las llamadas relaciones e historia de la nación chichimeca en una nueva versión establecida con el cotejo de los manuscritos más antiguos que se conocen*. Edited by Edmundo O'Gorman and Miguel León Portilla. 3rd ed. 2 vols. Biblioteca Nezahualcóyotl. Toluca: Instituto Mexiquense de Cultura, 1997.

Alvarado Tezozomoc, Fernando. *Crónica mexicana*. Edited by Gonzalo Díaz Migoyo and Germán Vázquez Chamorro. Madrid: Historia 16, 1997.

Anales de Tlatelolco: Unos anales históricos de la nación mexicana y códice de Tlatelolco. Edited by Heinrich Berlin and Robert H. Barlow. México, D.F.: Antigua Libr. Robredo, de José Porrua e Hijos, 1948.

Anghiera, Peter Martyr von [Pietro Martire d']. *Acht Dekaden über die Neue Welt*. Edited by Hans Klingelhöfer. 2nd ed. Darmstadt: Wiss. Buchges., 1973.

Auszug ettlicher Sendbrieff, dem aller durchleuchtigisten großmechtigisten Fürsten und Herren Herren Carl Römischen und Hyspanischen König etc. . . . durch ire verordent Hauptleut, von wegen einer newgefunden Inseln, der selben Gelegenheit und Inwoner Sitten und Gewonheiten inhaltend vor kurtzverschinen Tagen zugesandt. Nürnberg: Peypus, 1520.

Benavente, Toribio [de Motolinía]. *Historia de los indios de la Nueva España: Escrita a mediados del siglo XVI; teniendo a la vista las ediciones de Lord Kingsborough y de García Icazbalceta*. Edited by Daniel Sánchez García. Barcelona: Gili, 1914.

Benavente, Toribio [de Motolinía]. *Memoriales: O libro de las cosas de la Nueva España y de los naturales de ella*. Edited by Edmundo O'Gorman. 2. ed. México, D.F.: Universidad Autónoma de México, 1971.

Blackburn, Robin, and Heraclio Bonilla, eds. *Los conquistados: 1492 y la población indígena de las Américas*. Santafé de Bogotá: Tercer Mundo Editores, 1992.

Buenaventura Zapata y Mendoza, Juan. "Historia cronológica de la noble ciudad de Tlaxcala." In *Narradores indígenas y mestizos de la época colonial (siglos XVI–XVII): Zonas andina y mesoamericana*, edited by Rocío Cortés and Margarita Zamora, 139–151. Lima: Centro de Estudios Literarios "Antonio Cornejo Polar," 2016.

Castillo, Cristóbal del. *Historia de la venida de los mexicanos y otros pueblos: e historia de la conquista.* Edited by Federico Navarrete Linares. México, D.F.: Asociación de Amigos del Templo Mayor, 2001.

CDIA = *Colección de Documentos Inéditos relativos al descubrimiento, conquista y colonización de las posesiones españolas en América y Oceanía* [CDIA]. Edited by Luis Torres de Mendoza, Francisco de Cárdenas, and Joaquín Francisco Pacheco. 42 vols. Madrid: Imprenta de M.B. de Quirós, 1864.

CDIU = *Coleccion de Documentos Ineditos relativos al descubrimiento, conquista y organización de las antiguas posesiones españoles de Ultramar* [CDIU]. 25 vols. Madrid: Bernaldo de Quirós, 1884–1932.

CDM = *Colección de documentos para la historia de México* [CDM] (versión actualizada). Edited by Joaquín García Icazbalceta, 2 vols., México, 1858–1866. https://www.cervantesvirtual.com/ obra/coleccion-de-documentos-para-la-historia-de-mexico-version-actualizada--0/.

Cecil, Leslie G., and Timothy W. Pugh, eds. *Maya Worldviews at Conquest.* Boulder: University Press of Colorado, 2009.

Cervantes de Salazar, Francisco. *Crónica de la Nueva España.* Edited by Manuel Magallón. 2nd ed. Madrid: Ed. Atlas, 1971.

Chimalpahin Quauhtlehuanitzin, Domingo Francisco de San Antón Muñón. *Chimalpahin's Conquest: A Nahua Historian's Rewriting of Francisco López de Gómara's La Conquest de México.* Edited by Susan Schroeder, Anne J. Cruz, Cristian Roa-de-la Carrera, and David E. Tavares. Stanford: Stanford University Press, 2010.

Chimalpahin Quauhtlehuanitzin, Domingo Francisco de San Antón Muñón. *Codex Chimalpahin: Society and Politics in Mexico Tenochtitlan, Tlatelolco, Texcoco, Culhuacan, and Other Nahua Altepetl in Central Mexico.* Edited by Arthur J.O. Anderson and Susan Schroeder, Vol. 1. Norman: University of Oklahoma Press, 1997.

Chimalpahin Quauhtlehuanitzin, Domingo Francisco de San Antón Muñón. *Relaciones originales de Chalco Amaquemacan.* Edited by Silvia Rendón. México, D.F.: Fondo de Cultura Económica, 1965.

Chimalpahin Quauhtlehuanitzin, Domingo Francisco de San Antón Muñón. *Séptima relación de las différentes histoires originales.* Edited by Josefina García Quintana. México, D.F.: Universidad Nacional Autónoma de México, 2003.

Codex Chimalpahin—See Chimalpahin Quauhtlehuanitzin, Domingo Francisco de San Antón Muñón, "Codex Chimalpahin," 1997.

Codex Osuna. *Pintura del gobernador, alcaldes y regidores de México. Códice en geroglíficos mexicanos y en lenguas castellana y azteca, existente en la biblioteca del Excmo. Señor Duque de Osuna.* Madrid: Hernandez, 1878.

Codex Tovar—See Tovar, Juan de. "Historia de La Venida de Los Yndios," 1585.

Colección de documentos sobre Coyoacán. 2 vols. México, D.F.: Secretaría de Educación Pública, 1976.

Colón, Fernando. *Historia del Almirante Don Cristóbal Colón en la cual se da particular y verdadera relación de su vida y de sus hechos, y del descubrimiento de las Indias Occidentales, llamadas Nuevo-Mundo.* 2 vols. Madrid: Minuesa, 1892 [1571].

Cortés, Hernán. *Cartas de relación.* Edited by Manuel Alcalá. México, D.F.: Editorial Porrúa, 2005.

Cortés, Hernán. *Praeclara Ferdinandi Cortesii De Nova Maris Oceani Hyspania Narratio . . . .* Nürnberg: Peypus, 1524.

Crónica Mexicayotl: die Chronik des Mexikanertums des Alonso Franco, des Hernando de Alvarado Tezozomoc und des Domingo Francisco de San Antón Muñón Chimalpahin Quauhtlehuanitzin: aztekischer Text ins Deutsche übersetzt und erläutert. Edited by Berthold Rise. Sankt Augustin: Academia, 2004.

DC = Martínez, José Luis. ed. *Documentos Cortesianos 1518–1548.* 8 vols. México, D.F.: Universidad Nacional Autónoma de México, 1990.

Díaz, Juan. "Itinerario de la armada del Rey Católico a la isla de Yucatán [1520]." In *La conquista de Tenochtitlan,* edited by Germán Vázquez, 29–57. Madrid: Historia 16, 1988.

Díaz del Castillo, Bernal. *Historia verdadera de la conquista de la Nueva España*. Edited by Juan Gil and Carmen Sáenz de Santa María. Madrid: Fundación José Antonio de Castro, 2012.

Dürer, Albrecht. *Tagebuch der Reise in die Niederlande*. Edited by Friedrich Leitschuh. Leipzig: Brockhaus, 1884.

Durán, Diego. "Historia de las Indias de Nueva-España y Islas de Tierra Firme." Manuscript. Biblioteca Nacional de España, 1579. Biblioteca Digital Hispánica. http://bdh.bne.es/bnesea rch/CompleteSearch.do;jsessionid=D0CFB3BAE98E236970D1E28B8D5DDBA2?langu ageView=en&field=todos&text=Historia+de+las+Indias+de+Nueva-Espa%c3%b1a+y+ islas+de+Tierra+Firme&showYearItems=&exact=on&textH=&advanced=false&compl eteText=&pageSize=1&pageSizeAbrv=30&pageNumber=2.

Durán, Diego. *Historia de las Indias de Nueva-España y islas de Tierra Firme*. Edited by José Fernando Ramírez. 2 vols. México: Andrade y F. Escalante, 1867–1880 [1579].

El conquistador Anónimo. "Relación de algunas cosas de la Nueva España, y de la gran ciudad de Temestitán México; escrita por un compañero de Hernán Cortés (1858–1866)." Biblioteca Virtual Miguel de Cervantes. Accessed December 1, 2022. https://www.cervantesvirtual. com/obra-visor/coleccion-de-documentos-para-la-historia-de-mexico-version-actualizada- -0/html/21bcd5af-6c6c-4b27-a9a5-5edf8315e835_20.html.

Fernández de Oviedo, Gonzalo. *Historia general y natural de las Indias, Islas y Tierra-Firme del Mar Océano*. Madrid: Imprenta de la Real Academia de la Historia, 1851–1853[1532].

Fernández Domingo, Jesús Ignacio, ed. *Estudio del testamento de Don Hernando Cortés Marqués del Valle de Oaxaca*. Badajoz: Departamento de Publ. de la Diputación Provincial de Badajoz, 1999.

Fernández Sotelo, Rafael Diego, ed. *Herencia Española En La Cultura Material de Las regiones de México: Casa, Vestido y Sustento*. Zamora: El Colegio de Michoacán, 1993.

Herrera y Tordesillas, Antonio de. *Historia general de los hechos de los castellanos en las islas y tierrafirme del mar océano*. 17 vols. Madrid: Tipografía de Archivos, 1934–1957 [1601–1615].

Landa, Diego de. *Bericht aus Yucatán*. Edited by Carlos Rincón. 2nd ed. Leipzig: Reclam, 1993 [1864].

Las Casas, Bartolomé de. *Historia de las Indias*. Vol. 3. 5 vols. Obras Completas. Madrid: Alianza Editorial, 1994.

Las Casas, Bartolomé de. *Kurzgefasster Bericht von der Verwüstung der Westindischen Länder*. Edited by Hans Magnus Enzensberger. Frankfurt am Main: Insel-Verl, 1981 [1790].

Lehmann, Walter, Gerdt Kutscher, and Günter Vollmer, eds. *Geschichte der Azteken: Codex Aubin und verwandte Dokumente: aztekischer Text*. Berlin: Mann, 1981.

León Portilla, Miguel. *Coloquios y doctrina cristiana: Con que los doce frailes de San Francisco, enviados por el Papa Adriano VI y por el Emperador Carlos V, convirtieron a los indios de la Nueva España*. México, D.F.: Universidad Autónoma de México, 1986.

León Portilla, Miguel. *Rückkehr der Götter: Die Aufzeichnungen der Azteken über den Untergang ihres Reiches*. Frankfurt am Main: Vervuert, 1986.

Lockhart, James ed. *We People Here: Nahuatl Accounts of the Conquest of Mexico*. Berkeley: University of California Press, 1993.

López de Gómara, Francisco. *Historia general de las Indias y vida de Hernán Cortés*. Edited by Jorge Gurría Lacroix. Caracas: Biblioteca Ayacucho, 1991.

López de Gómara, Francisco. *La conquista de México*. Edited by José Luis de Rojas Gutiérrez de Gandarilla. Madrid: Dastin, 1987.

Marineo Sículo, Lucio. *Hernán Cortés: Su primera y olvidada biografía. La obra de Lucio Marineo Sículo, 1530*. Edited by Miguel León Portilla. México, D.F.: Editorial Ambos Mundos, 1985.

McAfee, Byron, and R. H. Barlow. "Anales de la conquista de Tlatelolco en 1473 y en 1521." *Memorias de la Academia Mexicana de la Historia*, Tlatelolco a través de los tiempos, 4, no. 3 (1945): 326–339.

Mendieta, Gerónimo de. *Historia eclesiástica indiana*. Edited by Joaquín García Icazbalceta and Antonio Rubial García. 2nd ed. 4 vols. México, D.F.: Consejo Nacional para la Cultura y las Artes, 1997 [1870].

Motolinía. See Benavente, Toribio de.

Muñoz Camargo, Diego. *Historia de Tlaxcala*. Edited by Alfredo Chavero. México, D.F.: Oficina Tip. de la Secretaría de Fomento, 1892 [1591].

Nebrija, Antonio de. *Gramática de la lengua castellana*. Edited by Antonio Quilis. Madrid: Editora Nacional, 1981.

Paso y Troncoso, Francisco del, ed. *Epistolario de Nueva España 1505–1818*. 2 vols. México: Porrúa, 1939.

Pomar, Juan Bautista. *Relaciones de Texcoco y de la Nueva España: Pomar-Zurita*. Edited by Joaquín García Icazbalceta. México, D.F.: Salvador Chavez Hayhos, 1975.

"Probanza Sobre Las Causas Que Se Dieron a La Suplicación de Las Provisiones Del Veedor Cristóbal de Tapia (Coyoacán, April 20, 1522)." *Boletín del Archivo General de la Nación* 9, no. 2 (1938): 181–235.

Proceso de residencia contra Pedro de Alvarado: Ilustrado con estampas sacadas de los antiguos códices mexicanos, y notas y noticias biográficas, críticas y arqueológicas. México, D.F.: Valdés y Redondas, 1847.

Relación de las ceremonias y ritos y población y gobierno de los indios de la provincia de Michoacán. Edited by José Tudela. Morelia: Balsal Ed., 1977.

Residencia. *Documentos para la historia de México: Archivo mexicano*. 2 vols. Sumario de la residencia tomada a D. Fernando Cortés. México, D.F.: Tipografía de Vicente García Torres, 1852–1853.

Rojas, Gabriel de. "Relación de Cholula." Edited by Fernando Gómez de Orozco. *Revista Mexicana de Estudios Históricos*, no. 1, 154–169. México: Editorial Cultura, October 1927 [1581].

Romero Solano, Luis. *Expedición cortesiana a las Molucas, 1527*. México, D.F.: Editorial Jus, 1950.

Sahagún, Bernardino de. *Florentine Codex: General History of the Things of New Spain, Book 12—The Conquest of Mexico*. Translated by Arthur J. O. Anderson and Charles E. Dibble. 2nd ed. Vol. 12. 13 vols. Santa Fe: The School of American Research and the University of Utah, 1975.

Sahagún, Bernardino de. *Historia general de las cosas de Nueva España*. Edited by Alfredo López Austin and Josefina García Quintana. 2 vols. Madrid: Alianza, 1988.

Sepúlveda, Juan Ginés de. *Del Nuevo Mundo*. Edited by Luis Rivero García. Obras completas. Vol. 11. Pozoblanco: Excmo. Ayuntamiento, 2005.

Solís, Antonio de. *Historia de la conquista de México, población y progresos de la América Septentrional, conocida por el nombre de Nueva España*. Edited by Edmundo O'Gorman. 3. ed. México, D.F.: Editorial Porrúa, 1978 [1684].

Suárez de Peralta, Juan. *Tratado del descubrimiento de las Indias: Noticias históricas de la Nueva España*. Edited by Teresa Silva Tena. México, D.F.: Consejo Nacional para la Cultura y las Artes, 1990.

Tapia, Andrés de. "Relación de algunas cosas de las que acaecieron al muy iluestre señor Don Hernando Cortés [1866]." In *La conquista de Tenochtitlan*, edited by Germán Vázquez, 59–123. Madrid: Historia 16, 1988.

Torquemada, Juan de. *Monarquia indiana: De los veinte y un libros rituales y monarquia indiana, con el origen y guerras de los indios occidentales, de sus poblazones, descubrimiento, conquista, conversión y otras cosas maravillosas de la mesma tierra*. Edited by Miguel León Portilla. 5th ed. 7 vols. México, D.F.: Universidad Nacional Autónoma de México, 1975.

Tovar, Juan de. *Códice Ramírez: Manuscrito del siglo XVI Intitulado: Relación del origen de los indios que habitan esta Nueva España, según sus historias*. México, D.F.: Editorial Innovación, 1979.

Tovar, Juan de. "Historia de La Venida de Los Yndios," 1585. *John Carter Brown Library*. https:// archive.org/details/tovarcodex00tova.

Tovar, Juan de. *Origen de los mexicanos*. Barcelona: Linkgua, 2011.

Vásquez de Tapia, Bernardino. "Relación de méritos y servicios [1939]." In *La conquista de Tenochtitlan*, edited by Germán Vázquez, 125–154. Madrid: Historia 16, 1988.

Zorita, Alonso de. *Edición crítica de la relación de la Nueva España y de la breve y sumaria relación escritas por Alonso de Zorita*. Edited by Wiebke Ahrndt. Translated by Luis Felipe Segura. Bonn: Sauerwein, 2001.

Cited Literature

Abulafia, David. *The Discovery of Mankind: Atlantic Encounters in the Age of Columbus.* New Haven: Yale University Press, 2008.

Adorno, Rolena. "Discourses on Colonialism: Bernal Díaz, Las Casas, and the Twentieth-Century Reader." *Modern Language Notes* 103, no. 2 (1988): 239–258.

Aimi, Antonio. *La "verdadera" visión de los vencidos: la conquista de México en las fuentes aztecas.* Alicante: Publicaciones de la Universidad de Alicante, 2009.

Akkeren, Ruud van. *La visión indígena de la conquista.* Guatemala: Serviprensa, 2007.

Alcántara Gallegos, Alejandro. "Los barrios de Tenochtitlan: Topografía, organización interna y tipología de sus predios." In *Mesoamérica y los ámbitos indígenas de la Nueva España,* edited by Pablo Escalante Gonzalbo, 167–198. Historia de la vida cotidiana en México. México, D.F.: El Colegio de México, 2004.

Altman, Ida. "Conquest, Coercion, and Indigenous Allies: The Role of Indios Amigos in the Campaigns in New Galicia." In *Indian Conquistadors: Indigenous Allies in the Conquest of Mesoamerica,* edited by Laura E. Matthew and Michel R. Oudijk, 145–174. Norman: University of Oklahoma Press, 2007.

Altman, Ida. *Emigrants and Society: Extremadura and America in the Sixteenth Century.* Berkeley: University of California Press, 1989.

Anders, Ferdinand. *Die Schätze des Montezuma: Utopie und Wirklichkeit.* Wien: Museum für Völkerkunde, 1996.

Andrews, Anthony P. "The Political Geography of the Sixteenth Century Yucatan Maya: Comments and Revisions." *Journal of Anthropological Research* 40, no. 4 (1984): 589–596.

Aracil Varón, María Beatriz. "Hernán Cortés y sus cronistas: la última conquista del héroe." *Atenea,* no. 499 (2009): 61–76. https://www.academia.edu/6204040/Hern%C3%A1n_C ort%C3%A9s_y_sus_cronistas_la_%C3%BAltima_conquista_del_h%C3%A9roe.

Aracil Varón, María Beatriz. *"Yo, Don Hernando Cortés": Reflexiones en torno a la escritura cortesiana.* Madrid: Iberoamericana, 2016.

Arnold, Philip P. "Eating Landscape: Human Sacrifice and Sustenance in Aztec Mexico." In *Aztec Ceremonial Landscapes,* edited by David Carrasco, 219–232. Niwot: University Press of Colorado, 1991.

Arranz Márquez, Luis. *Don Diego Colón, almirante, virrey y gobernador de las Indias.* Madrid: Consejo Superior de Investigaciones Científicas, 1982.

Asselbergs, Florine. "The Conquest in Images: Stories of Tlaxcalteca and Quauhquecholteca Conquistadors." In *Indian Conquistadors: Indigenous Allies in the Conquest of Mesoamerica,* edited by Laura Matthew and Michel Oudijk, 65–101. Norman: University of Oklahoma Press, 2007.

Aveni, Anthony F. "The Measure, Meaning, and Transformation of Aztec Time and Calendars." In *The Oxford Handbook of the Aztecs,* edited by Deborah L. Nichols and Enrique Rodríguez Alegría, 107–116. New York: Oxford University Press, 2017.

Ávila Sandoval, Santiago. "La vida cotidiana del último tlatoani mexica." In *Historia de la vida cotidiana en México,* edited by Pablo Escalante Gonzalbo, 1:279–300. Mesoamérica y los ámbitos indígenas de la Nueva España. Mexico, D.F.: El Colegio de México, 2004.

Báez-Jorge, Félix, and Sergio Vásquez Zárate. *Cempoala.* México, D.F.: Fondo de Cultura Económica, 2011.

Bargatzky, Thomas. "Aguilar Und Guerrero: Zwei versprengte Spanier in Yukatan im Zeitalter der Conquista." *Zeitschrift für Ethnologie* 106, no. 1/2 (1981): 161–175.

Barjau, Luis. *Hernán Cortés y Quetzalcóatl.* 2da ed. México, D.F.: Ediciones el tucán de Virginia, 2011.

Barjau, Luis. *La conquista de la Malinche.* México, D.F.: CONACULTA, 2009.

Barjau, Luis. *Voluntad e infortunio en la conquista de México.* México, D.F.: Instituto Nacional de Antropología e Historia, 2015.

Barrau, Oscar. "Framing the Literary: Jacob Cromberger of Seville and the Incipient Spanish American Narrative." *Colonial Latin American Review* 17, no. 1 (2008): 5–28.

Bassett, Molly H. *The Fate of Earthly Things: Aztec Gods and God-Bodies.* Austin: University of Texas Press, 2015.

Baudot, Georges. "Malintzin, imagen y discurso de mujer en el primer México virreinal." In *La Malinche, sus padres y sus hijos,* edited by Margo Glantz, 55–90. México, D.F.: Taurus, 2001.

Baudot, Georges. *Utopía e historia en México: Los primeros cronistas de la civilización mexicana (1520–1569).* Madrid: Espasa-Calpe, 1983.

Benítez, Fernando. *La ruta de Hernán Cortés.* 2nd ed. México, D.F.: Fondo de Cultura Económica, 1992.

Bennassar, Bartolomé. *Cortez der Konquistador: die Eroberung des Aztekenreiches.* Düsseldorf: Artemis und Winkler, 2002.

Benton, Bradley. "The Outsider: Alva Ixtlilxochitl's Tenuous Ties to the City of Tetzcoco." *Colonial Latin American Review* 23, no. 1 (2014): 37–52.

Berdan, Frances. *Aztec Archaeology and Ethnohistory.* New York: Cambridge University Press, 2014.

Berdan, Frances. "Trauma and Transition in Sixteenth-Century Central Mexico." In *The Meeting of Two Worlds: Europe and America, 1492–1650,* edited by Warwick Bray, 163–195. Oxford: Oxford University Press, 1993.

Bernhard, Roland. *Geschichtsmythen über Hispanoamerika: Entdeckung, Eroberung und Kolonisierung in Deutschen und Österreichischen Schulbüchern des 21. Jahrhunderts.* Göttingen: V & R unipress, 2013.

Bierhorst, John, ed. *Cantares mexicanos: Songs of the Aztecs.* Stanford: Stanford University Press, 1985.

Bierhorst, John, ed. *The Mythology of Mexico and Central America.* 2nd ed. Oxford: Oxford University Press, 2002.

Bleichmar, Daniela. "The Imperial Visual Archive: Images, Evidence, and Knowledge in the Early Modern Hispanic World." *Colonial Latin American Review* 24, no. 2 (2015): 236–266.

Boone, Elizabeth Hill, and Walter D Mignolo, eds. *Writing without Words: Alternative Literacies in Mesoamerica and the Andes.* Durham: Duke University Press, 1994.

Borah, Woodrow. "The Spanish and Indian Law: New Spain." In *The Inca and Aztec States, 1400–1800 Anthropology and History,* edited by George Allen Collier, Renato Rosaldo, and John D. Wirth, 265–288. New York: Academic Press, 1982.

Boruchoff, David A. "Indians, Cannibals, and Barbarians: Hernan Cortes and Early Modern Cultural Relativism." *Ethnohistory* 62, no. 1 (January 1, 2015): 17–38.

Brading, David Anthony. *The First America: The Spanish Monarchy, Creole Patriots, and the Liberal State, 1492–1867.* Cambridge: Cambridge University Press, 1991.

Bray, Warwick, ed. *The Meeting of Two Worlds: Europe and the Americas, 1492–1650.* Oxford: Oxford University Press, 1993.

Brienen, Rebecca Parker, and Margaret Ann Jackson, eds. *Invasion and Transformation: Interdisciplinary Perspectives on the Conquest of Mexico.* Boulder: University Press of Colorado, 2008.

Broda, Johanna. "The Sacred Landscape of Aztec Calendar Festivals: Myth, Nature and Society." In *Aztec Ceremonial Landscapes,* edited by David Carrasco, 74–120. Niwot: University Press of Colorado, 1991.

Brooks, Francis J. "Motecuzoma Xocoyotl, Hernán Cortés, and Bernal Díaz Del Castillo: The Construction of an Arrest." *The Hispanic American Historical Review* 75, no. 2 (1995): 149–183.

Brooks, Francis J. "Revising the Conquest of Mexico: Smallpox, Sources, and Populations." *The Journal of Interdisciplinary History* 24, no. 1 (1993): 1–29.

Brotherston, Gordon. "La Malintzin de los códices." In *La Malinche, sus padres y sus hijos,* edited by Margo Glantz, 19–37. México, D.F.: Taurus, 2001.

Brüggemann, Jürgen K. *Zempoala: El estudio de una ciudad prehispánica.* México, D.F.: Instituto Nacional de Antropología e Historia, 1991.

Bueno Bravo, Isabel. *La guerra en el imperio Azteca: Expansión, ideología y arte.* Madrid: Editorial Complutense, 2007.

Burkhart, Louise M. *The Slippery Earth: Nahua-Christian Moral Dialogue in 16th-Century Mexico.* Tucson: University of Arizona Press, 1989.

Caine, Barbara. *Biography and History.* Basingstoke: Palgrave Macmillan, 2010.

Calnek, Edward E. "The Internal Structure of Tenochtitlan." In *The Valley of Mexico*, edited by Eric Wolf, 287–302. Albuquerque: University of New Mexico Press, 1976.

Cardaillac, Louis. "Lo morisco peninsular y su proyección en la conquista de América." In *El mundo de los conquistadores*, edited by Martín Ríos Saloma, 437–456. México, D.F.: Universidad Nacional Autónoma de México, 2015.

Carman, Glen. *Rhetorical Conquests: Cortés, Gómara, and Renaissance Imperialism.* West Lafayette: Purdue University Press, 2006.

Carrasco, Davíd. *Aztec Ceremonial Landscapes.* Niwot: University Press of Colorado, 1991.

Carrasco Pizana, Pedro. *The Tenochca Empire of Ancient Mexico: The Triple Alliance of Tenochtitlan, Tetzcoco, and Tlacopan.* v. 234. Norman: University of Oklahoma Press, 1999.

Castañeda de la Paz, María. *Conflictos y alianzas en tiempos de cambio: Azcapotzalco, Tlacopan, Tenochtitlan y Tlatelolco (siglos XII-XVI).* México, D.F.: Universidad Nacional Autónoma de México, 2013.

Cervera Obregón, Marco Antonio. *El armamento entre los mexicas.* Madrid: Consejo Superior de Investigaciones Científicas, 2007.

Cervera Obregón, Marco Antonio. *Guerreros aztecas.* Madrid: Nowtilus, 2011.

Chamberlain, Robert Stoner. *Conquista y colonización de Yucatán, 1517–1550.* México, D.F.: Porrúa, 1982.

Chipman, Donald E. *Moctezuma's Children: Aztec Royalty under Spanish Rule, 1520–1700.* Austin: University of Texas Press, 2005.

Chuchiak IV, John F. "Forgotten Allies: The Origins and Roles of Native Mesoamerican Auxiliaries and Indios Conquistadores in the Conquest of Yucatán, 1526–1550." In *Indian Conquistadors: Indigenous Allies in the Conquest of Mesoamerica*, edited by Laura Matthew and Michel Oudijk, 175–226. Norman: University of Oklahoma Press, 2007.

Chuchiak IV, John F. "La conquista de Yucatán." In *Historia general de Yucatán*, edited by Sergio Quezada, Fernando Robles C., and Anthony P. Andrews, 2:29–58. Yucatán en el orden colonial. 1517–1811. Mérida: Universidad Autónoma de Yucatán, 2014.

Clendinnen, Inga. *Ambivalent Conquests: Maya and Spaniard in Yucatan, 1517–1570.* Cambridge: Cambridge University Press, 1987.

Clendinnen, Inga. *Aztecs: An Interpretation.* Cambridge: Cambridge University Press, 1993.

Clendinnen, Inga. "'Fierce and Unnatural Cruelty': Cortés and the Conquest of Mexico." *Representations*, no. 33 (Winter 1991): 65–100.

Clendinnen, Inga. *The Cost of Courage in Aztec Society: Essays on Mesoamerican Society and Culture.* New York: Cambridge University Press, 2010.

Coatsworth, John H. "Patterns of Rural Rebellion in Latin America: Mexico in Comparative Perspective." In *Riot, Rebellion, and Revolution: Rural Social Conflict in Mexico*, edited by Friedrich Katz, 21–62. Princeton: Princeton University Press, 1988.

Collier, George Allen, Renato Rosaldo, and John D. Wirth, eds. *The Inca and Aztec States, 1400–1800: Anthropology and History.* New York: Academic Press, 1982.

Connell, William F. *After Moctezuma: Indigenous Politics and Self-Government in Mexico City, 1524–1730.* Norman: University of Oklahoma Press, 2011.

Cook, Noble David. *Born to Die: Disease and New World Conquest, 1492–1650.* Cambridge: Cambridge University Press, 1999.

Cook, Noble David. "Sickness, Starvation, and Death in Early Hispaniola." *The Journal of Interdisciplinary History* 32, no. 3 (2002): 349–386.

Cortés, Rocío, and Margarita Zamora, eds. *Narradores Indígenas y Mestizos de La Época Colonial (Siglos XVI–XVII): Zonas Andina y Mesoamericana.* Lima: Centro de Estudios Literarios Antonio Cornejo Polar, 2016.

Crespo Cuesta, Eduardo Daniel. *Continuidades medievales en la conquista de América.* Pamplona: Eunsa, 2010.

Cuesta Domingo, Mariano. "Los cronistas oficiales de Indias: De López de Velasco a Céspedes Del Castillo." *Revista Complutense de Historia de América* 33 (2007): 115–150.

Deive, Carlos Esteban. *La Española y la esclavitud del indio.* Santo Domingo: Ed. Fundación García Arévalo, 1995.

Díaz, Mónica, ed. *To Be Indio in Colonial Spanish America.* Albuquerque: University of New Mexico Press, 2017.

Díaz Balsera, Viviana. "The Hero as Rhetor: Hernán Cortés's Second and Third Letters to Charles V." In *Invasion and Transformation: Interdisciplinary Perspectives on the Conquest of Mexico,* edited by Rebecca Parker Brienen and Margaret Ann Jackson, 57–74. Boulder: University Press of Colorado, 2008.

Díaz de Arce, Norbert. "Bezeichnungen für den Krieg bei den Azteken: die Metapher Teoatl Tlachinolli." *Indiana* 16 (2000): 7–28.

Diehl, Richard. "Tula and the Tolteca." In *The Aztec Empire,* edited by Felipe Solis, 124–129. New York: Guggenheim Museum, 2004.

Diel, Lori Boornazian. "The Codex Mexicanus Genealogy: Binding the Mexica Past and the Colonial Present," no. 24 (2015): 120–146.

Dirlik, Arif. "Performing the World: Reality and Representation in the Making of World Histor(ies)." *Journal of World History* 16, no. 4 (2005): 391–410.

Don, Patricia Lopes. *Bonfires of Culture: Franciscans, Indigenous Leaders, and the Inquisition in Early Mexico, 1524–1540.* Norman: University of Oklahoma Press, 2010.

Douglas, Eduardo de J. *In the Palace of Nezahualcoyotl: Painting Manuscripts, Writing the Pre-Hispanic Past in Early Colonial Period Tetzcoco, Mexico.* Austin: University of Texas Press, 2010.

Duverger, Christian. *Cortés.* Paris: Fayard, 2001.

Duverger, Christian. *Cortés et son double: Enquête sur une mystification.* Paris: Seuil, 2013.

Duverger, Christian. *Crónica de la eternidad: ¿quién escribió la historia verdadera de la conquista de la Nueva España?* México, D.F.: Taurus, 2012.

Earle, Rebecca. *The Body of the Conquistador: Food, Race, and the Colonial Experience in Spanish America, 1492–1700.* Cambridge: Cambridge University Press, 2012.

Elliott, John H. *Die neue in der alten Welt: Folgen einer Eroberung, 1492–1650.* Berlin: Wagenbach, 1992.

Elliott, John H. *Imperial Spain 1469–1716.* 2nd ed. London: Penguin, 2002.

Elliott, John H., Ramón María Serrera, José Luis Martínez, and Enrique Krauze. *Hernan Cortés y México.* Sevilla: Diputación Sevilla, 2000.

Escalante Gonzalbo, Pablo. "La ciudad, la gente y las costumbres." In *Historia de la vida cotidiana en México,* edited by Pilar Gonzalbo y Pablo Escalante, 1:199–230. México, D.F.: El Colegio de México, 2004.

Escalante Gonzalbo, Pablo. ed. *Historia de la vida cotidiana en México.* México, D.F.: El Colegio de México, 2004.

Escalante Gonzalbo, Pablo. "La cortesía, los efectos y la sexualidad." In *Historia general del Estado de México,* edited by María Teresa Jarquín Ortega and Manuel Miño Grijalva, 261–278. Zinacantepec: Colegio Mexiquense, 1998.

Escalante Gonzalbo, Pablo. "Los Otomies." In *Historia general del Estado de México,* edited by María Teresa Jarquín Ortega and Manuel Miño Grijalva, 2:161–185. Zinacantepec: Colegio Mexiquense, 1998.

Espinosa, Aurelio. *The Empire of the Cities: Emperor Charles V, the Comunero Revolt, and the Transformation of the Spanish System.* Boston: Brill, 2009.

Esteve Barba, Francisco. *Historiografía indiana.* 2a ed. Madrid: Gredos, 1992.

Evans, Susan Toby. "Aztec Palaces and Gardens: Intertwined Evolution." In *The Oxford Handbook of the Aztecs,* edited by Deborah L. Nichols and Enrique Rodríguez Alegría, 229–245. New York: Oxford University Press, 2017.

Fargher, Lane F., Richard E. Blanton, and Heredia Espinoza. "The Independent Republic of Tlaxcallan." In *The Oxford Handbook of the Aztecs,* edited by Deborah L. Nichols and Enrique Rodríguez-Alegría, 535–542. New York: Oxford University Press, 2017.

Florescano, Enrique. *Los orígenes del poder en Mesoamérica*. México, D.F.: Fondo de Cultura Económica, 2009.

Frankl, Víctor. "Die Begriffe des Mexikanischen Kaisertums und der Weltmonarchie in den 'Cartas de Relación' des Hernán Cortés." *Saeculum* 13 (1962): 1–34.

Gabbert, Wolfgang. *Kultureller Determinismus und die Eroberung Mexikos: Zur Kritik eines dichotomischen Geschichtsverständnisses*. Freiburg: Alber, 1995.

Gabbert, Wolfgang. "Warum Montezuma Weinte: Anmerkungen zur Frühphase der Europäischen Expansion in den Atlantischen Raum." In *Atlantik: Sozial- und Kulturgeschichte in der Neuzeit*, edited by Ulrike Schmieder and Hans-Heinrich Nolte, 29–47. Wien: Promedia, 2010.

García Cook, Angel. *Tlaxcala a la llegada de los españoles según las evidencias arqueológicas*. Mexico: Instituto Nacional de Antropología e Historia, 2014.

Loaeza, Pablo García. "Telling Violence: The Toxcatl Massacre at the Templo Mayor in Sixteenth-Century Sources." *Journal of Iberian and Latin American Studies* 22, no. 2 (2016): 109–123.

García Márquez, Agustín. *Los aztecas en el centro de Veracruz*. México, D.F.: Universidad Nacional Autónoma, 2005.

García Mendoza, Jaime. *La Provincia de la plata en el siglo XV: I Historia de los reales de minas de Temazcaltepec, Zultepec, Zacualpan y Taxco*. México, D. F: Publicia, 2011.

Gerhard, Peter. *A Guide to the Historical Geography of New Spain*. 2nd ed. Norman: University of Oklahoma Press, 1993.

Gibson, Charles. *The Aztecs under Spanish Rule: A History of the Indians of the Valley of Mexico; 1519–1810*. 2nd ed. Stanford: Stanford University Pr, 1991.

Gibson, Charles. *Tlaxcala in the Sixteenth Century*. New Haven: Yale UniversityPress, 1952.

Gillespie, Jeanne. *Saints and Warriors: Tlaxcalan Perspectives on the Conquest of Tenochtitlan*. New Orleans: University Press South, 2004.

Gillespie, Susan D. "Blaming Moctezuma." In *Invasion and Transformation: Interdisciplinary Perspectives on the Conquest of Mexico*, edited by Rebecca Parker Brienen and Margaret Ann Jackson, 25–56. Boulder: University Press of Colorado, 2008.

Gillespie, Susan D. *The Aztec Kings: The Construction of Rulership in Mexica History*. Tucson: Univ. of Arizona Pr., 1989.

Glantz, Margo. "Ciudad y escritura: La Ciudad de México en las cartas de relación." *Hispamérica* 19, no. 56–57 (1990): 165–174.

Glantz, Margo. ed. *La Malinche, sus padres y sus hijos*. México, D.F.: Taurus, 2001.

Glantz, Margo. "La Malinche: la lengua en la mano." In *La Malinche, sus padres y sus hijos*, edited by Margo Glantz, 91–114. México, D.F.: Taurus, 2001.

Goñi, Guillermo. *Las conquistas de México y Yucatán*. México, D.F.: Instituto Nacional de Antropología e Historia, 2008.

Gonzalbo Aizpuru, Pilar. "Vestir al Desnudo: Un Acercamiento a La Etica y La Estética Del Vestido En El Siglo XVI Novohispano." In *Herencia Española En La Cultura Material de Las Regiones de México: Casa, Vestido, Sustento*, edited by Rafael Diego Fernández Sotelo, 329–349. Zamora: El Colegio de Michoacán, 1993.

González Martínez, Joaquín Roberto. "Veracruz, perfiles regionales, económicos y poblacionales." In *Historia General de Veracruz*, edited by Martín Aguilar Sánchez and Juan Ortiz Escamilla, 19–64. Veracruz: Universidad Veracruzana, 2011.

González Torres, Yolotl. "El sacrificio humano: Poder y sumisión." In *El sacrificio humano en la tradición religiosa mesoamericana*, edited by Leonardo López Luján, 397–406. México, D.F.: Instituto Nacional de Antropologia e Historia, 2009.

Goodman, Nelson. *Ways of Worldmaking*. Indianapolis: Hackett, 1978.

Graulich, Michel. "« La mera verdad resiste a mi rudeza »: forgeries et mensonges dans l'Historia verdadera de la conquista de la Nueva España de Bernal Diaz del Castillo." *Journal de la société des américanistes* 82, no. 1 (1996): 63–95.

Graulich, Michel. *Le sacrifice humain chez les Aztèques*. Paris: Fayard, 2005.

Greenleaf, Richard E. *Zumárraga y la Inquisición mexicana 1536–1543*. México, D.F.: Fondo de Cultura Económica, 1988.

Grube, Nikolai, ed. *Maya: Gottkönige im Regenwald*. Potsdam: Ullmann, 2012.

Grube, Nikolai, and Simon Martin. "The Dynastic History of the Maya." In *Maya: Divine Kings of the Rain Forest*, edited by Nikolai Grube, Eva Eggebrecht, and Matthias Seidel, 148–171. Postdam: H. F. Ullmann, 2012.

Grunberg, Bernard. *Dictionnaire des Conquistadores de Mexico*. Paris: Harmattan, 2001.

Grunberg, Bernard. "Hernán Cortés y la guerra de los conquistadores." In *El mundo de los conquistadores*, edited by Martín Ríos Saloma, 557–576. México, D.F.: Universidad Nacional Autónoma de México, 2015.

Grunberg, Bernard. *Histoire de la conquête du Mexique*. Paris: L'Harmattan, 1995.

Grunberg, Bernard. "Las relaciones entre Cortés y sus hombres y el problema de la unidad en la conquista de México (Febrero 1519–Agosto 1521)." *Revista de Indias* 43, no. 171 (1983): 301–314.

Grunberg, Bernard. *L'univers des conquistadores: Les hommes et leur conquête dans le Mexique du XVIe siècle*. Paris: L'Harmattan, 1993.

Grunberg, Bernard. "The Origins of the Conquistadores of Mexico City." *The Hispanic American Historical Review* 74, no. 2 (1994): 259–283.

Gruzinski, Serge. *La Ciudad de México: Una historia*. México, D.F.: Fondo de Cultura Económica, 2004.

Gruzinski, Serge. *La colonisation de l'imaginaire: Sociétés indigènes et occidentalisation dans le Mexique Espagnol, XVIe-XVIIIe siècle*. Paris: Gallimard, 1988.

Gunsenheimer, Antje. "Geschichtstradierung in den yukatekischen Chilam Balam-Büchern: Eine Analyse der Herkunft und Entwicklung ausgewählter historischer Berichte." Universität Bonn, 2002.

Gutiérrez Escudero, Antonio. *Pedro de Alvarado: El conquistador del país de los quetzales*. Madrid: Anaya, 1988.

Hamann, Byron Ellsworth. "Object, Image, Cleverness: The Lienzo de Tlaxcala." *Art History* 36, no. 3 (2013): 518–545.

Hanks, William F. *Converting Words: Maya in the Age of the Cross*. Berkeley: University of California Press, 2010.

Hartnagel, Angelina. *Bernal Díaz Del Castillo, Doña Marina und die hohe Kunst der Historiographie: Eine Umfeldanalyse der Historia verdadera de la conquista de la Nueva España*. Frankfurt am Main: Peter Lang, 2013.

Hassig, Ross. *Aztec Warfare: Imperial Expansion and Political Control*. Norman: University of Oklahoma Press, 1988.

Hassig, Ross. *Mexico and the Spanish Conquest*. 2nd ed. Norman: University of Oklahoma Press, 2006.

Hassig, Ross. *Time, History, and Belief in Aztec and Colonial Mexico*. Austin: University of Texas Press, 2001.

Hausberger, Bernd. *Die Verknüpfung der Welt: Geschichte der frühen Globalisierung vom 16. bis zum 18. Jahrhundert*. Expansion, Interaktion, Akkulturation, Band 27. Wien: Mandelbaum Verlag, 2015.

Herrera, Robinson A. "Concubines and Wives: Reinterpreting Native-Spanish Intimate Unions in Sixteenth-Century Guatemala." In *Indian Conquistadors: Indigenous Allies in the Conquest of Mesoamerica*, edited by Laura Matthew and Michel Oudijk, 127–144. Norman: University of Oklahoma Press, 2007.

Hinz, Felix. *"Hispanisierung" in Neu-Spanien 1519–1568: Transformation kollektiver Identitäten von Mexica, Tlaxkalteken und Spaniern*. Vol. 3. Hamburg: Dr. Kovač, 2005.

Hirth, Kenneth G. *The Aztec Economic World: Merchants and Markets in Ancient Mesoamerica*. New York: Cambridge University Press, 2016.

Horn, Rebecca. "Indigenous Identities in Mesoamerica after the Spanish Conquest." In *Native Diasporas: Indigenous Identities and Settler Colonialism in the Americas*, edited by Gregory D. Smithers and Brooke N. Newman, 31–48. Lincoln: University of Nebraska Press, 2014.

Horn, Rebecca. *Postconquest Coyoacan: Nahua-Spanish Relations in Central Mexico, 1519–1650.* Stanford: Stanford University Press, 1997.

Huber, Vitus, *Beute und Conquista: Die politische Ökonomie der Eroberung Neuspaniens.* Frankfurt: Campus, 2018.

Huexotzinco Codex. Huexotzinco, Mexico, 1521. Manuscript/Mixed Material. https://www.loc.gov/item/mss47662-2657/.

Islas, Alfredo Ruiz. "Hernán Cortés y la isla California." *Iberoamericana* 7, no. 27 (2007): 39–58.

Jarquín Ortega, María Teresa y Manuel Miño Grijalva, eds. *Historia general del Estado de México.* 6 vols. Zinacantepec: Colegio Mexiquense, 1998.

Jiménez, Nora Edith. *Francisco López de Gómara: Escribir historias en tiempos de Carlos V.* México, D.F.: Colegio de Michoacán, 2001.

Johansson, Patrick. "La fundación de México-Tenochtitlan consideraciones 'cronológicas.'" *Arqueología Mexicana* 23, no. 135 (2015): 70–77.

Katz, Friedrich. "Rural Uprisings in Preconquest and Colonial Mexico." In *Riot, Rebellion, and Revolution: Rural Social Conflict in Mexico,* edited by Friedrich Katz, 65–94. Princeton: Princeton University Press, 1988.

Katz, Friedrich, ed. *Riot, Rebellion, and Revolution: Rural Social Conflict in Mexico,* Princeton: Princeton University Press, 1988.

Keegan, William F. *The People Who Discovered Columbus: The Prehistory of the Bahamas.* Gainesville: University Press of Florida, 1992.

Keen, Benjamin. "Recent Writing on the Spanish Conquest." *Latin American Research Review* 20, no. 2 (1985): 161–171.

Kellogg, Susan. *Law and the Transformation of Aztec Culture, 1500–1700.* Norman: University of Oklahoma Press, 1995.

Klaus, Susanne. *Uprooted Christianity: The Preaching of the Christian Doctrine in Mexico Based on Franciscan Sermons of the 16th Century Written in Nahuatl.* Schwaben: Saurwein, 1999.

Klauth, Carlo. *Geschichtskonstruktion bei der Eroberung Mexikos: am Beispiel der Chronisten Bernal Díaz del Castillo, Bartolomé de las Casas und Gonzales Fernández de Oviedo.* Hildesheim: Olms, 2012.

Kobayashi, José María. *La educación como conquista: Empresa franciscana en México.* México, D.F.: El Colegio de México, 1974.

Kohler, Alfred. *Karl V: 1500–1558, Eine Biographie.* München: Beck, 1999.

Köhler, Ulrich. *Vasallen des linkshändigen Kriegers im Kolibrigewand: über Weltbild, Religion und Staat der Azteken.* Berlin: Lit, 2009.

Kohut, Karl. "Literatura y cultura coloniales: Cuestiones teóricas y Nueva España." *Iberoamericana* 4, no. 14 (2004): 189–210.

König, Hans-Joachim. *Die Entdeckung und Eroberung Amerikas, 1492–1550.* Freiburg: Ploetz, 1992.

König, Hans-Joachim. "Plus Ultra: Ein Weltreichs- und Eroberungsprogramm? Amerika und Europa in politischen Vorstellungen im Spanien Karls V." In *Von Kolumbus bis Castro: Aufsätze zur Geschichte Lateinamerikas,* edited by Michael Riekenberg, Stefan Rinke, and Peer Schmidt, 73–100. Stuttgart: Heinz, 2006.

König, Hans-Joachim. *Von Kolumbus bis Castro: Aufsätze zur Geschichte Lateinamerikas.* Stuttgart: Heinz, 2006.

Krickeberg, Walter. *Las antiguas culturas mexicanas.* México, D.F.: Fondo de Cultura Económica, 1977.

Ladero Quesada, Miguel Ángel. *La España de los Reyes Católicos.* 4th ed. Madrid: Alianza Editorial, 2014.

Lafaye, Jacques. *Los conquistadores: figuras y escrituras.* 2nd ed. México, D.F.: Fondo de Cultura Económica, 1999.

Lázaro Avila, Carlos. *Las fronteras de América y los "Flandes Indianos."* Madrid: Consejo Superior de Investigaciones Científicas, 1997.

Lee, Jongsoo and Galen Brokaw, eds. *Texcoco: Prehispanic and Colonial Perspectives.* Boulder: University Press of Colorado, 2014.

Lee, Jongsoo. "The Aztec Triple Alliance: A Colonial Transformation of the Prehispanic Political and Tributary System." In *Texcoco: Prehispanic and Colonial Perspectives*, edited by Jongsoo Lee and Galen Brokaw, 63–92. Boulder: University Press of Colorado, 2014.

Lee, Jongsoo. "The Europeanization of Prehispanic Tradition: Bernardino de Sahagún's Transformation of Aztec Priests (Tlamacazque) into Classical Wise Men (Tlamatinime)." *Colonial Latin American Review* 26, no. 3 (2017): 291–312.

León Cazáres, María del Carmen. "Entre el breviario y la espada: Los mercedarios como capellanes en las huestes conquistadoras." In *El mundo de los conquistadores*, edited by Martín Ríos Saloma, 599–617. México, D.F.: Universidad Nacional Autónoma de México, 2015.

León Portilla, Miguel. *Bernardino de Sahagún*. Madrid: Historia 16, 1987.

León Portilla, Miguel. *Bernardino de Sahagún: Pionero de La Antropología*. México, D.F.: Universidad Nacional Autónoma de México, 1999.

León Portilla, Miguel. *Hernán Cortés y la Mar del Sur*. Madrid: Instituto de Cooperación Iberoamericana, 1985.

León Portilla, Miguel, and Carmen Aguilera. "Mapa de México Tenochtitlan y Sus Contornos Hacia 1550." Ciudad de México: Ediciones Era, 2016.

Levin Rojo, Danna, and Federico Navarrete Linares, eds. *Indios, mestizos y españoles: Interculturalidad e historiografía en la Nueva España*. Azcapotzalco: Universidad Autónoma Metropolitana, 2007.

Lienhard, Martin. *Disidentes, rebeldes, insurgentes: Resistencia indígena y negra en América Latina: Ensayos de historia testimonial*. Madrid: Iberoamericana, 2008.

Liss, Peggy K. *Orígenes de la nacionalidad mexicana 1521–1556: la formación de una nueva sociedad*. Translated by Agustín Bárcena. 2nd ed. México, D.F.: Fondo de Cultura Económica, 1995.

Loaeza, Pablo García. "Telling Violence: The Toxcatl Massacre at the Templo Mayor in Sixteenth-Century Sources." *Journal of Iberian and Latin American Studies* 22, no. 2 (2016): 109–123.

Lockhart, James. *The Nahuas after the Conquest: A Social and Cultural History of the Indians of Central Mexico, Sixteenth through Eighteenth Centuries*. Stanford: Stanford University Press, 1992.

Long, Janet, ed. *Conquista y comida: Consecuencias del encuentro de dos mundos*. México: Universidad Nacional Autónoma de México, 1996.

López Austin, Alfredo. *Cuerpo humano e ideología: las concepciones de los antiguos nahuas*. 2 vols. México, D.F.: Universidad Nacional Autónoma de México, 1984.

López Austin, Alfredo, and Leonardo López Luján. *Monte Sagrado, Templo Mayor: El cerro y la pirámide en la tradición religiosa mesoamericana*. México, D.F.: Universidad Nacional Autónoma de México, 2009.

López Luján, Leonardo, ed. *El Sacrificio Humano En La Tradición Religiosa Mesoamericana*. México: Universidad Nacional Autónoma de México, 2009.

"López Obrador asegura en su carta al Rey que los abusos de la conquista "aún generan encendidas polémicas"." *El País*. May 4, 2017. https://elpais.com/ internacional/2019/03/27/mexico/ 1553651641_263448.html.

Lovell, W. George, Christopher Hayden Lutz, and Wendy Kramer. *Strange Lands and Different Peoples: Spaniards and Indians in Colonial Guatemala*. Norman: University of Oklahoma Press, 2013.

Lupher, David A. *Romans in a New World: Classical Models in Sixteenth-Century Spanish America*. Ann Arbor: University of Michigan Press, 2003.

Madariaga, Salvador de. *Hernán Cortés: der Eroberer Mexikos*. Zürich: Manesse, 1997 [1941].

Maestre, María Dolores. *Frey Don Nicolás de Ovando, primer gobernador real de las Indias y tierra firme de la mar océana La Española, 1501, 1509 y 1511*. Sevilla: Padilla Libros, 2011.

Magaloni, Diana. "Painting a New Era: Conquest, Prophecy, and the World to Come." In *Invasion and Transformation: Interdisciplinary Perspectives on the Conquest of Mexico*, edited by Rebecca Parker Brienen and Margaret Ann Jackson, 125–150. Boulder: University Press of Colorado, 2008.

Magaloni, Diana. *Albores de la conquista: La Historia Pintada Del Códice Florentino*. Ciudad de México: Secretaría de Cultura, Dirección General de Publicaciones, 2016.

Manzanilla, Linda. "Teotihuacan." In *The Aztec Empire*, edited by Felipe Solis, 114–123. New York: Guggenheim Museum, 2004.

Manzo-Robledo, Francisco. *I, Hernán Cortés: The (Second) Trial of Residency*. New York: Peter Lang, 2013.

Maravall, José Antonio. *Las comunidades de Castilla: Una primera revolución moderna*. 2nd ed. Madrid: Alianza, 1979.

Marroquín Arredondo, Jaime. *Diálogos con Quetzalcóatl: Humanismo, etnografía y ciencia (1492–1577)*. Madrid: Iberoamericana, 2014.

Martínez Baracs, Andrea. *Un Gobierno de indios: Tlaxcala, 1519–1750*. Mexico: Fondo de Cultura Economica, 2008.

Martínez Hoyos, Francisco. *Breve historia de Hernan Cortés*. Madrid: Nowtilus, 2014.

Martínes, José Luis. *Hernán Cortés*. Breviarios del Fondo de Cultura Económica. México, D.F.: Fondo de Cultura Económica, 1992.

Martínez Martínez, María del Carmen. "Hernán Cortés en España (1540–1547): Negocios, pleitos y familia." In *El Mundo de los conquistadores*, edited by Martín Ríos Saloma, 577–598. México: Sílex-UNAM, 2015.

Martínez Silex, María del Carmen. *Veracruz 1519: Los hombres de Cortés*. León: Universidad de León, 2013.

Matthew, Laura. "Whose Conquest? Nahua, Zapoteca, and Mixtec Auxiliaries in the Conquest of Central America." In *Indian Conquistadors: Indigenous Allies in the Conquest of Mesoamerica*, edited by Laura Matthew and Michel Oudijk, 102–126. Norman: University of Oklahoma Press, 2007.

Matthew, Laura E. and Michel R. Oudijk, eds. *Indian Conquistadors: Indigenous Allies in the Conquest of Mesoamerica*, Norman: University of Oklahoma Press, 2007.

Matthew, Laura E. and Michel R. Oudijk, eds. "Conclusion." In *Indian Conquistadors: Indigenous Allies in the Conquest of Mesoamerica*, edited by Laura Matthew and Michel Oudijk, 317–324. Norman: University of Oklahoma Press, 2007.

McCaa, Robert. "Spanish and Nahuatl Views on Smallpox and Demographic Catastrophe in Mexico." *The Journal of Interdisciplinary History* 25, no. 3 (1995): 397–431.

McCafferty, Geoffrey, and Sharisse McCafferty. "Pregnant in the Dancing Place: Myths and Methods of Textile Production and Use." In *The Oxford Handbook of the Aztecs*, edited by Deborah L. Nichols and Enrique Rodríguez Alegría, 375–384. New York: Oxford University Press, 2017.

Medin, Tzvi. *Mito y pragmatismo e imperialismo: La conciencia social en la conquista del Imperio Azteca*. Frankfurt am Main: Vervuert, 2009.

Melgarejo Vivanco, José Luis. *Los Totonaca y su cultura*. Xalapa: Universidad Verracruzana, 1985.

Melville, Elinor G. K. *A Plague of Sheep: Environmental Consequences of the Conquest of Mexico*. Cambridge: Cambridge University Press, 1994.

Millon, René. "Teotihuacan: City, State and Civilization." In *Supplement to the Handbook of Middle American Indians*, edited by Jeremy Sabloff, 1:198–243. Austin: University of Texas Press, 1981.

Mira Caballos, Esteban. *Hernán Cortés: El fin de una leyenda*. Trujillo: Palacio de Barrantes Cervantes, 2010.

Miralles Ostos, Juan. *Hernán Cortés: Inventor de México*. Barcelona: Tusquets Editores, 2001.

Miralles Ostos, Juan. *Y Bernal Mintió: El lado oscuro de su historia verdadera de la conquista de la Nueva España*. Taurus Historia. México, D.F.: Taurus, 2008.

Mohar, Luz María. *El tributo México en el siglo XVI: Análisis de dos fuentes pictográficas*. México, D.F.: Centro de Investigaciones y Estudios Superiores en Antropología Social, 1987.

Morales, Francisco. "The Native Encounter with Christianity: Franciscans and Nahuas in Sixteenth-Century Mexico." *The Americas* 65, no. 2 (2008): 137–159.

Morehart, Christopher T. "Aztec Agricultural Strategies: Intensification, Landesque Capital, and the Sociopolitics of Production." In *The Oxford Handbook of the Aztecs*, edited by Deborah L. Nichols and Enrique Rodríguez Alegría, 263–279. New York: Oxford University Press, 2017.

Mundy, Barbara E. "Mapping the Aztec Capital: The 1524 Nuremberg Map of Tenochtitlan, Its Sources and Meanings." *Imago Mundi* 50 (1998): 11–33.

Mundy, Barbara E. *The Death of Aztec Tenochtitlan, the Life of Mexico City*. Austin: University of Texas Press, 2015.

Murià, José María, and Angélica Peregrina, eds. *Historia general de Jalisco*. Vol. 1. Desde los orígenes hasta mediados del siglo XVI. Zapopan: Porrúa, 2015.

Myers, Kathleen Ann. *Fernández de Oviedo's Chronicle of America: A New History for a New World*. Austin: University of Texas Press, 2007.

Navarrete Linares, Federico. "Beheadings and Massacres: Andean and Mesoamerican Representations of the Spanish Conquest." *Anthropology and Aesthetics* 53/54 (Spring–Autumn 2008): 59–78.

Navarrete Linares, Federico. "La Malinche, La Virgen y La Montaña: El juego de la identidad en los códices tlaxcaltecas." *História (São Paulo)* 26, no. 2 (2007): 288–310.

Navarrete Linares, Federico. *Los orígenes de los pueblos indígenas del Valle de México: Los altépetl y sus historias*. México, D.F.: Universidad Nacional Autónoma de México, 2011.

Nebel, Richard Karl. *Altmexikanische Religion und christliche Heilsbotschaft: Mexiko zwischen Quetzalcóatl und Christus*. Immensee: Neue Zeitschrift für Missionswiss, 1983.

Nichols, Deborah L. and Christopher A. Pool, eds. *The Oxford Handbook of Mesoamerican Archaeology*. Oxford: Oxford University Press, 2012.

Oliver, José R. *Caciques and Cemí Idols: The Web Spun by Taíno Rulers between Hispaniola and Puerto Rico*. Tuscaloosa: University of Alabama Press, 2009.

Olivier, Guilhem. "Humans and Gods in the Mexica Universe." In *The Oxford Handbook of the Aztecs*, edited by Deborah L. Nichols and Enrique Rodríguez Alegría, 572–583. New York: Oxford University Press, 2017.

Oudijk, Michel, and Matthew Restall. "Mesoamerican Conquistadors in the Sixteenth Century." In *Indian Conquistadors: Indigenous Allies in the Conquest of Mesoamerica*, edited by Laura Matthew and Michel Oudijk, 28–64. Norman: University of Oklahoma Press, 2007.

Owensby, Brian Philip. *Empire of Law and Indian Justice in Colonial Mexico*. Stanford: Stanford University Press, 2008.

Padrón, Ricardo. *The Spacious Word: Cartography, Literature, and Empire in Early Modern Spain*. Chicago: University of Chicago Press, 2004.

Pastrana Flores, Gabriel Miguel. *Historias de la conquista: aspectos de la historiografía de tradición náhuatl*. México, D.F.: Universidad Autónoma de México, 2004.

Paz, Octavio. "Hernán Cortés: Exorcismo y liberación." In *México en la obra de Octavio Paz; 1: El peregrino en su patria*, edited by Luis Mario Schneider, 100–112. México, D.F.: Fondo de Cultura Económica, 1988.

Peñafiel, Antonio. *Ciudades coloniales y capitales de la República Mexicana: La ciudad virreinal de Tlaxcala*. Mexico: Cosmos, 1978.

Pennock, Caroline. "Gender and Aztec Life Cycles." In *The Oxford Handbook of the Aztecs*, edited by Deborah L. Nichols and Enrique Rodríguez Alegría, 387–398. Oxford: Oxford University Press, 2017.

Pérez-Rocha, Emma, and Rafael Tena. *La nobleza indígena del centro de México después de la conquista*. México, D.F.: Instituto Nacional de Antropología e Historia, 2000.

Plunket, Patricia, and Gabriela Uruñela. "Cholula in Aztec Times." In *The Oxford Handbook of the Aztecs*, edited by Deborah L. Nichols and Enrique Rodríguez-Alegría, 523–533. New York: Oxford University Press, 2017.

Pomeranz, Kenneth. *The Great Divergence: China, Europe, and the Making of the Modern World Economy*. Princeton: Princeton University Press, 2009.

Pool, Christopher A. "The Formation of Complex Societies in Mesoamerica." In *The Oxford Handbook of Mesoamerican Archaeology*, edited by Deborah L. Nichols and Christopher A. Pool, 169–187. Oxford: Oxford University Press, 2012.

Portillo Cirio, Cándido. *Camaxtli: Dios tutelar de los tlaxcaltecas*. Tlaxcala: CAZATMEX, 2009.

Prem, Hanns J. *Die Azteken: Geschichte, Kultur, Religion*. München: C. H. Beck, 1999.

Prescott, William. *History of the Conquest of Mexico*. New York: Modern Library, 2001[1841].

Puiggrós, Rodolfo. *La España que conquistó el Nuevo Mundo*. 5th ed. Bogotá: El Áncora Ed., 1989.

Quezada, Sergio, Fernando Robles C., and Anthony P. Andrews, eds. *Historia general de Yucatán*. Mérida: Universidad Autónoma de Yucatán, 2014.

Rabasa, José. *Inventing America: Spanish Historiography and the Formation of Eurocentrism*. Norman: University of Oklahoma Press, 1993.

Ramos, Gabriela, and Yanna Yannakakis, eds. *Indigenous Intellectuals: Knowledge, Power, and Colonial Culture in Mexico and the Andes*. Durham: Duke University Press, 2014.

Ramos, Gabriela, and Yanna Yannakakis, eds. "Introduction." In *Indigenous Intellectuals: Knowledge, Power, and Colonial Culture in Mexico and the Andes*. Edited by Gabriela Ramos and Yanna Yannakakis, 1–20. Durham: Duke University Press, 2014.

Ramos Pérez, Demetrio. *Hernán Cortés: mentalidad y propósitos*. Madrid: Ediciones Rialp, 1992.

Rendón Garcini, Ricardo. *Breve historia de Tlaxcala*. México, D.F.: Fondo de Cultura Económica, 1996.

Restall, Matthew. *Maya Conquistador*. Boston: Beacon Press, 1998.

Restall, Matthew. "The New Conquest History." *History Compass* 10, no. 2 (2012): 151–60.

Restall, Matthew. "Spanish Creation of the Conquest of Mexico." In *Invasion and Transformation: Interdisciplinary Perspectives on the Conquest of Mexico*, edited by Rebecca Parker Brienen and Margaret Ann Jackson, 93–102. Boulder: University Press of Colorado, 2008.

Restall, Matthew. *When Montezuma Met Cortés: The True Story of the Meeting that Changed History*. New York: HarperCollins, 2018.

Rice, Prudence M. "Time, History, and Worldview." In *Maya Worldviews at Conquest*, edited by Leslie G. Cecil and Timothy W. Pugh, 17–38. Boulder: University Press of Colorado, 2009.

Riese, Berthold. *Das Reich der Azteken: Geschichte und Kultur*. München: C.H. Beck, 2011.

Riese, Berthold. *Die Maya: Geschichte, Kultur, Religion*. 5th ed. München: Beck, 2002.

Rinke, Stefan. *Kolumbus und der Tag von Guanahani: 1492, Ein Wendepunkt der Geschichte*. Stuttgart: Theiss, 2013.

Rinke, Stefan. *Lateinamerika*. Darmstadt: Theiss, 2015.

Ríos Castaño, Victoria. *Translation as Conquest: Sahagún and Universal History of the Things of New Spain*. Madrid: Iberoamericana, 2014.

Ríos Saloma, Martín, ed. *El mundo de los Conquistadores*. Mexico: Sílex-UNAM, 2015.

Ríos, Guadalupe Pinzón. "Descubriendo el Mar del Sur. Los puertos novohispanos en las exploraciones del Pacífico (1522–1565)." In *El Mundo de los Conquistadores*, edited by Martín Ríos Saloma, 749–773. México, D.F.: Sílex-UNAM, 2015.

Rivera-Pagán, Luis N. "Freedom and Servitude: Indigenous Slavery and the Spanish Conquest of the Caribbean." In *General History of the Caribbean: Volume I: Autochthonous Societies*, edited by Jalil Sued-Badillo, 316–362. New York: Palgrave Macmillan, 2003.

Roa-de-la Carrera, Cristián Andrés. *Histories of infamy: Francisco López de Gómara and the ethics of Spanish imperialism*. Translated by Scott Sessions. Boulder: University Press of Colorado, 2012.

Rodríguez, Verónica, and Monica Styles. "Domingo Francisco de San Antón Muñón Chimalpahin Cuatlehuanitzin (1579–1660)." In *Narradores indígenas y mestizos de la época colonial (Siglos XVI–XVII): Zonas andina y mesoamericana*, edited by Rocío Cortés and Margarita Zamora, 111–117. Lima: Centro de Estudios Literarios "Antonio Cornejo Polar," 2016.

Rodríguez-Sala, María Luisa. *Los cirujanos de hospitales de la Nueva España (siglos XVI y XVII): Miembros de un estamento profesional o de una comunidad científica?* México, D. F: Universidad Autónoma de México, 2005.

Rodríguez-Shadow, María. *La Mujer azteca*. 2nd ed. Toluca: Universidad Autónoma del Estado de México, 1991.

Rojas, José Luis de. *A cada uno lo suyo: El tributo indígena en la Nueva España en el siglo XVI*. Zamora: Colegio de Michoacán, 1993.

Rojas, José Luis de. *Tenochtitlan: Capital of the Aztec Empire*. Gainesville: University Press of Florida, 2012.

Rojas Rabiela, Teresa. "Las cuencas lacustres del altiplano central." *Arqueología Mexicana* 12, no. 68 (2004): 20–27.

Rojas Rabiela, Teresa. *Las siembras de ayer: la agricultura indígena del siglo XVI*. México, D.F.: Secretaría de Educación Pública, 1988.

Román Berrelleza, Juan Alberto. "El Papel de los infantes en las prácticas sacrificiales mexicas." In *El sacrificio humano en la tradición religiosa mesoamericana*, edited by Leonardo López Luján and Guilhem Olivier, 345–366. México, D.F.: Universidad Autónoma de México, 2009.

Romero Galván, José Rubén, and Pilar Máynez, eds. *El universo de Sahagún: pasado y presente*. México, D.F.: Universidad Autónoma de México, 2007.

Rouse, Irving. *The Tainos: Rise & Decline of the People Who Greeted Columbus*. New Haven: Yale University Press, 1992.

Ruiz y Torres, Josefina Edith. *A Puerta Cerrada: Lectura e inquisición en el siglo XVI novohispano*. México, D.F.: Ediciones Clandestino, 2014.

Sabloff, Jeremy, ed. *Supplement to the Handbook of Middle American Indians*. Austin: University of Texas Press, 1981.

Sanders, William T., Jeffrey R. Parsons, and Robert S. Santley. *The Basin of Mexico: Ecological Processes in the Evolution of a Civilization*. New York: Academic Press, 1979.

Santamarina Novillo, Carlos. "El sistema de dominación azteca el Imperio Tepaneca." PhD Dissertation, Universidad Complutense de Madrid, 2005.

Schmieder, Ulrike, and Hans-Heinrich Nolte, eds. *Atlantik: Sozial- und Kulturgeschichte in der Neuzeit*. Wien: Promedia-Verl, 2010.

Schreffler, Michael J. *The Art of Allegiance: Visual Culture and Imperial Power in Baroque New Spain*. University Park: Pennsylvania State University Press, 2007.

Schroeder, Susan. "Introduction." In *The Conquest All Over Again: Nahuas and Zapotecs Thinking, Writing, and Painting Spanish Colonialism*, edited by Susan Schroeder, 1–14. Brighton: Sussex Academic Press, 2010.

Schroeder, Susan, ed. *The Conquest All Over Again: Nahuas and Zapotecs Thinking, Writing, and Painting Spanish Colonialism*. Brighton: Sussex Academic Press, 2010.

Schroeder, Susan, ed. "Writing the Nahuatl Canon: Ethnicity, Identity, and Posterity According to Chimalpahin." In *To Be Indio in Colonial Spanish America*, edited by Mónica Díaz, 219–242. Albuquerque: University of New Mexico Press, 2017.

Schwaller, John Frederick, and Helen Nader. *The First Letter from New Spain: The Lost Petition of Cortés and His Company, June 20, 1519*. Austin: University of Texas Press, 2014.

Serrera Contreras, Ramón María. *La América de los Habsburgo (1517–1700)*. Sevilla: Universidad de Sevilla, 2011.

Sharer, Robert J. *The Ancient Maya*. 5th ed. Stanford: Stanford University Press, 1994.

Simson, Ingrid. *Amerika in der spanischen Literatur des Siglo de Oro: Bericht, Inszenierung, Kritik*. Frankfurt am Main: Vervuert, 2003.

Smith, Michael E., and Frederic Hicks. "Inequality and Social Class in Aztec Society." In *The Oxford Handbook of the Aztecs*, edited by Deborah L. Nichols and Enrique Rodríguez Alegría, 243–436. New York: Oxford University Press, 2017.

Smith, Michael E. *Aztec City-State Capitals*. Gainesville: University Press of Florida, 2008.

Smithers, Gregory D. and Brooke N. Newman, eds. *Native Diasporas: Indigenous Identities and Settler Colonialism in the Americas*. Lincoln: University of Nebraska Press, 2014.

Solis, Felipe, ed. *The Aztec Empire*. New York: Guggenheim Museum, 2004.

Solodkow, David M. *Etnógrafos coloniales: Alteridad y escritura en la conquista de América (siglo XVI)*. Madrid: Iberoamericana, 2014.

Soustelle, Jacques. *So Lebten die Azteken am Vorabend der spanischen Eroberung*. Stuttgart: Dt. Verl.-Anst., 1956.

Spores, Ronald. *The Mixtecs in Ancient and Colonial Times*. Norman: University of Oklahoma Press, 1984.

Stenzel, Werner. *Das kortesische Mexiko: Die Eroberung Mexikos und der darauf folgende Kulturwandel*. Frankfurt am Main: P. Lang, 2006.

Stenzel, Werner. "Quetzalcoatl von Tula: Die Mythogenese einer postkortesischen Legende." *Zeitschrift für Lateinamerika* 18 (1980): 1–92.

Stevens Arroyo, Antonio M. *Cave of the Jagua: The Mythological World of the Taínos.* 2nd ed. Scranton: University of Scranton Press, 2006.

Straub, Eberhard. *Das Bellum Iustum des Hernán Cortés in Mexico.* Köln: Böhlau, 1976.

Sued-Badillo, Jalil, *General History of the Caribbean: Volume I: Autochthonous Societies.* New York: Palgrave Macmillan, 2003.

Taboada, Hernán. *La sombra del islam en la Conquista de América.* México, D.F.: Fondo de Cultura Económica, 2004.

Tavárez, David. "Reclaiming the Conquest." In *Chimalpahin's Conquest,* edited by Susan Schroeder, 17–34. Stanford: Stanford University Press, 2010.

Thomas, Hugh. *Die Eroberung Mexikos: Cortés und Montezuma.* Frankfurt am Main: Fischer-Taschenbuch-Verl, 1993.

Thomas, Hugh. *The Golden Age: The Spanish Empire of Charles V.* London: Allen Lane, 2010.

Thomas, Hugh. *Who's Who of the Conquistadors.* London: Cassell, 2000.

Townsend, Camilla. *Fifth Sun: A New History of the Aztecs.* New York: Oxford University Press, 2019.

Todorov, Tzvetan. *Die Eroberung Amerikas: Das Problem des Anderen.* Translated by Wilfried Böhringer. Frankfurt am Main: Suhrkamp, 1985.

Toulet Abasolo, Lucina M. *Tlaxcala en la Conquista de México, D.F.: El Mito de la traición.* Tlaxcala: Tlaxcallan, 1996.

Townsend, Camilla. "Burying the White Gods: New Perspectives on the Conquest of Mexico." *The American Historical Review* 108, no. 3 (2003): 659–687.

Townsend, Camilla. "Don Juan Buenaventura Zapata y Mendoza." In *Narradores indígenas y mestizos de la época colonial (siglos XVI–XVII): Zonas andina y mesoamericana,* edited by Rocío Cortés and Margarita Zamora, 136–138. Lima: Centro de Estudios Literarios "Antonio Cornejo Polar," 2016.

Townsend, Camilla. *Annals of Native America: How the Nahuas of Colonial Mexico Kept Their History Alive.* Oxford: Oxford University Press, 2016.

Townsend, Camilla. *Malintzin's Choices: An Indian Woman in the Conquest of Mexico.* Albuquerque: University of New Mexico Press, 2006.

Trimborn, Hermann. "Zum Weltbild und Geschichtsbewußtsein in den Hochkulturen des alten Amerika." In *Archäologie und Geschichtsbewußtsein,* edited by Hermann Müller-Karpe, 105–110. München: Beck, 1982.

Turner, Guillermo. *Los soldados de la Conquista: Herencias culturales.* México, D.F.: Ediciones el Tucán de Virginia, 2013.

Umberger, Emily. "Schrift und Kalender." In *Die Azteken und ihre Vorläufer: Glanz und Untergang des alten Mexiko,* edited by Arne Eggebrecht, 126–131. Mainz am Rhein: P. von Zabern, 1986.

Vaca de Osma, José Antonio. *Hernán Cortés.* Madrid: Espasa Calpe, 2000.

Vail, Gabrielle. "Cosmology and Creation in Late Postclassic Maya, Literature and Art." In *Maya Worldviews at Conquest,* edited by Leslie G. Cecil and Timothy W. Pugh, 83–110. Boulder: University Press of Colorado, 2009.

Valdeón, Roberto A. *Translation and the Spanish Empire in the Americas.* Amsterdam: John Benjamins Publishing Company, 2014.

Valle, Rafael Heliodoro. *Bibliografía de Hernán Cortés.* Publicaciones de La Sociedad de Estudios Cortesianos. México, D.F.: Editorial Jus, 1953.

Van Deusen, Nancy E. "Coming to Castile with Cortés: Indigenous 'Servitude' in the Sixteenth Century." *Ethnohistory* 62, no. 2 (April 1, 2015): 285–308.

Vargas, Luis Alberto, and Leticia E. Casillas. "El encuentro de dos cocinas: México en el siglo XVI." In *Conquista y comida: Consecuencias del encuentro de dos mundos,* edited by Janet Long, 155–168. México, D. F: Universidad Autónoma de México, 1996.

Vas Mingo, Marta Milagros del. *Las capitulaciones de Indias en el siglo XVI.* Madrid: Cultura Hispánica, 1986.

Vasconcelos, José. *Hernán Cortés, creador de la nacionalidad*. México, D.F.: Xochitl, 1941.

Vélez Cipriano, Iván. *El Mito de Cortés: De héroe universal a ícono de la Leyenda Negra*. Madrid: Ediciones Encuentro, 2016.

Villella, Peter B. *Indigenous Elites and Creole Identity in Colonial Mexico, 1500–1800*. New York: Cambridge University Press, 2016.

Wagner, Henry Raup. *The Discovery of New Spain in 1518 by Juan de Grijalva*. Berkeley: The Cortes Society, 1942.

Warren, Joseph Benedict. *The Conquest of Michoacán: The Spanish Domination of the Tarascan Kingdom in Western Mexico, 1521–1530*. Norman: University of Oklahoma Press, 1985.

Watson, Kelly L. *Insatiable Appetites: Imperial Encounters with Cannibals in the North Atlantic World*. New York: New York University Press, 2015.

Wehrheim, Monika. "De enemigos a antecesores: Cortés, Clavijero y Pesado y la construcción de los Aztecas." *Romanische Forschungen* 3, no. 116 (2004): 346–360.

Whittaker, Gordon. "The Principles of Nahuatl Writing." *Göttinger Beiträge zur Sprachwissenschaft* 16 (2009): 47–81.

Wilkosz, Izabela. "Power, Performance and Propaganda: Sociopolitical Aspects of the Aztec Feast of Toxcatl." Doctoral Thesis, Freie Universität Berlin, 2014.

Wolf, Eric R., ed. *The Valley of Mexico*, 287–302. Albuquerque: University of New Mexico Press, 1976.

Wood, Stephanie Gail. *Transcending Conquest: Nahua Views of Spanish Colonial Mexico*. Norman: University of Oklahoma Press, 2003.

Wright, Elizabeth. "New World News, Ancient Echoes: A Cortés Letter and a Vernacular Livy for a New King and His Wary Subjects (1520–23)." *Renaissance Quarterly* 61, no. 3 (2008): 711–749.

INDEX

For the benefit of digital users, indexed terms that span two pages (e.g., 52–53) may, on occasion, appear on only one of those pages.

Figures are indicated by f following the page number